MostUsedWords.com presents

Spanish Frequency Dictionary

Advanced Vocabulary

5001 - 7500 Most Common Spanish Words

Book 3

First Printing, 2018

MostUsedWords.com

www.MostUsedWords.com

Contents

Why This Book?

Hello, dear reader.

Thank you for purchasing this book. We hope it serves you well on your language learning journey.

Not all words are created equal. The purpose of this frequency dictionary is to list the most common Spanish words in descending order, so you can learn this language as fast and efficiently as possible.

First, we would like to illustrate the value of a frequency dictionary. For the purpose of example, we have combined frequency data from various languages (mainly Romance, Slavic and Germanic languages) and made it into a single chart.

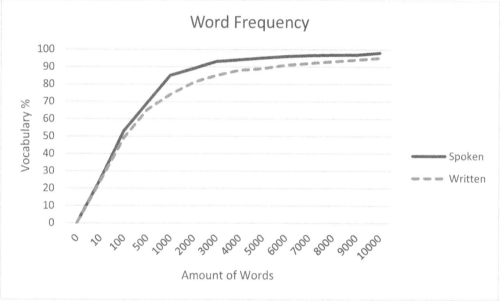

The sweet spots, according to the data seem to be:

Amount of Words	Spoken	Written
• 100	53%	49%
• 1.000	85%	74%
• 2.500	92%	82%
• 5.000	95%	89%
• 7.500	97%	93%
• 10.000	98%	95%

Above data corresponds with Pareto´s law.

Pareto's law, also known as the 80/20 rule, states that, for many events, roughly 80% of the effects come from 20% of the causes.

In language learning, this principle seems to be on steroids. It seems that just 20% of the 20% (95/5) of the most used words in a language account for roughly all the vocabulary you need.

To put this further in perspective: The Collins Spanish Dictionary (August 2016 edition) lists over 310.000 words in current use, while you will only need to know 1.62% (5000 words) to achieve 95% and 89% fluency in speaking and writing. Knowing the most common 10.000 words, or just 3.25%, will net you 98% fluency in spoken language and 95% fluency in written texts.

Keeping this in mind, the value of a frequency dictionary is immense. Study the most frequent words, build your vocabulary and progress quickly. One more frequency asked question needs to be answered.

Well, how many words do you need to know for varying levels of fluency?

While it's important to note that it is impossible to pin down these numbers and statistics with 100% accuracy, these are a global average of multiple sources. According to research, this is the amount of vocabulary needed for varying levels of fluency:

1. 250 words: the essential core of a language. Without these words, you cannot construct any meaningful sentences.
2. 750 words: are used every single day by every person who speaks the language.
3. 2500 words: should enable you to express everything you could possibly want to say, although some creativity might be required.
4. 5000 words: the active vocabulary of native speakers without higher education.
5. 10,000 words: the active vocabulary of native speakers with higher education.
6. 20,000 words: the amount you need to be able to recognize passively to read, understand, and enjoy a work of literature such as a novel by a notable author.

Caveats & Limitations.

1. A frequency list is never "The Definite Frequency List."

Depending on the source material analyzed, you may get different frequency lists. A corpus on spoken word differs from source texts based on a written language.

That is why we chose subtitles as our source, because, according to science, subtitles cover the best of both worlds: they correlate with both spoken and written language.

The frequency list is based on analysis of roughly 20 gigabytes of Spanish subtitles.

Visualize a book with almost 16 million pages, or 80.000 books of 200 pages each, to get an idea of the amount words that have been analyzed for this book.

If you were to read the source text used for this book, it would take you around 100 years of reading 24/7. A large base text is absolutely vital in order to develop an accurate frequency list.

Since 100 years of simply reading and then trying to process the text is a bit much for one person, we have called in additional power to help us establish the frequency rankings.

The raw data included over 1 million entries, or different "words". The raw data has been lemmatized; words are given in their dictionary form.

2. Creating a accurate frequency list is more complicated than it seems.

Above mentioned method of classification does come with it´s own complications. Take for example, the word

- **poder(se)**-*vb; m* – be able; power

Obviously, **poder** is most often used as a verb. However, you will see the word rank highly as one of the most common nouns. With our current methods, it is impossibe to determine exactly how often **poder** is used as a noun as opposed to the verb.

But while we developped an accurate method of estimating the correct position of "**poder**-*m* – power", (around the 500th most common word in Spanish), we decided we don't want duplicate entries in our frequency dictionaries. Why?

Poder is a single dictionary entry, and it's choosing between either "hey, you have duplicate entries, your list is wrong." and "hey, **poder** isn't the #9 most common noun, your list is wrong." (actual customer feedback, paraphrased.)

Because instances like **poder** are very few and inbetween, we kindly ask you to use your common sense while using this dictionary. Decide for yourself on not wether you should learn a translation or not.

Another difficulty are the conjugated verbs. Some conjugated vers can be classified as multiple parts of speech. Take for example **dicho**. It originally ranked somewhere around the 147th most common Spanish word.

As a conjugated verb, **dicho** is the past participle of "**decir**-*vb* – to say" and translates as "said", while as a noun it means "saying, expression".

No way, José, that "saying, expression" is the most 147th most used Spanish word. As previously stated, our words are lemmatized, and **decir** is already listed at place 77.

(Please refer to our upcoming book on Spanish verbs for detailed verb information, all regular and irregular conjugations and bilingual text example sentences.)

We did develop a method to accurately estimate the occurrence of **dicho** as a noun. By the time of writing "**dicho**-*m* – saying, expression" hoovers around the 11.702th place of the most common Spanish words. It is very unlikely that it will enter the 10.000 most common Spanish words, and thus will be out of the scope of our frequency dictionary series.

3. Nouns

We tried our best to keep out proper nouns, such as "**James**, **Ryan**, **Alice** as well as "**Rome**, **Washington**" or "the **Louvre**". Names of countries are an exception to the rule, and are included.

Some common proper nouns have multiple translations. For the ease of explanation, the following example is given in English.

"**Jack**" is a very common first name, but also a noun (a jack to lift up a vehicle) and a verb (to steal something). So is the word "**can**" It is a conjugation of the verb "to be able" as well as a noun (a tin can, or a can of soft drink).

With the current technology, it is unfortunately not possible to precisely identify the correct frequency placements of above words. We came up with a method to accurately estimate the correct placement of these words.

In example, a competitor's frequency dictionary on the English language listed the noun "**can**", like a can of coke, as the 247th most used word in the English language. Our methods would list it around the 3347th most used word. While not perfect, I *can* tell you that our method is more accurate than theirs.

4. This word doesn't belong there!

Some entries you might find odd in their respective frequency rankings. We were surprised a couple of times ourselves while creating this series. Keep in mind that the frequency list is compiled from a large amount of text, and may include words you wouldn't use yourself. But you might very well encounter them.

In our opinion, it is important you do know these words. Store them somewhere in your passive vocabulary, instead of trying to integrate them into your active vocabulary. But in the end, it's up to you wether you think you should learn a word, or skip it.

5. This is not a Spanish word!

You might find non-Spanish loanwords in this dictionary. We decided to include them, because if they´re being used in subtitle translation, it is safe to assume the word has been integrated into the Spanish general vocabulary.

6. Vulgarities

We also decided to keep out vulgarities, even though these are rather common in daily speech. We wanted to keep this book appropriate for readers of all ages. We tried to image what a modern-day middle American woman would take offense to, and drew the line there.

At the same time, some words absolutely needed to be clarified. In rare occasions, the usage of vocabulary items can differ severely between Spanish spoken in Latin America and Spanish spoken in Europe. It could lead to pretty awkward situations if you were not aware of these differences.

These words have been censored in way that one can still deduce their meaning, if one is already in the know. Kids, ask your parents. In example:

- **coger**-*vb* - to take, f*ck (LA)

7. Parallel text example sentences

Some sentences are easy, some are more difficult. Some are a direct translation, some are more loosely translated. Some mimic spoken language, some mimic written language. Some are more high-brow, some are more collequial. In short, we tried to include a mix of different types of language, just like you would encounter in real life.

Example sentences are great, because they show you Spanish word usage in context. You get to learn extra vocabulary from the sentences, since they're in parallel text. And since you'll encounter important, common words over and over again, you will ingrain those words faster in your long term memory.

8. Final thoughts

We are pretty confident our frequency ranking is as solid as it can be, keeping above pitfalls in mind. Still, this frequency list includes 25 extra words to compensate for any irregularities you might encounter. Or you might disagree with the addition of non-Spanish loanwords. So instead of the 5001 – 7500 most common words, you actually get the 5001-7525 most common words.

And one more thing.

The big secret to learning language is this: build your vocabulary, learn basic grammar and go out there and speak. Make mistakes, have a laugh and then learn from your mistakes. Wash, rinse, repeat..

We hope you enjoy this frequency dictionary and that it helps you in your journey of learning Spanish.

How To Use This Dictionary

abbreviation	*abr*	prefix	*pfx*
adjective	*adj*	preposition	*prp*
adverb	*adv*	pronoun	*prn*
article	*art*	suffix	*sfx*
auxiliary verb	*av*	verb	*vb*
conjunction	*con*	verb (reflexive)	*vbr*
contraction	*contr*	singular	*sg*
interjection	*int*	plural	*pl*
noun	*f(eminine), m(asculine)*	(coll)	*colloquial language*
numeral	*num*	(se)	*reflexive verb marker*
particle	*part*	(ES)	*European Spanish*
phrase	*phr*	(LA)	*Latin America Spanish*

Verbs

Some verbs can be used reflexively. Verbs that can be used reflexively are marked by "**(se)**". Only when the verb has a different meaning when used reflexively, we added the qualifier "**vbr**" to indicate the meaning of the reflexive verb.

Word Order

Different parts of speech are divided by "**;**". Generally speaking, the more common translations are given first.

Translations

We made the decision to give the most common translation(s) of a word, and respectively the most common part(s) of speech. It does, however, not mean that this is the only possible translations or the only part of speech the word can be used for.

International Phonetic Alphabet (IPA)

The pronunciation of foreign vocabulary can be tricky. To help you get it right, we added IPA entries for each entry. If you already have a base understanding of the pronunciation, you will find the IPA pronunciation straightforward. For more information, please visit www.internationalphoneticalphabet.org

Spanish English Frequency Dictionary

Rank	Spanish	English Translation(s)
	Part of Speech	Spanish Example Sentences
	[IPA]	-English Example Sentences

5001 indicio — **indication**
m
[ĩn̪.ˈdi.sjo]
El primer indicio de esta tormenta no es un trueno.
-The first hint of this storm is not a thunderclap.

5002 piña — **pineapple**
f
[ˈpi.ɲa]
Me gusta la piña azul de Jim.
-I like Jim's blue pineapple.

5003 reclutar — **recruit**
vb
[re.klu.ˈtar]
Esto no es una operación para reclutar partidarios.
-This is not an operation to recruit supporters.

5004 trayecto — **journey**
m
[tra.ˈjek̚.to]
Una vez que haya salido de la costa, el trayecto será corto pero muy sinuoso.
-Once you have left the coast, the journey is short but very winding.

5005 linaje — **lineage**
m
[li.ˈna.xe]
El presidente nombra a los secretarios basándose en lazos de linaje reconocidos.
-The president appoints the chiefs based on recognized lineage ties.

5006 manantial — **spring**
m
[ma.nãn̪.ˈtjal]
Los animales no beben del manantial.
-The animals don't drink from the spring.

5007 numeroso — **numerous**
adj
[nu.mɛ.ˈro.so]
Era rey de un pueblo numeroso.
-He was king over numerous people.

5008 negligencia — **negligence**
f
[ne.ɣli.ˈxẽn.sja]
Entre estos casos se incluyen desde la negligencia hasta agresiones y asesinatos.
-These cases include everything from negligence to assault and killings.

5009 coyote — **coyote**
m
[ko.ˈjo.te]
Parece que ahí entró un coyote.
-Looks like a coyote got in there.

5010 presenciar — **witness**
vb
[pre.sẽn.ˈsjar]
Es difícil presenciar algo tan abrumador.
-It's difficult to witness something so overwhelming.

5011 fulano — **some guy (coll)**
m
[fu.ˈla.no]
Fulano de Tal es un apelativo para una persona anónima.
-John Doe is a nickname for an anonymous person.

5012 milenio — **millennium**
m
[mi.ˈle.njo]
Pronto ingresaremos al primer siglo del tercer milenio.
-We will soon enter the first century of the third millennium.

5013 experimental — **experimental**
adj
[ɛks.pɛ.ri.mẽn̪.ˈtal]
Era una estación de energía experimental.
-It was an experimental power station.

5014 encarcelar — **imprison**
vb
[ẽŋ.kar.se.ˈlar]
El régimen ha decidido encarcelar a los oponentes.
-The regime has chosen to imprison opponents.

5015 analista — **analyst**
m/f
[a.na.ˈlis.ta]
No quiero terminar como analista financiero.
-I don't want to wind up a financial analyst.

5016 hermosura — **beauty**
f
[ɛr.mo.ˈsu.ra]
Si crees que puedes atraerme con tu hermosura, te equivocas y mucho.
-If you think you can entice me with your beauty then you are so wrong.

5017 erupción — **eruption**
f
[ɛ.rup.ˈsjõn]
Una erupción apareció en su cuello.
-A rash broke out on her neck.

5018 heroico — **heroic**
adj
[ɛ.ˈroi̯.ko]
Conociéndole, sería algo bastante heroico.
-Knowing him, it was something quite heroic.

5019 marfil — **ivory**
m
[mar.ˈfil]
Quiero usar un vestido marfil con hombros descubiertos.
-I want to wear an ivory gown with bare shoulders.

5020 malaria — **malaria**
f
[ma.ˈla.rja]
La malaria tiene graves consecuencias económicas y humanas para África.
-Malaria has a serious economic as well as human impact on Africa.

5021 precipicio — **cliff**
m
[pre.si.ˈpi.sjo]
Debería haberte lanzado por ese precipicio.
-I should've thrown you off that cliff back there.

5022 hebreo — **Hebrew; Jew**
adj; m
[e.ˈβre.o]
Aprenderé hebreo y estudiaré el Talmud.
-I will learn Hebrew and study the Talmud.

5023 hipnosis — **hypnosis**
f
[ip̚.ˈno.sis]
Le haré volver allí mediante hipnosis.
-I'm going to take you back there using hypnosis.

5024 persiana — **blind**
f
[pɛr.ˈsja.na]
Abre esa persiana, unos centímetros.
-Open that blind, just a few inches.

5025 nato — **born**
adj
[ˈna.to]
Eras un jinete nato, Jim.
-You were a natural horseman, Jim.

5026 parabrisas — **windshield**
m
[pa.ra.ˈβri.sas]
Tu parabrisas lleva roto un año.
-Your windshield's been broken for a year.

5027 demencia — **dementia**
f
[de.ˈmɛn.sja]
Se sabe que algunos hongos contaminantes causan fantasías, demencia, violencia.
-Some fungal contaminants have been known to cause delusions, dementia, and violence.

5028 poblar — **populate**
vb
[po.ˈβlar]
Organismos multicelulares empezaron a poblar todos estos océanos ancestrales, y prosperaron.
-Multicellular organisms began to populate all these ancestral oceans, and they thrived.

5029 incompetente — **incompetent**
adj
[ĩŋ.kõm.pɛ.ˈtẽn̪.te]
Para prevenir eso, tenemos que declararlo incompetente.
-To prevent that, we have to declare him incompetent.

5030 cuchilla — **blade**

	f		Estoy aplicando una gran fuerza en la cuchilla.
	[ku.ˈʧi.ja]		-I'm putting a tremendous amount of strain on the blade.
5031	**imitar**	**imitate**	
	vb		Solías imitar a personajes del libro.
	[i.mi.ˈtar]		-You used to imitate characters from the book.
5032	**receptor**	**recipient**	
	m		Cada una tiene un radio receptor dentro de ella.
	[re.sep̚.ˈtor]		-Each has a radio receiver inside it.
5033	**socialismo**	**socialism**	
	m		El thatcherismo surgió como la alternativa más aceptable al socialismo de
	[so.sja.ˈliṣ.mo]		estado.
			-Thatcherism emerged as the most plausible alternative to state socialism.
5034	**donar**	**donate**	
	vb		Mi padre está de acuerdo en donar tu corazón.
	[do.ˈnar]		-My father agrees to donate your heart.
5035	**significativo**	**significant**	
	adj		El cambio ha llegado rápido y ha sido significativo.
	[siɣ.ni.fi.ka.ˈti.βo]		-The change has come quickly and has been significant.
5036	**sonda**	**catheter**	
	f		Limpia la sonda con agua y jabón todos los días.
	[ˈsõn̪.da]		-Clean the catheter with soap and water every day.
5037	**extraer**	**extract**	
	vb		Ahora todos debemos extraer las conclusiones adecuadas de la experiencia.
	[ɛks.tra.ˈer]		-All of us must now draw the appropriate lessons from the experience.
5038	**despertador**	**alarm clock**	
	m		Cristóbal Colón era conocido por silenciar a su despertador repetidamente
	[dɛs.pɛr.ta.ˈðor]		golpeándolo con su puño. Desafortunadamente, su "despertador" era
			normalmente su primer oficial.
			-Christopher Columbus was notorious for repeatedly snoozing his alarm
			clock by hitting it with his fist. Unfortunately, his "alarm clock" was usually
			his first mate.
5039	**cactus**	**cactus**	
	m		Puedes visitar el museo del cactus.
	[ˈkak̚.tus]		-You can visit the Museum of the Cactus.
5040	**telefonear**	**call**	
	vb		Intenté telefonear a ambos desde el aeropuerto.
	[te.le.fo.ne.ˈar]		-I tried to phone you both from the airport.
5041	**académico**	**academic; academic**	
	adj; m		También pidió más apoyo para el sector académico.
	[a.ka.ˈðe.mi.ko]		-He also called for better support for the academic sector.
5042	**asombrar(se)**	**amaze**	
	vb		Aún puedes asombrar al mundo.
	[a.sõm.ˈbrar]		-You could yet astonish the world.
5043	**regional**	**regional**	
	adj		El proyecto también tratará de fomentar la cooperación regional.
	[re.xjo.ˈnal]		-The project will also seek to foster regional cooperation.
5044	**candado**	**padlock**	
	m		No tenemos tiempo de ocuparnos del candado.
	[kãn̪.ˈda.ðo]		-We don't have any time to fiddle with the lock.
5045	**musa**	**muse**	

f

['mu.sa]

Gracias por ser mi musa de la muerte.
-Thanks for being my death muse.

5046 captar

vb

[kap̚.'tar]

capture

Podría ser necesario estudiar las consecuencias de los diferentes enfoques, y cómo podían captar la variabilidad interanual.
-It may be necessary to consider the implications of the different approaches and how they can capture inter-annual variability.

5047 reinar

vb

[rei̯.'nar]

reign

Debe reinar un espíritu de consenso.
-A spirit of consensus must reign.

5048 antaño

adv

[ãn̪.'ta.ɲo]

formerly

Valiosos recursos que antaño estaban sujetos a consideraciones estratégicas enfrentadas se utilizan en la actualidad para fomentar una mayor cooperación.
-Valuable resources that were once subject to rival strategic considerations may now be used to foster greater cooperation.

5049 difundir

vb

[di.fũn̪.'dir]

spread

Además, el programa ha logrado captar y difundir las mejores prácticas de manera efectiva.
-In addition, the programme has managed to effectively capture and disseminate best practices.

5050 sacramento

m

[sa.kra.'mẽn̪.to]

sacrament

Dejó de tomar el sacramento después de que le visitaras.
-He stopped taking the sacrament after you visited.

5051 arruga

f

[a.'ru.ɣa]

wrinkle

Recuerdo cada arruga de su rostro.
-I remember every wrinkle on his face.

5052 transparente

adj

[trãns.pa.'rẽn̪.te]

transparent

Además, era indispensable que el proceso fuera transparente.
-It was, moreover, vital that the process is transparent.

5053 intolerable

adj

[ĩn̪.to.lɛ.'ra.βle]

unbearable

Después de eso, su vida se volvió intolerable.
-After that, his life became unbearable.

5054 pronóstico

m

[pro.'nos.ti.ko]

prediction

Por desgracia, este pronóstico se está cumpliendo ahora.
-Unfortunately, that prediction is now coming true.

5055 húngaro

adj; m

['ũŋ.ga.ro]

Hungarian; Hungarian person

No entendía una palabra de húngaro.
-I did not understand one word of Hungarian.

5056 escandaloso

adj

[ɛs.kãn̪.da.'lo.so]

scandalous

Les informaré sobre este contrato escandaloso.
-I'll tell them about this scandalous contract.

5057 imperdonable

adj

[ĩm.pɛr.ðo.'na.βle]

unforgivable

Sin embargo, abandonar nuestras acciones ahora sería imperdonable.
-To abandon our own actions now, however, would be unforgivable.

5058 francotirador

m

[frãn.ko.ti.ra.'ðor]

sniper

Tenía la esperanza de hallar así al francotirador.
-I was hoping that's how I'd find the sniper.

5059 vertical

adj

[bɛr.ti.'kal]

vertical

La carga estática vertical máxima la determina el fabricante.
-The maximum static vertical load is laid down by the manufacturer.

5060	**camionero**	**truck driver**
	m	Su hermano había sido camionero durante treinta años.
	[ka.mjo.ˈnɛ.ro]	-His brother had been a truck driver for thirty years.
5061	**revivir**	**revive**
	vb	Tenemos que responder a ese reto y revivir enérgicamente el debate sobre la reforma.
	[re.βi.ˈβir]	-We must respond to this challenge and energetically revive the reform debate.
5062	**frecuente**	**frequent**
	adj	Se ha demostrado que el consumo frecuente de pescado reduce el riesgo de padecer enfermedades cardíacas.
	[fre.ˈkwẽ̞.te]	-Frequent fish consumption has been shown to reduce the risk of heart disease.
5063	**ecuación**	**equation**
	f	Le he preparado una pequeña ecuación matemática.
	[e.kwa.ˈsjõn]	-I have prepared a little mathematical equation for you.
5064	**guisante**	**pea**
	m	No me gusta dejar un guisante solo en mi plato.
	[gi.ˈsã̞n.te]	-I don't like to leave one pea all alone on my plate.
5065	**maternidad**	**maternity**
	f	Mejores beneficios de maternidad también aumentan las tasas de natalidad.
	[ma.tɛr.ni.ˈðað]	-Better maternity benefits also raise birth rates.
5066	**prender**	**fasten, light**
	vb	Me encantaría prender uno de estos.
	[prẽ̞n.ˈdɛr]	-I would love to light one of these.
5067	**receso**	**break**
	m	Hablaré con usted después del receso.
	[re.ˈse.so]	-I'll talk to you after the break.
5068	**higiene**	**hygiene**
	f	Es importante tener buena higiene oral.
	[i.ˈxje.ne]	-Having good oral hygiene is important.
5069	**negación**	**denial**
	f	Tu nivel de negación es poco intenso.
	[ne.ɣa.ˈsjõn]	-Your level of denial is a little intense.
5070	**lomo**	**loin**
	m	El lomo está ligeramente relleno con escarola a la parrilla.
	[ˈlo.mo]	-The loin is lightly stuffed with grilled escarole.
5071	**opresión**	**oppression**
	f	Todos debemos actuar frente a la opresión.
	[o.pre.ˈsjõn]	-We must all act in the face of oppression.
5072	**reducción**	**reduction**
	f	También agradezco la reducción del papeleo.
	[re.ðuk.ˈsjõn]	-I also welcome the reduction in the paperwork.
5073	**irracional**	**irrational**
	adj	Seguimos haciendo lo que es irracional.
	[i.ra.sjo.ˈnal]	-We go on doing what is irrational.
5074	**gentileza**	**gentleness**
	f	Tiene mucha gentileza en sus ojos.
	[xẽ̞n.ti.ˈle.sa]	-He has such gentleness in his eyes.
5075	**detectar**	**detect**

	vb	Necesitamos un procedimiento para detectar y eliminarlos.
	[dɛ.tekˈtar]	-We need a procedure to detect and eliminate these.
5076	**comino**	**cumin**
	m	Las semillas de comino suelen sembrarse a principios de la primavera.
	[koˈmi.no]	-Cumin seeds are usually sown at the beginning of spring.
5077	**preciar(se)**	**value; pride yourself in**
	vb; vbr	Me agrada enormemente que vuelvas a apreciar mi conocimiento.
	[preˈsjar]	-It pleases me greatly that once again you value my knowledge.
5078	**principiante**	**beginner**
	m/f	Lo hizo bien para ser un principiante.
	[prĩn.siˈpjãn̪.te]	-He did well for a beginner.
5079	**pantera**	**panther**
	f	Porque es más inteligente que la pantera.
	[pãn̪ˈtɛ.ra]	-Because he's smarter than the panther.
5080	**cava**	**cava**
	m	Bueno, he comprado una botella de cava.
	[ˈka.βa]	-Anyway, I've bought a bottle of Cava.
5081	**latino**	**Latin; Latino**
	adj; m	Un proverbio latino reza que lo natural es bueno.
	[laˈti.no]	-A Latin proverb says that natural is good.
5082	**inmóvil**	**immobile**
	adj	Me quedé ahí, inmóvil, observándoles con envidia.
	[ĩmˈmo.βil]	-I stood there, immobile, looking up at them jealously.
5083	**empujón**	**push**
	m	Podríamos salir y darte un empujón.
	[ɛ̃m.puˈxõn]	-We could come out and give you a push.
5084	**travesía**	**voyage**
	f	El turismo es un viaje y una travesía.
	[tra.βeˈsi.a]	-Tourism is a journey and a voyage.
5085	**élite**	**elite**
	f	Son la élite del ejército alemán.
	[ˈe.li.te]	-They are the elite of the German army.
5086	**resplandor**	**brightness**
	m	La radiante revolución brilla con todo su resplandor.
	[rɛs.plãn̪ˈdor]	-The radiant revolution shines with all its brightness.
5087	**simulacro**	**drill**
	m	No recuerdo haber autorizado un simulacro táctico.
	[si.muˈla.kro]	-I don't recall authorizing a tactical drill.
5088	**repleto**	**full**
	adj	Este mundo está repleto de cosas interesantes que todavía no conoces.
	[repˈlɛ.to]	-This world is full of interesting things you have yet to know about.
5089	**escasez**	**shortage**
	f	Las predicciones sugieren que habrá escasez de trabajadores.
	[ɛsˈka.ses]	-Predictions suggest that there will be a shortage of workers.
5090	**festín**	**feast**
	m	Deberá esperar hasta después del festín.
	[fɛsˈtĩn]	-You'll have to wait until after the feast.
5091	**indiferencia**	**indifference**

	f	No puedo soportar más esta indiferencia.
	[ĩn̪.di.fɛ.ˈrɛ̃n.sja]	-I can't stand this indifference anymore.
5092	**bollo**	**bread roll, sweet bun**
	m	Yo solo he recibido un bollo.
	[ˈbo.jo]	-I only had one bread roll.
5093	**pinza**	**clothespin**
	f	Había una pinza para la ropa, el suelo, debajo de la cama.
	[ˈpĩn.sa]	-There was a clothespin lying there on the floor at the foot of the bed.
5094	**gringo**	**gringo; gringo (coll), foreigner (LA) (coll)**
	adj; m	Gracias por el efectivo, gringo.
	[ˈgrĩŋ.go]	-Thank you for the cash, gringo.
5095	**marioneta**	**puppet**
	f	Una marioneta no sabe que está siendo manipulada.
	[ma.rjo.ˈnɛ.ta]	-A puppet does not know that it is being controlled.
5096	**colono**	**settler, tenant farmer**
	m	Un colono resultó levemente herido en uno de los incidentes.
	[ko.ˈlo.no]	-A settler was slightly injured during one of the incidents.
5097	**subconsciente**	**subconscious**
	m	Ha estado en su subconsciente unas cuantas décadas.
	[suβ.kõns.ˈsjẽn̪.te]	-It has been in your subconsciousness for a few decades.
5098	**pera**	**pear**
	f	La única pera que queda en el árbol está podrida.
	[ˈpɛ.ra]	-The only pear left on the tree is rotten.
5099	**azafata**	**flight attendant**
	f	Era una azafata compartiendo un departamento.
	[a.sa.ˈfa.ta]	-She was a flight attendant sharing an apartment.
5100	**intriga**	**scheme**
	f	Necesitamos tu ayuda con una intriga.
	[ĩn̪.ˈtri.ɣa]	-We need your help with a scheme.
5101	**procurador**	**attorney**
	m	Yo soy el padre del procurador.
	[pro.ku.ra.ˈðor]	-I am the attorney's father.
5102	**odioso**	**odious**
	adj	Todo esto sería odioso si no fuera grotesco.
	[o.ˈðjo.so]	-All of this would be odious, were it not so grotesque.
5103	**arrepentimiento**	**remorse**
	m	Los tiranos no suelen mostrar arrepentimiento por su brutalidad.
	[a.re.pẽn̪.ti.ˈmjẽn̪.to]	-Tyrants seldom show remorse for their brutality.
5104	**dictador**	**dictator**
	m	Un dictador comunista nos arrebató nuestra patria.
	[dik̚.ta.ˈðor]	-Our homeland was taken from us by a communist dictator.
5105	**falsificación**	**counterfeit**
	f	Te arresto por cómplice en una operación de falsificación.
	[fal.si.fi.ka.ˈsjõn]	-I'm arresting you as an accomplice in a counterfeiting operation.
5106	**galán**	**handsome man**
	m	A mí me gustas más, mi apuesto galán.
	[ga.ˈlãn]	-I like you better, my handsome man.
5107	**trimestre**	**trimester**

	m	Cada trimestre se propondrán nuevos problemas.
	[tri.ˈmɛs.tre]	-New problems will be proposed each trimester.
5108	**fluido**	**fluid; free-flowing; fluently**
	m; adj; adv	Tengo el resultado preliminar del fluido.
	[ˈflwi.ðo]	-I got a preliminary result on the fluid.
5109	**expansión**	**expansion**
	f	Una vez acabada la expansión, usted y su tripulación serán recompensados.
	[ɛks.pãn.ˈsjõn]	-Once the expansion is complete, you and your crew will be rewarded.
5110	**bulto**	**lump**
	m	Este bulto en mi cabeza está creciendo.
	[ˈbul̪.to]	-This lump on my head is getting bigger.
5111	**redención**	**redemption**
	f	Tengo que creer que hay esperanza de redención.
	[re.ðɛ̃n.ˈsjõn]	-I have to believe that there is hope for redemption.
5112	**delicia**	**delight**
	f	Es una auténtica delicia para los amantes de la comida.
	[de.ˈli.sja]	-It is a true delight for food lovers.
5113	**supervisión**	**supervision**
	f	No se puede progresar sin normas o supervisión.
	[su.pɛr.βi.ˈsjõn]	-Without rules or supervision, you cannot make any progress.
5114	**ahogo**	**distress, difficulty breathing**
	m	Siempre siento ahogo en sitios cerrados.
	[a.ˈo.ɣo]	-I always choke in closed rooms.
5115	**descaro**	**impertinence**
	m	Tiene el descaro de aparcar justo delante.
	[dɛs.ˈka.ro]	-He has the nerve to park right out front.
5116	**repetición**	**repetition**
	f	La repetición no mejora su credibilidad.
	[re.pɛ.ti.ˈsjõn]	-Repetition does not enhance its credibility.
5117	**menudo**	**small**
	adj	Es menudo para la edad que tiene, pero ya sabe leer.
	[me.ˈnu.ðo]	-He's small for his age, but he can read already.
5118	**continental**	**continental**
	adj	Sirven un desayuno continental en este hotel.
	[kõn̪.ti.nɛ̃n̪.ˈtal]	-They serve a continental breakfast in this hotel.
5119	**llanta**	**tire**
	f	Y tenemos una huella de llanta.
	[ˈʎ̞ãn̪.ta]	-And we have a tire print.
5120	**casual**	**chance**
	adj	Fue descubierta de manera casual por un agricultor.
	[ka.ˈswal]	-It was discovered by chance by a farmer.
5121	**trepar**	**climb**
	vb	Debes sujetarlo si intenta trepar hacia afuera.
	[tre.ˈpar]	-You have to hold him if he tries to climb out.
5122	**soplo**	**breeze, breath**
	m	Un soplo tibio y silencioso.
	[ˈsop̚.lo]	-A breeze that's warm and silent.
5123	**plátano**	**banana**

	m	Deberíamos darle un plátano o algo.
	['pla.ta.no]	-We should get him a banana or something.
5124	**mentón**	**chin**
	m	El mentón y la frente también suelen ser mayores.
	[mɛ̃n.'tõn]	-The chin and forehead also tend to be larger.
5125	**mordisco**	**bite**
	m	Ese mordisco que me diste la semana pasada aún duele.
	[mor.'ðis.ko]	-That bite you gave me last week still throbs.
5126	**mutante**	**mutating; mutant**
	adj; m/f	Atrapé al líder de la rebelión mutante.
	[mu.'tãn.te]	-I have apprehended the leader of the mutant rebellion.
5127	**apretón**	**squeeze**
	m	Muy bien, dame un gran apretón.
	[a.prɛ.'tõn]	-All right, give me a big squeeze.
5128	**gaseosa**	**soda**
	f	Y un día, hace ocho años, mi hijo volcó gaseosa sobre la alfombra.
	[ga.se.'o.sa]	-And one day, eight years ago, my son spilled soda on our new carpet.
5129	**familiarizar(se)**	**become familiar with**
	vb	El objetivo del foro era familiarizar a los jóvenes con sus derechos cívicos.
	[fa.mi.lja.ri.'sar]	-The aim of the forum was to familiarize young people with their civil rights.
5130	**costura**	**seam, needlework**
	f	Una costura a la vista no es un defecto en su alfombra.
	[kos.'tu.ra]	-A visible seam is not a defect with your carpet.
5131	**albóndiga**	**meatball**
	f	Se me cayó la albóndiga en la piscina.
	[al.'βõn.di.ɣa]	-I dropped my meatball in the pool.
5132	**intestino**	**intestine**
	m	Esto entrará hasta llegar a tu intestino.
	[ĩn.tɛs.'ti.no]	-This is going in until it reaches your intestine.
5133	**imprenta**	**printing**
	f	Hasta la imprenta realmente no hubo propiedad intelectual.
	[ĩm.'prɛ̃n.ta]	-Until printing, there was no real intellectual property.
5134	**preliminar**	**preliminary**
	m	Me gustaría hacer otra observación preliminar.
	[pre.li.mi.'nar]	-I would like to make one other preliminary remark.
5135	**cristianismo**	**Christianity**
	m	Yo crecí pensando que el cristianismo era sinónimo de hipocresía.
	[kris.tja.'nis̪.mo]	-I was raised to believe Christianity was synonymous with hypocrisy.
5136	**llorón**	**whiny; crybaby**
	adj; m	Te estás comportando como un bebe llorón.
	[ʎo.'rõn]	-You're behaving like a sucking crybaby.
5137	**errado**	**wrong**
	adj	Creo que vamos por el camino errado.
	[ɛ.'ra.ðo]	-I think that we are on the wrong track.
5138	**residir**	**reside**
	vb	La preparación para las catástrofes no tiene que residir exclusivamente en el gobierno.
	[re.si.'ðir]	-Preparation for catastrophe does not have to reside exclusively with the government.
5139	**suavidad**	**softness**

f

[swa.βi.'ðað]

Me importa mucho la suavidad de mi piel.

-I care a great deal about the softness of my skin.

5140 censurar

vb

[sɛ̃n.su.'rar]

censor

La junta tiene el derecho de censurar las películas y obras teatrales que considere culturalmente inadecuadas.

-The board has the right to censor films and dramas which are considered culturally inappropriate.

5141 gozo

m

['go.so]

joy

En la izquierda tenéis algunas fotos de los protagonistas de nuestro gozo.

-In the left, you've got some photos of the protagonists of our joy.

5142 vigor

m

[bi.'ɣor]

vigor

Tienes el vigor del típico turista.

-You have the vigor of a typical tourist.

5143 jeque

m

['xe.ke]

sheik

El jeque Hassan estaba hablando de ese incidente.

-Sheikh Hassan was talking about that incident.

5144 tuberculosis

f

[tu.βɛr.ku.'lo.sis]

tuberculosis

Si tuviera tuberculosis tampoco sería culpa suya.

-If he had tuberculosis, it wouldn't be his fault either.

5145 cloaca

f

[klo.'a.ka]

sewer

Sin duda aquí huele como en una cloaca.

-It certainly smells like a sewer in here.

5146 gueto

m

['gɛ.to]

ghetto

El gueto está muy tranquilo últimamente.

-Things have been quiet in the ghetto lately.

5147 uranio

m

[u.'ra.njo]

uranium

Deberíamos empezar el tratamiento por la toxicidad del uranio como dijiste.

-We should start treatment for the uranium toxicity like you said.

5148 audio

msg

['au̯.ðjo]

audio

Puedes grabar independientemente el vídeo del audio.

-You can record the video independently of the audio.

5149 mandamiento

m

[mãn.da.'mjẽn.to]

commandment

No era un mandamiento en los tiempos de la Biblia.

-It wasn't a commandment in Bible times.

5150 modestia

f

[mo.'ðɛs.tja]

modesty

Apruebo vuestras intenciones así como vuestra modestia.

-I approve of your intentions as much as of your modesty.

5151 recipiente

m

[re.si.'pjẽn.te]

container

Vamos, déjame ver el recipiente.

-Come on, let me see the container.

5152 sanidad

f

[sa.ni.'ðað]

health service

Tienen sanidad disponible para todos.

-They have health care accessible to all.

5153 apuñalar

vb

[a.pu.ɲa.'lar]

stab

Las tijeras son para cortar pero pueden usarse también para apuñalar.

-Scissors are meant for cutting but can also be used to stab.

5154 imán

m

[i.'mãn]

magnet

Un imán puede coger y sostener muchos clavos a la vez.

-A magnet can pick up and hold many nails at a time.

5155 micro

mic, minibus

	m		Necesitamos meter un micro grabador adentro.
	['mi.kro]		-We need to get a micro recorder inside.
5156	**presumir**		**presume**
	vb		No te atrevas a presumir que me conoces.
	[pre.su.'mir]		-Don't you dare presume to know me.
5157	**borrador**		**draft, rubber**
	m		Tendrá el borrador en tres horas.
	[bo.ra.'ðor]		-You'll have a draft in three hours.
5158	**dominó**		**dominoes**
	m		Está allí con sus amigotes jugando al dominó.
	[do.mi.'no]		-He's there with his buddies, playing dominoes.
5159	**carnero**		**ram**
	m		Es muchísimo dinero por un carnero.
	[kar.'nɛ.ro]		-That's a lot of money for one ram.
5160	**patrimonio**		**heritage, wealth**
	m		Son parte del patrimonio cultural del mundo.
	[pa.tri.'mo.njo]		-They are a part of the world cultural heritage.
5161	**cobardía**		**cowardice**
	f		Debemos poner fin a esta cobardía.
	[ko.βar.'ði.a]		-We must put a stop to this cowardice.
5162	**suplente**		**substitute**
	m		La suplente no se detendrá hasta quitarme todo.
	[supˈ.'lẽn̪.te]		-That substitute won't stop until she takes everything from me.
5163	**estabilidad**		**stability**
	f		Todos queremos ver estabilidad en nuestra perturbada región.
	[ɛs.ta.βi.li.'ðað]		-We all want to see stability in our troubled region.
5164	**pose**		**pose**
	f		Usted parece no conseguir mantener la pose.
	['po.se]		-You seem to not get to maintain the pose.
5165	**recluta**		**recruit**
	m/f		Seguro que sería un buen recluta.
	[re.'klu.ta]		-I'm sure he'll make a fine recruit.
5166	**geografía**		**geography**
	f		Voy a hablar de historia, geografía y sociología.
	[xe.o.ɣra.'fi.a]		-I am going to talk about history, geography, and sociology.
5167	**caloría**		**calorie**
	f		Se necesitan unas 10 calorías para producir cada caloría de comida que consumimos en Occidente.
	[ka.lo.'ri.a]		-It takes about 10 calories to produce every calorie of food that we consume in the West.
5168	**inmune**		**immune**
	adj		Soy inmune a tu veneno paralizante.
	[ĩm.'mu.ne]		-I'm immune to your paralyzing poison.
5169	**palma**		**palm**
	f		Sujétalo en la palma y ciérrala.
	['pal.ma]		-Hold it in your palm and close it.
5170	**litera**		**bunk**
	f		Los listos escogen la litera primero.
	[li.'tɛ.ra]		-The smart ones go for his bunk first.
5171	**potro**		**colt**

m [ˈpo.tɾo]	Dele la oportunidad a este potro de mostrarle lo que puede hacer. -Give this colt a chance to show you what he can do.

5172 sacudir(se) — **shake; get rid off**
vb; vbr
[sa.ku.ˈðir]

Puedes sacudir un poco la cama.
-You can shake the bed a little.

5173 fundador — **founder**
m
[fũn̪.da.ˈðor]

Nos consuelan las palabras de nuestro fundador.
-We are comforted by the words of our founder.

5174 germen — **germ**
m
[ˈxɛɾ.mẽn]

Las sociedades pobres continuarán infectadas por el germen del conflicto.
-Poor societies will continue being affected by the germ of conflict.

5175 combatiente — **fighter**
m
[kõm.ba.ˈtjẽn̪.te]

Ningún terrorista puede ser un combatiente por la libertad.
-No terrorist can be a freedom fighter.

5176 fascismo — **fascism**
m
[fas.ˈsis̺.mo]

Cuando cayó el fascismo, surgieron las Naciones Unidas.
-As fascism fell, the United Nations rose.

5177 votante — **voter**
m
[bo.ˈtãn̪.te]

El segundo voto se concede a cualquier partido que decida el votante.
-The second vote is given to any party of the voter's choice.

5178 ombligo — **belly button**
m
[õm.ˈbli.ɣo]

No creo que Satán tenga ombligo.
-I don't think Satan has a belly button.

5179 entusiasta — **fan; enthusiastic**
m; adj [ẽn̪.tu.ˈsjas.ta]

Mi padre fue el más entusiasta. -My father was the most enthusiastic.

5180 jarabe — **syrup**
m
[xa.ˈra.βe]

Ahora conozco la historia del jarabe.
-I now know the history of syrup.

5181 acertijo — **riddle**
m
[a.sɛɾ.ˈti.xo]

Tenemos un acertijo medieval que resolver.
-We have a medieval riddle to solve.

5182 prohibición — **prohibition**
f
[pro.i.βi.ˈsjõn]

Podrán aplicarse sanciones a quienes no respeten esta prohibición.
-Sanctions can be applied to those who fail to respect this prohibition.

5183 hectárea — **hectare**
f
[ek̚.ˈta.re.a]

Se arrasan tres hectáreas de bosques para obtener una hectárea de coca.
-Three hectares of forest have to be destroyed to obtain one hectare of coca.

5184 apto — **suitable**
adj
[ˈap̚.to]

Busca un donante apto y pagaremos mucho menos.
-Come up with a suitable donor and we pay a lot less.

5185 rector — **dean**
m
[rek̚.ˈtor]

Estaba en una reunión con el rector.
-I was in a meeting with the dean.

5186 zurdo — **left-handed; left-handed person**
adj; m
[ˈsur.ðo]

Ni siquiera puedes jugarlo si eres zurdo.
-You can't even play it if you're left-handed.

5187 inolvidable — **unforgettable**
adj
[i.nol.βi.ˈða.βle]

Todo estará organizado para hacer su estancia inolvidable.
-Everything will be organized around you to make your stay unforgettable.

5188 adulterio — **adultery**
m
[a.ðul̩.ˈtɛ.rjo]
Según el tribunal afgano, había cometido adulterio.
-According to the Afghan judge, she had committed adultery.

5189 vinagre — **vinegar**
m
[bi.ˈna.ɣre]
Un poco de vinagre podría haberlo evitado.
-A little bit of vinegar would have probably done the trick.

5190 sequía — **drought**
f
[se.ˈki.a]
Me preocupa la sequía en Kenia.
-I'm concerned about the drought in Kenya.

5191 orar — **pray, make a speech**
vb
[o.ˈrar]
Puede ser importante orar en público o en familia.
-It may be important to pray in public or with our family.

5192 excesivo — **excessive**
adj
[ɛk.se.ˈsi.βo]
Me parece excesivo en estos momentos.
-I think it is excessive at this point in time.

5193 protegido — **protegé**
m
[pro.te.ˈxi.ðo]
Su protegido está hoy en el arcade.
-Your protegé is in the arcade today.

5194 octava — **octave**
f[ok̩.ˈta.βa]
No sé cuánto es una octava. -I don't know how much an octave is.

5195 invernadero — **greenhouse**
m
[ĩm.bɛr.na.ˈðɛ.ro]
El ambiente controlado del invernadero permite intensificar la producción agrícola.
-The controlled environment within the greenhouse allows agricultural production to be intensified.

5196 transacción — **transaction**
f
[trãn.sak.ˈsjõn]
Estoy hablando de una simple transacción.
-I'm talking about a simple transaction.

5197 genético — **genetic**
adj
[xe.ˈnɛ.ti.ko]
Era un ingeniero genético del proyecto.
-He was a genetic engineer on the project.

5198 venado — **deer**
m
[be.ˈna.ðo]
Estuviste bebiendo y atropellaste a un venado.
-You were drinking and you hit a deer.

5199 obligatorio — **mandatory**
adj
[o.βli.ɣa.ˈto.rjo]
Un examen obligatorio debe formar parte de la solución.
-A mandatory review must be an integral part of the solution.

5200 lápida — **tombstone**
f
[ˈla.pi.ða]
Escribiré mi nombre en tu lápida.
-I'll write my name on your tombstone.

5201 delegado — **delegate**
m
[de.le.ˈɣa.ðo]
En ausencia del delegado, se designará a un sustituto.
-In absence of the delegate, a proxy shall be designated.

5202 biografía — **biography**
f
[bjo.ɣra.ˈfi.a]
Algún día me gustaría escribir su biografía.
-I would like to write his biography one day.

5203 extravagante — **extravagant**
adj
[ɛks.tra.βa.ˈɣãn̩.te]
No sabía que podías permitirte algo tan extravagante.
-I didn't realize you could afford something this extravagant.

5204	**introducir(se)**	**introduce**
	vb	La Unión Europea podría introducir inmediatamente ese impuesto.
	[ĩṇ.tro.ðu.ˈsir]	-The European Union could introduce such a tax immediately.

5205	**guionista**	**screenwriter**
	m/f	Le conseguiré la ayuda de un guionista profesional.
	[gjo.ˈnis.ta]	-I'll get her some help from a professional screenwriter.

5206	**zumbido**	**buzz**
	m	Tu teléfono no detendrá su incesante zumbido.
	[sũm.ˈbi.ðo]	-Your phone will not stop its incessant buzzing.

5207	**provisional**	**provisional**
	adj	Te dí solo un indulto provisional.
	[pro.βi.sjo.ˈnal]	-I have given you only a provisional reprieve.

5208	**merodear**	**lurk**
	vb	Prefieren merodear en la oscuridad de sus nidos.
	[mɛ.ro.ðe.ˈar]	-Prefieren merodear en la oscuridad de sus nidos.

5209	**filipino**	**Philippine; Philippine person**
	adj; m[fi.li.ˈpi.no]	Es un espía filipino de primera. -He's a top Philippine spy.

5210	**impermeable**	**weatherproof; waterproof**
	m; adj	Es impermeable y tiene garantía completa.
	[ĩm.pɛr.me.ˈa.βle]	-It's waterproof and comes with a full warranty.

5211	**párroco**	**parish priest**
	m	Un párroco también resultó herido en el ataque.
	[ˈpa.ro.ko]	-A parish priest was wounded also in the assault.

5212	**ocasional**	**occasional**
	adj	Créame, puedo manejar la rabieta ocasional.
	[o.ka.sjo.ˈnal]	-Trust me, I can handle the occasional temper tantrum.

5213	**juzgado**	**court**
	m	Estoy deseando verte en el juzgado.
	[xuṣ.ˈɣa.ðo]	-I look forward to seeing you in court.

5214	**jaqueca**	**migraine**
	f	Hagamos algunos ejercicios para la jaqueca.
	[xa.ˈke.ka]	-Let's do some exercise for the migraine.

5215	**progresar**	**progress**
	vb	Todavía hay que progresar mucho para consolidar esa alianza.
	[pro.ɣre.ˈsar]	-Much progress has yet to be made in deepening that partnership.

5216	**aspirador**	**vacuum**
	m	Y este es el aspirador del que te estaba hablando.
	[as.pi.ra.ˈðor]	-And here's that vacuum cleaner I was talking to you about.

5217	**asignación**	**assignment**
	f	Tenemos una asignación muy especial para ustedes dos.
	[a.siɣ.na.ˈsjõn]	-We've got a very special assignment for you two.

5218	**excéntrico**	**eccentric; eccentric person**
	adj; m	Simplemente es sincero y algo excéntrico.
	[ɛk.ˈsẽṇ.tri.ko]	-He's just open and a little eccentric.

5219	**disparate**	**folly**
	m	Esperar que tolere sus limitaciones es un disparate.
	[dis.pa.ˈra.te]	-Expecting him to abide by your limitations is a folly.

5220	**mezquita**	**mosque**

	f [mɛs.ˈki.ta]	Parte de la mezquita se incendió. -Part of the mosque was set on fire.
5221	**barricada** f [ba.ri.ˈka.ða]	**barricade** El remolque vacío proporcionó la barricada perfecta. -The empty trailer provided the perfect barricade.
5222	**rastreador** adj; m [ras.tre.a.ˈðor]	**tracking; tracker** Debió haber quitado el rastreador del taxi. -She must have removed the cab's tracker.
5223	**cabrear** vb [ka.βre.ˈar]	**piss off** Eligió al policía equivocado para cabrear. -You picked the wrong cop to piss off.
5224	**desempleado** adj; m [de.sẽm.ple.ˈa.ðo]	**unemployed; unemployed person** Cientos de desempleados bajan del tren. -Hundreds of unemployed step out of the train.
5225	**vanguardia** f[bãŋ.ˈgwar.ðja]	**avant-garde, vanguard** Yo formo parte de la vanguardia. -I'm part of the avant-garde.
5226	**asiático** adj; m [a.ˈsja.ti.ko]	**Asian; Asian person** Tiene un jardín asiático en su casa en el que medita. -He has an Asian garden at his house where he meditates.
5227	**complicar(se)** vb [kõm.pli.ˈkar]	**complicate** Entiendo que esto puede complicar algunas cosas. -I can understand how this might complicate a few things.
5228	**consiguiente** adj [kõn.si.ˈɣjẽn̪.te]	**consequent** En el debate consiguiente se ha tratado de precisar más estos temas. -The subsequent debate attempted to clarify these issues.
5229	**aguardiente** m [a.ɣwar.ˈðjẽn̪.te]	**moonshine** Este es el mejor aguardiente que puedes probar. -This is just the best moonshine you'll ever taste.
5230	**por doquier** adv [por ðo.ˈkjɛr]	**all over the place** Edificios altos por doquier, como pilares. -High rises all over the place, like pillars.
5231	**entretener(se)** vb [ẽn̪.trɛ.te.ˈnɛr]	**entertain** Cuando escribo sobre personas intento entretener al lector. -When I write about people, I try to entertain the reader.
5232	**coleccionista** m/f [ko.lɛk.sjo.ˈnis.ta]	**collector** Preferiría vendérselo a un coleccionista de verdad. -I'd rather just sell it to a real collector.
5233	**eclipse** m [e.ˈklip.se]	**eclipse** Nos permite observar el eclipse sin dañarnos los ojos. -It allows us to look at the eclipse without injury to our eyes.
5234	**enfrentamiento** m [ẽɱ.frẽn̪.ta.ˈmjẽn̪.to]	**confrontation** Afortunadamente no se produjo ningún enfrentamiento. -Fortunately, a confrontation did not take place.
5235	**meteoro** m [mɛ.te.ˈo.ro]	**meteor** Ha estado tras el meteoro todo este tiempo. -He was after the meteor all this time.
5236	**emitir** vb [e.mi.ˈtir]	**broadcast** Bueno, Jane quería emitir la entrevista el día siguiente. -Well, Jane wanted to broadcast the interview the next day.

5237	**inseguro**	**unsafe, insecure**
	adj	Sin embargo, el mundo sigue siendo inseguro.
	[ĩn.se.ˈɣu.ro]	-However, the world is still unsafe.
5238	**alergia**	**allergy**
	f	Tengo alergia a la leche.
	[a.ˈlɛr.xja]	-I have an allergy to milk.
5239	**golosina**	**candy**
	f	Esto nunca habría sucedido si hubieras cogido esa golosina.
	[go.lo.ˈsi.na]	-This never would have happened if you had reached for that candy.
5240	**abad**	**abbot**
	m	Vamos a despertar al abad.
	[a.ˈβað]	-We will awake the abbot.
5241	**calavera**	**skull**
	f[ka.la.ˈβɛ.ra]	Envié la calavera a otro laboratorio. -I sent the skull out to another lab.
5242	**estirar(se)**	**stretch**
	vb	Bien, pueden estirar sus piernas.
	[ɛs.ti.ˈrar]	-All right, you can stretch your legs.
5243	**fugaz**	**brief**
	adj	Ese mismo día empezamos un romance fugaz.
	[ˈfu.ɣas]	-That very day our brief romance began.
5244	**ruiseñor**	**nightingale**
	m	Leí ese poema suyo de un ruiseñor.
	[rwi.se.ˈɲor]	-I read that poem of his about the nightingale.
5245	**cerrojo**	**bolt**
	m	Hay miles de libras de presión en ese cerrojo.
	[sɛ.ˈro.xo]	-There are a thousand pounds of pressure on that bolt.
5246	**andén**	**platform**
	m	Necesitamos el vídeo de seguridad de ese andén.
	[ãn̪.ˈdɛn]	-We need the security video from that platform.
5247	**impredecible**	**unpredictable**
	adj	Tom siempre me pareció un poco impredecible para empezar.
	[ĩm.pre.ðe.ˈsi.βle]	-Tom always struck me as a little unpredictable, to begin with.
5248	**túnica**	**tunic**
	f	Llevan la cruz debajo de la túnica.
	[ˈtu.ni.ka]	-They carry the cross under the tunic.
5249	**gigantesco**	**gigantic**
	adj	Entonces lo vertieron en un gigantesco molde de arcilla.
	[xi.ɣãn̪.ˈtɛs.ko]	-Then it was poured into a gigantic clay mould.
5250	**compartimiento**	**compartment**
	m	El fuego se expandió al siguiente compartimiento.
	[kõm.par.ti.ˈmjẽn̪.to]	-The fire has spread to the next compartment.
5251	**contemplar**	**contemplate, take into account**
	vb	Deje que se queden aquí y contemplen sus crímenes.
	[kõn̪.tẽm.ˈplar]	-Let them stay out here and contemplate their crimes.
5252	**repasar**	**check**
	vb	Puedo volver a repasar mis documentos pero me acordaría de algo así.
	[re.pa.ˈsar]	-I can check my records again, but I'd remember something like that.
5253	**gozar**	**enjoy**

	vb	Todos podremos gozar con baile y con música en directo.
	[go.'sar]	-All of us will enjoy dance and live music.
5254	**sartén**	**frying pan**
	f	Pásame esa sartén de ahí abajo.
	[sar.'tɛ̃n]	-Grab that frying pan for me down there.
5255	**recepcionista**	**receptionist**
	m/f	El también es jefe del recepcionista.
	[re.sɛp.sjo.'nis.ta]	-He's the receptionist's boss, too.
5256	**clérigo**	**cleric**
	m	Me han dicho que mi clérigo estaba arrestado.
	['klɛ.ri.ɣo]	-I was told my cleric was arrested.
5257	**descuido**	**carelessness**
	m[dɛs.'kwi.ðo]	Considérenlo un descuido de mi parte. -Chalk this one up to carelessness on my part.
5258	**insomnio**	**insomnia**
	m	Tengo erupciones, palpitaciones e insomnio.
	[ĩn.'sõm.njo]	-I get skin rashes, heart palpitations, and insomnia.
5259	**seriedad**	**seriousness**
	f	Por ello debemos abordarlo con la máxima seriedad.
	[sɛ.rje.'ðað]	-That is why it must be approached with extreme seriousness.
5260	**concluir**	**conclude**
	vb	Quisiera concluir con estas breves observaciones.
	[kõŋ.'klwir]	-Allow me to conclude with these brief observations.
5261	**contribuir**	**contribute**
	vb	¿Te gustaría contribuir al programa?
	[kõn.tri.'βwir]	-Would you like to contribute to the program?
5262	**valija**	**suitcase**
	f	Llenaron una valija con algunos objetos pequeños.
	[ba.'li.xa]	-They filled a suitcase with a number of small objects.
5263	**gradual**	**gradual**
	adj	Se observa una mejora gradual del sistema judicial.
	[gra.'ðwal]	-We are witnessing a gradual improvement in the justice system.
5264	**desconectado**	**disconnected**
	adj	Está desconectado; no tiene sentido.
	[dɛs.ko.nek̚.'ta.ðo]	-It's disconnected; there's no point.
5265	**oscurecer**	**get dark**
	vb	Escucha, está empezando a oscurecer.
	[os.ku.re.'sɛr]	-Listen, it's starting to get dark.
5266	**racial**	**racial**
	adj	Algunos dijeron lo mismo de la integración racial.
	[ra.'sjal]	-There were those who said the same of racial integration.
5267	**venenoso**	**poisonous**
	adj	Un lagarto venenoso podría escapar del zoológico y morderte.
	[be.ne.'no.so]	-A poisonous lizard could escape from the zoo and bite you.
5268	**adaptación**	**adaptation**
	f	En algunos casos, dicha adaptación parece estar funcionando.
	[a.ðap̚.ta.'sjõn]	-In some cases, such an adaptation appears to be working.
5269	**comentar**	**discuss, mention**

vb
[ko.mẽn̩.ˈtar]

Solo puedo comentar esta cuestión como economista.
-I can only discuss this issue as an economist.

5270 dimisión **resignation**

f
[di.mi.ˈsjõn]

Francamente, estoy sorprendido de que no hayas presentado la dimisión.
-Frankly, I'm surprised you haven't tendered your resignation.

5271 decadencia **decline**

f
[de.ka.ˈðẽn.sja]

La decadencia del Japón ha sido palpable.
-Japan's decline has been palpable.

5272 mezquino **mean**

adj
[mɛs.ˈki.no]

Si he sido mezquino contigo, lo siento.
-If I was mean to you, I'm sorry.

5273 hazaña **feat**

f[a.ˈsa.ɲa]

Es un ejemplo reciente de un país que logró esa hazaña. -It is a recent
example of a country that achieved this feat.

5274 aislado **isolated**

adj
[ai̯s̩.ˈla.ðo]

Creció aislado, justo como pensábamos.
-He grew up isolated, just like we thought.

5275 temblor **tremor**

m
[tẽm.ˈblor]

El temblor debe haber provocado un derrumbe.
-The tremor must have shaken the rocks loose.

5276 admisión **admission**

f
[að.mi.ˈsjõn]

Declararse culpable es una admisión total de culpabilidad.
-A plea of guilty is a full admission of guilt.

5277 ama de casa **housewife**

f
[ˈa.ma ðe ˈka.sa]

Una ama de casa tiene muchos deberes domésticos.
-A housewife has many domestic duties.

5278 reliquia **relic**

f
[re.ˈli.kja]

Llevo dos años viendo esa reliquia.
-I've watched that relic for two years now.

5279 solemne **solemn**

adj
[so.ˈlẽm.ne]

Pedimos su apoyo en esta tan solemne declaración.
-We ask for your support in this most solemn declaration.

5280 belga **Belgian; Belgian person**

adj; m
[ˈbɛl.ɣa]

Tengo una pregunta para la científica belga.
-I have a question for the Belgian scientist.

5281 temible **fearsome**

adj
[te.ˈmi.βle]

Esta temible criatura desatará oleadas de destrucción por doquier en Azeroth.
-This fearsome creature will unleash destruction upon towns across Azeroth.

5282 sorber **slurp**

vb
[sor.ˈβɛr]

¿Puedo por favor sorber en paz?
-Can I please slurp in peace?

5283 concordar **agree**

vb
[kõŋ.kor.ˈðar]

Me temo que no puedo concordar contigo, Jim.
-I can't agree with you, Jim.

5284 monto **sum**

m
[ˈmõn̩.to]

En efecto, el monto de dinero es minúsculo.
-Indeed, the sum of money is minuscule.

5285 bombón **chocolate, beauty (coll)**

	m	Igual te apetece un bombón.
	[bõm.ˈbõn]	-Maybe you'd like a chocolate.
5286	**conducto**	**channel**
	m	El conducto del agua fluye por aquí debajo.
	[kõn̪.ˈduk̚.to]	-The water channel runs under here.
5287	**recomendar**	**recommend**
	vb	Sin esa información sería difícil recomendar medida alguna.
	[re.ko.mẽn̪.ˈdar]	-Without that information, it would be difficult to recommend any action.
5288	**extracción**	**extraction**
	f[ɛks.trak.ˈsjõn]	Enviaremos unidades al punto de extracción. -We'll send units to the extraction point.
5289	**amateur**	**amateur**
	adj	Veamos qué está haciendo ese amateur.
	[a.ma.ˈteu̯r]	-Let's go see what this amateur is doing.
5290	**diecinueve**	**nineteen**
	num	En 2002 se graduaron diecinueve niñas en este programa.
	[dje.si.ˈnwe.βe]	-Nineteen girls graduated from this programme in 2002.
5291	**latido**	**beat**
	m	Cada contracción de los ventrículos representa un latido.
	[la.ˈti.ðo]	-Each contraction of the ventricles represents one heartbeat.
5292	**válido**	**valid**
	adj	Esto es válido tanto para vehículos estacionados como en circulación.
	[ˈba.li.ðo]	-This is valid both when the vehicle is stationary and in motion.
5293	**bombardear**	**bomb**
	vb	Nos mandaron aquí a bombardear una fábrica.
	[bõm.bar.ðe.ˈar]	-We were sent here to bomb a factory.
5294	**trasto**	**piece of junk**
	m	Ni siquiera sabemos si este trasto funcionará o no.
	[ˈtras.to]	-We don't even know if this piece of junk will work.
5295	**reconfortante**	**heartwarming**
	adj	Es reconfortante ver a una madre tan orgullosa.
	[re.kõm̩.for.ˈtãn̪.te]	-It's heartwarming to see such a proud mother.
5296	**serbio**	**Serbian; Serb**
	adj; m	Un granjero serbio vive en esa granja.
	[ˈsɛr.βjo]	-A Serbian farmer lives in that farm.
5297	**hipo**	**hiccup**
	m	Cuando estoy angustiado, me da hipo.
	[ˈi.po]	-When I get anxious, I hiccup.
5298	**blindar**	**armor**
	vb	Tenemos que blindar la bomba contra el calor para evitar una explosión prematura.
	[blĩn̪.ˈdar]	-We have to shield the bomb against heat to avoid a premature explosion.
5299	**locomotora**	**locomotive; locomotor**
	f; adj	Necesitaríamos una locomotora para mover todo eso.
	[lo.ko.mo.ˈto.ra]	-We'd need a locomotive to move all that.
5300	**aplicación**	**application**
	f	Esto hará que sea posible que toda la aplicación sea diseñada.
	[ap̚.li.ka.ˈsjõn]	-This will make it possible for the entire application to be designed.
5301	**meditación**	**meditation**

f
[me.ði.ta.ˈsjõn]

Pensé que esto sería una meditación guiada.
-I thought this was supposed to be a guided meditation.

5302 médula

marrow

f
[ˈme.ðu.la]

Ya hemos obtenido toda la médula.
-We've already got all of the marrow.

5303 reproducción

reproduction

f
[re.pro.ðuk.ˈsjõn]

Intento mejorar las especies mediante su reproducción.
-I'm trying to improve the species via reproduction.

5304 link

link

m
[ˈlĩŋk]

Haz clic en el siguiente link para leer el libro.
-Click the following link to read the book.

5305 anal

anal

adj
[a.ˈnal]

No querrás tener otra de esas fisuras anales.
-You don't want to get another one of those anal fissures.

5306 amargura

bitterness

f
[a.mar.ˈɣu.ra]

Hay mucha amargura e ira entre la población joven.
-There is much bitterness and anger within the youth population.

5307 doméstico

domestic

adj
[do.ˈmɛs.ti.ko]

Este tipo tiene antecedentes por asalto doméstico.
-This guy has got a prior for domestic assault.

5308 preparado

qualified

m
[pre.pa.ˈra.ðo]

No estoy preparado para ser padre.
-I'm not really qualified to be a dad.

5309 tiza

chalk

f
[ˈti.sa]

Toma este trozo de tiza y escribe en la pizarra.
-Take this piece of chalk and write on the blackboard.

5310 egoísmo

selfishness

m
[e.ɣo.ˈiṣ.mo]

Pero lo perdimos por mi egoísmo.
-But we lost it because of my selfishness.

5311 melón

melon

m
[me.ˈlõn]

La cara de la mujer parece un melón.
-The woman's face looks like a melon.

5312 porvenir

future

m
[por.βe.ˈnir]

Forjemos un nuevo porvenir para nuestras naciones.
-Let us forge a new future for our nations.

5313 bacalao

cod

m
[ba.ka.ˈla.o]

Pues tienen que probar el bacalao.
-Well, you have got to try the cod.

5314 resentimiento

resentment

m
[re.sẽn.ti.ˈmjẽn.to]

Pareces tener un gran resentimiento hacia ella.
-You seem to have a real resentment towards her.

5315 genuino

genuine

adj
[xe.ˈnwi.no]

Es muy natural y genuino como persona.
-He's very natural and genuine as a person.

5316 dardo

dart

m
[ˈdar.ðo]

Fui alcanzado por un dardo envenenado pero ella me salvó.
-I was hit by a poisonous dart, but she saved me.

5317 obediente

obedient

	adj	Necesitas aprender a ser un perro obediente.
	[o.βe.ˈðjẽn̪.te]	-You need to learn to be an obedient dog.
5318	**liquidar**	**finish, eliminate**
	vb	Él nos quiere liquidar aquí.
	[li.ki.ˈðar]	-He wants to finish us here.
5319	**finalizar**	**conclude**
	vb	Permítanme finalizar de un modo positivo.
	[fi.na.li.ˈsar]	-But allow me to conclude in a positive way.
5320	**astucia**	**cunning**
	f	Patrick, me atribuyes demasiada astucia.
	[as.ˈtu.sja]	-Patrick, you credit me with far too much cunning.
5321	**accesorio**	**accessory; secondary**
	m; adj	Revisa el accesorio para encontrar información del fabricante.
	[ak.se.ˈso.rjo]	-Check the accessory for any manufacturer information.
5322	**demandante**	**plaintiff**
	m/f	Sigue allá, buscando un demandante.
	[de.mãn̪.ˈdãn̪.te]	-He's still down there looking for a plaintiff.
5323	**rellenar**	**fill**
	vb	Aquí hay algunos formularios que deben rellenar.
	[re.je.ˈnar]	-Here are some forms you need to fill out.
5324	**totalidad**	**entirety**
	f	Graben la totalidad de este espectáculo si quieren.
	[to.ta.li.ˈðað]	-Record the show in its entirety for all we care.
5325	**explotación**	**exploitation**
	f	Creíamos que la explotación ilegal era consecuencia del conflicto.
	[ɛks.plo.ta.ˈsjõn]	-We had thought that the illegal exploitation was a consequence of the conflict.
5326	**guillotina**	**guillotine**
	f	Regresarás a la guillotina de inmediato.
	[gi.jo.ˈti.na]	-You'll be back on the guillotine in no time.
5327	**costoso**	**expensive**
	adj	Es demasiado costoso y siempre perdemos.
	[kos.ˈto.so]	-It's too expensive and we always lose.
5328	**anticipo**	**advance**
	m	Me quedo hasta conseguir mi anticipo.
	[ãn̪.ti.ˈsi.po]	-I'm staying till I get my advance.
5329	**prudencia**	**caution**
	f	Redoblaré mi prudencia en el futuro.
	[pru.ˈðẽn.sja]	-I will redouble my caution in the future.
5330	**borrachera**	**drunkenness**
	f	Vaya a dormir su borrachera como es costumbre.
	[bo.ra.ˈʧɛ.ra]	-Go sleep off your drunkenness, as usual.
5331	**bufete**	**firm of lawyers**
	m	Escuché que abrió su propio bufete.
	[bu.ˈfɛ.te]	-I hear you started your own law firm.
5332	**miniatura**	**miniature; miniature**
	f; adj	Las pilas miniatura se utilizan en diversos productos que requieres fuentes compactas de energía eléctrica.
	[mi.nja.ˈtu.ra]	-Miniature batteries are used in a variety of products that require compact sources of electrical power.

5333	**reencarnación**	**reincarnation**
	f	Pero noté que estás interesado en la reencarnación.
	[re.ẽŋ.kar.na.ˈsjõn]	-But I did notice that you're interested in reincarnation.

5334	**aterrorizado**	**terrified**
	adj	Comencemos el espectáculo con nuestro primer joven aterrorizado.
	[a.tɛ.ro.ri.ˈsa.ðo]	-Let's start our show with our first terrified young fellow.

5335	**sombrío**	**somber**
	adj	El lado sombrío de las cosas no me atrae.
	[sõm.ˈbri.o]	-The somber side of things does not appeal to me.

5336	**favorable**	**favorable**
	adj	Tus plegarias encontraron una favorable respuesta.
	[fa.βo.ˈra.βle]	-Then your prayers met with a favorable response.

5337	**sudeste**	**southeast**
	m	Los escaladores llegaron al borde sudeste.
	[su.ˈðɛs.te]	-The climbers got on the southeast ridge.

5338	**sinfonía**	**symphony**
	f	Pero necesitamos hacerlo escuchando la sinfonía completa.
	[sĩɱ.fo.ˈni.a]	-But we need to do that while listening to the entire symphony.

5339	**espiral**	**spiral**
	f	Todavía pienso que tenemos que trabajar en la espiral.
	[ɛs.pi.ˈral]	-I still think we need to work on the spiral.

5340	**denegar**	**deny**
	vb	El gobierno sigue la política de denegar refugio a los terroristas.
	[de.ne.ˈɣar]	-It is government policy to deny safe haven to terrorists.

5341	**maratón**	**marathon**
	m	El doctor me prohibió participar en la maratón.
	[ma.ra.ˈtõn]	-The doctor forbade me to take part in the marathon.

5342	**animación**	**animation**
	f	Sabía más que nosotros de animación.
	[a.ni.ma.ˈsjõn]	-He knew more about animation than we did.

5343	**devoto**	**devotee; devout**
	m; adj	Porque él es un devoto del Señor.
	[de.ˈβo.to]	-Because he's a devotee of the Lord.

5344	**mediar**	**mediate**
	vb	Comprenden sus complejidades y pueden mediar en forma imparcial.
	[me.ˈðjar]	-They understand their complexities and can mediate impartially.

5345	**idéntico**	**identical**
	adj	Extrañamente, era idéntico al tuyo.
	[i.ˈðẽṉ.ti.ko]	-Oddly enough, it was identical to yours.

5346	**financiar**	**finance**
	vb	Los ahorros pueden utilizarse para financiar otros servicios.
	[fi.nãn.ˈsjar]	-The savings can be used as a source to finance additional services.

5347	**barranco**	**cliff**
	m	No puedo tirarlos por un barranco.
	[ba.ˈrãŋ.ko]	-I can't just drive them off a cliff.

5348	**pionero**	**pioneering; pioneer**
	adj; m	Fue pionero en óptica, ingeniería y astronomía.
	[pjo.ˈnɛ.ro]	-He was a pioneer in optics, engineering, and astronomy.

5349	**esgrima**	**fencing**

f
[εş.ˈɣri.ma]
Valeria va a enseñarme esgrima.
-Valeria is going to teach me fencing.

5350 tarro — jar

m
[ˈta.ro]
Las conservas deben ser guardadas en un tarro con selle hermético.
-Preserves must be stored in a jar with an airtight seal.

5351 lanzador — pitcher

m
[lãn.sa.ˈðor]
En serio, soy muy buen lanzador.
-Seriously, I'm really a good pitcher.

5352 visón — mink

m
[bi.ˈsõn]
Me encanta mi nuevo visón falso.
-I love my new faux mink.

5353 hobby — hobby

m
[ˈoβ.βi]
Coleccionar estas cosas era mi hobby privado.
-That was my private hobby, collecting those things.

5354 cacharro — junky; wreck

adj; m
[ka.ˈʧa.ro]
Mira el cacharro que estoy manejando ahora.
-Look at the jalopy I'm driving now.

5355 improvisar — improvise

vb
[ĩm.pro.βi.ˈsar]
Tenía que improvisar una cama con algo.
-I had to improvise a bed out of something.

5356 veinticuatro — twenty-four

num
[bei̯n.ti.ˈkwa.tro]
Tiene veinticuatro horas para conseguirnos una casa.
-You have twenty-four hours to get us a house.

5357 barrer — sweep

vb
[ba.ˈrɛr]
Largo, tienes una acera que barrer.
-Get out, you've got a sidewalk to sweep.

5358 muralla — wall

f
[mu.ˈra.ja]
Tom golpeó la muralla con el puño.
-Tom struck the wall with his fist.

5359 estéril — sterile

adj
[εs.ˈtɛ.ril]
Intenta vengarse de mí por ser estéril.
-He's trying to get back at me for being sterile.

5360 chusma — rabble

f
[ˈʧuş.ma]
Utilizaremos el ejército para limpiar la chusma.
-We'll use the army to clean out the rabble.

5361 pepino — cucumber

m
[pe.ˈpi.no]
Siempre quise probar un pepino de mar.
-I always wanted to try a sea cucumber.

5362 beneficencia — charity

f
[be.ne.fi.ˈsẽn.sja]
Quizás podríamos hablar luego de otra beneficencia.
-Maybe we can talk a little later about another charity.

5363 anotación — annotation

f
[a.no.ta.ˈsjõn]
Una pequeña anotación que nadie notará.
-A small annotation that nobody will notice.

5364 eficiencia — efficiency

f
[e.fi.ˈsjẽn.sja]
Sin embargo, seguimos intentando mejorar su eficiencia.
-However, we are still trying to improve its efficiency.

5365 electoral — electoral

adj
[e.lekˈto.ˈral]

Anteriormente el órgano electoral central dependía del Parlamento.
-In the past, the central electoral body was under the Parliament.

5366 sanguíneo — **sanguine**

adj
[sãŋ.ˈgi.ne.o]

Estos son los resultados del análisis sanguíneo del mes pasado.
-These are the results of my blood test from a month ago.

5367 carnal — **carnal**

adj
[kar.ˈnal]

Hay una atracción carnal que es simplemente primitiva en su esencia.
-There's a carnal attraction that's just primitive in its essence.

5368 ampliar — **enlarge**

vb
[ãm.ˈpljar]

Nosotros queríamos ampliar la cocina.
-We wanted to enlarge the kitchen.

5369 pudrir(se) — **rot**

vb
[pu.ˈðrir]

¡No me voy a pudrir aquí!
-I'm not rotting away here!

5370 conmover — **move**

vb
[kõm.mo.ˈβɛr]

Se apoyan en la manipulación para conmover a su audiencia.
-They rely on manipulation to move their audience.

5371 mecha — **wick**

f
[ˈme.tʃa]

Todavía no has mojado tu mecha.
-You have not yet dipped your wick.

5372 amazona — **amazon**

f
[a.ma.ˈso.na]

Diana es una amazona que se convirtió en americana.
-Diana's an Amazon who's become an American.

5373 reclutamiento — **recruitment**

m
[re.klu.ta.ˈmjẽn̯.to]

Si fuese reclutamiento, sería ilegal.
-If it were recruitment, it would be illegal.

5374 vaciar — **empty**

vb
[ba.ˈsjar]

Debo vaciar mi cabeza de palabras.
-I have to empty my head of the words.

5375 solidaridad — **solidarity**

f
[so.li.ða.ri.ˈðað]

La solidaridad no entiende de tamaño.
-Solidarity does not differentiate when it comes to size.

5376 subida — **rise**

f
[su.ˈβi.ða]

Presuntamente, este aumento de restricciones ha contribuido a la subida del precio del arroz.
-These increased restrictions have allegedly contributed to the rise in the price of rice.

5377 trastorno — **disorder**

m
[tras.ˈtor.no]

El doctor piensa que tiene algún trastorno raro.
-The doctor seems to think he's suffering from some rare disorder.

5378 magnitud — **magnitude**

f
[maɣ.ni.ˈtuð]

Ella creía importante subrayar la magnitud del problema.
-She considered that it was important to stress the magnitude of the problem.

5379 dique — **dike**

m
[ˈdi.ke]

Tienen que atravesar el río y saltar el dique.
-They have to get across the river and over the dike.

5380 penoso — **pitiful, embarrassing**

adj
[pe.ˈno.so]

No me hagas ver como un penoso perdedor.
-Don't make me look like some pitiful loser.

5381	**restaurar**	**restore**
	vb	No recaudamos dinero para restaurar el puente.
	[rɛs.tau̯.ˈrar]	-We're not raising money to restore the bridge.

5382	**distinción**	**distinction**
	f	Es importante aclarar la distinción entre pueblos indígenas y minorías.
	[dis.tĩn.ˈsjõn]	-It was important to clarify the distinction between indigenous peoples and minorities.

5383	**nómina**	**salary**
	f	No me lo puedo permitir con mi nómina.
	[ˈno.mi.na]	-I can't afford this with my salary.

5384	**úlcera**	**ulcer**
	f	Pensé que no tenías una úlcera.
	[ˈul.sɛ.ra]	-I thought you didn't have an ulcer.

5385	**espagueti**	**spaghetti**
	m	No debes comer demasiado helado y espagueti.
	[ɛs.pa.ˈɣɛ.ti]	-You must not eat too much ice-cream and spaghetti.

5386	**incendiar**	**burn down**
	vb	Parece capaz de incendiar una plantación.
	[ĩn.sɛ̃n.ˈdjar]	-He looks like he might burn down a plantation.

5387	**publicación**	**publication**
	f	Es preciso especificar el contenido mínimo de tal publicación.
	[pu.βli.ka.ˈsjõn]	-It is necessary to specify the minimum content of such publication.

5388	**evaluar**	**evaluate**
	vb	Todavía es demasiado pronto para evaluar los resultados de sus actividades.
	[e.βa.ˈlwar]	-It is still too early to evaluate the results of its activities.

5389	**abundante**	**abundant**
	adj	El abastecimiento alimentario de Australia es abundante y los datos sugieren que las deficiencias nutricionales deben ser poco comunes.
	[a.βũn.ˈdãn.te]	-Australia's food supply is abundant, and data suggest that nutritional deficiencies should be uncommon.

5390	**inventor**	**inventor**
	m	También quería ser un gran inventor.
	[ĩm.bɛ̃n.ˈtor]	-He also wanted to be a big inventor.

5391	**semáforo**	**traffic light**
	m	Hubo un accidente en el semáforo.
	[se.ˈma.fo.ro]	-There was an accident at the traffic light.

5392	**tocador**	**dressing table**
	m	Puede haberse caído detrás del tocador.
	[to.ka.ˈðor]	-It may have fallen behind the dressing table.

5393	**biológico**	**biological**
	adj	Existe el peligro de perturbar el equilibrio biológico.
	[bjo.ˈlo.xi.ko]	-There is a risk of disturbance to the biological balance.

5394	**irreal**	**unreal**
	adj	Hay algo totalmente irreal en todo esto.
	[i.re.ˈal]	-There's something very unreal about all of this.

5395	**podar**	**prune**
	vb	No puedo podar este árbol. Es demasiado alto.
	[po.ˈðar]	-I cannot prune this tree. It's too high.

5396	**proseguir**	**continue**

vb[pro.se.ˈɣir]

Ahora debemos proseguir la labor iniciada. -Now we have to continue the work which has been started.

5397	**sandalia**	**sandal**
	f	Hace un tiempo encontraron una sandalia en el estanque.
	[sãn̪.ˈda.lja]	-A while ago, they found a sandal in the pond.
5398	**fundar**	**found**
	vb	Fueron a fundar sus propias iglesias.
	[fũn̪.ˈdar]	-They went on to found their own churches.
5399	**platillo**	**plate**
	m	Regresaré si preparan un platillo extra.
	[pla.ˈti.ʝo]	-I'll be around if you fix an extra plate.
5400	**despensa**	**pantry**
	f	No comas galletas en la despensa.
	[dɛs.ˈpẽn.sa]	-Don't eat biscuits in the pantry.
5401	**tirado**	**stranded**
	adj	No puedes dejar tirado a Barry en el escenario.
	[ti.ˈra.ðo]	-You can't leave Barry stranded on the stage.
5402	**fango**	**mud**
	m	Los estoy limpiando y tomando muestras de fango.
	[ˈfãŋ.go]	-I'm cleaning them and taking mud samples.
5403	**mercenario**	**mercenary; mercenary**
	m; adj	No seré recordado como el mercenario de un tirano.
	[mɛr.se.ˈna.rjo]	-I won't be remembered as a tyrant's mercenary.
5404	**ensueño**	**fantasy**
	m	La otra casa fue tu ensueño, no el mío.
	[ẽn.ˈswe.ɲo]	-That other house was your dream, not mine.
5405	**sustituir**	**replace**
	vb	Dime por qué necesitan sustituir las camillas viejas.
	[sus.ti.ˈtwir]	-Tell me why they need to replace the old stretchers.
5406	**jalar**	**pull**
	vb	Renuncié, pero todavía puedo jalar algunos hilos.
	[xa.ˈlar]	-I quit, but I can still pull some strings.
5407	**generar**	**generate**
	vb	Es crucial generar información de primera mano.
	[xe.nɛ.ˈrar]	-It is crucial to generate first-hand information.
5408	**rendimiento**	**performance**
	m	Esas medidas también mejorarán su rendimiento escolar.
	[rẽn̪.di.ˈmjẽn̪.to]	-Such measures will also improve their performance in schools.
5409	**incomodar**	**make uncomfortable**
	vb	No vas a incomodar a nadie en prisión.
	[ĩŋ.ko.mo.ˈðar]	-You won't bother anyone in prison.
5410	**conserva**	**canned food**
	f	Las conservas deben ser guardadas en un tarro con selle hermético.
	[kõn.ˈsɛr.βa]	-Preserves must be stored in a jar with an airtight seal.
5411	**agricultor**	**farmer**
	m	Digamos que soy pescador y agricultor.
	[a.ɣri.kul̪.ˈtor]	-Let's say I'm a fisherman and a farmer.
5412	**trastornar**	**drive mad**
	vb[tras.tor.ˈnar]	Porque no te quería trastornar durante tus exámenes. -Because I didn't want to upset you during your final exams.

5413	**alfiler**	**pin**
	m	No encuentro un alfiler para el pañuelo.
	[al.fi.ˈlɛr]	-I can't find a pin for the handkerchief.
5414	**exactitud**	**accuracy**
	f	Puedes comprobar su exactitud si quieres.
	[ɛk.sakˈ.ti.ˈtuð]	-You can check them for accuracy if you like.
5415	**crónico**	**chronic**
	adj	Sufrían secuelas psicológicas, como estrés postraumático crónico y depresión.
	[ˈkro.ni.ko]	-They suffer from psychological consequences, such as chronic post-traumatic stress and depression.
5416	**manifiesto**	**manifest; evident**
	m; adj	Capitán, aquí una copia del manifiesto actualizado.
	[ma.ni.ˈfjɛs.to]	-Captain, here's a copy of the updated manifest.
5417	**calificar**	**mark**
	vb	Ambos queremos calificar para la gira profesional.
	[ka.li.fi.ˈkar]	-We were both trying to qualify for the pro tour.
5418	**abrazo**	**hug**
	m	Siempre sabes cuándo necesito un abrazo.
	[a.ˈβra.so]	-You always know when I need a hug.
5419	**afligir(se)**	**grieve, suffer from**
	vb	Está casado y no quiere afligir a su mujer.
	[a.fli.ˈxir]	-He is married and does not want to hurt his wife.
5420	**encadenar**	**chain**
	vb	Solía encadenar a sus víctimas a una pared.
	[ɛ̃ŋ.ka.ðe.ˈnar]	-He used to chain his victims to a wall.
5421	**introducción**	**introduction**
	f	La introducción de medidas positivas sería una herramienta para facilitar el proceso.
	[ĩn̪.tro.ðuk.ˈsjõn]	-The introduction of positive measures would be a tool for facilitating this process.
5422	**guitarrista**	**guitarist**
	m/f	Sabemos que fue un gran guitarrista.
	[gi.ta.ˈris.ta]	-We do know he was a great guitarist.
5423	**pelar**	**peel**
	vb	No puedo pelar papas. No tengo cuchillo.
	[pe.ˈlar]	-I cannot peel potatoes. I don't have a knife.
5424	**afirmación**	**affirmation**
	f	Empecemos con nuestra afirmación del día.
	[a.fir.ma.ˈsjõn]	-Let's start with our affirmation of the day.
5425	**psiquiatría**	**psychiatry**
	f	Es alguien que no sabe nada de psiquiatría.
	[si.kja.ˈtri.a]	-He's someone who doesn't know a thing about psychiatry.
5426	**rabioso**	**rabid**
	adj	Se me lanzó cual hurón rabioso.
	[ra.ˈβjo.so]	-He came at me like a rabid ferret.
5427	**ilustre**	**illustrious**
	adj	Este viejo lugar tiene un pasado ilustre.
	[i.ˈlus.tre]	-This old place has had an illustrious past.
5428	**matador**	**matador; deadly**

m; adj
[ma.ta.ˈðor]

Hay una leyenda de un matador famoso.
-There's a legend of a famous matador.

5429 singular

special; unique

m; adj
[sĩŋ.gu.ˈlar]

Vivimos en un mundo singular y diverso.
-We live in a world that is both unique and diverse.

5430 sirio

Syrian; Syrian

adj; m
[ˈsi.rjo]

Estaba casada con un mercante sitio.
-She was married to a Syrian merchant.

5431 puntuación

punctuation

f
[pũn̪.twa.ˈsjõn]

El propósito de la puntuación es ayudar al lector.
-The purpose of punctuation is to help the reader.

5432 clientela

clientele

f
[kljẽn̪.ˈte.la]

No quiero intimidar a la clientela.
-I don't want to intimidate the clientele.

5433 patente

clear; patent

f; adj
[pa.ˈtẽn̪.te]

Legalmente, supongo que tiene una patente.
-Legally, I suppose he does have a patent.

5434 copiloto

copilot

m/f
[ko.pi.ˈlo.to]

Entonces es posible que contactara con el copiloto.
-So it's possible he made contact with the copilot.

5435 obsceno

obscene

adj
[oβs.ˈse.no]

No necesitas repetir todo el lenguaje obsceno.
-Yo don't need to repeat all of the obscene language.

5436 credencial

identity document; accrediting

f; adj
[kre.ðẽn.ˈsjal]

Primero que nada, mi credencial dice que soy astrónomo.
-First off, my badge says I'm an astronomer.

5437 inspeccionar

inspect

vb
[ĩns.pɛk.sjo.ˈnar]

Parece que hemos venido a inspeccionar la carretera.
-Looks like they're here to inspect the road.

5438 deshonesto

dishonest

adj
[de.so.ˈnɛs.to]

No debí venir aquí y ser deshonesto.
-I should not have come here and been dishonest.

5439 melancolía

melancholy

f
[me.lãŋ.ko.ˈli.a]

Es solo un poco de melancolía.
-It's just a moment of melancholy.

5440 chuleta

chop; sassy (coll)

f; adj
[ʧu.ˈlɛ.ta]

Pero solo he comido una chuleta de cordero.
-But I only ate one lamb chop.

5441 entregar(se)

deliver

vb
[ẽn̪.tre.ˈɣar]

Este proveedor solo utilizará esta información para entregar el elemento pedido.
-This vendor will only use this information to deliver the item you ordered.

5442 paralelo

parallel; parallel

m; adj[pa.ra.ˈle.lo]

El camino va paralelo al río. -The road runs parallel to the river.

5443 malta

malt

f
[ˈmal̪.ta]

Recuerdo su panfleto sobre la malta perfectamente.
-I remember your pamphlet on malt ever so well.

5444 comunitario

communal

adj
[ko.mu.niˈta.rjo]

Se han previsto actividades de reintegración a nivel comunitario.
-Reintegration activities at the communal level have been planned.

5445 avatar — avatar

m
[a.βaˈtar]

Crea tu avatar para que aparezca aquí y en otros blogs.
-Create your avatar to appear here and on other blogs.

5446 foca — seal

f
[ˈfo.ka]

Esta foca tiene memoria de elefante.
-This seal has the memory of an elephant.

5447 mercadería — merchandise

f
[mɛr.ka.ðɛˈri.a]

Se aprovecharon de mi fe religiosa para venderme mercadería defectuosa.
-They took advantage of my religious faith to sell me faulty merchandise.

5448 aspirar — inhale

vb
[as.piˈrar]

Ni siquiera sabes como aspirar.
-You don't even know how to inhale.

5449 apunte — note

m
[aˈpũn̪.te]

Terminaré con un apunte muy personal.
-I will end on a very personal note.

5450 vajilla — tableware

f
[baˈxi.ja]

Una vez casi me compro un juego de vajilla.
-I almost got a set of tableware once.

5451 preferencia — preference

f
[pre.fɛˈrẽn.sja]

Algunos organizadores expresaron su preferencia por personas que ya conocían.
-Some organizers expressed a preference for people who were known to them.

5452 hostilidad — hostility

f
[os.ti.li.ˈðað]

Lo que no consigo entender es su inexplicable hostilidad hacia mí.
-What I can't understand is their inexplicable hostility toward me.

5453 congregación — congregation

f
[kõŋ.gre.ɣaˈsjõn]

Háganos saber cómo podemos apoyar a su congregación.
-Please let us know how we can support your congregation.

5454 manifestante — demonstrator

m/f
[ma.ni.fɛsˈtã̪n.te]

Otro manifestante sostiene un signo que apenas se ve sobre su hombro izquierdo.
-Another demonstrator holds a sign, just barely visible over his left shoulder.

5455 decisivo — decisive

adj
[de.si.ˈsi.βo]

Decidí hacer un movimiento decisivo y audaz.
-I decided to make a bold and decisive move.

5456 imprimir — print

vb
[ĩm.pri.ˈmir]

Abra el documento que desee imprimir.
-Open the document that you want to print.

5457 colmillo — fang

m
[kol.ˈmi.ʝo]

Tengo un par de marcas de colmillo en el abdomen.
-I have a couple of fang marks in the abdomen.

5458 gallinero — henhouse

m
[ga.ʝi.ˈnɛ.ro]

Hay un zorro en mi gallinero.
-There's a fox in my henhouse.

5459 equipamiento — equipment

m
[e.ki.pa.ˈmjẽn̪.to]

Resulta que él no compra el equipamiento.
-It turns out he doesn't buy any of his equipment.

5460	**calamar**	**dummy; squid**
	adj; m	Se pensaba que el calamar gigante era una leyenda hasta 2004.
	[ka.la.ˈmar]	-The giant squid was thought to be a myth until 2004.
5461	**jubilar(se)**	**get rid of; retire**
	vb; vbr	Creo que finalmente me voy a jubilar.
	[xu.βi.ˈlar]	-I think I am finally going to retire.
5462	**fascinar**	**fascinate**
	vb	El sabía cómo fascinar a Lili.
	[fas.si.ˈnar]	-He knew how to fascinate Lili.
5463	**arteria**	**artery**
	f	Bloquearon la arteria hepática, cortaron el flujo sanguíneo.
	[ar.ˈtɛ.rja]	-They blocked the hepatic artery, cut off the blood flow.
5464	**citación**	**citation**
	f	Enviaré a alguien para hacer una citación.
	[si.ta.ˈsjõn]	-I'll send someone to issue a citation.
5465	**ventura**	**fortune**
	f	Vengo para oír la buena ventura, no la mala.
	[bẽn̪.ˈtu.ra]	-I came to hear good fortune, not bad.
5466	**coronación**	**coronation**
	f	No querrán perderse su propia coronación.
	[ko.ro.na.ˈsjõn]	-You don't want to miss your own coronation.
5467	**recital**	**recital**
	m	Mi recital es mañana y necesito practicar.
	[re.si.ˈtal]	-My recital is tomorrow and I need to practice.
5468	**frustración**	**frustration**
	f	En tercer lugar quisiera expresar mi frustración.
	[frus.tra.ˈsjõn]	-Thirdly, I would like to express my frustration.
5469	**corresponsal**	**correspondent**
	m/f	Como corresponsal de guerra es importante ser imparcial.
	[ko.rɛs.põn.ˈsal]	-As a war correspondent, it's important that I'd be seen as unbiased.
5470	**hipocresía**	**hypocrisy**
	f	Tenemos que poner fin a esta hipocresía.
	[i.po.kre.ˈsi.a]	-We need to put an end to this hypocrisy.
5471	**gremio**	**guild, union**
	m	Tienes mucha fuerza en ese gremio.
	[ˈgre.mjo]	-You got a lot of pull with that union.
5472	**ente**	**entity**
	m	Se te considera un ente hostil.
	[ˈẽn̪.te]	-You are classified as a hostile entity.
5473	**inválido**	**invalid; disabled person**
	adj; m	Los tribunales pueden declarar inválido un matrimonio.
	[ĩm.ˈba.li.ðo]	-A marriage may be declared invalid by the court.
5474	**competente**	**competent**
	adj	También queda por resolver la cuestión del tribunal competente.
	[kõm.pɛ.ˈtẽn̪.te]	-The issue of the competent court also remained to be resolved.
5475	**realista**	**realist; realistic**
	m; adj	Nos corresponde a nosotros considerar si es realista o no.
	[re.a.ˈlis.ta]	-It is up to us to consider whether this is realistic or not.
5476	**cuadrilátero**	**ring; four-sided**

m; adj
[kwa.ðri.ˈla.tɛ.ro]

Estaré de vuelta en el cuadrilátero pronto.
-I'll be back in the ring soon.

5477 contradicción — **contradiction**

f
[kõn.tra.ðik.ˈsjõn]

No creo que exista ninguna contradicción en esto.
-I do not believe that there should be any contradiction in this.

5478 estatus — **status**

m
[ɛs.ˈta.tus]

Nos preocupa especialmente el estatus del sistema de seguridad europea.
-We are particularly concerned about the status of the European security system.

5479 apagón — **blackout**

m
[a.pa.ˈɣõn]

No podemos hacer nada hasta después del apagón.
-There's nothing we can do until after the blackout.

5480 naipe — **playing card**

m
[ˈnaj.pe]

Si se trata de una imitación, pueden no saber sobre el naipe.
-If this is a copycat, they may not know about the playing card.

5481 blasfemia — **blasphemy**

f
[blas.ˈfe.mja]

Prefiero no ser testigo de tal blasfemia.
-I'd rather not bear witness to such blasphemy.

5482 satisfactorio — **satisfactory**

adj
[sa.tis.fak.ˈto.rjo]

Este resultado puede considerarse muy satisfactorio.
-I'd rather not bear witness to such blasphemy.

5483 detenido — **stopped, arrested; prisoner**

adj; m
[dɛ.te.ˈni.ðo]

Horas después fue detenido por la policía.
-Hours later, he was arrested by the police.

5484 esquema — **diagram**

m
[ɛs.ˈke.ma]

Supongo que podría dibujarte un esquema.
-I suppose I could draw you a diagram.

5485 conteo — **count**

m
[kõn.ˈte.o]

Se llevó a cabo un conteo rápido de los resultados.
-A quick count of the results was conducted.

5486 defunción — **death**

f
[de.fũn.ˈsjõn]

Toda las municipalidades han estado expidiendo certificados de nacimiento, matrimonio y defunción.
-Birth, marriage, and death certificates are being issued by all municipalities.

5487 reclamo — **decoy**

m
[re.ˈkla.mo]

La próxima vez que me envíes de reclamo, te agradecería un aviso previo.
-Next time you send me in as a decoy, a heads-up would be nice.

5488 dentadura — **dentures**

f
[dẽn.ta.ˈðu.ra]

Esa es la dentadura que buscamos.
-Those are the dentures we're looking for.

5489 madurez — **maturity**

f
[ma.ˈðu.res]

Varias nuevas tecnologías han alcanzado recientemente mayor madurez comercial.
-A number of new technologies have recently attained greater commercial maturity.

5490 cubano — **Cuban; Cuban person**

adj; m
[ku.ˈβa.no]

Disculpe. He asumido que era cubano.
-Sorry. I just assumed you were Cuban.

5491 oliva — **olive; olive**

adj; f
[o.ˈli.βa]

Según testimonios de los vecinos, varios de los agresores llevaban un uniforme verde oliva.
-According to testimony given by neighbors, several of the assailants were wearing an olive green uniform.

5492 fastidiar(se)

vb; vbr
[fas.ti.ˈðjar]

annoy; put up with

Di que no me volverás a fastidiar.
-Say you'll never annoy me again.

5493 bondadoso

adj
[bõn̪.da.ˈðo.so]

kind

Tienes un instinto dulce y bondadoso.
-You have such a sweet, kind instinct.

5494 patinaje

m
[pa.ti.ˈna.xe]

skating

Un deporte de invierno con el que mucha gente disfruta es el patinaje.
-A winter sport that many people enjoy is ice skating.

5495 encuesta

f
[ẽŋ.ˈkwɛs.ta]

survey

En esta encuesta participaron un total de 2.500 familias escogidas aleatoriamente.
-A total of 2,500 households randomly selected participated in the survey.

5496 centenar

num
[sẽn̪.te.ˈnar]

hundred

Aun así, solo se ha investigado un centenar de ellas.
-Yet only about a hundred have been investigated.

5497 inquietante

adj
[ĩŋ.kjɛ.ˈtãn̪.te]

disturbing

Esa cifra es tan impresionante como inquietante.
-This figure is as impressive as it is disturbing.

5498 escalofriante

adj
[ɛs.ka.lo.ˈfrjãn̪.te]

spooky

Es escalofriante, pero cuéntame más.
-This is spooky, but tell me more.

5499 tapar

vb
[ta.ˈpar]

cover

El FBI intentó tapar esto tanto como pudo.
-The FBI tried to cover this up as much as they could.

5500 lujoso

adj
[lu.ˈxo.so]

luxurious

Este es el apartamento más lujoso del centro de Barcelona.
-This is the most luxurious apartment in the center of Barcelona.

5501 seguimiento

m
[se.ɣi.ˈmjẽn̪.to]

tracking

Tengo un sistema haciendo seguimiento de sospechosos.
-I have a system tracking suspects.

5502 anatomía

f[a.na.to.ˈmi.a]

anatomy

Necesitas más experiencia en anatomía femenina. -You need more experience in the female anatomy.

5503 hallazgo

m
[a.ˈjas̬.ɣo]

discovery

Fue él quien informó del hallazgo.
-It was him who informed of the discovery.

5504 colectivo

adj; m
[ko.lek̚.ˈti.βo]

collective; group

Es indispensable que hagamos un esfuerzo colectivo para combatirlo.
-It is imperative that we make a collective effort to combat it.

5505 calzado

adj; m
[kal.ˈsa.ðo]

wearing shoes; footwear

Necesitamos obtener toda su ropa y su calzado.
-We need to obtain all clothing and footwear.

5506 alfabeto

m
[al.fa.ˈβɛ.to]

alphabet

Estas son las letras del alfabeto genético.
-These are the letters of the genetic alphabet.

5507	**abanico**		**fan, variety**
	m		Simplemente sostén este abanico delante del estomago.
	[a.βa.ˈni.ko]		-You just have to hold this fan right before your stomach.
5508	**desventaja**		**disadvantage**
	f		Tu miedo será nuestra mayor desventaja.
	[dεs̬.βε̃n̪.ˈta.xa]		-Your fear will prove to be our greatest disadvantage.
5509	**cascabel**		**bell**
	m		Veo que aún llevas el cascabel.
	[kas.ka.ˈβεl]		-I see you're still wearing the bell.
5510	**realización**		**realization**
	f		No existe una vía única para su realización.
	[re.a.li.sa.ˈsjõn]		-There is no single road to their full realization.
5511	**porte**		**demeanor**
	m		Su porte era fresco pero también relajado.
	[ˈpor.te]		-His demeanor was crisp yet easy-going.
5512	**vestimenta**		**clothing**
	f		Usa esa vieja manta como vestimenta.
	[bεs.ti.ˈmẽn̪.ta]		-He's using that old blanket as clothing.
5513	**mástil**		**mast**
	m		Sufrió un tirón muscular colocando el mástil.
	[ˈmas.til]		-He pulled a muscle putting the mast up.
5514	**cabellera**		**hair**
	f		Tenía una cabellera roja muy hermosa.
	[ka.βe.ˈʝε.ra]		-He had such beautiful red hair.
5515	**parálisis**		**paralysis**
	f		No deberíamos tolerar más esta parálisis.
	[pa.ˈra.li.sis]		-We should not tolerate this paralysis any longer.
5516	**boxear**		**box**
	vb		Aprendió a boxear para sobrevivir.
	[bok.se.ˈar]		-He learned to box in order to survive.
5517	**deslumbrante**		**dazzling**
	adj		El príncipe descubrió que la chica deslumbrante era ella.
	[dεs̬.lũm.ˈbrã̃n̪.te]		-The prince found out that the dazzling girl was her.
5518	**carguero**		**freight; freighter**
	adj; m[kar.ˈɣε.ro]		Apenas tenemos suficiente para regresar al buque carguero. -We barely got enough to get back to the freighter.
5519	**vídeojuego**		**vídeo game**
	m		Es igual que cuando creas un vídeojuego.
	[ˈbi.ðe.o.xwe.ɣo]		-It's the same when you make a video game.
5520	**azufre**		**sulfur**
	m		Tú utilizas azufre, ¿verdad Sully?
	[a.ˈsu.fre]		-You use sulfur, right, Sully?
5521	**firmeza**		**firmness**
	f		Déjame mostrarte la firmeza de mis creencias.
	[fir.ˈme.sa]		-Let me show you the firmness of my beliefs.
5522	**capellán**		**chaplain**
	m		Eso es lo que te dijo el capellán esta mañana.
	[ka.pe.ˈʝãn]		-That's what the chaplain told you this morning.
5523	**fabricación**		**manufacturing**

	f	En su conjunto representan una proporción importante de los costes de fabricación.
	[fa.βri.ka.ˈsjõn]	-Together they account for a major proportion of the manufacturing cost.
5524	**indicación**	**indication**
	f	Me complace señalar el reconocimiento de esta indicación.
	[ĩn̪.di.ka.ˈsjõn]	-I am pleased to note the recognition of this indication.
5525	**placentero**	**pleasurable**
	adj	Bueno, físicamente puede ser bastante placentero.
	[pla.sẽn̪.ˈtɛ.ro]	-Well, on a physical level, it can be rather pleasurable.
5526	**gráfico**	**graphic**
	adj	Necesita ser gráfico para captar su atención.
	[ˈgra.fi.ko]	-It needs to be graphic to get their attention.
5527	**abatir(se)**	**take down; fold up, become depressed**
	vb; vbr	Podría abatir a un ciervo pequeño.
	[a.βa.ˈtir]	-She could take down a small deer.
5528	**adorno**	**ornament**
	m	Cada adorno es en sí mismo una forma de expresión.
	[a.ˈðor.no]	-Each ornament is in itself a form of expression.
5529	**dependiente**	**dependent; shop assistant**
	adj; m	Ya dije que es demasiado dependiente.
	[de.pẽn̪.ˈdjẽn̪.te]	-I already said he's being too dependent.
5530	**rizar**	**curl**
	vb	Creo que puedo rizar una cinta.
	[ri.ˈsar]	-I think I can curl a ribbon.
5531	**caimán**	**caiman**
	m	El caimán latirostris es un depredador muy eficiente.
	[kai̯.ˈmãn]	-The caiman latirostris is pretty efficient as a predator.
5532	**desaguar**	**drain**
	vb	En ningún caso una terraza se desagua en otra terraza.
	[de.sa.ˈɣwar]	-Under no circumstances does a terrace drain onto another terrace.
5533	**bañar(se)**	**bathe**
	vb[ba.ˈɲar]	Que otro ser humano me tenga que bañar es humillante. -To have another human being bathe me is humiliating.
5534	**fértil**	**fertile**
	adj	Ojalá estuviéramos en la parte fértil del valle.
	[ˈfɛr.til]	-I wish we were in the fertile part of the valley.
5535	**semanal**	**weekly**
	adj	Además del descanso semanal los trabajadores tienen derecho a vacaciones pagadas.
	[se.ma.ˈnal]	-In addition to a weekly rest, an employed person is entitled to a paid vacation.
5536	**magnate**	**tycoon**
	m	Estás enamorada de un magnate despiadado.
	[maɣ.ˈna.te]	-You're in love with a ruthless tycoon.
5537	**barajar**	**shuffle**
	vb	Puede barajar cartas de diferentes maneras.
	[ba.ra.ˈxar]	-You can shuffle cards in a variety of ways.
5538	**indemnización**	**compensation**
	f	También se podrá reclamar una indemnización por agresión.
	[ĩn̪.dẽm.ni.ˈsa.sjõn]	-A claim for compensation for assault will also be available.

5539	**avería**	**breakdown**
	f	Es muy tarde para una avería.
	[a.βɛ.ˈri.a]	-It's kind of late for a breakdown.
5540	**porra**	**nightstick**
	f	Reconocería en cualquier lugar esa porra.
	[ˈpo.ra]	-I'd know that nightstick anywhere.
5541	**característico**	**characteristic**
	adj	En este edificio característico encontrará varias habitaciones.
	[ka.rakˈtɛ.ˈris.ti.ko]	-In its characteristic building, you will find several rooms.
5542	**psíquico**	**psychic**
	adj	Déjeme adivinar... es un psíquico.
	[ˈsi.ki.ko]	-Let me guess... you're a psychic.
5543	**facial**	**facial**
	adj	Existen pocos equipos especializados en el campo del rejuvenecimiento facial.
	[fa.ˈsjal]	-There are few specialist teams in the field of facial rejuvenation.
5544	**delirio**	**delirium**
	m	El tratamiento de las afecciones que causen delirio puede reducir su riesgo.
	[de.ˈli.rjo]	-Treating the conditions that cause delirium can reduce its risk.
5545	**heladera**	**refrigerator**
	f	Traeré un huevo de mi heladera.
	[e.la.ˈðɛ.ra]	-I'll bring an egg from my refrigerator.
5546	**canario**	**from the Canary Islands, canary yellow; Canary Islander, canary**
	adj; m	Es como el canario en la mina de carbón.
	[ka.ˈna.rjo]	-It's like the canary in the coal mine.
5547	**barbaridad**	**atrocity**
	f	¿Pero qué barbaridad está diciendo?
	[bar.βa.ri.ˈðað]	-But what atrocity are you suggesting?
5548	**ideología**	**ideology**
	f	Lo crucial es situar la ideología donde pertenece.
	[i.ðe.o.lo.ˈxi.a]	-The crucial thing is to locate ideology where it belongs.
5549	**radiador**	**radiator**
	m	Estaba atado al radiador en su habitación de hotel.
	[ra.ðja.ˈðor]	-He was chained to the radiator in her hotel room.
5550	**testimonio**	**testimony**
	m	Puede encontrar una transcripción de su testimonio aquí.
	[tɛs.ti.ˈmo.njo]	-You can find a transcript of her testimony here.
5551	**altavoz**	**speaker**
	m	Está bien que el altavoz funcionara.
	[al̪.ˈta.βos]	-It's a good thing the loudspeaker worked.
5552	**insensato**	**foolish; foolish**
	adj; m	Sería insensato descartar a priori la última posibilidad.
	[ĩn.sɛ̃n.ˈsa.to]	-It would be foolish to rule out the last possibility a priori.
5553	**elemental**	**elementary**
	adj	Es elemental aprobar e implementar rápidamente estas propuestas.
	[e.le.mɛ̃n̪.ˈtal]	-The rapid adoption and implementation of these proposals are elementary.
5554	**desordenado**	**disorganized**
	adj	Estaríamos metiéndonos en una situación bastante desordenada.
	[de.sor.ðe.ˈna.ðo]	-We'd be walking into a pretty messy situation.
5555	**traductor**	**translator**

	m	Este comentario es del traductor responsable del alemán.
	[tra.ðuk̚.ˈtor]	-This comment is from the translator who was in charge of German.
5556	**meñique**	**little finger**
	m	Eran tan pequeños que no podía meter mi meñique entre en ellos.
	[me.ˈɲi.ke]	-They were so small I couldn't get my little finger between them.
5557	**tirón**	**pull**
	m	Un tirón de la cuerda significa subir despacio.
	[ti.ˈrõn]	-One tug on the rope means pull up slowly.
5558	**restricción**	**restriction**
	f	Por lo tanto, es necesario eliminar esa restricción.
	[rɛs.trik.ˈsjõn]	-It is, therefore, necessary to remove that restriction.
5559	**melocotón**	**peach**
	m	Su sabor es exquisitamente afrutado, con un toque entre naranja y melocotón, muy especial.
	[me.lo.ko.ˈtõn]	-Its flavor is exquisitely fruity with a touch between orange and peach, very special.
5560	**restringir**	**restrict**
	vb	Puede conceder o restringir accesos a algunos informes.
	[rɛs.trĩŋ.ˈxir]	-You can grant or restrict view access to some reports.
5561	**fatiga**	**fatigue**
	f	Tenía la reputación de interesarme en pacientes con fatiga crónica.
	[fa.ˈti.ɣa]	-I had a reputation of being interested in patients with chronic fatigue.
5562	**bosnio**	**Bosnian; Bosnian person**
	adj; m	Yo tengo un pasaporte bosnio.
	[ˈboş.njo]	-I have a Bosnian passport.
5563	**carril**	**lane**
	m	En estos momentos se están haciendo obras para crear otro carril de autobuses.
	[ka.ˈril]	-At the moment, construction work for another bus lane is ongoing.
5564	**centinela**	**sentinel**
	m/f	El centinela me dijo que teníamos huéspedes de honor.
	[sẽṇ.ti.ˈne.la]	-The sentinel told me of our honored guests.
5565	**indigno**	**unworthy**
	adj	En primer lugar, es indigno.
	[ĩṇ.ˈdiɣ.no]	-In the first place, that is unworthy.
5566	**superioridad**	**superiority**
	f	Esperaba con ansia tu superioridad intelectual.
	[su.pɛ.rjo.ri.ˈðað]	-I was so looking forward to your intellectual superiority.
5567	**dotado**	**gifted**
	adj	Tal vez la Tierra no sea el único planeta dotado de vida.
	[do.ˈta.ðo]	-Perhaps the Earth is not the only planet gifted with life.
5568	**buceo**	**diving**
	m	Me reincorporaron al programa de buceo.
	[bu.ˈse.o]	-They put me back in the diving program.
5569	**problemático**	**problematic**
	adj	Hay un aspecto problemático que me gustaría mencionar.
	[pro.βle.ˈma.ti.ko]	-There is one problematic aspect that I would like to mention.
5570	**externo**	**external**
	adj	Podríamos conectarla a un sistema externo.
	[ɛks.ˈtɛr.no]	-We could connect her to an external system.

5571 mililitro — **milliliter**
m
[mi.li.ˈli.tro]
Hay 40 mililitros de sangre en ese frasco.
-There are 40 milliliters of blood in that jar.

5572 debut — **debut**
m
[de.ˈβut]
Quiere lucir bien para su debut.
-She wants to look good for her debut.

5573 serenidad — **calm**
f
[sɛ.re.ni.ˈðað]
Permíteme decir que admiro tu serenidad.
-Please let me tell you that I admire you for being so calm.

5574 indudable — **undeniable**
adj
[ĩn̪.du.ˈða.βle]
Esa imagen ofrecerá una prueba indudable de la inmortalidad del alma.
-That image will offer undeniable proof, of the soul's immortality.

5575 flotante — **floating**
adj
[flo.ˈtãn̪.te]
Este lugar es... Como un gran panteón flotante.
-This place is... It's like a big floating graveyard.

5576 rotación — **rotation**
f
[ro.ta.ˈsjõn]
Tengo a seis chicos en mi rotación.
-I've got six guys in my rotation.

5577 creatividad — **creativity**
f
[kre.a.ti.βi.ˈðað]
La creatividad es la habilidad para combinar elementos conocidos de formas nuevas e inusuales.
-Creativity is the ability to combine known elements in a new and unusual way.

5578 convocar — **summon**
vb
[kõm.bo.ˈkar]
Es malvado, un brujo que puede convocar demonios.
-He's evil, a sorcerer who can summon demons.

5579 lechero — **milk; milkman**
adj; m
[le.ˈtʃɛ.ro]
El lechero viene cerca de las seis cada mañana.
-The milkman came around at six every morning.

5580 provocación — **provocation**
f
[pro.βo.ka.ˈsjõn]
Posteriormente fue acusada del delito de "provocación".
-She was subsequently charged with the crime of "provocation".

5581 remar — **row**
vb
[re.ˈmar]
Fuimos al lago a remar en bote.
-We went to the lake to row a boat.

5582 relevo — **replacement**
m
[re.ˈle.βo]
Debo encontrar un relevo mientras tanto.
-I must find a replacement in the meantime.

5583 prescindir — **get by without**
vb
[prɛs.sĩn̪.ˈdir]
Incluso, ya puedo prescindir de él.
-I can already get by without him.

5584 estadía — **stay**
f
[ɛs.ta.ˈði.a]
Espero que su estadía sea provechosa y relajante.
-I hope his stay will be fruitful and relaxing.

5585 coste — **cost**
m
[ˈkos.te]
El coste global del proyecto será bastante elevado.
-The overall cost of the operation is going to be pretty enormous.

5586 aerolínea — **airline**
f
[a.ɛ.ro.ˈli.ne.a]
Creo que elegimos la aerolínea equivocada.
-I think we just chose the wrong airline.

5587	**torrente**	**torrent**
	m	Esto desató un torrente de asistencia internacional.
	[to.ˈrɛ̃n̪.te]	-This triggered a torrent of international aid.
5588	**heredar**	**inherit**
	vb	Solo está esperando para heredar la propiedad.
	[ɛ.re.ˈðar]	-She's just waiting to inherit the estate.
5589	**Sor**	**Sister**
	f	Es Sor Clementina, nuestro gendarme.
	[ˈsor]	-She's sister Clementina, our police officer.
5590	**genital**	**genital**
	adj	Soy uróloga, especialista en reconstrucción genital.
	[xe.ni.ˈtal]	-I'm a urologist, specializing in genital reconstruction.
5591	**designar**	**appoint**
	vb	Podrán designar a un médico para examinar a la persona.
	[de.siɣ.ˈnar]	-They may appoint a doctor to examine the person.
5592	**inclinación**	**inclination**
	f	Los países desarrollados y en desarrollo muestran una similar inclinación a limitar la inmigración.
	[ĩŋ.kli.na.ˈsjõn]	-Developed and developing countries show a similar inclination towards restricting immigration.
5593	**de antemano**	**beforehand**
	adv[de ãn̪.te.ˈma.no]	Las empresas necesitan garantías a fin de planificar de antemano. -Enterprises need guarantees in order to plan ahead.
5594	**proporción**	**proportion**
	f	Había una gran proporción de menores detenidos.
	[pro.por.ˈsjõn]	-There was a large proportion of young children in detention.
5595	**represión**	**repression**
	f	La represión ideológica continúa en demasiadas naciones.
	[re.pre.ˈsjõn]	-The repression of conscience continues in too many nations.
5596	**equivocarse**	**be wrong**
	vbr	Sin duda, la libertad también incluye el derecho incluso a equivocarse.
	[e.ki.βo.ˈkar.se]	-Indeed, freedom also includes the right even to be wrong.
5597	**bisabuelo**	**great-grandfather**
	m	Creo que sé dónde está enterrado su bisabuelo.
	[bi.sa.ˈβwe.lo]	-I think that I know where your great-grandfather is buried.
5598	**derretir**	**melt**
	vb	Necesito derretir esto con un helado.
	[dɛ.rɛ.ˈtir]	-I need to melt this with some ice cream.
5599	**suspenso**	**failing grade, suspense (LA)**
	m	Creo que hay mucho suspenso en esta pintura.
	[sus.ˈpɛ̃n.so]	-I think that there is a lot of suspense in this painting.
5600	**taladrar**	**drill**
	vb	No podríamos haber escogido un punto peor para taladrar.
	[ta.la.ˈðrar]	-We couldn't have picked a worse spot to drill.
5601	**erótico**	**erotic**
	adj	Desearía que tuviéramos algo de cine erótico antiguo normal.
	[ɛ.ˈro.ti.ko]	-I just wish we had some regular, old-fashioned erotic cinema.
5602	**mazo**	**mallet**
	m	Usaré mi mazo para dejarte inconsciente.
	[ˈma.so]	-I will use my mallet and knock you unconscious.

5603	**sanar**	**heal**
	vb	Todos tenemos heridas que queremos sanar.
	[sa.ˈnar]	-We all have wounds that we want to heal.

5604	**supuesto**	**supposed; case**
	adj; m	No tienes ninguna información de este supuesto agente norcoreano.
	[su.ˈpwɛs.to]	-You've got no information on this supposed North Korean agent.

5605	**referente a**	**regarding**
	adj	No aceptaré ninguna pregunta referente a él.
	[re.fɛ.ˈrẽn̪.te a]	-I will not be taking any questions regarding him.

5606	**botiquín**	**first-aid kit**
	m	Tengo un botiquín en la camioneta.
	[bo.ti.ˈkĩn]	-I've got a first-aid kit in the van.

5607	**inmobiliaria**	**real-estate; real state agency**
	adj; f	El propietario de una empresa inmobiliaria fue acusado de discriminación
	[ĩm.mo.βi.ˈlja.rja]	contra algunos clientes.
		-The owner of a housing agency was charged for discrimination against
		customers.

5608	**puma**	**puma**
	m[ˈpu.ma]	Su animal favorito es el puma. -His favorite animal is the puma.

5609	**vegetariano**	**vegetarian**
	adj	Ya sé, probaré ese restaurante vegetariano.
	[be.xɛ.ta.ˈrja.no]	-I know, I'll try that vegetarian restaurant.

5610	**bautizo**	**baptism**
	m	Compré esto para el bautizo de Melanie.
	[bau̯.ˈti.so]	-I bought this for Melanie's baptism.

5611	**sonoro**	**loud**
	adj	Creo que el saxofón es más sonoro.
	[so.ˈno.ro]	-I think the saxophone is louder.

5612	**naufragio**	**shipwreck**
	m	El naufragio no resultó tan bien como esperaba.
	[nau̯.ˈfra.xjo]	-The shipwreck hasn't turned out as well as I'd hoped.

5613	**estela**	**wake**
	f	He visto un objeto naranja flotando detrás de mí en la estela de la barca.
	[ɛs.ˈte.la]	-I saw an orange object floating behind me in the wake of the boat.

5614	**invasor**	**invader; invading**
	m; adj	Haga lo necesario para neutralizar al invasor.
	[ĩm.ba.ˈsor]	-Use whatever means to neutralize the invader.

5615	**coordinación**	**coordination**
	f	Eso demuestra que debe haber coordinación.
	[ko.or.ði.na.ˈsjõn]	-This shows that there has to be coordination.

5616	**chic**	**chic**
	adj	Les parece chic tener un delfín como mascota.
	[ˈt͡ʃik]	-They think it's chic to have a dolphin for a pet.

5617	**ligado**	**bound**
	adj	Podrías estar ligado a ellas ahora.
	[li.ˈɣa.ðo]	-You might be bound by them right now.

5618	**participante**	**participant; participating**
	m/f; adj	Se aceptará solo un diseño por participante.
	[par.ti.si.ˈpãn̪.te]	-Only one design per participant will be accepted.

5619	**carpeta**		**folder**
	f		Copia los elementos seleccionados a otra carpeta.
	[kar.ˈpɛ.ta]		-Copy the selected items to another folder.
5620	**violinista**		**violinist**
	m/f		Hay un violinista que necesito encontrar.
	[bjo.li.ˈnis.ta]		-There's a violinist I need to find.
5621	**descontento**		**discontented; displeasure**
	adj; m		Parecías un chico descontento con la sociedad.
	[dɛs.kõn̪.ˈtẽn̪.to]		-You seemed like a kid discontented with society.
5622	**nadador**		**swimmer**
	m		Él es mejor nadador que yo.
	[na.ða.ˈðor]		-He is a better swimmer than I.
5623	**microscopio**		**microscope**
	m		Se examinará cada pozo con un microscopio.
	[mi.kros.ˈko.pjo]		-Each well shall be examined using a microscope.
5624	**inclinar(se)**		**bend, persuade; bow, tend toward**
	vb; vbr[ĩŋ.kli.ˈnar]		Tienes que inclinar también el cuerpo. -You have to bend your body too.
5625	**demolición**		**demolition**
	f		Parece que podría estar haciendo alguna demolición.
	[de.mo.li.ˈsjõn]		-It looks like you might be doing some demolition.
5626	**levantamiento**		**uprising**
	m		No debemos mezclarnos en el levantamiento.
	[le.βãn̪.ta.ˈmjẽn̪.to]		-We shouldn't be involved in the uprising.
5627	**memorable**		**memorable**
	adj		Es mejor ser memorable que aburrido.
	[me.mo.ˈra.βle]		-It's better to be memorable than boring.
5628	**resbalar(se)**		**slip**
	vb		Supongo que uno puede resbalar y caerse del techo.
	[rɛs̠.βa.ˈlar]		-I guess you can just slip and fall off the roof.
5629	**florecer**		**bloom**
	vb		De repente la vida puede florecer.
	[flo.re.ˈsɛr]		-All of a sudden life is able to just bloom.
5630	**agitación**		**agitation**
	f		Lo que ha percibido como agitación era en realidad un placer de lo más intenso y tranquilo.
	[a.xi.ta.ˈsjõn]		-What you perceived as agitation was indeed most intense tranquil enjoyment.
5631	**buscador**		**searcher**
	m		Es una especie de buscador de almas.
	[bus.ka.ˈðor]		-It is kind of a soul searcher.
5632	**magnético**		**magnetic**
	adj		Tendremos que aumentar el gradiante magnético.
	[maɣ.ˈnɛ.ti.ko]		-We'll have to increase the magnetic gradient.
5633	**equipar(se)**		**equip**
	vb		Se necesita equipar albergues para las personas que han sido seriamente afectadas por el segundo terremoto.
	[e.ki.ˈpar]		-We need to equip shelters for people seriously affected by the second earthquake.
5634	**balanza**		**scales**

	f		Esas eran las balanzas que desequilibraste.
	[ba.ˈlãn.sa]		-Those were the scales you threw off balance.
5635	**nevar**	**snow**	
	vb		Según el pronóstico del tiempo va a nevar mañana.
	[ne.ˈβar]		-According to the weather forecast, it is going to snow tomorrow.
5636	**inversor**	**investor**	
	m		El inversor puede vender estas acciones a terceros.
	[ĩm.bɛr.ˈsor]		-The investor can sell these shares to a third party.
5637	**senil**	**senile**	
	adj		Ese hombre o está senil o lleva demasiado tiempo bajo el sol.
	[se.ˈnil]		-Either that man's senile or he's been out in the sun too long.
5638	**racismo**	**racism**	
	m[ra.ˈsiṣ.mo]		Este es un ejemplo de los efectos estructurales del racismo y la discriminación. -This is an example of the structural impact of racism and discrimination.
5639	**arpa**	**harp**	
	f		Preferiría aprender a tocar el arpa.
	[ˈar.pa]		-I would rather learn to play the harp.
5640	**pico**	**pick, peak, small amount**	
	m		Tengo un pico, dos palas y una carretilla.
	[ˈpi.ko]		-I have a pick, two shovels, and a wheelbarrow.
5641	**vallar**	**fence; fenced enclosure**	
	vb; m		Quiero construir y vallar un camino que atraviese las tierras.
	[ba.ˈjar]		-I want to construct and fence a road over the land.
5642	**cese**	**cessation**	
	m		Seguimos pidiendo el cese de esta práctica.
	[ˈse.se]		-We continue to call for the cessation of this practice.
5643	**saldar**	**pay off**	
	vb		Necesito vuestra ayuda para saldar esa cuenta.
	[sal̪.ˈdar]		-I need your help to pay off that debt.
5644	**olimpiada**	**Olympics**	
	f		Quizás vayan a la olimpiada.
	[o.lĩm.ˈpja.ða]		-Maybe they're going to the Olympics.
5645	**cafetero**	**fond of coffee**	
	adj		De verdad que él es muy cafetero.
	[ka.fɛ.ˈtɛ.ro]		-He is really fond of coffee.
5646	**anteayer**	**day before yesterday**	
	adv		El acuerdo se firmó anteayer.
	[ãn̪.te.a.ˈjɛr]		-The agreement was signed the day before yesterday.
5647	**amnistía**	**amnesty**	
	f		Está escrito aquí mismo que anunciaron una amnistía.
	[ãm.nis.ˈti.a]		-It is written right here that they announced an amnesty.
5648	**bambú**	**bamboo**	
	m		Trajimos suficiente bambú para construir una nueva ducha.
	[bãm.ˈbu]		-We brought enough bamboo to build a whole new shower.
5649	**jorobado**	**hunched; hunchback**	
	adj; m		El jorobado de Notre Dame, probablemente.
	[xo.ro.ˈβa.ðo]		-The hunchback of Notre Dame, probably.
5650	**excavación**	**excavation**	

f

[ɛk.sa.βa.ˈsjõn]

Continuando nuestra excavación encontramos otra cosa.
-As we continued our excavation, we found one other thing.

5651 eslabón   **link**

m

[ɛş.la.ˈβõn]

Necesitamos encontrar el eslabón débil, ahora.
-We need to find the weak link, now.

5652 llanura   **plain**

f

[ɟja.ˈnu.ra]

El área alrededor de este río es una gran llanura.
-The area around this river is a large plain.

5653 enfermizo   **sickly**

adj

[ɛ̃ɱ.fɛr.ˈmi.so]

Bueno, es muy inseguro y algo enfermizo.
-Well, he's very insecure and somewhat sickly.

5654 notario   **public notary**

m

[no.ˈta.rjo]

Lo haremos la semana que viene, con un notario.
-We'll do that next week, at the public notary.

5655 democrático   **democratic**

adj

[de.mo.ˈkra.ti.ko]

La idea es establecer un diálogo democrático.
-The idea is to establish a democratic dialogue.

5656 burgués   **middle-class; rich person**

adj; m

[bur.ˈɣes]

Ambos venimos de un ambiente intolerablemente burgués.
-Both of us come from obscenely middle-class homes.

5657 afilar(se)   **sharpen; become thin**

vb; vbr

[a.fi.ˈlar]

Sería un gatito aprendiendo a afilar las garras.
-You'd be a kitten who's learning to sharpen its claws.

5658 sádico   **sadistic; sadist**

adj; m

[ˈsa.ði.ko]

Estáis esperando a que ese sádico se entregue.
-So you're waiting for this sadist to turn himself in.

5659 aceptación   **acceptance**

f

[a.sep̚.ta.ˈsjõn]

Promueven el espíritu de tolerancia, aceptación y cooperación.
-They promote the spirit of tolerance, acceptance, and cooperation.

5660 minoría   **minority**

f

[mi.no.ˈri.a]

Resulta evidente que cada minoría tiene sus intereses y preocupaciones especiales.
-It becomes evident that each minority has its special interests and concerns.

5661 tentador   **tempting**

m

[tɛ̃n̪.ta.ˈðor]

Aunque debo decir que es tentador.
-Got to say, though, it's tempting.

5662 medieval   **medieval**

adj

[me.ðje.ˈβal]

El poblado medieval estaba dentro de la fortaleza, por protección.
-The medieval village was inside the fortress, for protection.

5663 matriz   **womb**

f

[ˈma.tris]

Es la matriz para todas las crías de abeja.
-It is the womb for all of the baby bees.

5664 recaudar   **collect**

vb

[re.kau̯.ˈðar]

Su principal función es recaudar los impuestos municipales.
-Their main function is to collect taxes from the municipality.

5665 fundir(se)   **melt; melt, burn out**

vb; vbr

[fũn̪.ˈdir]

Se utiliza un sistema de recuperación de energía único para fundir el chocolate.
-A unique energy retrieval system is used to melt chocolate.

5666 abominable   **abominable**

	adj	Pero entiendo perfectamente su comportamiento abominable.
	[a.βo.mi.'na.βle]	-But I fully understand their abominable behavior.
5667	**suroeste**	**southwest**
	adj	Mola que te guste el suroeste.
	[su.ro.'ɛs.te]	-It's cool that you like the southwest.
5668	**incapacidad**	**inability**
	f	La incapacidad de recordar es lo que constituye la amnesia.
	[ĩŋ.ka.pa.si.'ðað]	-It is the inability to remember that constitutes amnesia.
5669	**galón**	**gallon**
	m	Es solo medio galón de leche.
	[ga.'lõn]	-It's only a half gallon of milk.
5670	**desdichado**	**unhappy**
	m	Ser desdichado es un estado mental.
	[dɛs.ði.'ʧa.ðo]	-Being unhappy is a state of mind.
5671	**rito**	**rite**
	m	Solo estoy intentando detener el gran rito.
	['ri.to]	-I'm only trying to stop the grand rite.
5672	**ladrar**	**bark**
	vb	Va a ladrar en su primera noche.
	[la.'ðrar]	-He's going to bark the first night.
5673	**destello**	**flash, sparkle**
	m	El destello es como un grito de ayuda.
	[dɛs.'te.jo]	-The flash is like a scream for help.
5674	**excavar**	**dig**
	vb	No pueden excavar en la tierra helada.
	[ɛk.sa.'βar]	-They can't dig the frozen soil.
5675	**vasto**	**vast**
	adj	Este desierto era un vasto océano.
	['bas.to]	-This dessert was once a vast ocean.
5676	**allanamiento**	**flattening, forced entry**
	m	Alex, no hay evidencia de allanamiento.
	[a.ja.na.'mjẽn.to]	-Alex, there's no evidence of a break-in.
5677	**proyectil**	**projectile**
	m	Hombre, busquemos este proyectil mañana.
	[pro.jek̚.'til]	-Man, let's look for this projectile tomorrow.
5678	**atorar(se)**	**obstruct; get tongue-tied**
	vb; vbr	Se ha debido atorar en la impresora.
	[a.to.'rar]	-It must've gotten caught in the printer.
5679	**limitación**	**limitation**
	f	Pero eso es una limitación también.
	[li.mi.ta.'sjõn]	-But that is a limitation, as well.
5680	**veintidós**	**twenty-two**
	num	Tiene veintidós hijos y una docena de esposas.
	[bein̪.ti.'ðos]	-He has twenty-two children and a dozen wives.
5681	**danés**	**Danish; Danish person**
	adj; m	Espero poder revelar la identidad del candidato danés mañana.
	[da.'nes]	-I hope I can reveal the identity of the Danish candidate tomorrow.
5682	**inquisición**	**inquisition**

	f	No vine aquí para una inquisición.
	[ĩŋ.ki.si.ˈsjõn]	-I didn't come here for an inquisition.
5683	**instantáneo**	**instant**
	adj	Búscame un botiquín y pegamento instantáneo.
	[ĩns.tãn̪.ˈta.ne.o]	-Find me a first aid kit and some instant glue.
5684	**casilla**	**box**
	f	Señale con una cruz la casilla correspondiente.
	[ka.ˈsi.ʝa]	-Place a cross in the appropriate box.
5685	**ómnibus**	**bus**
	m	Me sorprendió verte bajar de ese ómnibus.
	[ˈõm.ni.βus]	-I was surprised to see you get off that bus.
5686	**refinar**	**refine**
	vb	Después puede refinar los resultados de la búsqueda.
	[re.fi.ˈnar]	-You can then refine the search results.
5687	**fregar**	**wash**
	vb	Friega tus platos antes de irte a la cama.
	[fre.ˈɣar]	-Wash your dishes before you go to bed.
5688	**cúpula**	**dome, leadership**
	f	Esa cúpula está a punto de caerse sobre nuestras cabezas.
	[ˈku.pu.la]	-That dome's about to come crashing down on all our heads.
5689	**depredador**	**predatory; predator**
	adj; m	Es tan depredador como cualquier animal del parque.
	[de.pre.ða.ˈðor]	-He is as much a predator as any animal in the park.
5690	**silvestre**	**wild**
	adj	Solo estás fascinada por ese rosal silvestre porque está floreciendo.
	[sil.ˈβɛs.tre]	-You're only fascinated by that wild rose because it's flourishing.
5691	**imponente**	**imposing**
	adj	Toda ciudad tiene una catedral imponente.
	[ĩm.po.ˈnɛ̃n̪.te]	-Every city has an imposing cathedral.
5692	**brasileño**	**Brazilian; Brazilian person**
	adj; m	Viene a comer el embajador brasileño.
	[bra.si.ˈle.ɲo]	-We have the Brazilian Ambassador coming over for lunch.
5693	**intermedio**	**intermediate; intermission**
	adj; m	Este usuario puede contribuir con un nivel intermedio de inglés.
	[ĩn̪.tɛr.ˈme.ðjo]	-This user is able to contribute with an intermediate level of English.
5694	**cono**	**cone**
	m	Me siento como un cono de tráfico gigante.
	[ˈko.no]	-I feel like a giant traffic cone.
5695	**escáner**	**scanner**
	m	Estoy recibiendo movimiento en el escáner.
	[ɛs.ˈka.nɛr]	-I'm picking up movement on the scanner.
5696	**licenciar(se)**	**award a degree, license; get a degree**
	vb; vbr	Podríamos licenciar su obra y presentarle un nuevo mundo de ingresos.
	[li.sɛ̃n.ˈsjar]	-We could license his work and introduce him to a whole new world of revenue.
5697	**nublar(se)**	**cloud**
	vb	Es lo suficiente para nublar tu visión.
	[nu.ˈβlar]	-It is powerful enough to cloud your vision.
5698	**infante**	**infant**

	m/f	Se permite solo un infante por adulto.
	[ĩm.ˈfãn̪.te]	-Only one infant per adult is permitted.
5699	**descubierto**	**uncovered**
	m	He descubierto algunas cosas perturbadoras.
	[dɛs.ku.ˈβjɛɾ.to]	-I've uncovered some pretty disturbing things.
5700	**desembarcar(se)**	**unload; disembark**
	vb; vbr[de.sẽm.baɾ.ˈkaɾ]	Tenemos que desembarcar los paquetes antes de mediodía. -We have to unload the packages before noon.
5701	**rígido**	**rigid**
	adj	Un código de conducta rígido no surtirá efecto.
	[ˈri.xi.ðo]	-A rigid code of conduct is not effective.
5702	**delatar**	**betray**
	vb	Pensé que los caballos me delatarían.
	[de.la.ˈtaɾ]	-I thought the horses would betray me.
5703	**brusco**	**abrupt**
	adj	Supongo que he sido un poco brusco.
	[ˈbɾus.ko]	-I guess I have been a little abrupt.
5704	**competidor**	**competitor; competitor**
	adj; m	Espero demostraros que soy un competidor.
	[kõm.pɛ.ti.ˈðoɾ]	-I hopefully prove to you that I'm a competitor.
5705	**secar(se)**	**dry**
	vb	Debería dejarlo secar, pero soy un poco impaciente.
	[se.ˈkaɾ]	-I should let it dry, but I'm a little impatient.
5706	**portavoz**	**spokesperson**
	m/f	Susan se ofreció a ser su portavoz.
	[poɾ.ˈta.βos]	-Susan took it upon herself to become his spokesperson.
5707	**hinchar(se)**	**swell; stuff yourself**
	vb; vbr	Si caminamos, mis piernas se van a hinchar.
	[ĩn̪.ˈtʃaɾ]	-If we walk, my legs will swell.
5708	**fabricante**	**manufacturing; manufacturer**
	adj; m	Deberá notificar su decisión al fabricante.
	[fa.βɾi.ˈkãn̪.te]	-It must notify its decision to the manufacturer.
5709	**abstinencia**	**withdrawal**
	f	Cuando despierte, no sentirá la abstinencia.
	[aβs.ti.ˈnẽn.sja]	-When she wakes up, she won't be in withdrawal.
5710	**razonamiento**	**reasoning**
	m	Nos cuesta trabajo seguir este razonamiento.
	[ra.so.na.ˈmjẽn̪.to]	-We find it difficult to follow this reasoning.
5711	**recordatorio**	**reminder**
	m	Los dejo con un pequeño recordatorio.
	[re.koɾ.ða.ˈto.rjo]	-I'll leave you with a small reminder.
5712	**diminuto**	**tiny**
	adj	Observen esta imagen de un punto azul y diminuto.
	[di.mi.ˈnu.to]	-Look at this image of the tiny, blue dot.
5713	**cosmos**	**cosmos**
	m	También contiene toda la información conocida del cosmos.
	[ˈkos̝.mos]	-It also contains all the known information of the cosmos.
5714	**compadecer**	**pity**

	vb		Eres demasiado bueno para compadecerte de ti mismo.
	[kõm.pa.ðe.ˈsɛɾ]		-And you're too good to pity yourself.

5715 corneta — cornet; cornet player

f; m/f

[koɾ.ˈnɛ.ta]

Una señora pregunta por el corneta.
-The cornet player is wanted by a lady.

5716 crucificar — crucify

vb[kɾu.si.fi.ˈkaɾ]

¿Le ordenó alguna vez crucificar a los prisioneros? -Did he ever order you to crucify the prisoners?

5717 viruela — smallpox

f

[bi.ˈɾwe.la]

Para identificar el virus original como viruela, debimos secuenciarlo.
-In order to identify the original virus as smallpox, we had to sequence it.

5718 deslizar(se) — slip, sneak

vb

[dɛʂ.li.ˈsaɾ]

Solo tengo que deslizar estas tijeras bajo la banda.
-I just need to slip these shears under the band.

5719 mitología — mythology

f

[mi.to.lo.ˈxi.a]

Quería aprender mitología, pero no había dónde estudiarlo.
-I wanted to learn mythology, but there is nowhere you can study.

5720 guisar — stew

vb

[gi.ˈsaɾ]

Yo quería prepararla para guisar.
-I wanted to set it to stew.

5721 impaciencia — impatience

f

[ĩm.pa.ˈsjẽn.sja]

Su impaciencia se acaba, capitán.
-Your impatience is at an end, Captain.

5722 dúo — pair

m

[ˈdwo]

Ustedes sí que son un dúo alegre.
-You two are a cheerful pair.

5723 inflación — inflation

f

[ĩm.fla.ˈsjõn]

La tasa de inflación actual es muy elevada.
-The current rate of inflation is extremely high.

5724 exorcismo — exorcism

m

[ɛk.soɾ.ˈsiʂ.mo]

Descubrí que ella había cometido los asesinatos durante un exorcismo.
-I found out that she had committed these murders during an exorcism.

5725 currículum — curriculum

m

[ku.ˈɾi.ku.lũm]

Envíanos tu currículum, tu candidatura es muy importante.
-Send us your curriculum, as your candidature is important.

5726 cocer — boil

vb

[ko.ˈsɛɾ]

Cualquier tío puede cocer unos fideos.
-Any guy can boil a pot of noodles.

5727 incienso — incense

m

[ĩn.ˈsjẽn.so]

Volveré a por ti cuando se consuma el incienso.
-I'll be back to get you once the incense is finished.

5728 componente — built in; component

adj; m
[kõm.po.ˈnẽn̪.te]

Este componente seguirá desempeñando un papel crucial en el programa propuesto.
-This component will continue to play a vital role in the proposed programme.

5729 orador — public speaker

m

[o.ɾa.ˈðoɾ]

No te preocupes. Soy un orador bastante bueno.
-But don't worry. I'm sort of a good public speaker.

5730 aviador — pilot

m
[a.βja.ˈðor]
La esposa del piloto es una auténtica belleza.
-The pilot's wife is a real beauty.

5731 verja — fence

f[ˈbɛr.xa]
Menos mal que pusieron una verja. -Good thing they put up the fence.

5732 lucio — pike

m
[ˈlu.sjo]
Puede ser una trucha, pero no un lucio.
-It may be a trout, but not a pike.

5733 clasificación — classification

f
[kla.si.fi.ka.ˈsjõn]
No tenemos una clasificación por género.
-We do not have the classification by gender.

5734 medusa — jellyfish

f
[me.ˈðu.sa]
Creo que puede picarte la medusa.
-I think you can just get stung by the jellyfish.

5735 sífilis — syphilis

f
[ˈsi.fi.lis]
Estoy buscando a alguien con sífilis.
-I'm looking for someone with syphilis.

5736 cráter — crater

m
[ˈkra.tɛr]
Ese cráter es donde solía estar.
-That crater is where it used to be.

5737 infalible — infallible

adj
[ĩɱ.fa.ˈli.βle]
Está diciendo que nadie es infalible.
-She's saying that no one is infallible.

5738 lamento — lament

m
[la.ˈmẽn̪.to]
Su lamento sigue siendo tan elocuente hoy como entonces.
-His lament remains as poignant today as it was then.

5739 tapadera — cover

f
[ta.pa.ˈðɛ.ra]
Esto lo utilizó el ladrón como tapadera.
-This was used by the thief as a cover.

5740 aparcar — park

vb
[a.par.ˈkar]
Hay muchos otros lugares para aparcar.
-There are plenty of other places to park.

5741 caverna — cavern

f
[ka.ˈβɛr.na]
Esta no es una caverna natural.
-This isn't a natural cavern.

5742 incertidumbre — uncertainty

f
[ĩn.sɛr.ti.ˈðũm.bre]
Vivimos tiempos de cambio e incertidumbre.
-We live in times of change and uncertainty.

5743 sembrar — sow

vb
[sẽm.ˈbrar]
Hoy es el momento de sembrar, para así mañana poder cosechar.
-Today is the time to sow so that tomorrow we will be able to harvest.

5744 ordenanza — ordinance

f
[or.ðe.ˈnãn.sa]
Esa ordenanza ya ni siquiera viene en los libros.
-That ordinance isn't even on the books anymore.

5745 patriotismo — patriotism

m
[pa.trjo.ˈtiş.mo]
Tendré que apelar a su patriotismo.
-I'll have to appeal to their patriotism.

5746 saborear — savor

vb
[sa.βo.re.ˈar]
Déjanos saborear este momento mientras dure.
-Let us savor this moment while it lasts.

5747 **concesión** — concession

f[kõn.se.ˈsjõn]

Esto tal vez no parezca demasiada concesión. -This may not seem like much of a concession.

5748 **cesto** — **basket**

m

[ˈsɛs.to]

Saca tus sucios dedos del cesto.
 -Take your scabby fingers out of the basket.

5749 **enfriar(se)** — **cool; get cold, catch a cold**

vb; vbr

[ẽɱ.ˈfrjar]

Sácalo del horno y deja que se enfríe.
 -Remove from the oven and allow to cool.

5750 **proteína** — **protein**

f

[pro.te.ˈi.na]

Hay otra forma de secretar tanta proteína.
 -There's another way to secrete that much protein.

5751 **innumerable** — **innumerable**

adj

[ĩn.nu.mɛ.ˈra.βle]

La belleza natural del pico más alto de Japón atrae a innumerable gente a sus laderas.
 -The natural beauty of Japan's highest peak draws countless people to its slopes.

5752 **sudoeste** — **south-west**

m

[su.ðo.ˈɛs.te]

Yo vivo en el sudoeste de Irlanda.
 -I live in the south west of Ireland.

5753 **aristócrata** — **aristocrat**

m/f

[a.ris.ˈto.kra.ta]

Entonces sabré el calibre de este aristócrata inglés.
 -Then I will know the caliber of this English aristocrat.

5754 **duración** — **length of time**

f

[du.ra.ˈsjõn]

También debe indicarse la duración prevista del acogimiento.
 -Also, the expected duration of the placement must be indicated.

5755 **maquinista** — **machinist**

m/f

[ma.ki.ˈnis.ta]

¿Te acuerdas de Jean? Tu amigo maquinista.
 -You remember Jean, your machinist friend?

5756 **vega** — **meadow**

f

[ˈbe.ɣa]

Sus terrenos son todos propios de vega, cultivados en su mayoría por cítricos y algunos parrales.
 -Its terrains are the ones of the meadow, cultivated with citrus and some vineyards.

5757 **pintada** — **graffiti**

f

[pĩn̪.ˈta.ða]

Era una amenaza, eso es lo que la pintada significaba.
 -It was a threat, that's what the graffiti meant.

5758 **alerta** — **alarm; alert; on the alert**

f; adj; adv

[a.ˈlɛr.ta]

Es imprescindible que nos sigamos manteniendo alerta.
 -It is imperative that we continue to be alert.

5759 **canela** — **cinnamon**

f

[ka.ˈne.la]

Me recuerda cuanto odio la canela.
 -Reminds me of how much I hate cinnamon.

5760 **colmena** — **hive**

f

[kol.ˈme.na]

Estaba escuchando las abejas en la colmena.
 -I was listening to the bees in the hive.

5761 **decepcionante** — **disappointing**

adj

[de.sɛp.sjo.ˈnãn̪.te]

Francamente, considero que es tanto decepcionante y vergonzoso.
 -Quite frankly, I find it both disappointing and embarrassing.

5762 **urbano** — **urban**

adj
Un guerrero urbano no necesita eso.
[ur.ˈβa.no]
-An urban warrior has no need for that.

5763 iraquí — **Iraqi; Iraqi person**
adj; m
Esto no fue mencionado por la parte iraquí.
[i.ra.ˈki]
-This was not mentioned by the Iraqi side.

5764 extorsión — **extortion**
f
Estuvo preso por extorsión y fraude interestatal.
[ɛks.tor.ˈsjõn]
-He's done time for extortion and interstate fraud.

5765 procesión — **procession**
f
Le pedí que no permitiera esta procesión.
[pro.se.ˈsjõn]
-I had asked you not to allow this procession.

5766 crepúsculo — **twilight**
m
Con un crepúsculo así, mañana hará buen tiempo.
[kre.ˈpus.ku.lo]
-With such a twilight, it will be fine tomorrow.

5767 azote — **scourge, spank**
m
Fueron el azote de dos galaxias.
[a.ˈso.te]
-They've been the scourge of two galaxies.

5768 patrocinador — **sponsor**
m
De hecho, fuimos el patrocinador original.
[pa.tro.si.na.ˈðor]
-As a matter of fact, we were the original sponsor.

5769 cacahuete — **peanut**
m
Están fritos en aceite de cacahuete.
[ka.ka.ˈwɛ.te]
-They're fried in peanut oil.

5770 eliminación — **elimination**
f
Esto les permitirá iniciar el proceso de eliminación.
[e.li.mi.na.ˈsjõn]
-This will enable them to start the process of elimination.

5771 colisión — **collision**
f
Para mí, la colisión sería inminente.
[ko.li.ˈsjõn]
-To me, a collision would seem imminent.

5772 pelotudo — **slow, dumb (LA) (coll); young adult (LA)**
adj; m
El borracho pelotudo todavía no cobró el sueldo.
[pe.lo.ˈtu.ðo]
-The drunk idiot hasn't got paid yet.

5773 ajeno — **somebody else's**
adj
Voy a fingir que estaba jugando con dinero ajeno.
[a.ˈxe.no]
-I'll just pretend I was playing with somebody else's money.

5774 conquistador — **conqueror, Casanova; seductive**
m; adj
Fue atacada sin previo aviso por un despiadado conquistador.
[kõŋ.kis.ta.ˈðor]
-She was attacked without a word of warning by a ruthless conqueror.

5775 chal — **shawl**
m
En serio, abuela, cómprate un chal.
[ˈtʃal]
-Seriously, Grandma, buy a shawl.

5776 cortejar — **court**
vb
Mi aprendiz quiere cortejar a Lillian.
[kor.te.ˈxar]
-My apprentice wants to court Lillian.

5777 feto — **fetus**
m
Ya veo la forma del feto desarrollándose.
[ˈfɛ.to]
-I already see the form of the fetus developing.

5778 pilotar — **pilot**

		vb	Está herido y no puede pilotar.
		[pi.lo.ˈtar]	-He's wounded and cannot pilot.

5779 sustentar(se) — **sustain, support**

vb
[sus.tẽn̪.ˈtar]

No puede sustentar a su familia con su sueldo mensual.
-He cannot support his family on his monthly income.

5780 calmo — **calm**

adj
[ˈkal.mo]

Un gerente debe mantenerse calmo en situaciones como esta.
-A manager has to keep calm at times like this.

5781 combinar — **combine**

vb
[kõm.bi.ˈnar]

Cuando compuse esto quise combinar varios estilos...
-When I wrote this, I tried to combine different styles...

5782 fugarse — **break out**

vbr
[fu.ˈɣar.se]

Dijo que alguien estaba planeando fugarse de la cárcel y matarte.
-He said someone is planning to break out of prison and kill you.

5783 electricista — **electrician**

m/f
[e.lek̚.tri.ˈsis.ta]

Y después llegó el electricista con su máquina.
-And then the electrician with his machine came in.

5784 sandía — **watermelon**

f
[sãn̪.ˈdi.a]

Ayer compré una sandía de tres libras.
-Yesterday I bought a three-pound watermelon.

5785 milímetro — **millimeter**

m
[mi.ˈli.mɛ.tro]

No cedan un milímetro de terreno.
-Don't give up a millimeter of ground.

5786 simulación — **simulation**

f
[si.mu.la.ˈsjõn]

Se recomienda probar una simulación primero.
-It is recommended to try a simulation first.

5787 génesis — **origin**

f
[ˈxe.ne.sis]

La discriminación interviene en la génesis de los movimientos de refugiados.
-Discrimination plays a role in the genesis of refugee movements.

5788 inhumano — **inhumane**

adj
[i.nu.ˈma.no]

Es inhumano echarme con este tiempo.
-It's Inhumane to kick me out in this weather.

5789 astillar — **splinter**

vb
[as.ti.ˈjar]

Los trabajadores los van a astillar.
-The workers will splinter them.

5790 predicar — **preach**

vb
[pre.ði.ˈkar]

No he venido hoy aquí para predicar.
-I didn't come here to preach today.

5791 promover — **promote**

vb
[pro.mo.ˈβɛr]

Él trabajó duro para promover la paz.
-He worked hard to promote peace.

5792 halagar — **flatter**

vb
[a.la.ˈɣar]

Tengo que halagar y perseguir a determinados clientes.
-I have to flatter and pursue certain clients.

5793 adecuar(se) — **adjust**

vb [a.ðe.ˈkwar]

No tienes por qué adecuar tu vida a la mía. -Don't adjust your life to mine.

5794 hipódromo — **racecourse**

m
[i.ˈpo.ðro.mo]

Estaba en una fiesta con mi padre y Maggie en el hipódromo.
-I was at a party with my dad and Maggie over by the racecourse.

5795	**danzar**	**dance**
	vb	Tus padres pueden danzar con sus ancestros.
	[dãn.ˈsar]	-Your parents can dance with their ancestors.
5796	**caño**	**pipe**
	m	Me has golpeado con un caño.
	[ˈka.ɲo]	-You hit me with a pipe.
5797	**felicitar**	**congratulate**
	vb	Quisiera felicitar a los autores del informe exhaustivo.
	[fe.li.si.ˈtar]	-I would like to congratulate the authors of the comprehensive report.
5798	**deportista**	**sporty; athlete**
	adj; m/f	Me gusta él porque es deportista.
	[de.por.ˈtis.ta]	-I like him because he's sporty.
5799	**lapicero**	**pencil**
	m	El lapicero, ¡se me ha caído!
	[la.pi.ˈsɛ.ro]	-The pencil, I dropped it!
5800	**engordar**	**gain weight**
	vb	Si siempre comes tanto, vas a engordar.
	[ẽŋ.gor.ˈðar]	-If you always eat that much, you'll gain weight.
5801	**apelar**	**appeal**
	vb	Él indicó inmediatamente al juez que deseaba apelar.
	[a.pe.ˈlar]	-He immediately indicated to the judge that he wanted to appeal.
5802	**favorecer**	**favour**
	vb	Parecen favorecer la opción de una victoria militar.
	[fa.βo.re.ˈsɛr]	-They seem to favor the option of a military victory.
5803	**ingrato**	**ungrateful**
	adj	Te sacaré de este ingrato país.
	[ĩŋ.ˈgra.to]	-I'm taking you away from this ungrateful country.
5804	**desempeño**	**performance**
	m	El objetivo siempre es mejorar tu propio desempeño.
	[de.sẽm.ˈpe.ɲo]	-The goal is always to improve one's own performance.
5805	**espeso**	**thick**
	adj	El pelaje del conejo es espeso.
	[ɛs.ˈpe.so]	-The rabbit's fur is thick.
5806	**cuadrante**	**quadrant**
	m	Viene del cuadrante superior izquierdo.
	[kwa.ˈðrãn̪.te]	-It's coming down from the upper left quadrant.
5807	**clasificar(se)**	**classify; win a place**
	vb; vbr	Creo que podemos clasificar eso como una confesión espontánea.
	[kla.si.fi.ˈkar]	-I think we can classify that as a spontaneous utterance.
5808	**manipulación**	**handling**
	f	Todos juntos condenamos la manipulación y el fraude electoral.
	[ma.ni.pu.la.ˈsjõn]	-We all stand together in our condemnation of manipulation and electoral fraud.
5809	**protestante**	**Protestant**
	adj	Sí, pero mi marido era protestante.
	[pro.tɛs.ˈtãn̪.te]	-Yes, but my husband was a Protestant.
5810	**místico**	**mystic; mystic**
	adj; m	No parece haber nada místico en esto.
	[ˈmis.ti.ko]	-There doesn't seem to be anything mystical about this.

5811	**fascinación**	**fascination**
	f	Temo que haya desarrollado una fascinación por el fuego.
	[fas.si.na.ˈsjõn]	-I'm afraid he's developed a fascination with fire.
5812	**cresta**	**crest**
	f	La cresta del río ha pasado.
	[ˈkrɛs.ta]	-The river crest's gone by.
5813	**gratuito**	**free, uncalled for**
	adj	El proceso era sencillo y totalmente gratuito.
	[gra.ˈtwi.to]	-The process was simple and entirely free of charge.
5814	**diabetes**	**diabetes**
	f	Tienes diabetes, te caerías muerto.
	[dja.ˈβɛ.tes]	-You have diabetes, you'll drop dead.
5815	**camuflaje**	**camouflage**
	m	Solo demostraba el valor del camuflaje.
	[ka.mu.ˈfla.xe]	-I was just demonstrating the value of camouflage.
5816	**antibiótico**	**antibiotic; antibiotic**
	adj; m	Todavía tenemos unas pocas botellas de antibiótico.
	[ãn̪.ti.ˈβjo.ti.ko]	-We still have a few bottles of antibiotic.
5817	**siciliano**	**Sicilian; Sicilian person**
	adj; m	Me encanta ese vino siciliano que tienes.
	[si.si.ˈlja.no]	-I love that Sicilian wine of yours.
5818	**masturbación**	**masturbation**
	f	Sin la masturbación, los hombres y las mujeres se volverán locos.
	[mas.tur.βa.ˈsjõn]	-Without masturbation, men and women will go insane.
5819	**aterrorizar(se)**	**terrorise**
	vb	No deberías aterrorizar a nadie más.
	[a.tɛ.ro.ri.ˈsar]	-Yo should not terrorize anyone else.
5820	**inmaduro**	**immature, unripe**
	adj	Sería inmaduro por su parte pensarlo.
	[ĩm.ma.ˈðu.ro]	-It would be immature of them to think so.
5821	**soso**	**dull, boring**
	adj	A mí me parece un payaso soso y sin complicaciones.
	[ˈso.so]	-He seems to be a dull, uncomplicated clown.
5822	**coalición**	**coalition**
	f	Propongo que creemos una coalición con las empresas.
	[ko.a.li.ˈsjõn]	-I propose that we establish a coalition with industrial firms.
5823	**estático**	**static**
	adj	El concepto de medio ambiente es cambiante y no puede permanecer estático.
	[ɛs.ˈta.ti.ko]	-The concept of the environment was a changing one and could not remain static.
5824	**gorrión**	**sparrow**
	m[go.ˈrjõn]	Nos interesa hasta el último gorrión. -We are interested even in the lowliest sparrow.
5825	**avalancha**	**avalanche**
	f	Desaparecieron en aquella avalancha hace cien años.
	[a.βa.ˈlãn̪.tʃa]	-They were lost in that avalanche a hundred years ago.
5826	**posponer**	**postpone**

	vb [pos.po.ˈnɛr]		Debemos posponer nuestros planes relacionados con la granja durante un tiempo. -We must postpone our plans related to the farm for a while.
5827	**poético**	**poetic**	
	adj [po.ˈɛ.ti.ko]		Personalmente, me parece bastante poético. -Personally, I think it's rather poetic.
5828	**asar**	**roast**	
	vb [a.ˈsar]		Van a asar malvaviscos en esta chimenea. -They are going to roast marshmallows in this fireplace.
5829	**tóxico**	**toxic**	
	adj [ˈtok.si.ko]		Fabricar paneles solares es un proceso increíblemente tóxico. -Making solar panels is an incredibly toxic process.
5830	**desecho**	**waste**	
	m [de.ˈse.t͡ʃo]		A la larga, los propios neumáticos se convierten en desecho. -Ultimately, the tires themselves become waste.
5831	**sobornar**	**bribe**	
	vb [so.βor.ˈnar]		No necesitamos sobornar a los testigos. -We don't need to bribe the witnesses.
5832	**indefinido**	**indefinite**	
	adj [ĩn̪.de.fi.ˈni.ðo]		El uso del artículo indefinido es importante. -The use of the indefinite article is significant.
5833	**cerro**	**hill**	
	m [ˈsɛ.ro]		Los adultos de la aldea se dirigieron al cerro y los enfrentamientos continuaron. -Adults from the village headed to the hill and clashes continued.
5834	**clic**	**click**	
	m [ˈklik]		Primero selecciona algún texto u objeto, luego haz clic en este icono. -First select some text or an object, then click this icon.
5835	**disfrute**	**enjoyment**	
	m [dis.ˈfru.te]		No entiendo tu disfrute en quebrantar la ley. -I do not understand your enjoyment in breaking the law.
5836	**anomalía**	**anomaly**	
	f [a.no.ma.ˈli.a]		Esperamos que esa anomalía involuntaria se rectifique. -We hope that that unintended anomaly will be rectified.
5837	**auditorio**	**hearing; auditorium**	
	adj; m [au̯.ði.ˈto.rjo]		Pensé que estarías en el auditorio. -I thought you'd be in the auditorium.
5838	**resucitar**	**resurrect**	
	vb [re.su.si.ˈtar]		Intentó resucitar su cuerpo usando magia. -She tried to resurrect his body using magic.
5839	**ansia**	**craving**	
	f[ˈãn.sja]		Sentía ansia por el aire de la montaña. -I felt a craving for the mountain air.
5840	**próspero**	**prosperous**	
	adj [ˈpros.pɛ.ro]		Escojamos un futuro seguro y próspero para todos. -Let us choose a secure and prosperous future for all.
5841	**víveres**	**supplies**	
	mpl [ˈbi.βɛ.res]		Me temo que hemos perdido los víveres y las medicinas. -I'm afraid we've lost the food and the medical supplies.
5842	**mercader**	**merchant**	

m/f
[mɛr.ka.ˈðɛr]

Parece ser un mercader experimentado.
-You appear to be an experienced merchant.

5843 aventurero

adj; m
[a.βɛ̃n.tu.ˈrɛ.ro]

adventurous; adventurer

Este chico es un aventurero internacional.
-This guy is an international adventurer.

5844 armónico

adj
[ar.ˈmo.ni.ko]

harmonious

Las calles y plazuelas de la ciudad constituyen un conjunto verdaderamente armónico.
-The streets and squares of the city are a truly harmonious whole.

5845 deducir

vb
[de.ðu.ˈsir]

deduce

Esto debería ser bastante fácil de deducir.
-This should be fairly easy to deduce.

5846 pasarela

f
[pa.sa.ˈre.la]

walkway

Se vino abajo una pasarela en el centro.
-A walkway collapsed over at the center.

5847 impulsivo

adj
[ĩm.pul.ˈsi.βo]

impulsive

Creí que quería ser más impulsivo.
-I thought he wanted to be more impulsive.

5848 anti

pfx
[ˈãn̪.ti]

anti

El dispositivo fue equipado con un mecanismo antirobo.
-The device was fitted with an anti-theft mechanism.

5849 impreso

adj; m
[ĩm.ˈpre.so]

printed; flyer

Decidimos ocultarlo con un filtro impreso.
-We decided to hide it with a printed filter.

5850 pío

m
[ˈpi.o]

tweet

Y ella dijo que los pájaros hacen "pío".
-And she said that birds go "tweet."

5851 molde

m
[ˈmol̪.de]

mould

El grupo presenció la destrucción del molde de fundición de combustible sólido.
-The group witnessed the destruction of the solid fuel pouring mould.

5852 rural

adj
[ru.ˈral]

rural

Sigue habiendo diferencias entre las áreas urbanas y rurales.
-There are still differences between urban areas and rural areas.

5853 travesura

f
[tra.βe.ˈsu.ra]

mischief

Dile que continuamos con nuestra travesura.
-Tell her we continue to work our mischief.

5854 despreciar

vb[dɛs.pre.ˈsjar]

despise

Debes despreciarme por haberte decepcionado. -You must despise me for having let you down.

5855 entristecer(se)

vb
[ɛ̃n̪.tris.te.ˈsɛr]

sadden

Entristecer a un hombre moribundo es un crimen, lo sé.
-To sadden a dying man is a crime, I know.

5856 chapa

f
[ˈtʃa.pa]

sheet

Luego puse una chapa perforada aquí.
-Then I've laid some perforated sheet here.

5857 percibir

vb
[pɛr.si.ˈβir]

perceive

El estrés compromete en especial la habilidad de percibir.
-Stress especially compromises one's ability to perceive.

5858 cáscara

shell

f · Tenés que comerte la cáscara también.
['kas.ka.ra] · -You have to eat the shell as well.

5859 furgón — **van**
m · Los tipos del furgón están armados también.
[fur.'ɣõn] · -The guys in the van are armed too.

5860 historieta — **cartoon strip**
f · Pero parece algo sacado de una historieta.
[is.to.'rje.ta] · -But he's like something out of a comic book.

5861 inmobiliario — **real-estate**
adj · China ha invertido demasiado en desarrollo inmobiliario.
[ĩm.mo.βi.'lja.rjo] · -China has invested too much in real-estate development.

5862 ocaso — **sunset**
m · El perdedor arderá antes del ocaso.
[o.'ka.so] · -The loser will burn before sunset.

5863 concepción — **conception**
f · El hijo será protegido desde su concepción.
[kõn.sɛp.'sjõn] · -The child shall be protected from the time of conception.

5864 proveer — **supply**
vb · Queremos crear y proveer embalajes y servicios innovadores que sorprendan
[pro.βe.'ɛr] · el mercado.
-We want to develop and supply innovative packaging and services to amaze
the market.

5865 despliegue — **deployment**
m · Se espera que el despliegue esté terminado a finales de abril.
[dɛs.'plje.ɣe] · -The deployment is expected to be completed by the end of April.

5866 gerencia — **management**
f · Sírvete champán, cortesía de la gerencia.
[xɛ.'r̃ɛn.sja] · -Help yourself to champagne, courtesy of the management.

5867 australiano — **Australian; Australian person**
adj; m · Tenía una cita con un chico australiano.
[au̯s.tra.'lja.no] · -She was on a date with some Australian guy.

5868 preñar — **impregnate**
vb · Voy a preñar a mi esposa.
[pre.'ɲar] · -I will impregnate my wife.

5869 elogio — **compliment**
m[e.'lo.xjo] · Ese es el único elogio que escuché de mi padre. -That's the only compliment
I've ever heard from my father.

5870 ceguera — **blindness**
f · No te importa que los efectos secundarios incluyen ceguera.
[se.'ɣɛ.ra] · -You don't care if the side effects may include blindness.

5871 iniciación — **initiation**
f · No puedes unirte hasta pasar la iniciación.
[i.ni.sja.'sjõn] · -You can't join until you go through initiation.

5872 susceptible — **susceptible**
adj · La haría demasiado susceptible a nuevos tumores.
[sus.sep̚.'ti.βle] · -It would make her too susceptible to new tumors.

5873 seleccionar — **select**
vb · Primero debe seleccionar la política a modificar.
[se.lɛk.sjo.'nar] · -You must first select a policy to be changed.

5874 socialista — **socialist**

adj
[so.sja.ˈlis.ta]

No seremos parte de esta perversión socialista.
-We will not be party to this socialist perversion.

5875 urna   **vase**

f

['ur.na]

Han pasado mil años y esta urna sigue allí.
-A thousand years have passed and this vase is still there.

5876 tapón   **plug, cover**

m

[ta.ˈpõn]

No podemos dejarles abrir ese tapón.
-We can't let them pull that plug.

5877 mamífero   **mammal; mammal**

m; adj

[ma.ˈmi.fɛ.ro]

Hay un mamífero que pone huevos.
-There is a mammal that lays eggs.

5878 desacato   **contempt**

m

[de.sa.ˈka.to]

Tranquilícese o tendré que acusarla de desacato.
-Quiet down or I will have to fine you for contempt.

5879 monopolio   **monopoly**

m

[mo.no.ˈpo.ljo]

Aquí tiene el monopolio del mercado negro.
-He has a monopoly on the black market here.

5880 milagroso   **miraculous**

adj

[mi.la.ˈɣro.so]

No esperemos ningún resultado milagroso.
-So let us not expect any miraculous results.

5881 alineación   **line-up**

f

[a.li.ne.a.ˈsjõn]

Aparentemente, tengo que identificarlo en una alineación o algo así.
-Apparently, I've got to spot him in a line-up or something.

5882 contratista   **contractor**

m/f

[kõn̪.tra.ˈtis.ta]

El gasto correspondiente debía ser recuperado del contratista.
-The associated cost was to be recovered from the contractor.

5883 osar   **dare**

vb

[o.ˈsar]

¡Cómo puede osar decir mentiras!
-How can you dare tell lies!

5884 renovar   **renew**

vb

[re.no.ˈβar]

Hoy vengo a renovar aquella promesa.
-Today, I have come to renew that pledge.

5885 muela   **molar**

f['mwe.la]

Esa muela obviamente lleva aquí años. -That molar has obviously been here for ages.

5886 bautismo   **baptism**

m

[bau̯.ˈtis̪.mo]

Me gustaría acompañarte a tu bautismo.
-I'd like to go with you to your baptism.

5887 cañería   **pipe**

f

[ka.ɲɛ.ˈri.a]

Bajo por la cañería para divertirme.
-I climb down the pipe for fun's sake.

5888 virtual   **virtual**

adj

[bir.ˈtwal]

Estamos orgullosos de poder ofrecerles el siguiente tour virtual.
-We are proud to be able to give the following virtual tour.

5889 arete   **earring**

m

[a.ˈrɛ.te]

Y ella tiene el otro arete.
-And she has the other earring.

5890 gamba   **prawn**

f
['gãm.ba]

Te ves como una gamba gigante.
-You look like a giant prawn.

5891 aura — aura

f
['aṵ.ra]

Debo mantener mi aura de misterio.
-I have to retain my aura of mystery.

5892 fumador — smoker

m
[fu.ma.'ðoɾ]

Le dije que tenemos a un fumador.
-I told him we got a smoker.

5893 allende — **on the other side**

adv
[a.'jẽn̯.de]

Pero él viene de allende.
-But he comes from the other side.

5894 busto — **bust**

m
['bus.to]

Una se mostró interesada en un busto de Frederic Remington.
-One expressed interest in a Frederic Remington bust.

5895 acoger(se) — **accept, take in; find shelter**

vb; vbr
[a.ko.'xeɾ]

Si lo hicieran, tendrían que acoger refugiados.
-If they did, they'd have to accept refugees.

5896 despedida — **farewell**

f
[dɛs.pe.'ði.ða]

Esta nueva sinfonía es mi despedida.
-This new symphony, it's my farewell.

5897 situar(se) — **place**

vb
[si.'twaɾ]

Quisiera situar esta propuesta en su contexto.
-I would like to place this proposal in its context.

5898 liviano — **light**

adj
[li.'βja.no]

Este es un traje muy liviano.
-This is a very lightweight suit.

5899 abdomen — **abdomen**

m
[aβ.'ðo.mẽn]

Solo hallamos una pequeña hemorragia en su abdomen inferior.
-The only thing we found was a little bleeding in your lower abdomen.

5900 viceversa — **vice versa**

adv
[bi.se.'βeɾ.sa]

El planeta puede sobrevivir sin la humanidad, pero no viceversa.
-The planet can survive without humankind, but not vice versa.

5901 bacteria — **bacterium**

f[bak̚.'tɛ.rja]

Tomó mucho trabajo infectar a esta bacteria. -It took a lot of crafty work to infect this bacterium.

5902 cajero — **cashier, cash point**

m
[ka.'xɛ.ro]

Dirígete al cajero para más detalles.
-Please refer to the cashier for further details.

5903 fiable — **trustworthy**

adj
['fja.βle]

Quiero decir, este es un testigo fiable.
-I mean, this is a trustworthy witness.

5904 vocal — **vocal; vowel**

adj; f
[bo.'kal]

Detecto fuertes señales de tensión vocal.
-I detect strong vocal stress patterns.

5905 aceituna — **olive**

f
[a.sei̯.'tu.na]

Me acaban de tirar una aceituna.
-They just threw an olive at me.

5906 rascacielos — **skyscraper**

	m	En fin, estoy trabajando en diseñar otro rascacielos.
	[ras.ka.ˈsje.los]	-Anyway, I'm just working on designing yet another skyscraper.
5907	**procesar**	**process**
	vb	Necesitamos esa información para procesar el pago del producto.
	[pro.se.ˈsar]	-We need these details to process the payment of the product.
5908	**rubí**	**ruby**
	m	Suponíamos que cuando recuperase el rubí también detendría al culpable.
	[ru.ˈβi]	-We assumed that when you retrieved the ruby, you would also apprehend the culprit.
5909	**asombro**	**astonishment**
	m	Quisiera compartir con usted mi asombro.
	[a.ˈsõm.bro]	-I would like to share with you my astonishment.
5910	**castidad**	**chastity**
	f	Hay cosas peores que la castidad.
	[kas.ti.ˈðað]	-There are worse things than chastity.
5911	**cantera**	**quarry**
	f	Probablemente termines trabajando en la cantera.
	[kãn̪.ˈtɛ.ra]	-You'll probably end up getting a job at the quarry.
5912	**implorar**	**implore**
	vb	¿A quién más, mi señor, podría yo implorar?
	[ĩm.plo.ˈrar]	-Whom else, my lord, could I implore?
5913	**cripta**	**crypt**
	f	Esta cripta lleva hasta debajo del banco.
	[ˈkrip̚.ta]	-This crypt goes all the way under the bank.
5914	**gubernamental**	**governmental**
	adj	De ahí seguimos el procedimiento gubernamental.
	[gu.βɛr.na.mẽn̪.ˈtal]	-From there, we follow the governmental procedure.
5915	**irregular**	**irregular**
	adj	Cobran sus sueldos en forma irregular.
	[i.re.ɣu.ˈlar]	-Their salaries are paid on an irregular basis.
5916	**caricia**	**caress**
	f	Recuerdo esa caricia, tu olor.
	[ka.ˈri.sja]	-I remember that caress, your odor.
5917	**ortografía**	**orthography**
	f	Su ortografía no era perfecta.
	[or.to.ɣra.ˈfi.a]	-Her orthography was not perfect.
5918	**estético**	**cosmetic**
	adj	No es mi trabajo más estético.
	[ɛs.ˈtɛ.ti.ko]	-It's not my most cosmetic work.
5919	**ultra**	**over; ultra; extremist**
	pfx; adj; m/f	Es ultra veloz y muy preciso.
	[ˈul̪.tra]	-It is ultra fast and very precise.
5920	**desilusión**	**disappointment**
	f	Ahora os traigo una pequeña desilusión.
	[de.si.lu.ˈsjõn]	-Now I have a small disappointment for you.
5921	**excremento**	**excrement**
	m	Huele como a alguna mezcla de químicos, con algo de excremento.
	[ɛks̺.re.ˈmẽn̪.to]	-It smells like chemicals of some kind, with a mixture of excrement.
5922	**considerado**	**considerate**

	adj	Ha sido considerado, educado y riguroso.
	[kõn.si.ðɛ.ˈra.ðo]	-He was considerate, courteous, and thorough.

5923 vicioso — **depraved, vicious**

adj
[bi.ˈsjo.so]

Es importante salir del circulo vicioso.
-It is important to leave the vicious circle.

5924 perfume — **perfume**

m
[pɛr.ˈfu.me]

Te he traído algo de perfume.
-I've brought you some perfume.

5925 sanguijuela — **leech**

f
[sãŋ.gi.ˈxwe.la]

Esa sanguijuela se aprovecha de todo el mundo.
-That leech takes advantage of everyone.

5926 adolescencia — **adolescence**

f
[a.ðo.lɛs.ˈsɛn.sja]

Arruinaste mi adolescencia, lo sabes.
-You blighted my adolescence, you know that.

5927 cantor — **singing; singer**

adj; m
[kãn̪.ˈtor]

Mi madrina me dijo que eres cantor.
-My godmother told me you are a singer.

5928 contaminar — **contaminate**

vb
[kõn̪.ta.mi.ˈnar]

No querrías contaminar las pruebas.
-You don't want to contaminate the evidence.

5929 contribuyente — **taxpayer**

m/f
[kõn̪.tri.βu.ˈjẽn̪.te]

Déjele hablar, es un contribuyente.
-Let him talk, he is a taxpayer.

5930 jugoso — **juicy**

adj
[xu.ˈɣo.so]

Sabes que todavía te debo un jugoso favor.
-You know I still owe you one big juicy favor.

5931 olímpico — **Olympian; Olympian**

adj; m
[o.ˈlĩm.pi.ko]

¿Quieres que hablemos del ideal olímpico?
-Do you want to talk about the Olympian ideal?

5932 prodigio — **wonder**

m
[pro.ˈði.xjo]

¿Es su belleza una bendición o un prodigio?
-Is your beauty a boon or a wonder?

5933 aéreo — **aerial**

adj
[a.ˈɛ.re.o]

Los jóvenes escaparon durante un bombardeo aéreo.
-The boys escaped during an aerial bombardment.

5934 certificar — **certify**

vb
[sɛr.ti.fi.ˈkar]

El notario público es la autoridad competente para celebrar y certificar un matrimonio civil.
-The notary public is the authority competent to conclude and certify a civil marriage.

5935 vello — **fuzz**

m
[ˈbe.jo]

¿Finalmente te está saliendo vello en lugares raros?
-Are you finally getting fuzz in weird places?

5936 limpiador — **cleaning; wiper (LA)**

adj; m
[lĩm.pja.ˈðor]

Solo hay trabajo como limpiador de retretes.
-The only work out there for me is cleaning toilets.

5937 réplica — **replica**

f
[ˈrep̚.li.ka]

Esta es una réplica de un huevo de dinosaurio.
-This is a replica of a dinosaur's egg.

5938 exigencia — **demand**

f
[ɛk.si.ˈxẽn.sja]

Tal exigencia contravendría el derecho internacional.
-Such a demand would be contrary to international law.

5939 teclado — keyboard

m
[te.ˈkla.ðo]

Tendrías que poder levantar el teclado.
-You should be able to lift the keyboard.

5940 artillero — artillery; artilleryman

adj; m
[ar.ti.ˈʝɛ.ro]

¿Pero nosotros necesitamos apoyo artillero?
-But do we need artillery support?

5941 contención — containment

f
[kõn̪.tẽn.ˈsjõn]

No tengo acceso al campo de contención.
-I do not have access to the containment field.

5942 deletrear — spell out

vb
[de.lɛ.tre.ˈar]

Usaba las fichas del scrabble para deletrear.
-He used scrabble tiles to spell out.

5943 otorgar — award

vb
[o.tor.ˈɣar]

El juez también puede otorgar una indemnización por otros daños materiales, a su discreción.
-The judge may also award compensation for other material damages at his or her discretion.

5944 monarquía — monarchy

f
[mo.nar.ˈki.a]

No cree en la vieja monarquía.
-He doesn't believe in the old Monarchy.

5945 bateador — batter

m
[ba.te.a.ˈðor]

El bateador también hizo su parte.
-The batter did his part too.

5946 mensual — monthly

adj
[mẽn.ˈswal]

Eso aliviaría tu carga financiera mensual.
-That'll ease off your monthly financial burden.

5947 preocupante — alarming

adj[pre.o.ku.ˈpãn̪.te]

El control sanitario es muy preocupante, sobre todo, en los niños. -The health situation is alarming, especially for the children.

5948 mosquetero — musketeer

m
[mos.kɛ.ˈtɛ.ro]

Seré un mosquetero cuando las vacas vuelen.
-I'll be a musketeer when cows fall from the sky.

5949 manojo — handful

m
[ma.ˈno.xo]

Solo un manojo de gente estudia estos idiomas.
-Only a handful of people study these languages.

5950 fragancia — fragrance

f
[fra.ˈɣãn.sja]

Detecto una fragancia en el aire.
-I detect a fragrance in the air.

5951 estímulo — stimulus, incentive

m
[ɛs.ˈti.mu.lo]

Esta falta de estímulo me resulta realmente decepcionante.
-I find this lack of stimulus to be truly disappointing.

5952 inservible — unusable

adj
[ĩn.sɛr.ˈβi.βle]

¿Y ahora su mano está completamente inservible?
-So is your hand completely unusable now?

5953 sobresaliente — protruding; outstanding

adj; m
[so.βre.sa.ˈljẽn̪.te]

Fueron muy gentiles y su trabajo es sobresaliente.
-They were very nice, and their work is outstanding.

5954 itinerario — itinerary

	m		Simplemente ajústese al itinerario que le di.
	[i.ti.nɛ.ˈra.rjo]		-Just stick with the route that I gave you.
5955	**exótico**		**exotic**
	adj		Estamos pensando en un país de lujo exótico.
	[ɛk.ˈso.ti.ko]		-We're thinking of a land of exotic luxury.
5956	**cliché**		**cliche**
	m		La palabra "cliché" viene del francés.
	[kli.ˈʧe]		-The word "cliche" comes from French.
5957	**minar**		**mine**
	vb		¿Cómo demonios estoy intentando minar tu decisión?
	[mi.ˈnar]		-How the hell am I trying to undermine your decision?
5958	**prematuro**		**premature**
	adj		Resulta prematuro especular sobre esta cuestión.
	[pre.ma.ˈtu.ro]		-It is premature to speculate on this question.
5959	**purgatorio**		**purgatory**
	m		Tu recompensa será un purgatorio eterno para ti en este mundo.
	[pur.ɣa.ˈto.rjo]		-Your reward will be an eternal purgatory for you in this world.
5960	**fraile**		**friar**
	m		El fraile dijo que escribir con la izquierda es pecado.
	[ˈfrai̯.le]		-The friar said that writing with the left is a sin.
5961	**abono**		**fertilizer**
	m		En ese período, debe aplicarse abono cuatro veces.
	[a.ˈβo.no]		-Fertilizer should be applied four times during this period.
5962	**diversos**		**various**
	adj		Y ahora escucharé atentamente los comentarios de los diversos oradores.
	[di.ˈβɛr.sos]		-I will now listen carefully to the comments from the various speakers.
5963	**pedazo**		**chunk**
	m[pe.ˈða.so]		Le falta un pedazo, justo en el medio. -There's a chunk missing right in the center.
5964	**cetro**		**scepter**
	m		Muchos han muerto buscando el cetro.
	[ˈsɛ.tro]		-Many have died in pursuit of the scepter.
5965	**cupón**		**coupon**
	m		No necesito un cupón de usted.
	[ku.ˈpõn]		-I don't need a coupon from you.
5966	**disminuir**		**decrease**
	vb		No necesitas disminuir tu tiempo conmigo.
	[diş.mi.ˈnwir]		-You don't need to decrease your time with me.
5967	**cosmético**		**cosmetic; cosmetic**
	adj; m		Asistiréis de inmediato al tratamiento cosmético.
	[koş.ˈmɛ.ti.ko]		-You'll attend immediately to the cosmetic treatment.
5968	**chacal**		**jackal**
	m		Un zorro atrapado es más peligroso que un chacal.
	[ʧa.ˈkal]		-A cornered fox is more dangerous than a jackal.
5969	**vikingo**		**Viking; Viking**
	adj; m		Estaba en el cofre de tesoro del vikingo.
	[bi.ˈkĩŋ.go]		-It was in the Viking's treasure chest.
5970	**bombilla**		**bulb**

f
[bõm.ˈbi.ja]
Convertiste mi pepino en una bombilla.
-You've turned my pickle into a light bulb.

5971 cochino — **dirty; pig**
adj; m
[ko.ˈʧi.no]
No, es desagradable, viejo cochino.
-No, it's disgusting, you dirty old man.

5972 Alpes — **Alps**
mpl
[ˈal.pes]
Esta fue nuestra primera visita a los nevados Alpes.
-This was our first visit to the snowy Alps.

5973 pretendiente — **suitor**
m
[pɾɛ.tẽn̪.ˈdjẽn̪.te]
Todo joven quería ser su pretendiente.
-Every boy of age desired to be her suitor.

5974 abertura — **opening**
f
[a.βɛɾ.ˈtu.ra]
Seguirá presionando hasta conseguir una abertura.
-She'll keep the pressure on until she gets an opening.

5975 interrogación — **interrogation**
f
[ĩn̪.tɛ.ro.ɣa.ˈsjõn]
Puede utilizar nuestras salas de interrogación.
-You're welcome to use our interrogation rooms.

5976 premeditar — **premeditate**
vb
[pre.me.ði.ˈtar]
A mí este crimen no me parece premeditado.
-This crime doesn't look premeditated to me.

5977 susurro — **whisper**
m
[su.ˈsu.ro]
No se oía siquiera un susurro.
-Not even a whisper could be heard.

5978 peregrino — **pilgrim**
m
[pɛ.re.ˈɣri.no]
Desde entonces se entrega a su vocación de peregrino perpetuo.
-He set himself thus in his vocation of the perpetual pilgrim.

5979 nacionalidad — **nationality**
f[na.sjo.na.li.ˈðað]
Toda persona tiene derecho a elegir libremente su nacionalidad. -Everybody has the right to a free choice of his or her nationality.

5980 azotar — **whip**
vb
[a.so.ˈtar]
Nunca le vi azotar un caballo así.
-I never saw him whip a horse that way.

5981 entretanto — **meanwhile**
adv
[ẽn̪.tre.ˈtãn̪.to]
Aun así, entretanto irrumpen varios hechos innegables.
-Meanwhile, though, a few hard facts intrude.

5982 tentar — **tempt**
vb
[tẽn̪.ˈtar]
Y estoy feliz de tentar el destino.
-And I'm happy to tempt fate.

5983 reforzar — **strengthen**
vb
[re.for.ˈsar]
También debemos reforzar nuestras normas y reglamentos.
-We also need to strengthen our rules and regulations.

5984 constancia — **persistence**
f
[kõns.ˈtãn.sja]
Le agradezco su tenacidad y persistencia aquí.
-I thank you for your tenacity and persistence here.

5985 emprender — **undertake**
vb
[ẽm.prẽn̪.ˈdɛr]
También puede emprender investigaciones por iniciativa propia.
-He is also able to undertake investigations on his own initiative.

5986 desolar — **devastate**

	vb	Van a desolar la ciudad.
	[de.so.ˈlar]	-They are going to devastate the city.
5987	**rumorearse**	**be rumoured**
	vbr	Se empieza a rumorear de nosotros.
	[ru.mo.re.ˈar.se]	-People are beginning to talk about us.
5988	**luminoso**	**bright**
	adj	Era un día frío y luminoso de abril, y los relojes marcaban la una de la tarde.
	[lu.mi.ˈno.so]	-It was a bright cold day in April, and the clocks were striking thirteen.
5989	**lino**	**linen**
	m	Me queda demasiado bien el lino.
	[ˈli.no]	-I look too good in linen.
5990	**restante**	**remaining**
	adj	El 4,6% son hablantes de los demás idiomas.
	[rɛs.ˈtãn̪.te]	-The remaining 4.6 percent are speakers of the other languages.
5991	**desviar(se)**	**divert**
	vb	Prepárese a desviar la potencia al dar la señal.
	[dɛs̞.ˈβjar]	-Prepare to divert power on my signal.
5992	**conllevar**	**entail**
	vb	Tienes que tomar decisiones, asumiendo las responsabilidades que puedan conllevar.
	[kõn̪.ɟje.ˈβar]	-You have to make decisions, assuming the responsibilities that these can entail.
5993	**oxidar(se)**	**rust**
	vb	Si no lo sacas y lo usas, se va a oxidar.
	[ok.si.ˈðar]	-If you don't take it out and use it, it's going to rust.
5994	**tropezar(se)**	**stumble**
	vb [tro.pe.ˈsar]	Era pesada y le hizo tropezar. -It was heavy and made him stumble.
5995	**genocidio**	**genocide**
	m	Fue el primer genocidio del siglo XX.
	[xe.no.ˈsi.ðjo]	-This was the first genocide of the twentieth century.
5996	**penetración**	**penetration**
	f	Conté 40 puñaladas de varias profundidades de penetración.
	[pe.nɛ.tra.ˈsjõn]	-I counted 40 stab wounds of various depths of penetration.
5997	**intelecto**	**intellect**
	m	Solo estoy celoso de tu intelecto.
	[ĩn̪.te.ˈlek̚.to]	-It's just that I'm jealous of your intellect.
5998	**anulación**	**annulment**
	f	Como sabes, he conseguido la anulación.
	[a.nu.la.ˈsjõn]	-As you know, I've gotten the annulment.
5999	**inundar**	**flood**
	vb	Mientras tanto, intenta no inundar más jardines.
	[i.nũn̪.ˈdar]	-In the meanwhile, try not to flood more gardens.
6000	**navideño**	**Christmas**
	adj	Voy a hacer un milagro navideño.
	[na.βi.ˈðe.ɲo]	-I am going to perform a Christmas miracle.
6001	**demorar(se)**	**delay; arrive late**
	vb; vbr	No tratamos de demorar el trabajo.
	[de.mo.ˈrar]	-We are not trying to delay the work.
6002	**guardarropa**	**wardrobe**

	m		Mi hija tiene mejor guardarropa que yo.
	[gwar.ða.ˈro.pa]		-My daughter has a better wardrobe than I do.
6003	**maniquí**		**mannequin**
	m		Es un maniquí con una camiseta amarilla.
	[ma.ni.ˈki]		-It's a mannequin with a yellow shirt.
6004	**barrote**		**bar**
	m		¿Ves algún barrote en las ventanas?
	[ba.ˈro.te]		-You see any bars on the windows?
6005	**cuchara**		**spoon**
	f		Ahora si puedes pasarme mi cuchara gigante...
	[ku.ˈʧa.ra]		-Now if you'll hand me my giant spoon...
6006	**mestizo**		**racially mixed; mixed race**
	adj; m		Dice que le llamaron mestizo.
	[mɛs.ˈti.so]		-He says they called him a half-breed.
6007	**intermediario**		**intermediary**
	m		Un intermediario se ocupó de todo.
	[ĩn̪.tɛr.me.ˈðja.rjo]		-Everything was taken care of through an intermediary.
6008	**brote**		**outbreak**
	m		Tengo un brote de virus herpético.
	[ˈbro.te]		-I have an outbreak of a herpetic virus.
6009	**temeroso**		**afraid**
	adj		Bueno, es natural estar un poco temeroso.
	[te.mɛ.ˈro.so]		-Well, it's natural to be a little afraid.
6010	**aproximación**		**approximation**
	f[a.prok.si.ma.ˈsjõn]		Esto no es una aproximación, explicó él. -This is not an approximation, he explained.
6011	**sangrado**		**bleed**
	adj		Probablemente experimentará calambres y sangrado. Es algo natural.
	[sãŋ.ˈgra.ðo]		-You will probably experience some cramping and bleeding. This is natural.
6012	**hélice**		**propeller**
	f		Esa hélice podría haber causado muchos más daños.
	[ˈe.li.se]		-That propeller could have done a great deal more damage.
6013	**incógnito**		**incognito; incognito**
	adj; m		Trato de pasar de incógnito, es raro.
	[ĩŋ.ˈkoɣ.ni.to]		-I'm trying to be incognito, it's weird.
6014	**almeja**		**clam, pussy (coll)**
	f		Ella se aferra como una nutria tratando de abrir una almeja.
	[al.ˈme.xa]		-She holds on like an otter trying to break open a clam.
6015	**indígena**		**native; native person**
	adj; m		Le encanta la cultura indígena estadounidense.
	[ĩn̪.ˈdi.xe.na]		-He has a thing about Native American culture.
6016	**reforma**		**reform**
	f		La reforma propuesta se queda corta.
	[re.ˈfor.ma]		-The proposed reform does not go far enough.
6017	**articular**		**joint; articulate**
	adj; vb		Para los japoneses es difícil articular el sonido de la ele.
	[ar.ti.ku.ˈlar]		-It is difficult for the Japanese to articulate the sound of the l.
6018	**voltio**		**volt**

m

['boḷ.tjo]

¿Puedes iniciar con un voltio, por favor?
-Can you start it at 1 volt, please?

6019 cláusula

f

['klau̯.su.la]

clause

Esa cláusula viola el derecho internacional.
-This clause is a violation of international law.

6020 óxido

m

['ok.si.ðo]

rust

Solo tengo que quitarle el óxido.
-I just have to get the rust off of it.

6021 capricornio

adj

[ka.pri.'kor.njo]

Capricorn

Me gustaría que dibujen un capricornio.
-I'd like you to draw a Capricorn.

6022 vértigo

m

['bɛr.ti.ɣo]

vertigo

Durante el examen se quejó de vértigo, dolor en el tórax y debilidad general.
-During the examination, he had complained about vertigo, pain in the thorax, and general weakness.

6023 atrocidad

f

[a.tro.si.'ðað]

atrocity

Yo intento evitar que suceda semejante atrocidad.
-I'm trying to stop that kind of atrocity from happening.

6024 gama

f

['ga.ma]

range

También estaría disponible en una gama de colores.
-It would also be available in a range of colors.

6025 complicidad

f[kõm.pli.si.'ðað]

involvement

Mi complicidad termina aquí, con la cesta de la colada. -My involvement ends here, with the laundry basket.

6026 precipitar(se)

vb

[pre.si.pi.'tar]

hurry

No hay necesidad de precipitar las cosas.
-There's no need to rush fate.

6027 intrigante

m

[ĩn.tri.'ɣãn̪.te]

intriguing

Creo que encontrará esto intrigante.
-I think you'll find this intriguing.

6028 proporcionar

vb

[pro.por.sjo.'nar]

provide

Los sectores públicos no pueden proporcionar servicios adecuados.
-The public sectors are not able to provide adequate services.

6029 tardanza

f

[tar.'ðãn.sa]

delay

Buenos días a todos, disculpen mi tardanza.
-Good morning to everybody, sorry for the delay.

6030 burguesía

f

[bur.ɣe.'si.a]

the middle-class

La familia de Frank es parte de la burguesía.
-Frank's family is part of the middle-class.

6031 apareamiento

m

[a.pa.re.a.'mjẽn.to]

mating

Las jaulas se inspeccionan a diario a partir de los 18 días tras el apareamiento.
-Cages are inspected daily beginning 18 days after mating.

6032 modificar

vb

[mo.ði.fi.'kar]

modify

Hemos ofrecido modificar el embargo a cambio de reformas.
-We have offered to modify the embargo in exchange for reforms.

6033 rebote

m

[re.'βo.te]

bounce

Señor, estamos listos para el rebote.
-Sir, we're ready for the bounce.

6034 mutación

mutation

f
[mu.ta.'sjõn]

Ya sabes, la naturaleza de tu mutación.
-You know, the nature of your mutation.

6035 galante — **gallant**

adj
[ga.'lãn̪.te]

Capitán, tan galante como siempre.
-Captain, are as gallant as ever.

6036 arrastre — **dragging**

m
[a.'ras.tre]

Y entonces hubo ese ruido de arrastre y...
-And then there was this dragging noise and...

6037 follón — **racket**

m
[fo.'jõn]

Montaste un follón mientras venías.
-You made a racket coming up.

6038 jerga — **slang**

f
['xɛr.ɣa]

Pensé que estábamos usando la jerga callejera.
-I thought we were doing street slang.

6039 cumplimiento — **compliance**

m
[kũm.pli.'mjẽn̪.to]

Un organismo de supervisión público vigilará el cumplimiento de estas reglas.
-A public supervisory body will monitor compliance with these rules.

6040 aleta — **fin**

f[a.'lɛ.ta]

El atún de aleta amarilla es muy valorado para sashimi. -Yellowfin tuna is highly prized for sashimi.

6041 párpado — **eyelid**

m
['par.pa.ðo]

Si el objeto está en el párpado, trate de lavarlo suavemente con agua.
-If the object is on an eyelid, try to gently flush it out with water.

6042 apasionante — **thrilling**

adj
[a.pa.sjo.'nãn̪.te]

El episodio de esta noche es el quinto capítulo de nuestra apasionante historia.
-Tonight's episode is part five of our thrilling story.

6043 desconfianza — **distrust**

f
[dɛs.kõm̩.'fjãn.sa]

La desconfianza entre las partes aumenta.
-Distrust between the parties is growing.

6044 ocular — **eye; lens**

adj; m
[o.ku.'lar]

Estos dos fármacos disminuyen la presión ocular mediante diferentes mecanismos.
-These two drugs lower the pressure in the eye by different mechanisms.

6045 borroso — **blurred**

adj
[bo.'ro.so]

Después de ese día, todo me parecía borroso.
-After that day, everything seems blurred to me.

6046 burocracia — **bureaucracy**

f
[bu.ro.'kra.sja]

Y por último no queremos una burocracia excesiva.
-And finally, we do not want any superfluous bureaucracy.

6047 machete — **machete**

m
[ma.'tʃɛ.te]

No queremos ser asesinados a machete.
-We do not wish to be killed by machete.

6048 revuelto — **messy; scrambled eggs**

adj; m
[re.'βwɛl̪.to]

Tienes el pelo un poco revuelto.
-Your hair's a little messy.

6049 antojo — **whim**

m
[ãn̪.'to.xo]

Debe ser lindo poder ir a todos lados a tu antojo.
-It must be nice being able to go places on a whim.

6050 grotesco — **hideous**

adj

[gro.ˈtɛs.ko]

Eso es mucho más grotesco.

-It's much more hideous.

6051 sujetar   **hold**

vb

[su.xɛ.ˈtar]

Este robot es capaz de sujetar un huevo sin romperlo.

-This robot can hold an egg without breaking it.

6052 ateo   **atheistic; atheist**

adj; m

[a.ˈte.o]

No puedes amenazar a un ateo con el infierno.

-You can't threaten an atheist with hell.

6053 sarcasmo   **sarcasm**

m

[sar.ˈkas̠.mo]

No tengo paciencia para tu sarcasmo.

-I don't have the patience for your sarcasm.

6054 impactante   **stunning**

adj

[ĩm.pak̚.ˈtãn̪.te]

Es británico y su trabajo es realmente impactante.

-He is British and his work is just stunning.

6055 tenebroso   **gloomy**

adj[te.ne.ˈβro.so]

Siempre temieron a ese oscuro y tenebroso país del este. -They always feared that dark and gloomy country in the east.

6056 pestaña   **eyelash**

f

[pɛs.ˈta.ɲa]

Encontraron una pestaña en el ala sur.

-They found an eyelash in the south wing.

6057 trenza   **braid**

f

[ˈtrẽn.sa]

Todos los poderes de una bruja se hallan en su trenza.

-All the powers of a witch reside in her braid.

6058 encierro   **confinement**

m

[ẽn.ˈsjɛ.ro]

Al menos no tiene que compartir su encierro.

-At least it does not have to share its confinement.

6059 preferible   **preferable**

adj

[pre.fɛ.ˈri.βle]

Sería preferible mantener el carácter genérico del texto.

-It would be preferable to maintain the generic nature of the text.

6060 contraste   **contrast**

m

[kõn̪.ˈtras.te]

Crea un contraste que pueden distinguir.

-It's creating a contrast that they can indeed see.

6061 reflexión   **reflection**

f

[re.flɛk.ˈsjõn]

Me gustaría terminar con una reflexión personal.

-I would like to finish with a personal reflection.

6062 recitar   **recite**

vb

[re.si.ˈtar]

Mucha gente lo escuchaba recitar sus poesías.

-Many people were listening to him recite his poems.

6063 macarrones   **macaroni**

mpl

[ma.ka.ˈro.nes]

Creo que no debías cocinar los macarrones.

-I don't think you're supposed to cook the macaroni.

6064 requisito   **requirement**

m

[re.ki.ˈsi.to]

Este requisito se verificará mediante un cálculo.

-This requirement shall be verified by a calculation.

6065 mira   **sight**

f

[ˈmi.ra]

Ves su cara por la mira.

-You see his face through the sight.

6066 conservatorio   **conservatory**

	m	Podría ir al conservatorio de Lyon.
	[kõn.sɛr.βa.ˈto.rjo]	-He could go to the Conservatory in Lyon.

6067 **voltear(se)** — **turn around**

vb
[bol̪.te.ˈar]

Pero entonces se puede voltear, sin advertencia... y pegarte.
-But then he can turn around without any warning and... hit you.

6068 **hormigón** — **concrete**

m
[or.mi.ˈɣõn]

Creo que es roble sobre hormigón.
-It's oak, I think, over concrete.

6069 **misionero** — **missionary; missionary**

adj; m
[mi.sjo.ˈnɛ.ro]

Jim fue a Corea como misionero cristiano.
-Jim went to Korea as a Christian missionary.

6070 **influir** — **influence**

vb
[ĩm̩.ˈflwir]

Los profesores pueden influir en sus alumnos.
-Teachers can influence their students.

6071 **merienda** — **afternoon snack**

f[mɛ.ˈrjẽn̪.da]

Nosotros hablaremos durante la merienda. -We will talk during the afternoon snack.

6072 **ladera** — **lateral; hillside**

adj; f
[la.ˈðɛ.ra]

Cultivamos algunas verduras en la ladera.
-We grow a few vegetables up on the hillside.

6073 **estorbar** — **obstruct**

vb
[ɛs.tor.ˈβar]

Sabes muy bien que no me gusta estorbar.
-You know I don't like to get in the way.

6074 **credo** — **creed**

m
[ˈkre.ðo]

Esto también es parte de nuestro credo democrático.
-That is a part of our democratic creed, too.

6075 **torso** — **torso**

m
[ˈtor.so]

Su torso era ancho y largo en contraste con sus extremidades inferiores.
-Their torso was wide and long in contrast with its inferior extremities.

6076 **esquizofrenia** — **schizophrenia**

f
[ɛs.ki.so.ˈfre.nja]

Este nivel de esquizofrenia nos supera.
-This level of schizophrenia is quite beyond us.

6077 **educativo** — **educational**

adj
[e.ðu.ka.ˈti.βo]

Prosigue la reforma del contenido educativo.
-The reform of the educational content is ongoing.

6078 **átomo** — **atom**

m
[ˈa.to.mo]

Hemos liberado el poder del átomo.
-We've unleashed the power of the atom.

6079 **infiltrar** — **infiltrate**

vb
[ĩm̩.fil̪.ˈtrar]

Ya sabes, eres el hombre perfecto para infiltrarse en una banda motorista.
-You know, you're the perfect man to infiltrate a biker gang.

6080 **entidad** — **organization**

f
[ɛ̃n̪.ti.ˈðað]

La entidad podrá cobrar una cuota que no sea excesiva.
-An organization may charge a fee that is not excessive.

6081 **corrida** — **bullfight**

f
[ko.ˈri.ða]

Después por la tarde tiene lugar una corrida de toros.
-Later in the afternoon takes place a bullfight.

6082 **cianuro** — **cyanide**

m
[sja.ˈnu.ro]

No limpiaron los desperdicios de cianuro.
-They didn't clean up the cyanide waste.

6083 inquietud — **restlessness**

f
[ĩŋ.kjɛ.ˈtuð]

Podría haberle ahorrado un montón de inquietud.
-I could have saved you a lot of anxiety.

6084 memorial — **memorial**

m
[me.mo.ˈrjal]

No debería ir a ese memorial tampoco.
-He shouldn't be going to that memorial either.

6085 temerario — **reckless**

adj
[te.mɛ.ˈra.rjo]

Está haciendo algo temerario y peligroso.
-You're doing a reckless and a dangerous thing.

6086 especulación — **speculation**

f
[ɛs.pe.ku.la.ˈsjõn]

Debemos poner fin inmediatamente a esta especulación letal.
-We must put an immediate end to this lethal speculation.

6087 narrador — **narrator**

m[na.ra.ˈðor]

Además, el narrador era británico. -Plus, the narrator was British.

6088 irritar(se) — **irritate**

vb
[i.ri.ˈtar]

Solo le gusta irritar a las personas.
-He just likes to irritate people.

6089 chelín — **shilling**

m
[tʃe.ˈlĩn]

La gente pagaría un chelín por ver esto.
-People would pay a shilling to see this.

6090 reconciliación — **reconciliation**

f
[re.kõn.si.lja.ˈsjõn]

No puede haber reconciliación sin verdad.
-Without truth, there can be no reconciliation.

6091 calamidad — **calamity**

f
[ka.la.mi.ˈðað]

Estoy afrontando esta calamidad como cualquier otro ciudadano.
-I'm facing this calamity just like every other citizen.

6092 remover — **stir, remove**

vb
[re.mo.ˈβɛr]

Bien, pudimos remover completamente el tumor abdominal.
-Well, we were able to completely remove the abdominal tumor.

6093 lienzo — **canvas**

m
[ˈljẽn.so]

Me gustaría probar con el lienzo.
-I'd like to try my hand at the canvas.

6094 aterrar — **terrify**

vb
[a.tɛ.ˈrar]

Debes aterrorizar a la gente con eso.
-You must terrify people with that.

6095 vietnamita — **Vietnamese; Vietnamese person**

adj; m/f
[bjɛt̚.na.ˈmi.ta]

Serás enorme en la comunidad vietnamita.
-You'll be huge in the Vietnamese community.

6096 ciruela — **plum**

f
[si.ˈrwe.la]

Realmente no está mal para ser ciruela.
-That's actually not bad for a plum.

6097 velero — **sailing boat**

m
[be.ˈlɛ.ro]

Quiero volver al velero con Rocky.
-I want to go back to the sailboat with Rocky.

6098 barraca — **hut**

f
[ba.ˈra.ka]

El número está escrito en la barraca.
-The number is on the hut.

6099	**gaviota**	**seagull**
	f	Hubiera tenido mucho más éxito siendo gaviota o pez.
	[ga.ˈβjo.ta]	-I'd have been much more successful as a seagull or a fish.
6100	**repulsivo**	**repulsive**
	adj	Nunca haría algo tan asqueroso y repulsivo.
	[re.pul.ˈsi.βo]	-I would never do something so repulsive and disgusting.
6101	**malestar**	**discomfort**
	m	Otros efectos secundarios muy comunes eran el dolor y malestar.
	[ma.lɛs.ˈtar]	-Other very common side effects were pain and discomfort.
6102	**granito**	**granite**
	m	Encontré partículas microscópicas de granito embebidas en el petróleo.
	[gra.ˈni.to]	-I found that there were microscopic particles of granite embedded in petroleum.
6103	**mantel**	**tablecloth**
	m	Podría haberte traído un mantel del restaurante.
	[mãn̪.ˈtɛl]	-I could have brought you a tablecloth from the restaurant.
6104	**pinchazo**	**prick, pinch**
	m	Vale, sentirá un pequeño pinchazo.
	[pĩn̪.ˈʧa.so]	-Okay, this will just pinch a little.
6105	**desilusionar(se)**	**let down**
	vb	No puedes desilusionar a tu padre.
	[de.si.lu.sjo.ˈnar]	-You can't let down the old man.
6106	**refrán**	**saying**
	m	Eso es un antiguo refrán inglés.
	[re.ˈfrãn]	-That is an old English saying.
6107	**administrar**	**manage**
	vb	También necesita administrar cuidadosamente los recursos que ya han sido asignados.
	[að.mi.nis.ˈtrar]	-It also needs to manage carefully the resources that have already been allocated.
6108	**revelar(se)**	**reveal**
	vb	Ni siquiera quiero revelar su nombre.
	[re.βe.ˈlar]	-I don't even want to reveal his name.
6109	**farmacéutico**	**pharmaceutical; pharmacist**
	adj; m	Perdone, estoy buscando al farmacéutico.
	[far.ma.ˈseu̯.ti.ko]	-Excuse me, I'm looking for the pharmacist.
6110	**esforzarse**	**make an effort**
	vbr	La comunidad internacional debe esforzarse y hacer algo.
	[ɛs.for.ˈsar.se]	-The international community needs to make an effort to do something.
6111	**aspirante**	**candidate**
	m/f	Yo soy el nuevo aspirante.
	[as.pi.ˈrãn̪.te]	-I am the new candidate.
6112	**recobrar(se)**	**recover**
	vb	Una vez robado, el material nuclear es extraordinariamente difícil de recobrar.
	[re.ko.ˈβrar]	-Once stolen, nuclear material is extraordinarily difficult to recover.
6113	**muscular**	**muscular**
	adj	Solo será una pequeña hemorragia muscular interna.
	[mus.ku.ˈlar]	-It's probably just a small internal muscular hemorrhage.
6114	**guita**	**money (coll)**

	f		Por los muebles que tienen, no pueden tener mucha guita.
	['gi.ta]		-By the look of their furniture, they can't have much money.
6115	**psicótico**	**psychotic**	
	adj		Estoy obligado a negociar con un psicótico.
	[si.'ko.ti.ko]		-I'm being forced into negotiating with a psychotic.
6116	**sucesión**	**succession**	
	f		Es inapropiado hablar prematuramente sobre su sucesión.
	[su.se.'sjõn]		-It is inappropriate to talk premature about his succession.
6117	**constructor**	**building; builder**	
	adj; m		Es además pintor, maestro constructor y dramaturgo.
	[kõns.truk̚.'tor]		-He's also a painter, a master builder, and a playwright.
6118	**retomar**	**resume**	
	vb		Finalmente, puede retomar su épico viaje.
	[rɛ.to.'mar]		-At last, he can resume his epic journey.
6119	**apacible**	**gentle**	
	adj		Viviremos en esta ciudad apacible.
	[a.pa.'si.βle]		-We'll live in this gentle town.
6120	**audacia**	**audacity**	
	f		Tu audacia es impresionante, Chloe.
	[au̯.'ða.sja]		-Your audacity is impressive, Chloe.
6121	**visibilidad**	**visibility**	
	f		Llovía y la visibilidad era mala.
	[bi.si.βi.li.'ðað]		-It was raining and the visibility was poor.
6122	**contrabandista**	**contraband; smuggler**	
	adj; m		Esta vez quiero que seáis un contrabandista.
	[kõn.tra.βãn.'dis.ta]		-I want you to be a smuggler this time.
6123	**corporativo**	**corporate**	
	adj		Hace préstamos cuestionables con dinero corporativo.
	[kor.po.ra.'ti.βo]		-He makes questionable loans with big corporate money.
6124	**pibe**	**boy (coll)**	
	m		Soy un pibe argentino que vive acá.
	['pi.βe]		-I'm an Argentine boy that lives here.
6125	**adrede**	**intentionally**	
	adv		¿Por qué te pones en peligro adrede a diario?
	[a.'ðre.ðe]		-Why are you intentionally putting yourself in danger, day after day?
6126	**turístico**	**tourist**	
	adj		Dijo que estaba revisando un problema turístico.
	[tu.'ris.ti.ko]		-He said he was checking out a tourist problem.
6127	**asfixia**	**suffocation**	
	f		Se produjeron dos casos de muerte por asfixia.
	[as.'fik.sja]		-There had been two cases of death from suffocation.
6128	**meditar**	**meditate**	
	vb		Aprenderá a meditar para controlar su dolor.
	[me.ði.'tar]		-He will learn to meditate to control all pain.
6129	**jardinería**	**gardening**	
	f		Le pidió a su hermano que le ayudara con la jardinería.
	[xar.ði.nɛ.'ri.a]		-He had his brother help him with the gardening.
6130	**moco**	**mucus**	

	m	No conozco ningún animal de granja que produzca un moco como este.
	['mo.ko]	-I don't know any farm animal that produces a mucus like that.

6131 **pendejada** — **bullshit (LA) (coll)**

f

[pẽn.de.'xa.ða]

Si te dice alguna pendejada, dile que soy yo el que pregunta.
-If she gives you any bullshit, tell her it's me that's asking.

6132 **sucursal** — **branch**

f

[su.kur.'sal]

Encontré algo en la sucursal sudamericana.
-I did find something in our South American branch.

6133 **renacer** — **revive**

vb

[re.na.'sɛr]

Ayudarán a todo a renacer.
-They will help revive everything.

6134 **indulto** — **pardon**

m

[ĩn.'dul̪.to]

Dijeron que me conseguiste un indulto.
-They said that you got me a pardon.

6135 **consumir** — **consume**

vb

[kõn.su.'mir]

No puedes dejar que una imagen consuma toda tu vida.
-You can't let this one image consume your whole life.

6136 **trivial** — **trivial**

adj

[tri.'βjal]

Siento haberlos molestado por algo tan trivial.
-I'm sorry to inconvenience you with something this trivial.

6137 **aparentar** — **feign**

vb

[a.pa.rẽn̪.'tar]

Tú no necesitas aparentar interés.
-You don't need to feign interest.

6138 **platino** — **platinum; platinum**

adj; m

[pla.'ti.no]

Me han denegado una tarjeta platino.
-They turned me down on my platinum card.

6139 **rigor** — **exactitude, rigour**

m

[ri.'ɣor]

También necesitamos que haya rigor presupuestario.
-Equally, we need to have budgetary rigor.

6140 **banjo** — **banjo**

m

['bãŋ.xo]

El banjo es un instrumento increíble.
-It's an amazing instrument, the banjo.

6141 **cineasta** — **filmmaker**

m/f

[si.ne.'as.ta]

Preguntémosle al cineasta qué le parece.
-Let's ask the filmmaker what he thinks.

6142 **intrusión** — **intrusion**

f

[ĩn.tru.'sjõn]

Seguro que le gustaría la intrusión.
-I'm sure she'd appreciate the intrusion.

6143 **distribuidor** — **distributor**

m

[dis.tri.βwi.'ðor]

Hay solamente un distribuidor aquí en California.
-There's only one distributor out here in California.

6144 **transportador** — **transporter**

m

[trãns.por.ta.'ðor]

Si dejo el transportador así, me despedirán.
-If I left the transporter like this, I'd be fired.

6145 **envenenamiento** — **poisoning**

m

[ẽm.be.ne.na.'mjẽn̪.to]

Es tan repentino que sospechamos de un envenenamiento por radiación.
-It's so sudden we suspect radiation poisoning.

6146 **bayoneta** — **bayonet**

f
[ba.jo.ˈnɛ.ta]

Han habido muchos combates de bayoneta.
-There have been a lot of bayonet skirmishes.

6147 **asta**

horn

f
[ˈas.ta]

¿Tienen el asta de un pobre alce colgada en el bar?
-They got some poor elk's horn hanging over the bar?

6148 **persistente**

persistent

adj
[pɛr.sis.ˈtẽn.te]

Déjame advertirte, puedo ser muy persistente.
-Let me warn you I can be very persistent.

6149 **presagio**

omen

m[pre.ˈsa.xjo]

Desde el principio fue un presagio. -From the beginning, it was an omen.

6150 **ardor**

burning sensation

m
[ar.ˈðor]

Sentirá una ligera sensación de ardor.
-You'll feel a slight burning sensation.

6151 **iceberg**

iceberg

m
[i.se.ˈβɛrɣ]

También podría ser la punta de un iceberg sumergido.
-It could also be the tip of a submerged iceberg.

6152 **cerámica**

ceramic

f
[sɛ.ˈra.mi.ka]

Escucha agua golpeando contra una pared cerámica.
-He listens to water beating against a ceramic wall.

6153 **imparcial**

impartial

adj
[ĩm.par.ˈsjal]

Esperamos que la evaluación sea justa e imparcial.
-We hope that the assessment will be fair and impartial.

6154 **estuche**

case

m
[ɛs.ˈtu.tʃe]

Tom está guardando sus bolígrafos en el estuche.
-Tom is putting his pens into the pencil case.

6155 **cebra**

zebra

f
[ˈse.βra]

Tengo tanta hambre que podría comerme una cebra entera.
-I'm so hungry I could eat a whole zebra.

6156 **resentirse**

feel resentful

vbr
[re.sẽn.ˈtir.se]

Las víctimas de los conflictos pueden resentirse si nadie rinde cuentas por su sufrimiento.
-Conflict victims may feel resentful if no one is called to account for their suffering.

6157 **vejiga**

bladder

f
[be.ˈxi.ɣa]

Tiene la vejiga floja desde que era crío.
-He's got a bum bladder ever since he was a kid.

6158 **computador**

computer; computer (LA)

adj; m
[kõm.pu.ta.ˈðor]

Un computador no puede tener voluntad propia.
-A computer can't have a will of its own.

6159 **optimismo**

optimism

m
[op̚.ti.ˈmis̬.mo]

Comparto este optimismo por varias razones.
-I share this optimism for a number of reasons.

6160 **dirigente**

leader; leading

m/f; adj
[di.ri.ˈxẽn.te]

Va a ser una dirigente poderosa.
-She's going to be a powerful leader.

6161 **liar(se)**

mishandle (ES), roll; get embroiled

vb; vbr
[ˈljar]

Ella me enseñó cómo liar un cigarro.
-She taught me how to roll a cigarette.

6162 **metrópoli**

metropolis

	f	En la actualidad, la metrópoli continúa creciendo.
	[mɛ.ˈtro.po.li]	-The metropolis continues to grow today.
6163	**inexplicable**	**inexplicable**
	adj	Acaba de suceder y es inexplicable.
	[i.nɛks.pli.ˈka.βle]	-It just happened, and it's inexplicable.
6164	**aturdido**	**confused**
	adj[a.tur.ˈði.ðo]	¡Les he aturdido con toda esta cháchara! -I confused them with my chatter!
6165	**maestría**	**mastery**
	f	Usted ha demostrado tener talento y una maestría excepcional en
	[ma.ɛs.ˈtri.a]	circunstancias muy difíciles.
		-You have demonstrated talent and exceptional mastery under very trying circumstances.
6166	**dureza**	**hardness**
	f	Siempre he preferido la dureza del suelo.
	[du.ˈre.sa]	-I will always prefer the hardness of the floor.
6167	**estragos**	**havoc**
	mpl	Enfermedades y epidemias causan grandes estragos en la vida de niños,
	[ɛs.ˈtra.ɣos]	hombres y mujeres.
		-Disease and sickness wreak havoc on the lives of children, men, and women.
6168	**desastroso**	**disastrous**
	adj	La polución tiene un efecto desastroso sobre la ecología de una región.
	[de.sas.ˈtro.so]	-Pollution has a disastrous effect on the ecology of a region.
6169	**espécimen**	**specimen**
	m	No quiero darle un espécimen contaminado.
	[ɛs.ˈpe.si.mɛn]	-I don't want to give you a contaminated specimen.
6170	**fracción**	**fraction**
	f	Es solo una fracción de centímetro.
	[frak.ˈsjõn]	-That's only a fraction of a centimeter.
6171	**tajar**	**cut**
	vb	Le he visto tajar docenas de buenos caballeros.
	[ta.ˈxar]	-I've seen you cut down a dozen great knights.
6172	**discriminación**	**discrimination**
	f	Él luchó contra la discriminación racial.
	[dis.kri.mi.na.ˈsjõn]	-He fought against racial discrimination.
6173	**proyector**	**projector**
	m	Tal vez debería apagar el proyector.
	[pro.jek.ˈtor]	-Maybe you should just turn the projector off.
6174	**paleta**	**palette, lollipop**
	f	Hay una paleta en la esquina superior derecha de la hoja.
	[pa.ˈlɛ.ta]	-There's a palette in the upper right-hand corner of this planning sheet.
6175	**orgánico**	**organic**
	adj	Tenemos una barra de pan orgánico integral.
	[or.ˈɣa.ni.ko]	-We've got one loaf organic bread, brown.
6176	**nirvana**	**nirvana**
	m	La claustrofilia puede llevarte al completo nirvana sensorial.
	[nir.ˈβa.na]	-Claustrophilia can bring you to full sensory nirvana.
6177	**devastador**	**devastating**
	adj	Perder a alguien tan cercano es devastador.
	[de.βas.ta.ˈðor]	-To lose someone so close it's devastating.

6178	**aportar**		**contribute**
	vb		Queremos participar y aportar nuestra contribución.
	[a.por.ˈtar]		-We want to join in and contribute our share.
6179	**represalia**		**reprisal**
	f		En represalia, han decidido destituirme.
	[re.pre.ˈsa.lja]		-In reprisal, they've decided to depose me.
6180	**aseo**		**bathroom**
	m		Todas las habitaciones disponen de baño privado con ducha, aseo y minibar.
	[a.ˈse.o]		-All of the rooms feature a private bathroom with shower and toilet, and a minibar.
6181	**arquero**		**archer**
	m		El arquero hace más que disparar flechas.
	[ar.ˈkɛ.ro]		-The archer does more than just shoot arrows.
6182	**terrenal**		**earthly**
	adj		Necesito liberarme de mi prisión terrenal.
	[tɛ.re.ˈnal]		-I must be released from my earthly prison.
6183	**confrontación**		**confrontation**
	f		Hubo una confrontación y venció la mayoría.
	[kõɱ.frõn̪.ˈta.sjõn]		-Then there was a confrontation and the majority won.
6184	**predicción**		**prediction**
	f		Solo quiero confirmar que mi predicción era cierta.
	[pre.ðik.ˈsjõn]		-I just want to confirm that my prediction was correct.
6185	**clandestino**		**clandestine**
	adj		Antes trabajaba como agente clandestino del gobierno.
	[klã̠n.dɛs.ˈti.no]		-I used to work for a clandestine government agency.
6186	**precisar**		**require, specify**
	vb		Es importante precisar claramente el objetivo del programa.
	[pre.si.ˈsar]		-It is important to clearly specify the focus of the programme.
6187	**paño**		**cloth**
	m		Mayuko trapeó una mesa con un paño.
	[ˈpa.ɲo]		-Mayuko wiped a table with a cloth.
6188	**barcaza**		**barge**
	f		Una barcaza se acerca al puente.
	[bar.ˈka.sa]		-A barge is approaching the bridge.
6189	**elenco**		**cast**
	m		El elenco de actores debe ser aprobado.
	[e.ˈlɛ̃ŋ.ko]		-The casting of actors must be approved.
6190	**caparazón**		**shell**
	m		Aprenden a salir de su caparazón.
	[ka.pa.ra.ˈsõn]		-They learn to come out of their shell.
6191	**clítoris**		**clitoris**
	m		Lo usamos para determinar la sensibilidad del clítoris.
	[ˈkli.to.ris]		-We use it to determine the sensitivity of the clitoris.
6192	**evasión**		**evasion**
	f		Disculpe, eso parece una evasión.
	[e.βa.ˈsjõn]		-Forgive me, that sounds like an evasion.
6193	**zapatero**		**shoemaker**
	m		Hora de cerrar la tienda, zapatero.
	[sa.pa.ˈtɛ.ro]		-Time to close up the shop, shoemaker.

6194	**acecho**	**stalking**
	m[a.ˈse.tʃo]	Un híbrido. Un coche perfecto para el acecho. -Hybrid. Great car for stalking.
6195	**computación**	**computer studies (LA)**
	f	Ella hizo un curso básico de matemáticas y luego computación.
	[kõm.pu.ta.ˈsjõn]	-She took a pure mathematics course, then computer studies.
6196	**irrumpir**	**burst in**
	vb	Necesitamos algo para decirte cuando irrumpir, una señal.
	[i.rũm.ˈpir]	-We need something to tell you when to burst in, a signal.
6197	**restauración**	**restoration**
	f	Entonces me impliqué en la restauración del auto.
	[res.tau̯.ra.ˈsjõn]	-Then I got involved in the restoration of the car.
6198	**recámara**	**chamber**
	f	Las chicas la llevarán a su recámara.
	[re.ˈka.ma.ra]	-The girls will take you to your chamber.
6199	**someter**	**submit**
	vb	Además, entiende que otros grupos también desean someter propuestas escritas.
	[so.me.ˈter]	-It was his understanding that other groups likewise wished to submit written proposals.
6200	**maleza**	**undergrowth**
	f	Cuidado al pisar, hay mucha maleza por aquí.
	[ma.ˈle.sa]	-Watch your step, there's a lot of undergrowth here.
6201	**codicioso**	**greedy**
	adj	Eso es lo que pasa cuando te pones codicioso.
	[ko.ði.ˈsjo.so]	-That's what happens when you get greedy.
6202	**diplomacia**	**diplomacy**
	f	Es una tarea que requerirá mucha diplomacia y tacto.
	[dipˈ.lo.ˈma.sja]	-It's an assignment that'll require a lot of diplomacy and tact.
6203	**silbar**	**whistle**
	vb	Se puso a silbar una melodía.
	[sil.ˈβar]	-He began to whistle a tune.
6204	**expuesto**	**exposed**
	adj	El público quedó expuesto a la devastación.
	[εks.ˈpwes.to]	-The audience was exposed to the devastation.
6205	**paradoja**	**paradox**
	f	Según él, fue una paradoja interesante.
	[pa.ra.ˈðo.xa]	-According to him, it was an interesting paradox.
6206	**absolver**	**absolve**
	vb	No hay penitencia que me pueda absolver de este pecado tan oscuro.
	[aβ.sol.ˈβer]	-There's no penance that can absolve me of this darkest sin.
6207	**concejo**	**council**
	m	No les hablaste sobre el concejo.
	[kõn.ˈse.xo]	-You didn't tell them about the council.
6208	**ceño**	**frown**
	m	Ese ceño no te queda bien.
	[ˈse.ɲo]	-That frown doesn't suit you.
6209	**tribuna**	**stand**
	f[tri.ˈβu.na]	Hoy declaramos desde esta tribuna que estamos de su lado. -Today we declare from this rostrum that we stand by her side.
6210	**radiografiar**	**X-ray**

	vb	Me gustaría radiografiar esas costillas.
	[ra.ðjo.ɣra.ˈfjar]	-I'd like to X-ray those ribs.
6211	**artritis**	**arthritis**
	f	No tendré artritis en estos dedos.
	[ar.ˈtri.tis]	-I'll have no arthritis in these fingers.
6212	**paracaidista**	**parachutist**
	m/f	Estuvo bien conocer y charlar con un paracaidista.
	[pa.ra.kai̯.ˈðis.ta]	-It was nice to meet and talk with a parachutist.
6213	**molecular**	**molecular**
	adj	Mi hermano puede controlar su densidad molecular.
	[mo.le.ku.ˈlar]	-My brother has the ability to control his molecular density.
6214	**abdominal**	**abdominal; crunch**
	adj; f	También tiene una profunda herida abdominal de puñalada.
	[aβ.ðo.mi.ˈnal]	-He also has a deep abdominal stab wound.
6215	**espontáneo**	**spontaneous**
	adj	No fue algo espontáneo sino provocado.
	[ɛs.põn̪.ˈta.ne.o]	-It was not spontaneous but was whipped up.
6216	**paisano**	**from the same place; civilian**
	adj; m	Soy un paisano, no quiero ser deportado.
	[pai̯.ˈsa.no]	-I'm a civilian, I don't want to be deported.
6217	**traficar**	**traffic**
	vb	Es dueña de un lugar que se usó para traficar narcóticos.
	[tra.fi.ˈkar]	-She owns a business that's been used to traffic narcotics.
6218	**fósil**	**fossil**
	m	Ninguna institución arqueológica en el mundo compraría un fósil robado.
	[ˈfo.sil]	-There isn't an archaeological institution in the world that would buy a stolen fossil.
6219	**cacao**	**cocoa**
	m	Le puse demasiada crema de cacao.
	[ka.ˈka.o]	-I put a little too much cream de cocoa in it.
6220	**rehacer**	**redo**
	vb	Deberíamos rehacer tu perfil e incluir eso.
	[re.a.ˈsɛr]	-We should redo your profile and put that in it.
6221	**municipio**	**municipality**
	m	No necesitáis el municipio para esto.
	[mu.ni.ˈsi.pjo]	-You don't need the municipality for that.
6222	**nombramiento**	**appointment**
	m	El nombramiento del funcionario ha vencido.
	[nõm.bra.ˈmjẽn̪.to]	-The appointment of the staff member has expired.
6223	**embrujar**	**bewitch**
	vb	Puedo enseñarles a embrujar la mente.
	[ẽm.bru.ˈxar]	-I can teach you how to bewitch the mind.
6224	**padecer**	**suffer**
	vb	También pueden padecer traumas y desasosiego dentro de la familia.
	[pa.ðe.ˈsɛr]	-They may also suffer from trauma and unrest within the family.
6225	**averiado**	**broken down**
	adj	Señor, mi coche se ha averiado.
	[a.βɛ.ˈrja.ðo]	-Mister, my car's broken down.
6226	**cisterna**	**tanker**

f
[sis.ˈtɛr.na]

La carga de cada vehículo cisterna se pesará y registrará por separado.
-Each tanker load shall be weighed and recorded separately.

6227 **apretado** — **cramped**
adj
[a.prɛ.ˈta.ðo]

Estaba tan apretado que no podíamos sentarnos.
-It was so cramped, we couldn't sit.

6228 **caseta** — **hut**
f
[ka.ˈsɛ.ta]

Tengo una caseta en la playa de ahí abajo.
-I have a hut on the beach down there.

6229 **diluvio** — **downpour**
m
[di.ˈlu.βjo]

Pasé una semana en una trinchera bajo un diluvio.
-I spent a week in a foxhole in the pouring rain.

6230 **textura** — **texture**
f
[tɛks.ˈtu.ra]

La carne es tierna y su textura poco fibrosa.
-The meat is tender and has a low-grain texture.

6231 **inclinado** — **inclined**
adj
[ĩŋ.kli.ˈna.ðo]

Al principio, estaba inclinado a escribir esto como un corte.
-At first, I was inclined to write it off as a cut.

6232 **destacar** — **stand out**
vb
[dɛs.ta.ˈkar]

Tenemos que hacer destacar nuestra solicitud.
-We have to make our application stand out.

6233 **consumidor** — **consumer**
m
[kõn.su.mi.ˈðor]

El consumidor tiene derecho a saber esto.
-The consumer has a right to know this.

6234 **capacitar** — **train**
vb
[ka.pa.si.ˈtar]

Tiene planes para reestructurar y capacitar su personal.
-It has plans to restructure and to train its staff.

6235 **vendaje** — **bandage**
m
[bẽn.ˈda.xe]

Solo un vendaje ligero y hemos acabado.
-Just a light bandage and we're done.

6236 **idealista** — **idealistic; idealist**
adj; m
[i.ðe.a.ˈlis.ta]

Ella era curiosa, inteligente e idealista.
-She was inquisitive, intelligent, and idealistic.

6237 **redactor** — **editor**
m
[re.ðak.ˈtor]

Soy redactor de arte, no investigador.
-I'm an art editor, not an investigator.

6238 **cabecera** — **headboard**
f
[ka.βe.ˈsɛ.ra]

Pero olvidamos las velas de la cabecera.
-But we forgot about the candles on the headboard.

6239 **irritable** — **irritable**
adj
[i.ri.ˈta.βle]

Estoy cansado, hambriento y un poco irritable.
-I'm tired, hungry and just a little bit irritable.

6240 **indulgente** — **indulgent**
adj
[ĩn.dul.ˈxẽn.te]

El profesor anterior era muy indulgente.
-The former teacher was too indulgent.

6241 **conveniencia** — **advantage**
f
[kõm.be.ˈnjẽn.sja]

Quizás podamos utilizarla para nuestra conveniencia.
-Maybe we can use it to our advantage.

6242 **calentador** — **water heater**

m
[ka.lẽn̪.ta.ˈðor]

He venido para arreglar vuestro calentador.
-I'm here to fix your water heater.

6243 anarquista

m/f; adj
[a.nar.ˈkis.ta]

anarchist; anarchist

No creo que sea guay ser un anarquista.
-I don't think it is cool be an anarchist.

6244 ágil

adj
[ˈa.xil]

agile

Es muy ágil y activo a pesar de tener las patas cortas.
-It is very agile and active in spite of short legs.

6245 colosal

adj
[ko.lo.ˈsal]

colossal

Tuve que permitirte cometer ese error colosal.
-I had to let you make that colossal blunder.

6246 atormentar

vb
[a.tor.mẽn̪.ˈtar]

torment

No deberías atormentar al pobre hombre.
-You shouldn't torment the poor fellow.

6247 titán

m
[ti.ˈtãn]

titan

Pareces un titán con ese disfraz.
-You look like a titan with that costume.

6248 constituir

vb
[kõns.ti.ˈtwir]

constitute

Esta cláusula podría también constituir una nueva ayuda.
-This clause could also constitute new aid.

6249 orquídea

f
[or.ˈki.ðe.a]

orchid

Esta es una orquídea que solo se encuentra en la región del Amazonas.
-This is an orchid found only in the Amazon region.

6250 asegurador

adj; m
[a.se.ɣu.ra.ˈðor]

insurance; insurer

El asegurador puede exigir la notificación de cualquier cambio en las circunstancias del contrato.
-The insurer may request notification of any changes in circumstances in the contract.

6251 vizconde

m
[bis.ˈkõn̪.de]

viscount

El vizconde se los llevó esta mañana.
-The Viscount took them this morning.

6252 oyente

m/f
[o.ˈjẽn̪.te]

listener

No necesito un oyente, pero gracias igualmente.
-I don't need a listener, sir, but I thank you anyway.

6253 ampolla

f
[ãm.ˈpo.ja]

vial, blister

Lave la ampolla suavemente con agua y jabón antiséptico.
-Wash the blister gently with germ-fighting (antiseptic) soap and water.

6254 derrotado

adj
[dɛ.ro.ˈta.ðo]

defeated

Me hubiera gustado ver al matón derrotado.
-I would like to have seen the bully defeated.

6255 agrícola

adj
[a.ˈɣri.ko.la]

agricultural

El número de mujeres en el sector agrícola es particularmente alto.
-The number of women in the agricultural sector is particularly high.

6256 cafeína

f[ka.fe.ˈi.na]

caffeine

Aquí no servimos nada con cafeína. -We don't serve anything with caffeine here.

6257 insulina

f
[ĩn.su.ˈli.na]

insulin

Murió ayer por sobredosis de insulina.
-He died yesterday of an overdose of insulin.

6258 detonación

detonation

f
[dɛ.to.na.ˈsjõn]

Si hay otra detonación, me vengaré.
-If there's another detonation, I'll take my revenge.

6259 **guerrilla**

guerrilla

f
[gɛ.ˈri.ja]

Los grupos de guerrilla han continuado incorporando en sus filas a menores de 15 años.
-The guerrilla groups have continued enlisting children under 15 years of age.

6260 **concebir**

conceive

vb
[kõn.se.ˈβir]

Soy algo que ni siquiera puedes concebir.
-I am something that you can't even conceive.

6261 **maligno**

malign

adj
[ma.ˈliɣ.no]

En consecuencia, el nacionalismo puede ser maligno o benigno.
-Nationalism could, therefore, be malignant or benign.

6262 **horizontal**

horizontal

adj
[o.ri.sõn̯.ˈtal]

Encontrarás bourbon básicamente en cada superficie horizontal.
-You'll find bourbon on basically every horizontal surface.

6263 **vano**

futile

adj
[ˈba.no]

Después de otro vano sermón, lo dejarás quedarse.
-After another futile sermon, you'll let him stay.

6264 **chistar**

talk back, make a sound

vb
[tʃis.ˈtar]

Pusiste el dedo en una vela encendida anoche sin chistar.
-You had your finger in a lit candle last night and didn't even flinch.

6265 **detestable**

despicable

adj
[dɛ.tɛs.ˈta.βle]

Ese acto me parece detestable, señor.
-Such an act is detestable to me, sir.

6266 **presentador**

presenter

m
[pre.sẽn̯.ta.ˈðor]

Ser un buen presentador requiere mucha práctica.
-Being a good presenter requires much practice.

6267 **benéfico**

charity

adj
[be.ˈne.fi.ko]

Tengo que prepararme para el almuerzo benéfico.
-I have to get ready for this charity brunch.

6268 **columpio**

swing

m
[ko.ˈlũm.pjo]

No es gran cosa, pero quizás quieras volver a sentarte en el columpio.
-It's not a big deal, but maybe you want to sit back on the swing.

6269 **damasco**

apricot

m
[da.ˈmas.ko]

Este bizcocho es de damasco, creo.
-This muffin is apricot, I think.

6270 **nodriza**

nursemaid

f
[no.ˈðri.sa]

Mi nodriza me enseño a ser educada.
-My nursemaid taught me to be educated.

6271 **distraer(se)**

distract

vb[dis.tra.ˈɛr]

Por favor, no intente distraer nuestra atención. -Please do not attempt to distract our attention.

6272 **persuadir**

persuade

vb
[pɛr.swa.ˈðir]

Jim intentó persuadir a Ana para comer pizza.
-Jim tried to persuade Ana to eat pizza.

6273 **amarrar**

tie

vb
[a.ma.ˈrar]

Me gustaría amarrar esto si pudiera.
-I'd like to tie this back if I could.

6274 **desembarco**

landing

m
[de.sẽm.ˈbar.ko]

Necesitaremos soporte naval para el desembarco.
-We'll need naval support for a landing.

6275 silbido — **whistle**

m
[sil.ˈβi.ðo]

Se supone que eso era un silbido.
-That was supposed to be a whistle.

6276 robusto — **robust**

adj
[ro.ˈβus.to]

Nuestro sistema es mucho más robusto.
-Our system is much more robust.

6277 júbilo — **joy**

m
[ˈxu.βi.lo]

Los gritos de júbilo se mezclaban con las lágrimas.
-Cries of joy were mingled with tears.

6278 gramática — **grammar**

f
[gra.ˈma.ti.ka]

Necesitas estudiar tu gramática, hijo.
-You need to study your grammar, son.

6279 retórico — **rhetorical**

adj
[rɛ.ˈto.ri.ko]

Es una especie de acuerdo retórico.
-It's a kind of rhetorical agreement.

6280 descomposición — **decomposition**

f
[dɛs.kõm.po.si.ˈsjõn]

Tenemos cuatro cuerpos en varios estados de descomposición.
-We've got four bodies in various states of decomposition.

6281 indigestión — **indigestion**

f
[ĩn.di.xɛs.ˈtjõn]

Ya sabes, siempre me da indigestión.
-You know, it always gives me indigestion.

6282 anécdota — **anecdote**

f
[a.ˈnɛk.ðo.ta]

No le convertiré en una anécdota.
-I will not turn him into an anecdote.

6283 contratiempo — **setback**

m
[kõn.tra.ˈtjẽm.po]

No quiero preocuparte, pero tenemos un diminuto contratiempo.
-I don't want to worry you, but we have a teensy setback.

6284 incompetencia — **incompetence**

f
[ĩn.kõm.pɛ.ˈtẽn.sja]

El pueblo estadounidense no tolerará tal incompetencia.
-The American people won't stand for such incompetence.

6285 tenor — **tenor**

m
[te.ˈnor]

El tenor del informe es bastante negativo.
-The tenor of the report is fairly negative.

6286 regresivo — **regressive**

adj
[re.ɣre.ˈsi.βo]

Este síndrome regresivo puede limitarse a los ratones.
-This regressive syndrome may be limited to the mice.

6287 erudito — **expert; erudite person**

adj; m[ɛ.ru.ˈði.to]

Era muy erudito y experto en historia, filosofía y ciencia. -He was highly intellectual and was an expert in history, philosophy, and science.

6288 novelista — **novelist**

m/f
[no.βe.ˈlis.ta]

Mi objetivo en la vida es ser un novelista.
-My goal in life is to be a novelist.

6289 espanto — **terror**

m
[ɛs.ˈpãn.to]

Está luchando contra la carga de un gran espanto.
-He's struggling beneath the load of the great terror.

6290 horrendo — **horrendous**

adj
[o.ˈrɛ̃n̪.do]

Ese fue el horrendo resultado de ese ataque con bomba.
-This was the horrendous result of that bomb attack.

6291 traicionero

adj
[trai̯.sjo.ˈnɛ.ro]

treacherous

El camino de delante sigue siendo traicionero.
-The path ahead remains treacherous.

6292 miga

f
[ˈmi.ɣa]

crumb

No me dejaste ni una miga.
-You didn't even leave me a crumb.

6293 balístico

adj
[ba.ˈlis.ti.ko]

ballistic

Haga un análisis balístico de la explosión.
-Run a ballistic analysis of the explosion.

6294 tranquilizante

adj; m
[trã̃n.ki.li.ˈsã̃n̪.te]

reassuring; tranquilizer

Puedo darte más tranquilizante si quieres.
-I can give you more tranquilizer if you want.

6295 álamo

m
[ˈa.la.mo]

poplar

Esto es un álamo adecuado para hacer esculturas.
-This is a poplar which is suitable for carving.

6296 domar

vb
[do.ˈmar]

tame

Tuve que domar a un puma.
-I had to tame a cougar.

6297 derrumbar(se)

vb
[dɛ.rũm.ˈbar]

demolish, break down

Tenemos suficiente para derrumbar al impostor.
-We have enough to break down the impostor.

6298 intersección

f
[ĩn̪.tɛr.sɛk.ˈsjõn]

intersection

Llegamos a una intersección donde nos dispararon.
-We hit an intersection where we were shot at.

6299 consolar

vb
[kõn.so.ˈlar]

comfort

Siempre estás esperando a un marinero al que consolar.
-You're always waiting for a sailor to comfort.

6300 telégrafo

m
[te.ˈle.ɣra.fo]

telegraph

Diremos que fue error del telégrafo.
-We'll say it was the telegrapher's mistake.

6301 cordial

m
[kor.ˈðjal]

cordial

Me esperaba una bienvenida más cordial aquí.
-I had expected a more cordial welcome here.

6302 expulsión

f
[ɛks.pul.ˈsjõn]

expulsion

Se suprimió la expulsión por delitos graves.
-Expulsion for serious criminal offenses was to be abolished.

6303 cáliz

m
[ˈka.lis]

goblet

Vale, siento haber roto el cáliz.
-Okay, I'm sorry I broke the goblet.

6304 camarógrafo

m
[ka.ma.ˈro.ɣra.fo]

cameraman

Siempre he tratado de estar cerca del camarógrafo.
-I've always tried to stay close to the cameraman.

6305 escaparate

m
[ɛs.ka.pa.ˈra.te]

closet (LA), shop window

Estoy poniendo un taburete y una mesa en nuestro escaparate.
-I am placing a stool and a table in our shop window.

6306 calambre

cramp

	m		Le dio un calambre mientras nadaba.
	[ka.ˈlãm.bɾe]		-He got a cramp while he was swimming.
6307	**molécula**		**molecule**
	f		Una molécula está formada por átomos.
	[mo.ˈle.ku.la]		-A molecule is made up of atoms.
6308	**simular**		**pretend**
	vb		Solía simular que tenía un amigo imaginario.
	[si.mu.ˈlar]		-I used to pretend I had an imaginary friend.
6309	**oasis**		**oasis**
	m		Mientras podamos avanzaremos hacia el oasis.
	[o.ˈa.sis]		-While we can, we'll push on towards the oasis.
6310	**muleta**		**crutch**
	f		Te mereces algo mejor que ser mi muleta emocional.
	[mu.ˈlɛ.ta]		-You deserve better than being my emotional crutch.
6311	**sauce**		**willow**
	m		Hay un sauce enorme en la granja.
	[ˈsau̯.se]		-There's a huge willow tree at the farm.
6312	**pileta**		**basil (LA), pool (LA)**
	f		También tenemos pileta climatizada y trajes de baño para todos.
	[pi.ˈlɛ.ta]		-We also have a heated pool and enough swimsuits for everyone.
6313	**resonancia**		**resonance**
	f		La resonancia mediática siempre es significativa.
	[re.so.ˈnãn.sja]		-The media resonance is always great.
6314	**expectativa**		**expectation**
	f		Lamentablemente, esta expectativa sencillamente no es realista.
	[ɛks.pek̚.ta.ˈti.βa]		-Unfortunately, that expectation is simply not realistic.
6315	**mambo**		**mambo, issue (LA)**
	m		Empezaremos de nuevo con el mambo.
	[ˈmãm.bo]		-We're going to start again with the mambo.
6316	**restar**		**deduct**
	vb		No se olviden de restar el uno.
	[rɛs.ˈtar]		-Don't forget to subtract the one.
6317	**absolución**		**absolution**
	f		Es pecaminoso no ofrecer la oportunidad de absolución.
	[aβ.so.lu.ˈsjõn]		-It is sinful to offer no chance of absolution.
6318	**sureste**		**southeast**
	m		Tenemos reclusos en el patio sureste.
	[su.ˈrɛs.te]		-We've got inmates in the southeast quad.
6319	**audiencia**		**hearing**
	f		Solo siéntate para que podamos empezar esta audiencia.
	[au̯.ˈðjẽn.sja]		-Just sit down so we can start this hearing.
6320	**interponer(se)**		**interject; intervene**
	vb; vbr		Disculpen, ¿puedo interponer algo yo?
	[ĩn.tɛr.po.ˈnɛr]		-Excuse me, can I interject something?
6321	**fusilamiento**		**execution by firing squad**
	m		Fue la noche anterior a su fusilamiento.
	[fu.si.la.ˈmjẽn.to]		-It was the night before her execution by firing squad.
6322	**cuarteto**		**quartet**

	m	
	[kwar.ˈtɛ.to]	Y los cinco cantáis ese cuarteto. -And the five of you sing that quartet.
6323	**alubia**	**bean**
	f	
	[a.ˈlu.βja]	Se llevó la alubia de recuerdo. -He took the bean as a souvenir.
6324	**adquisición**	**acquisition**
	f	
	[að.ki.si.ˈsjõn]	Esa es la última adquisición para mi biblioteca. -This is the latest acquisition to my library.
6325	**pandillero**	**member of a gang**
	m	
	[pãn̪.di.ˈʝɛ.ro]	Pensó que era un pandillero, y me dejó marchar. -He thought I was a gangbanger, and he let me go.
6326	**propulsión**	**propulsion**
	f	
	[pro.pul.ˈsjõn]	Parece que ella escribió el libro sobre propulsión. -Looks like she wrote the book on propulsion.
6327	**fiasco**	**fiasco**
	m	
	[ˈfjas.ko]	Necesita contraatacar después de este fiasco. -You need to counter-attack after this fiasco.
6328	**presuntuoso**	**conceited**
	adj	
	[pre.sũn̪.ˈtwo.so]	Le encuentro arrogante, presuntuoso y autoritario. -I find him to be arrogant, conceited, and peremptory.
6329	**carrete**	**reel**
	m	
	[ka.ˈrɛ.te]	Todavía no han encontrado el carrete. -They still haven't found the reel.
6330	**reptil**	**reptile**
	m	
	[rep̚.ˈtil]	Quiero el reptil más peligroso que tengas. -I want the most dangerous reptile you've got.
6331	**neblina**	**mist**
	f	
	[ne.ˈβli.na]	Una cortina de neblina bloqueó nuestra visión. -A curtain of mist blocked our view.
6332	**equivaler**	**be equal to**
	vb	
	[e.ki.βa.ˈlɛr]	Ello podía equivaler a una condena a prisión perpetua sin posibilidad de libertad condicional. -This can amount to a sentence of life imprisonment without the possibility of parole.
6333	**joroba**	**hump**
	f	
	[xo.ˈro.βa]	Te saldrá una joroba cuando envejezcas. -You'll get a hump when you get older.
6334	**colonial**	**colonial**
	adj [ko.lo.ˈnjal]	Tenemos todo el derecho a oponernos a esta guerra colonial. -We have every right to oppose this colonial war.
6335	**regentar**	**manage**
	vb	
	[re.xẽn̪.ˈtar]	Desafortunadamente, tengo un bar que regentar. -Unfortunately, I've got a bar to run.
6336	**adoración**	**adoration**
	f	
	[a.ðo.ra.ˈsjõn]	Lo crié con mucho amor y adoración. -I brought him up with much love and adoration.
6337	**informática**	**computing**
	f	
	[ĩm.for.ˈma.ti.ka]	Esperamos con interés que se creen mejores oportunidades mediante la ampliación del uso de la informática.

-We are looking forward to opportunities being created through the expanding use of informatics.

6338	**espinaca**		**spinach**
	f		La espinaca es rica en minerales y vitaminas.
	[ɛs.pi.ˈna.ka]		-Spinach is rich in minerals and vitamins.
6339	**rentable**		**profitable**
	adj		Es más rentable venir a Dubái.
	[r̃ɛ̃n.ˈta.βle]		-It's more profitable to come to Dubai.
6340	**chalet**		**cottage**
	m		Recuerdo observar el chalet desde aquí.
	[ʧa.ˈlɛt]		-I remember looking at the cottage from about here.
6341	**planificación**		**planning**
	f		La planificación y aplicación deberán coordinarse.
	[pla.ni.fi.ka.ˈsjõn]		-The planning and implementation have to be coordinated.
6342	**vicario**		**vicar**
	m		No necesito su consejo, vicario.
	[bi.ˈka.rjo]		-I don't need your counsel, vicar.
6343	**adaptar(se)**		**adapt**
	vb		Es difícil adaptar esta historia para niños.
	[a.ðap̚.ˈtar]		-It is hard to adapt this story for children.
6344	**arándano**		**blueberry**
	m		Tiene el tamaño de un arándano.
	[a.ˈrã̃n.da.no]		-It's about the size of a blueberry.
6345	**coronar**		**crown**
	vb		Venimos para coronar la victoria con la amistad.
	[ko.ɾo.ˈnar]		-We have come to crown victory with friendship.
6346	**estéreo**		**stereo; stereo**
	adj; m		He averiguado cómo usar tu estéreo.
	[ɛs.ˈtɛ.re.o]		-I figured out how to use your stereo.
6347	**mellizo**		**twin; twin**
	adj; m		Odiaría pensar que tengo un mellizo maligno.
	[me.ˈʝi.so]		-I'd hate to think I have an evil twin.
6348	**influyente**		**influential**
	adj		Ahora soy un miembro influyente de esta comunidad.
	[ĩm.flu.ˈʝẽn.te]		-I'm an influential member of this community now.
6349	**escultor**		**sculptor**
	m[ɛs.kuļ.ˈtor]		Seguro que serás un escultor reconocido. -I'm sure you'll be a famous sculptor.
6350	**joyero**		**jeweller, jewellery box**
	m		Solo se trataba de una pequeña discusión con un joyero.
	[xo.ˈʝɛ.ro]		-It was just a little argument with a jeweler.
6351	**liquidación**		**settlement**
	f		El acuerdo de liquidación está terminado.
	[li.ki.ða.ˈsjõn]		-The settlement agreement's all done.
6352	**repertorio**		**repertoire**
	m		Tengo un repertorio muy amplio, señor.
	[re.pɛr.ˈto.rjo]		-I have a very large repertoire, sir.
6353	**clarinete**		**clarinet; clarinettist**
	m; m/f		Yo no toco el clarinete.
	[kla.ri.ˈnɛ.te]		-I don't play the clarinet.

6354	**cinematográfico**		**cinematographic**

6354 **cinematográfico** — **cinematographic**
adj
[si.ne.ma.to.ˈɣra.fi.ko]
Tras sus primeros cien años de vida, la técnica y el lenguaje cinematográfico han evolucionado enormemente.
-After its first one hundred years, the techniques and the cinematographic language have greatly evolved.

6355 **derrocar** — **overthrow**
vb
[dɛ.ro.ˈkar]
Trabajo para derrocar un estado corrupto y antidemocrático.
-I'm working to overthrow a corrupt, anti-democratic state.

6356 **valorar** — **value**
vb
[ba.lo.ˈrar]
Apreciarán el increíble tesoro que les ofrezco.
-You will appreciate the incredible value I'm offering.

6357 **huerta** — **vegetable garden**
f
[ˈwɛr.ta]
La anciana se mantenía ocupada en su huerta.
-The old lady busied herself on her vegetable garden.

6358 **lavadero** — **sink, laundry room**
m
[la.βa.ˈðɛ.ro]
Hay un lavadero en la planta baja.
-There is a laundry room on the ground floor.

6359 **hemisferio** — **hemisphere**
m
[e.mis.ˈfɛ.rjo]
Los Estados Unidos están en el hemisferio norte.
-The United States is in the Northern Hemisphere.

6360 **cuántico** — **quantum**
adj
[ˈkwã̃n.ti.ko]
Estamos literalmente desintegrando las cosas a un nivel cuántico.
-We are literally tearing things apart on a quantum level.

6361 **derramamiento** — **shedding**
m
[dɛ.ra.ma.ˈmjẽ̞n.to]
Le di mi palabra de que cooperaríamos para evitar el derramamiento de una sola gota de sangre.
-I gave you my word that we would cooperate to avoid the shedding of a single drop of blood.

6362 **hablador** — **talkative**
adj
[a.βla.ˈðor]
Bueno, de repente no eres tan hablador.
-Well, you're suddenly not so talkative.

6363 **ronco** — **hoarse**
adj
[ˈrõŋ.ko]
Estoy ronco, pero no te preocupes.
-I'm hoarse, but don't worry.

6364 **ansiar** — **yearn**
vb
[ãn.ˈsjar]
No sabes lo que es ansiar tanto el roce de alguien.
-You don't know what it's like to yearn for the touch of another.

6365 **atraso** — **backwardness**
m
[a.ˈtra.so]
Nuestros verdaderos enemigos son la pobreza y el atraso.
-The real enemies for us are poverty and backwardness.

6366 **vigía** — **lookout**
m/f
[bi.ˈxi.a]
Necesitamos un vigía, alguien en algún techo.
-We need a lookout, someone on a roof somewhere.

6367 **modificación** — **modification**
f
[mo.ði.fi.ka.ˈsjõn]
Cinco de los tanques no necesitan modificación alguna.
-Five of the tanks do not require any modification.

6368 **pique** — **pique**
m
[ˈpi.ke]
Haré que parezca un pique.
-I'll make it just look like pique.

6369 **mediano** — **medium-sized**

adj
[me.ˈðja.no]
Esto equivale a un país mediano de la Unión Europea.
-This is the equivalent of a medium-sized EU country.

6370 drenaje
m
[dɾe.ˈna.xe]
drainage
La aplicación de medidas de mejoramiento del drenaje y de restauración de tierras necesita mucho tiempo.
-Drainage improvement measures and land recovery take a long time to implement.

6371 desconectar
vb
[dɛs.ko.nek̚.ˈtar]
disconnect
Tendremos que desconectar los sistemas averiados.
-We're going to have to disconnect the damaged systems.

6372 fertilidad
f
[fɛr.ti.li.ˈðað]
fertility
Soy un doctor especializado en fertilidad.
-I'm a doctor specialized in fertility.

6373 destornillador
m
[dɛs.tor.ni.ja.ˈðor]
screwdriver
Tú no tienes tu destornillador.
-You don't have your screwdriver.

6374 prefectura
f
[pre.fek̚.ˈtu.ra]
prefecture
Cada prefectura está dirigida por un prefecto.
-Each prefecture is headed by a prefect.

6375 especializado
adj
[ɛs.pe.sja.li.ˈsa.ðo]
specialized
Este es el único zoológico especializado en fauna sudamericana.
-This zoo is the unique one specialized in South American fauna.

6376 continuidad
f
[kõn.ti.nwi.ˈðað]
continuity
Es esencial garantizar la continuidad del programa.
-It is essential to ensure the continuity of the programme.

6377 alcoba
f
[al.ˈko.βa]
bedroom
Me encantaría, pero estoy ocupada guardando mis ropas en mi alcoba.
-I'd love to, but I'm busy moving my clothes into my bedroom.

6378 primogénito
m
[pri.mo.ˈxe.ni.to]
firstborn
Prometieron ponerle mi nombre al primogénito.
-They promised to name the first born after me.

6379 acordeón
m[a.kor.ðe.ˈõn]
accordion
Lleva tocando el acordeón 7 años. -He's been playing the accordion for 7 years.

6380 incomparable
adj
[ĩŋ.kõm.pa.ˈra.βle]
incomparable
Único por fuera e incomparable por dentro.
-Unique on the outside and incomparable on the inside.

6381 persuasión
f
[pɛr.swa.ˈsjõn]
persuasion
Hemos trabajado en técnicas de persuasión toda la semana.
-We worked on persuasion tactics all week.

6382 coliseo
m
[ko.li.ˈse.o]
coliseum
El transporte hacia el coliseo continuará en breve.
-Transport to the Coliseum will continue shortly.

6383 agresividad
f
[a.ɣre.si.βi.ˈðað]
aggressiveness
Encuentras su agresividad atractiva, pero yo no.
-You find his aggressiveness attractive, but I don't.

6384 sanitario
m; adj
[sa.ni.ˈta.rjo]
bathroom; sanitary
¿Saben dónde está el sanitario?
-Do you know where the bathroom is?

6385 frigorífico
refrigerator

m
[fri.ɣo.ˈri.fi.ko]

En el frigorífico había ocultas varias armas.
-A number of weapons were concealed in the refrigerator.

6386 curación — **healing**

f
[ku.ra.ˈsjõn]

No confundas sufrimiento con curación, Victor.
-Just don't confuse suffering with healing, Victor.

6387 bautizar — **baptize**

vb
[bau̯.ti.ˈsar]

Trató de bautizar a Iris en la bañera.
-You were trying to baptize Iris in the bathtub.

6388 incomprensible — **incomprehensible**

adj
[ĩŋ.kõm.prẽn.ˈsi.βle]

Esto me parece lamentable y también incomprensible.
-I find this really regrettable and also incomprehensible.

6389 impensable — **unthinkable**

adj
[ĩm.pẽn.ˈsa.βle]

Es impensable que podamos siquiera permitirlo.
-It is unthinkable that we can even allow it.

6390 beneficiar — **benefit**

vb
[be.ne.fi.ˈsjar]

No todo lo que hagamos nos tiene que beneficiar.
-Not everything we do has to benefit us.

6391 enmascarar — **mask**

vb
[ẽm.mas.ka.ˈrar]

El shock del accidente suele enmascarar lesiones.
-The shock of the accident can often mask injuries.

6392 obstrucción — **obstruction**

f
[oβs.truk.ˈsjõn]

Quizás corregimos la obstrucción a tiempo.
-Could just mean we caught the obstruction early.

6393 diésel — **diesel**

m
[ˈdje.sɛl]

Hay 4 motores disponibles, 2 diésel y 2 gasolina.
-There are 4 engines available, 2 diesel and 2 gasoline.

6394 pulmonía — **pneumonia**

f
[pul.mo.ˈni.a]

Casi cojo una pulmonía, pero lo encontré.
-I almost caught pneumonia, but I found it.

6395 bisturí — **scalpel**

m[bis.tu.ˈri]

Desearía tener un bisturí ahora mismo. -I wish I had a scalpel right now.

6396 fotográfico — **photographic**

adj
[fo.to.ˈɣra.fi.ko]

Seguro no buscaba que fuera fotográfico.
-I'm sure it wasn't intended to be photographic.

6397 verbal — **verbal**

adj
[bɛr.ˈβal]

Eso es prácticamente un contrato verbal.
-That is practically a verbal contract.

6398 respetuoso — **respectful**

adj
[rɛs.pɛ.ˈtwo.so]

Gracias por ser tan respetuoso conmigo.
-Thank you for being so respectful toward me.

6399 perspicaz — **keen**

adj
[pɛrs.ˈpi.kas]

Hay una inteligencia perspicaz bajo toda esta psicosis.
-There is a keen intelligence underneath all this psychosis.

6400 herpes — **herpes**

m
[ˈɛr.pes]

Podrías tener herpes o algo.
-You could have herpes or something.

6401 reñir — **tell off, fight**

vb
[re.ˈɲir]

No llamó porque no quería reñir.
-She hasn't called to avoid a fight.

6402 gobernante — **ruling; leader**
adj; m
[go.βɛr.ˈnãn̪.te]
La democracia hará que la familia gobernante avance.
-Democracy will push the ruling family forward.

6403 ecuador — **equator**
m
[e.kwa.ˈðor]
El ecuador divide al globo en dos hemisferios.
-The equator divides the globe into two hemispheres.

6404 detallar — **detail**
vb
[dɛ.ta.ˈjar]
La mesera llegará pronto para detallar los especiales del día.
-The waitress will be here soon to detail the specials of the day.

6405 trámite — **process**
m
[ˈtra.mi.te]
Una de las principales quejas es la lentitud de los trámites.
-One of the main complaints is slow processing.

6406 gabardina — **raincoat**
f
[ga.βar.ˈði.na]
Sí, es una gabardina estupenda.
-Yes, it's a fine looking raincoat.

6407 fusible — **fusible; fuse**
adj; m
[fu.ˈsi.βle]
Bonito lugar para guardar un fusible.
-That's a fine place to put a fuse.

6408 glaciar — **glacier**
m
[gla.ˈsjar]
Bob, llegaron las muestras del glaciar.
-Bob, the samples from the glacier have arrived.

6409 historiador — **historian**
m
[is.to.rja.ˈðor]
Cuando era joven, quise ser historiador.
-When I was young, I wanted to be a historian.

6410 pulir — **polish**
vb
[pu.ˈlir]
Solo necesitas pulir un poco tu actuación.
-It's just that your act could use a little polish.

6411 asfalto — **asphalt**
m[as.ˈfal̪.to]
Estas huellas en el asfalto me parecen bastante recientes. -These impressions in the asphalt look pretty fresh to me.

6412 lujo — **luxury**
m
[ˈlu.xo]
Evidentemente lo considera un lujo superfluo.
-Obviously, it sees it as an unnecessary luxury.

6413 península — **peninsula**
f
[pe.ˈnĩn.su.la]
Queda un campo de minas en la península.
-One minefield remains on the peninsula.

6414 indicador — **indicator**
m
[ĩn̪.di.ka.ˈðor]
Este indicador debe reflejar el costo total del personal.
-This indicator should reflect the total costs of the employee workforce.

6415 pedal — **pedal**
m
[pe.ˈðal]
Tengo sangre en el pedal izquierdo.
-I've got blood on the left pedal.

6416 dudoso — **dubious**
adj
[du.ˈðo.so]
Creo que es un procedimiento dudoso.
-I regard that as a dubious procedure.

6417 meteorológico — **meteorological**
adj
[mɛ.te.o.ro.ˈlo.xi.ko]
Además se ha instalado equipo meteorológico en varios lugares.
-In addition, meteorological equipment has been installed at various sites.

6418 leñador — **woodcutter**

	m	Veamos la cabaña del leñador.
	[le.ɲa.ˈðor]	-Let's see the woodcutter's cottage.

6419 victorioso — **victorious**
adj
[biḱ.to.ˈrjo.so]
¡Regresaré victorioso a esta casa!
-I will return to this house victorious!

6420 revuelo — **stir**
m
[re.ˈβwe.lo]
Su informe armó todo un revuelo aquí.
-Your report's causing quite a stir around here.

6421 arrepentirse — **regret**
vbr
[a.re.pẽn̪.ˈtir.se]
La gente que intenta chantajearme suelen arrepentirse.
-People who try to blackmail me usually regret it.

6422 helar — **freeze**
vb
[e.ˈlar]
Es una maravilla que no te hayas helado.
-It's a wonder you didn't freeze.

6423 mortero — **mortar**
m
[mor.ˈtɛ.ro]
Necesitaré un mortero y una piedra.
-I'll need a mortar and a pestle.

6424 cotidiano — **daily, routine**
adj
[ko.ti.ˈðja.no]
La muerte se ha convertido para ellos en un hecho cotidiano.
-Death has become a daily event for them.

6425 incremento — **increase**
m
[ĩŋ.kre.ˈmẽn̪.to]
El incremento en el número de biocidas es alarmante.
-The increase in the number of biocidal products is alarming.

6426 apéndice — **appendix**
m
[a.ˈpẽn̪.di.se]
El apéndice sangrará demasiado y morirá rápido.
-The appendix will bleed too much and he will die fast.

6427 registrador — **registrar**
m[re.xis.tra.ˈðor]
El registrador redactará inmediatamente un acta de registro del nacimiento. -
The registrar will immediately draw up a deed of this registration of birth.

6428 debido — **properly**
adj
[de.ˈβi.ðo]
Ambas cuestiones deben ser encaradas como es debido.
-Both issues need to be properly addressed.

6429 alimenticio — **food**
adj
[a.li.mẽn̪.ˈti.sjo]
Cada programa proporciona un suplemento alimenticio a las familias.
-Each programme provides a food supplement to families.

6430 cojín — **cushion**
m
[ko.ˈxĩn]
No querréis acabar como este cojín...
-You don't want to end up like this cushion.

6431 confidente — **confidant**
m
[kõɱ.fi.ˈðẽn̪.te]
Tal vez simplemente necesitas un confidente.
-Perhaps you are simply in need of a confidante.

6432 agotamiento — **exhaustion**
m
[a.ɣo.ta.ˈmjẽn̪.to]
Conozco muy bien esa sensación de agotamiento.
-I know that feeling of exhaustion too well.

6433 anticipar(se) — **anticipate**
vb
[ãn̪.ti.si.ˈpar]
Puede anticipar posibles desafíos futuros y capacidades operacionales.
-It can anticipate future challenges and operational skills.

6434 condecorar — **decorate**

vb
[kõn̪.de.ko.ˈrar]
Te vamos a condecorar a ti.
-We're going to decorate you.

6435 aeródromo — aerodrome
m
[a.ɛ.ˈro.ðro.mo]
Ha rechazado invertir en el aeródromo.
-He's refused to invest in the aerodrome.

6436 sarampión — measles
m
[sa.rãm.ˈpjõn]
No estaré siempre con el sarampión.
-I won't always have measles.

6437 depositar — deposit
vb
[de.po.si.ˈtar]
Me gustaría depositar esto, gracias.
-I'd like to deposit this, thank you.

6438 usuario — user
m
[u.ˈswa.rjo]
¿Cómo puedo convertirme en un usuario de confianza?
-How can I become a trusted user?

6439 éter — ether
m
[ˈɛ.tɛr]
No solo los hospitales utilizan éter.
-It's not just hospitals that use ether.

6440 pinchar — poke, inject
vb
[pĩn̪.ˈtʃar]
Ahora no es el momento de pinchar al oso.
-Now's not the time to poke the bear.

6441 comanche — Comanche; Comanche Indian
adj; m/f
[ko.ˈmãn̪.tʃe]
Lo aprendí de una cocinera comanche.
-I learned it of a cook Comanche.

6442 trabar(se) — lock, start up; get tangled up
vb; vbr[tra.ˈβar]
Debería trabar tu puerta desde afuera. -I should lock your room from the outside.

6443 enciclopedia — encyclopedia
f
[ɛ̃n.si.klo.ˈpe.ðja]
He decidido leerme la enciclopedia entera.
-I've decided to read the whole encyclopedia.

6444 arqueólogo — archaeologist
m
[ar.ke.ˈo.lo.ɣo]
Pero intento hacerlo como un arqueólogo.
-I'm trying to do it like an archaeologist.

6445 implantar — implant
vb
[ĩm.plãn̪.ˈtar]
Decidieron implantar embriones humanos en madres de alquiler humanas.
-They decided to implant human embryos in surrogate human mothers.

6446 expandir — expand, spread
vb
[ɛks.pãn̪.ˈdir]
Estoy aquí para expandir mi clientela.
-I'm here to expand my client base.

6447 recaudación — collection
f
[re.kau̯.ða.ˈsjõn]
La tasa general de recaudación sigue siendo insatisfactoria.
-The overall rate of the collection remains disappointing.

6448 pubertad — puberty
f
[pu.βɛr.ˈtað]
Esas mujeres me ayudaron a pasar mi pubertad.
-Those ladies got me through puberty.

6449 propulsor — propellant; promoter
adj; m
[pro.pul.ˈsor]
No se entregó ningún propulsor líquido para su destrucción.
-No liquid propellant had been presented for destruction.

6450 acuático — aquatic

adj
[aˈkwa.ti.ko]
Las acciones deberán contribuir a mejorar el medio ambiente acuático.
-The actions must contribute to enhancing the aquatic environment.

6451 rugir — **roar**
vb
[ruˈxir]
El león se puso a rugir cuando nos aproximamos.
-The lion began to roar as we approached.

6452 penicilina — **penicillin**
f
[pe.ni.si.ˈli.na]
Esa maleta está llena de nuestra penicilina.
-That suitcase is full of our penicillin.

6453 capitolio — **Capitol**
m
[ka.pi.ˈto.ljo]
Es el segundo más grande después del capitolio.
-Second only in size to the capitol.

6454 llano — **flat**
adj
[ˈʎa.no]
El resto del territorio es llano u ondulado.
-The rest is flat or rolling terrain.

6455 estampilla — **stamp (LA), seal (ES)**
f
[ɛs.tãm.ˈpi.ʝa]
Tom finalmente consiguió la rara estampilla que quería.
-Tom finally got hold of the rare stamp he wanted.

6456 mechero — **lighter**
m
[me.ˈtʃɛ.ro]
Está ahí sentado encendiendo un mechero.
-He's sitting in there lighting a lighter.

6457 fastidiado — **fed up, broken (ES)**
adj
[fas.ti.ˈðja.ðo]
Tenéis que estar locos, están todos fastidiados con vosotros.
-You must be nuts, they're all fed up with you.

6458 malla — **mesh**
f[ˈma.ʝa]
La dimensión de la malla será igual o superior a 110 milímetros. -The mesh size shall be equal or more than 110 millimeters.

6459 publicista — **publicist**
m/f
[pu.βli.ˈsis.ta]
Chica, necesitas un nuevo publicista.
-Girl, you have got to get a new publicist.

6460 seta — **mushroom**
f
[ˈsɛ.ta]
Encontraron una seta en una fiesta.
-You found a mushroom at a rave.

6461 ambiental — **environmental**
adj
[ãm.bjẽn̯.ˈtal]
El tema ambiental exige unas consideraciones adicionales.
-Further thought needs to be given to the environmental issue.

6462 desconcertante — **upsetting**
adj
[dɛs.kõn.sɛr.ˈtãn̯.te]
Este es un mundo precioso y desconcertante.
-This is a beautiful, upsetting world.

6463 oxigenar(se) — **oxygenate; get fresh air**
vb; vbr
[ok.si.xe.ˈnar]
La sangre no podía oxigenar sus tejidos.
-The blood was unable to oxygenate her tissue.

6464 anticipación — **in advance**
f
[ãn̯.ti.si.pa.ˈsjõn]
Recuerde que podrá solicitar comidas especiales con debida anticipación.
-Remember that you can request special meals for your flights in advance.

6465 emotivo — **emotional**
adj
[e.mo.ˈti.βo]
Puedo prometerles que esto fue un momento emotivo en mi laboratorio.
-I can promise you this was an emotional moment in my laboratory.

6466 tejar — **tile; tile factory**

	vb; m	Yo debería tejar mi patio.
	[te.ˈxar]	-I should tile my patio.
6467	**faena**	**chore**
	f	Creía que sería un reto interesante, pero es una faena aburrida.
	[fa.ˈe.na]	-I thought it'd be an interesting challenge, but it's a boring chore.
6468	**cooperativo**	**cooperative**
	adj	Ahora será un poco más cooperativo.
	[ko.o.pɛ.ra.ˈti.βo]	-He'll be a little more cooperative now.
6469	**viga**	**beam**
	f	Señor, solo necesitamos quitar esa viga y podremos sacarle del vehículo.
	[ˈbi.ɣa]	-Sir, we just need to remove this beam, and we can free you from the vehicle.
6470	**duplicado**	**duplicate**
	m	Solo tiene que pedir un duplicado.
	[dup̚.li.ˈka.ðo]	-You only have to request a duplicate.
6471	**desactivar**	**deactivate**
	vb	Si intentas desactivar el mecanismo, estallará.
	[de.sak̚.ti.ˈβar]	-If you attempt to deactivate the device, you will detonate.
6472	**repollo**	**cabbage**
	m	Tenemos pescado, espinacas, repollo y mucho más.
	[re.ˈpo.ʝo]	-We have fish, spinach, cabbage, and a lot more.
6473	**sepultura**	**burial**
	f[se.puʝ.ˈtu.ra]	No pudimos darles una sepultura digna. -We couldn't give them a decent burial.
6474	**crucifijo**	**crucifix**
	m	Le dimos a Ana un crucifijo de plata en su quinceañera.
	[kru.si.ˈfi.xo]	-We got Ana silver crucifix for her quiceañera.
6475	**interceptar**	**intercept**
	vb	Tienes que interceptar todas sus llamadas.
	[ĩn̪.tɛr.sep̚.ˈtar]	-You have to intercept all his calls.
6476	**arterial**	**arterial**
	adj	Hiciste lo correcto con el sangrado arterial.
	[ar.tɛ.ˈrjal]	-You did the right thing with the arterial bleed.
6477	**intimidar**	**intimidate**
	vb	No quiero intimidar a la clientela.
	[ĩn̪.ti.mi.ˈðar]	-I don't want to intimidate the clientele.
6478	**benefactor**	**benevolent; benefactor**
	adj; m	Descubriré la identidad de mi benefactor.
	[be.ne.fak̚.ˈtor]	-I'll find out the identity of my benefactor.
6479	**melancólico**	**melancholic**
	adj	Daremos un paseo melancólico junto al lago.
	[me.lãŋ.ˈko.li.ko]	-We'll take a melancholic walk around the lake.
6480	**acariciar**	**caress**
	vb	Déjate acariciar por el sol y disfruta de nuestra piscina climatizada.
	[a.ka.ri.ˈsjar]	-Let the sun caress you and enjoy our heated swimming pool.
6481	**observatorio**	**observatory**
	m	Jim estaba de camino al observatorio.
	[oβ.sɛr.βa.ˈto.rjo]	-Jim was on his way to the observatory.
6482	**portafolio**	**portfolio**

	m [por.ta.ˈfo.ljo]		Trae un portafolio lleno de clientes. -She brings a full portfolio of clients with her.
6483	**colecta**	**collection**	
	f [ko.ˈlek̚.ta]		Solo estamos haciendo una colecta para él. -We're just having a collection for him.
6484	**devorar**	**devour**	
	vb [de.βo.ˈrar]		Debe devorar el alma de sus víctimas. -He must devour the souls of his victims.
6485	**seducción**	**seduction**	
	f [se.ðuk.ˈsjõn]		Esta parte de la seducción es bastante sencilla. -This part of the seduction is quite simple, really.
6486	**hachís**	**hash**	
	m [a.ˈtʃis]		Sí, tienen bastante hachís dentro. -Yes, they've got quite a lot of hash in them.
6487	**odisea**	**odyssey**	
	f [o.ði.ˈse.a]		Para muchos de ellos la odisea culmina en tragedia. -For many of them, the odyssey ends in tragedy.
6488	**concursante**	**competing; contestant**	
	adj; m/f [kõŋ.kur.ˈsãn̪.te]		Yo seré el concursante, preséntame. -I'll be the contestant, you bring me out.
6489	**clon**	**clone**	
	m[ˈklõn]		El clon necesita acceso total a la memoria. -The clone needs full memory access.
6490	**gratificante**	**gratifying**	
	adj [gra.ti.fi.ˈkãn̪.te]		Este es un avance gratificante que debe mantenerse. -This is a gratifying development that must be maintained.
6491	**gestión**	**paperwork, management**	
	f [xɛs.ˈtjõn]		Las autoridades municipales se encargan de su gestión. -The authorities of the local commune are responsible for managing them.
6492	**pleito**	**lawsuit**	
	m [ˈplei̯.to]		Ganaste cinco millones de dólares en un pleito. -You won $5 million in a lawsuit.
6493	**aspiración**	**breathing, aspiration**	
	f [as.pi.ra.ˈsjõn]		Nuestra generación tiene el privilegio de cumplir esta aspiración. -It is the privilege of our generation to fulfill this aspiration.
6494	**arado**	**plow**	
	m [a.ˈra.ðo]		Es un nuevo tipo de arado. -It's a new type of plow.
6495	**calidez**	**warmth**	
	f [ka.ˈli.ðes]		Pronto conocerás la calidez de nuestro abrazo. -Soon you will know the warmth of our embrace.
6496	**denso**	**thick**	
	adj [ˈdẽn.so]		El problema es que el humo era demasiado denso. -The problem is the smoke was too thick.
6497	**convivir**	**live together with**	
	vb [kõm.bi.ˈβir]		Ojalá pudiera convivir con tu madre. -I wish that I could live together with your mother.
6498	**radiografía**	**radiography**	

f

[ra.ðjo.ɣra.ˈfi.a]

Dicen tener tuberculosis y quieren una radiografía diaria.
-They claim to have tuberculosis and want to be X-rayed daily.

6499 hojalata   **tin**

f

[o.xa.ˈla.ta]

Mira, esto no es otra cosa que hojalata inservible.
-Look, 'tis but worthless tin.

6500 primicia   **scoop**

f

[pri.ˈmi.sja]

Obtendré la primicia del siglo yo solita.
-I'll grab the scoop of the century all by myself.

6501 dialecto   **dialect**

m

[dja.ˈlek̚.to]

Conozco los límites del dialecto local.
-I know the limits of the local dialect.

6502 mojado   **wet**

adj

[mo.ˈxa.ðo]

Asegurémonos de no dejar esto mojado.
-Let's make sure not to let this wet.

6503 conducción   **driving**

f

[kõn̪.duk.ˈsjõn]

Te estoy multando por exceso de velocidad y conducción temeraria.
-I'm citing you for speeding and reckless driving.

6504 extremista   **extreme; extremist**

adj; m/f

[ɛks.tre.ˈmis.ta]

Yo solo pienso que esto suena algo extremista.
-I just think it sounds a bit extreme.

6505 mortalidad   **mortality**

f

[mor.ta.li.ˈðað]

Supongo que solo necesitaba recordar su mortalidad.
-Guess he just needed to be reminded of his mortality.

6506 izar   **hoist**

vb

[i.ˈsar]

Necesitas dos manos para izar los embalajes.
-You need two hands to hoist the crates.

6507 exageración   **exaggeration**

f

[ɛk.sa.xɛ.ra.ˈsjõn]

Todos los días sería una exageración.
-Every day would be an exaggeration.

6508 heroísmo   **heroism**

m

[ɛ.ro.ˈiş.mo]

El verdadero heroísmo se define por el sacrificio.
-True heroism is defined by sacrifice.

6509 cochera   **garage (LA), depot**

f

[ko.ˈʧɛ.ra]

No pude salir de mi cochera porque había un vehículo en medio del camino.
-I couldn't get out of my garage because there was a car in the way.

6510 fundamento   **foundation**

m

[fũn̪.da.ˈmẽn̪.to]

Las matemáticas son el fundamento de todas las ciencias.
-Mathematics are the foundation of all sciences.

6511 supervisar   **supervise**

vb

[su.pɛr.βi.ˈsar]

El moderador del sitio debe supervisar las publicaciones.
-The site moderator should supervise postings.

6512 vertedero   **garbage dump**

m

[bɛr.te.ˈðɛ.ro]

Lo he encontrado cerca del vertedero.
-I found it near the garbage dump.

6513 unánime   **unanimous**

adj

[u.ˈna.ni.me]

Te dije que necesitábamos un voto unánime.
-I told you we needed a unanimous vote.

6514 paladar   **palate**

m
[pa.la.ˈðar]

Tenemos que trabajar para refinar tu paladar.
-We have got to work on refining your palate.

6515 auricular

adj; m
[au̯.ri.ku.ˈlar]

auricular; headset

Este es el auricular de comunicación que verán en muchos trajes espaciales.
-This is the communication headset you'll see on lots of space suits.

6516 carrusel

m
[ka.ru.ˈsɛl]

carousel

Estábamos en el carrusel del parque.
-We were on the carousel in the park.

6517 sorteo

m
[sor.ˈte.o]

raffle

Ellos hicieron un sorteo aquí.
-The made a raffle here.

6518 asteroide

m
[as.tɛ.ˈroi̯.ðe]

asteroid

Este asteroide pasó cerca de la Tierra.
-This asteroid passed close to Earth.

6519 estrangular

vb
[ɛs.trãŋ.gu.ˈlar]

strangle

Creo que alguien está intentando estrangularme.
-I think someone's trying to strangle me.

6520 cuatrocientos

num[kwa.tro.ˈsjẽn̪.tos]

four hundred

Esta biblioteca tiene más de cuatrocientos años. -This library has existed for more than four hundred years.

6521 timidez

f
[ti.ˈmi.ðes]

shyness

Tiene la profunda timidez del verdadero artista.
-He has the profound shyness of the true artist.

6522 recompensar

vb
[re.kõm.pẽn.ˈsar]

reward

No puedes recompensar esa clase de comportamiento.
-You can't reward that kind of behavior.

6523 clímax

m
[ˈkli.maks]

climax

Representa el clímax de sus búsquedas.
-It represents the climax of his searches.

6524 comarca

f
[ko.ˈmar.ka]

region

Existen multitud de tesoros escondidos por la comarca.
-There are many treasures hidden throughout the region.

6525 hambruna

f
[ãm.ˈbru.na]

famine

Si llueve ahora, habrá hambruna.
-If it rains now, there'll be a famine.

6526 meca

f
[ˈme.ka]

mecca

Viena también es una meca para los amantes del chocolate.
-Vienna is also a mecca for chocolate lovers.

6527 chorro

m
[ˈtʃo.ro]

stream

Puede que observe un pequeño chorro o gota de fluido.
-You may see a small stream or drop of fluid.

6528 incondicional

adj; m/f
[ĩŋ.kõn̪.di.sjo.ˈnal]

unconditional; stalwart

Ello es algo que consideramos prioridad incondicional.
-That is something that we consider to be an unconditional priority.

6529 marisco

m
[ma.ˈris.ko]

shellfish

Bueno... qué desperdicio de marisco.
-Well... that's a waste of shellfish.

6530 ribera

riverbank

	f		Ellos irán a la ribera a reunirse en el bosque esta noche.
	[ri.ˈβɛ.ra]		-They'll go to the riverbank and gather in the woods tonight.

6531 desapercibido — **unnoticed**
adj
[de.sa.pɛr.si.ˈβi.ðo]
No quiero que el trabajo duro de personas importantes pase desapercibido.
-I don't want the hard work of you important people to go unnoticed.

6532 psicosis — **psychosis**
f
[si.ˈko.sis]
No, estás alimentando su psicosis.
-No, you're feeding into his psychosis.

6533 hepatitis — **hepatitis**
f
[e.pa.ˈti.tis]
Se ha puesto en marcha una campaña de tratamiento de la hepatitis viral.
-A viral hepatitis treatment programme is currently underway.

6534 flan — **flan**
m
[ˈflãn]
Amo las natillas, pero odio el flan.
-I love custard, but I hate flan.

6535 afición — **hobby, fans**
f
[a.fi.ˈsjõn]
Lo importante es tener tu propia afición.
-The important thing is to have your own hobby.

6536 insaciable — **insatiable**
adj
[ĭn.sa.ˈsja.βle]
Su insaciable curiosidad será su muerte.
-His insatiable curiosity will be the death of him.

6537 capitular — **capitulate; town hall**
vb; adj
[ka.pi.tu.ˈlar]
No podemos capitular en la guerra del crimen.
-We cannot capitulate in the war on crime.

6538 trinar — **chirp, be very angry**
vb
[tri.ˈnar]
Esa cosa trinaba día y noche.
-That thing chirped night and day.

6539 mora — **blackberry**
f
[ˈmo.ra]
Te traje té y panecillos de mora.
-I brought you tea and blackberry scones.

6540 turba — **mob**
f
[ˈtur.βa]
Odiaría vernos linchados por una turba de porristas airados.
-I'd hate to see us lynched by an angry mob of cheerleaders.

6541 controversia — **controversy**
f
[kõn.tro.ˈβɛr.sja]
Si queremos pasión, necesitamos controversia.
-If we want passion, we need controversy.

6542 justificación — **justification**
f
[xus.ti.fi.ka.ˈsjõn]
No existe justificación para esa dilación.
-There is no justification for such a delay.

6543 escéptico — **skeptic; skeptic**
adj; m
[ɛs.ˈsep̚.ti.ko]
No puedo evitar ser un escéptico.
-I can't help it if I'm skeptical.

6544 controlador — **controlling; controller**
adj; m
[kõn.tro.la.ˈðor]
Podías identificar un controlador y neutralizarlo.
-You could identify a controller and neutralize it.

6545 inoportuno — **inopportune**
adj
[i.no.por.ˈtu.no]
Has llegado en un momento bastante inoportuno.
-You've come at an extremely inopportune time.

6546 descartar — **discard**

	vb	
	[dɛs.kar.ˈtar]	Mi imaginación no me permite descartar la idea.
		-My imagination just won't let me discard the idea.
6547	**futbolista**	**football player**
	m/f	
	[fut.βo.ˈlis.ta]	Un joven futbolista debe tener la posibilidad de equivocarse para crecer.
		-A young football player must have the chance to make mistakes to grow up.
6548	**arqueología**	**archeology**
	f	
	[ar.ke.o.lo.ˈxi.a]	La arqueología revela los secretos del pasado.
		-Archeology reveals the secrets of the past.
6549	**lácteo**	**dairy; lactose**
	adj; m	
	[ˈlak̚.te.o]	No puedo imaginar que exista mucho peligro en el centro lácteo.
		-I can't imagine there being much danger at the dairy hub.
6550	**ciénaga**	**swamp**
	f	
	[ˈsje.na.ɣa]	Vi esa ciénaga cuando venía aquí.
		-I saw this swamp when he came here.
6551	**guerrillero**	**guerrilla; guerrilla**
	adj; m[gɛ.ri.ˈjɛ.ro]	Perdí al hijo que se convirtió en guerrillero. -I lost the son who became a guerrilla.
6552	**extraoficial**	**unofficial**
	adj	
	[ɛks.tra.o.fi.ˈsjal]	Lo que sea que esté haciendo es extraoficial.
		-Whatever he's doing is unofficial.
6553	**enredar(se)**	**tangle, confuse, mess with (ES)**
	vb	
	[ɛ̃n.re.ˈðar]	Lake hizo algo para enredar el jurado en su caso.
		-Lake did something to mess with the jury on his case.
6554	**renovación**	**renovation**
	f	
	[re.no.βa.ˈsjõn]	Aún quiero colaborar con esta renovación.
		-I still want to chip in on this renovation.
6555	**puñalada**	**stab**
	f	
	[pu.ɲa.ˈla.ða]	Es una puñalada rápida al corazón.
		-It's a quick stab in the heart.
6556	**imprescindible**	**essential**
	adj	
	[ĩm.prɛs.sĩn̪.ˈdi.βle]	Es imprescindible realizar un informe sobre las lenguas.
		-It is essential for a report on languages to be drawn up.
6557	**multimillonario**	**multimillionaire**
	adj	
	[mul̪.ti.mi.jo.ˈna.rjo]	El problema fue que el productor era un multimillonario.
		-The problem was that the producer was a multimillionaire.
6558	**inseparable**	**inseparable**
	adj	
	[ĩn.se.pa.ˈra.βle]	Desde entonces, Pancracio se convirtió en su compañero inseparable.
		-Ever since, Pancracio became his inseparable partner.
6559	**tocadiscos**	**record player**
	m	
	[to.ka.ˈðis.kos]	Tienes un tocadiscos en tu habitación.
		-You have a record player in your room.
6560	**emblema**	**emblem**
	m	
	[ɛ̃m.ˈble.ma]	Era el emblema del emperador.
		-It was the emblem of the emperor.
6561	**disimular**	**disguise**
	vb	
	[di.si.mu.ˈlar]	Lo necesitaba para disimular mi voz.
		-I needed that to disguise my voice.
6562	**pastelería**	**patisserie**

f
[pas.te.lɛ.ˈri.a]

Hay una pastelería justo al otro lado de la calle.
-There is a patisserie just across the street.

6563 descendencia

f
[dɛs.sẽn̩.ˈdẽn.sja]

offspring

Los machos estaban involucrados en proteger la descendencia.
-The males got involved in protecting offspring.

6564 sumergir(se)

vb
[su.mɛr.ˈxir]

immerse

Pero necesita suficiente como para sumergir un cuerpo.
-But he needs enough in which to immerse a body.

6565 próstata

f
[ˈpros.ta.ta]

prostate

Desearía tener un mejor diagnóstico sobre mi próstata.
-I wish I had a better prognosis on my prostate.

6566 integral

adj
[ĩn̩.te.ˈɣral]

comprehensive

Nuestra forma de abordar la inmigración es integral.
-Our approach to migration is comprehensive.

6567 cuesta

f[ˈkwɛs.ta]

slope

Laurila quiere sorprenderlos en esa cuesta. -Laurila wants to surprise them on that slope.

6568 postrar(se)

vb
[pos.ˈtrar]

prostrate

No me postraré ante ustedes para conservar mi cargo.
-I will not prostrate myself before you to keep my position.

6569 colaborador

adj; m
[ko.la.βo.ra.ˈðor]

cooperative; contributor, co-worker

Ha sido periodista y colaborador de varios periódicos.
-He has been a journalist and contributor to several periodicals.

6570 stock

m
[ˈs.tokk]

stock

Necesitábamos su nombre para vender stock.
-We needed his name to sell the stock.

6571 contramaestre

m
[kõn̩.tra.ma.ˈɛs.tre]

boatswain

El contramaestre ordena a todos aligerarla.
-The boatswain calls all hands to lighten it.

6572 elocuente

adj
[e.lo.ˈkwẽn̩.te]

eloquent

Ahora se disculpa por no ser elocuente.
-Now he's excusing himself for not being eloquent.

6573 coleccionar

vb
[ko.lɛk.sjo.ˈnar]

collect

Mi padre amaba coleccionar estos cuando estaba vivo.
-My father loved to collect these when he was alive.

6574 fijación

f
[fi.xa.ˈsjõn]

fixation

En casos extremos esa fijación es común.
-In extreme cases, such a fixation is common.

6575 dinámico

adj
[di.ˈna.mi.ko]

dynamic

Es importante mantener un enfoque dinámico.
-It is important to keep an approach dynamic.

6576 turbar

vb
[tur.ˈβar]

disturb

Lamento, una vez más, turbar tu sueño.
-I am sorry, once again, to disturb your slumber.

6577 plutonio

m
[plu.ˈto.njo]

plutonium

Ese plutonio se convertirá en combustible para centrales nucleares civiles.
-That plutonium will be converted to fuel for civil nuclear power plants.

6578 descompuesto

broken down

adj
[dɛs.kõm.ˈpwɛs.to]

Pensé que el baño estaba descompuesto.
-I thought the toilet was broken.

6579 fortalecer

vb
[for.ta.le.ˈsɛr]

strengthen

Debería fortalecer la vigilancia y los mecanismos de presentación de informes.
-It should strengthen the monitoring and reporting mechanisms.

6580 astro

m
[ˈas.tro]

star

Se quedó mirando al astro celestial hasta que lo dejó ciego.
-He stared up at the heavenly body until it made him blind.

6581 impenetrable

adj
[ĩm.pe.nɛ.ˈtra.βle]

impenetrable

Es completamente impenetrable al mundo exterior.
-It is completely impenetrable to the outside world.

6582 conjurar

vb
[kõŋ.xu.ˈrar]

conjure

No puedo conjurar nada para mí mismo.
-Can't conjure a thing for me.

6583 paternidad

f
[pa.tɛr.ni.ˈðað]

paternity

Será muy fácil establecer la paternidad.
-It'll be easy enough to establish paternity.

6584 candidatura

f
[kãn.di.ða.ˈtu.ra]

candidacy

He vuelto a repasar su discurso de candidatura.
-I took another pass at your candidacy speech.

6585 tifus

m
[ˈti.fus]

typhus

Hemos tenido 4.000 muertes por inanición y tifus.
-We've had 4,000 deaths by starvation and typhus.

6586 publicitario

adj; m
[pu.βli.si.ˈta.rjo]

advertising; publicist

También podríamos hablar del efecto publicitario.
-We could also speak about the advertising effect.

6587 astillero

m
[as.ti.ˈʝɛ.ro]

shipyard

Todavía es posible salvar este astillero.
-It is still possible to save this shipyard.

6588 alarmante

adj
[a.lar.ˈmãn.te]

alarming

Esto es alarmante y exige acción inmediata.
-This is alarming and calls for urgent action.

6589 ruin

adj
[ˈrwĩn]

despicable

Les dije que eras demasiado ruin como para asustarte.
-I told them you were too mean to be afraid.

6590 delincuencia

f
[de.lĩŋ.ˈkwẽn.sja]

delinquency

Esta es una predicción de la delincuencia suburbana en París.
-This is a forecast on Paris suburban delinquency.

6591 accesible

adj
[ak.se.ˈsi.βle]

accessible

Esta información será accesible al público.
-This information shall be accessible to the public.

6592 facilitar

vb
[fa.si.li.ˈtar]

facilitate

Esos esfuerzos son necesarios porque debemos facilitar las conversaciones.
-Such efforts are called for because of the need to facilitate the talks.

6593 checo

adj; m
[ˈtʃe.ko]

Czech; Czech person

Propongo que decida el pueblo checo.
-I say, let the Czech people decide.

6594 hábitat

habitat

	m		Estamos haciendo escaneos para evaluar el potencial de este hábitat.
	[ˈa.βi.tat]		-We're conducting scans to evaluate the potential of this habitat.

6595 **incurable** — **incurable**

adj
[ĩŋ.ku.ˈra.βle]

Esta enfermedad contagiosa viene afligiendo a la humanidad desde tiempos inmemoriales y sigue siendo incurable.
-This contagious disease has afflicted mankind since time immemorial and it remains incurable.

6596 **confederación** — **confederation**

f
[kõm̩.fe.ðɛ.ra.ˈsjõn]

El Reino funciona en forma muy semejante a una confederación.
-The Kingdom functioned much like a confederation.

6597 **incontable** — **countless**

adj
[ĩŋ.kõn̩.ˈta.βle]

Ha estado nevando por aquí un incontable número de veces.
-It had been snowing here countless times.

6598 **dichoso** — **happy**

adj
[di.ˈtʃo.so]

En este dichoso mundo hay más soledad que cualquier otra cosa.
-In this happy world, there is more loneliness than anything else.

6599 **adoptivo** — **adoptive**

adj
[a.ðop̚.ˈti.βo]

No tienen un hogar adoptivo donde recuperarse.
-They don't have an adoptive home in which to recover.

6600 **canica** — **marble**

f
[ka.ˈni.ka]

Parece una común y ordinaria canica.
-It looks like a common, ordinary marble.

6601 **confín** — **border**

m
[kõm̩.ˈfĩn]

Por muchos siglos, este fue el confín del mundo conocido.
-For many centuries, this was the end of the known world.

6602 **andante** — **walking**

adj
[ãn̩.ˈdãn̩.te]

No tomo consejos de un bolso andante.
-I'm not taking advice from a walking purse.

6603 **aritmético** — **arithmetic; arithmetician**

adj; m
[a.rit̚.ˈmɛ.ti.ko]

Sin embargo, esta cifra contenía un error aritmético.
-However, this figure contained an arithmetical error.

6604 **electo** — **elected; elected member**

adj; m
[e.ˈlek̚.to]

Soy un representante electo del pueblo.
-I'm an elected representative of the people.

6605 **dióxido** — **dioxide**

m
[ˈdjok.si.ðo]

Estos países tienen derecho a cobrar sus cuotas de dióxido de carbono.
-These countries are entitled to cash in on their carbon dioxide quotas.

6606 **colesterol** — **cholesterol**

m
[ko.lɛs.tɛ.ˈrol]

Se recomienda una dieta saludable, baja en colesterol.
-A healthy, low-cholesterol diet is recommended.

6607 **angustiar(se)** — **upset**

vb
[ãŋ.gus.ˈtjar]

No sé, pero estaba angustiada.
-I don't know, but she was upset.

6608 **cautiverio** — **captivity**

m
[kau̯.ti.ˈβɛ.rjo]

Hicieron un híbrido genético, lo criaron en cautiverio.
-You made a genetic hybrid, raised it in captivity.

6609 **diámetro** — **diameter**

m
[ˈdja.mɛ.tro]

El diámetro máximo es un poco más de un kilómetro.
-Maximum diameter is a little over a kilometer.

6610 **sureño** — **southern; southerner**

adj; m
[suˈre.ɲo]
Ese diputado sureño es tu mayor obstáculo.
-That southern congressman is your biggest obstacle.

6611 caucho — **rubber**

m
[ˈkau̯.ʧo]
Las importaciones incluyen caucho, madera y productos pesqueros.
-Exports include rubber, timber, and fisheries products.

6612 descalzo — **barefoot**

adj
[dɛsˈkal.so]
Él estaba descalzo cuando le recogimos.
-He was barefoot when we picked him up.

6613 baboso — **slimy**

adj
[baˈβo.so]
También estoy pegajoso, sucio, sudoroso y baboso.
-I'm also sticky, dirty, sweaty, and slimy.

6614 esquivar — **dodge**

vb
[ɛs.kiˈβar]
Sabía cómo esquivar a mis sombras.
-I knew how I might dodge my shadows.

6615 sumar — **add**

vb
[suˈmar]
Supongo que finalmente está empezando a sumar.
-I guess it's finally starting to add up.

6616 incentivo — **incentive**

m
[ĩn.sẽ̝ˈti.βo]
55 millones de dólares es un enorme incentivo.
-$55 million is a lot of incentive.

6617 excusado — **superfluous; restroom**

adj; m
[ɛk.suˈsa.ðo]
Alguien te llama desde el excusado.
-Somebody's calling your name from the toilet.

6618 primordial — **primary**

adj
[pri.morˈðjal]
Esta seguirá siendo nuestra preocupación primordial.
-This will continue to be our primary preoccupation.

6619 privilegiar — **grant a privilege to**

vb
[pri.βi.leˈxjar]
Para dejarlo claro, queremos privilegiar el principio de la preferencia.
-To put it plainly, we wish to favor the principle of preference.

6620 predecible — **predictable**

adj
[pre.ðeˈsi.βle]
Buscamos una cooperación estructurada, predecible y exigente.
-We are looking for a structured, predictable, and demanding partnership.

6621 conversión — **conversion**

f
[kõm.bɛrˈsjõn]
Esta conversión me parece muy sospechosa.
-This conversion strikes me as highly dubious.

6622 monedero — **purse**

m
[mo.ne.ˈðɛ.ro]
Encontré 20 dólares extra en mi monedero.
-I found an extra $20 in my purse.

6623 viñedo — **vineyard**

m
[biˈɲe.ðo]
Pidió que esparcieran sus cenizas en el viñedo.
-He asked that his ashes be scattered in the vineyard.

6624 malicia — **malice**

f
[maˈli.sja]
Porque tendría mucho miedo de su malicia.
-Because I would be so afraid of your malice.

6625 resfrío — **cold**

m
[rɛsˈfri.o]
No quiero que agarres un resfrío.
-I don't want you to get a cold.

6626 terrateniente — **landowner**

		m/f	Soy un terrateniente respetado con unos empleados leales.
		[tɛ.ra.te.ˈnjɛ̃n̪.te]	-I'm a respectable landowner, with a staff that's loyal.

6627 voltaje — voltage

m

[bol̪.ˈta.xe]

La corriente es directa, pero el voltaje varía.

-The current is direct, but the voltage varies.

6628 panfleto — pamphlet

m

[pãɱ.ˈflɛ.to]

Quizá deberías escribirla un panfleto o algo así.

-Maybe you should write her a pamphlet or something.

6629 alardear — boast

vb

[a.lar.ðe.ˈar]

Las chicas van a este show para alardear sobre sus novios.

-Girls go on the show to boast about their boyfriends.

6630 jazmín — jasmine

m

[xaṣ.ˈmĩn]

Es encantador, el aroma a jazmín.

-It is lovely, the scent of jasmine.

6631 faja — sash

f

[ˈfa.xa]

Este cordón es una faja sagrada.

-This rope is a sacred sash.

6632 metropolitano — urban; subway

adj; m

[mɛ.tro.po.li.ˈta.no]

Actualmente, la consejería organiza una serie de conferencias sobre el transporte metropolitano urbano.

-The ministry is currently supporting a series of conferences on urban metropolitan transport.

6633 peaje — toll

m

[pe.ˈa.xe]

Cada kilómetro de vía que recorre un tren conlleva un peaje obligatorio sin límite superior.

-There is a mandatory toll with no upper limit for every kilometer of track that a train covers.

6634 herejía — heresy

f

[ɛ.re.ˈxi.a]

Se está juzgando una herejía científica aquí.

-It is scientific heresy that is being tried here.

6635 agresor — attacking; attacker

adj; m

[a.ɣre.ˈsor]

Ángela tampoco puede identificar a su agresor.

-Angela can't identify her attacker, either.

6636 contracción — contraction

f

[kõn̪.trak.ˈsjõn]

Ahora debe empujar en cada contracción.

-Now, you must push with each contraction.

6637 raptar — kidnap

vb

[rap̚.ˈtar]

No sé nada de un plan para raptar a nadie.

-I don't know anything about no plot to kidnap nobody.

6638 cautela — caution

f

[kau̯.ˈte.la]

Solo la cautela los mantiene vivos.

-Only by caution do they remain alive.

6639 distribuir — distribute

vb

[dis.tri.ˈβwir]

Necesitamos algo que podamos distribuir a gran escala.

-We need something we can distribute on a mass scale.

6640 ozono — ozone

m

[o.ˈso.no]

No deberías haber intentado robar nuestro ozono.

-You shouldn't have tried to steal our ozone.

6641 virtuoso — virtuous; virtuoso

adj; m
[bir.ˈtwo.so]

La educación propicia un ciclo virtuoso de desarrollo.
-Education leads to a virtuous cycle of development.

6642 bordado — **embroidery**
m
[bor.ˈða.ðo]

Tengo un bordado que quiero terminar.
-I have some embroidery I'd like to attend to.

6643 promotor — **promoter**
m
[pro.mo.ˈtor]

Como promotor exclusivo tengo derecho a organizar partidos.
-As your exclusive promoter, I have the right to arrange matches.

6644 pichón — **squab**
m[pi.ˈʧõn]

Me gusta casi cualquier cosa excepto el sushi y pichón. -I like pretty much anything, except sushi and squab.

6645 escurridizo — **evasive, slippery**
adj
[ɛs.ku.ri.ˈði.so]

Eres igual de escurridizo que una anguila.
-You're slippery as an ell.

6646 perjudicial — **harmful**
adj
[pɛr.xu.ði.ˈsjal]

Sería muy perjudicial para la criatura.
-It would be very harmful to the child.

6647 deforme — **misshapen**
adj
[de.ˈfor.me]

Y el diámetro es ancho y deforme.
-And the diameter is wide and misshapen.

6648 eludir — **avoid**
vb
[e.lu.ˈðir]

Y sabiéndolo, la podremos eludir.
-And in knowing that, we can avoid her.

6649 hamaca — **hammock**
f
[a.ˈma.ka]

Hay una hamaca con mosquitero incorporado.
-There is a hammock with mosquito net built-in.

6650 acosar — **harass**
vb
[a.ko.ˈsar]

Claro, son tan buenos amigos que decidió acosar a su esposa.
-Sure, you are such good friends you decided to harass his wife.

6651 pincel — **paint brush**
m
[pĩn.ˈsɛl]

Leslie me dice que eres bueno con el pincel.
-Leslie tells me you're good with a paintbrush.

6652 insistente — **insistent**
adj
[ĩn.sis.ˈtẽn̯.te]

Bueno, fue bastante insistente por teléfono.
-Well, you were rather insistent on the phone.

6653 festivo — **festive, holiday**
adj
[fɛs.ˈti.βo]

Pero bueno, técnicamente es festivo.
-But I mean, it is technically a holiday.

6654 soberbio — **proud**
adj
[so.ˈβɛr.βjo]

Y Michael comprendió que él también había sido demasiado soberbio.
-And Michael realized that he, too, had been too proud.

6655 ráfaga — **burst**
f
[ˈra.fa.ɣa]

Sin cambios desde la última ráfaga.
-No change since the recent burst.

6656 alquitrán — **tar**
m
[al.ki.ˈtrãn]

El río parece lleno de alquitrán.
-The river looks as if it's full of tar.

6657 escaso — **lacking**

adj
[ɛs.ˈka.so]

La vida nocturna es un poco escasa.
-The night life's a little lacking.

6658 indirecto   **indirect**

adj
[ĩn.di.ˈrek.to]

El sistema de calentamiento puede ser directo, indirecto o eléctrico.
-The heating system may be direct, indirect or electric.

6659 avispa   **wasp**

f
[a.ˈβis.pa]

Es como tener una avispa en el vehículo.
-It's like having a wasp in the car.

6660 contraataque   **counterattack**

m[kõn.tra.a.ˈta.ke]

Sus hombres van a estar en primera fila en nuestro contraataque. -You men will be the first wave in our counterattack.

6661 ofrecimiento   **offer**

m
[o.fre.si.ˈmjẽn.to]

Le agradezco su ofrecimiento de enviarme más información.
-Thank you for your offer to send me more information.

6662 compostura   **composure**

f
[kõm.pos.ˈtu.ra]

Debo admitir que admiro tu compostura.
-I must say, I admire your composure.

6663 calumnia   **slander**

f
[ka.ˈlũm.nja]

La calumnia es una grave infracción.
-Slander is a serious offense.

6664 saga   **saga**

f
[ˈsa.ɣa]

Espero que termines con esta saga.
-I hope you put an end to this saga.

6665 toser   **cough**

vb
[to.ˈsɛr]

El vino era tan fuerte que me hizo toser.
-The wine was so strong it makes me cough.

6666 impar   **odd**

adj
[ĩm.ˈpar]

Hay un número impar en el registro telefónico.
-There's an odd number in the phone record.

6667 pantufla   **slipper**

f
[pãn.ˈtu.fla]

Éramos como dos perros luchando por una vieja pantufla.
-We were like two dogs fighting over an old slipper.

6668 impotencia   **impotence**

f
[ĩm.po.ˈtẽn.sja]

Solo me embarga una sensación de impotencia.
-I'm only seized with a feeling of impotence.

6669 devolución   **refund**

f
[de.βo.lu.ˈsjõn]

Parece que podremos otorgarte una devolución.
-It looks like we will be able to get you a refund.

6670 coherente   **coherent**

adj
[ko.ɛ.ˈrẽn.te]

También nos preocupaba dar un formato coherente al informe.
-We were also concerned to give the report a coherent form.

6671 albañil   **builder**

m/f
[al.βa.ˈɲil]

Si realmente quieres vivir aquí, puedo pagarle a un albañil.
-If you really want to live here, I can pay for a builder.

6672 simbólico   **symbolic**

adj
[sĩm.ˈbo.li.ko]

Obviamente es simbólico, actúa a dos niveles.
-Obviously, it's symbolic, it works on both levels.

6673 ilimitado   **unlimited**

| | adj | |
| | [i.li.mi.'ta.ðo] | |

Tendrás un torrente casi ilimitado de gas natural.
-You'll have an almost unlimited stream of natural gas.

6674 **residencial** — **residential**

adj
[re.si.ðẽn.'sjal]

Así es como visualizaríamos una aplicación residencial.
-This is how we would envision a residential application.

6675 **aplaudir** — **applaud**

vb
[ap̚.lau̯.'ðir]

Quiero aplaudir sus esfuerzos en este sentido.
-I want to applaud her efforts to that end.

6676 **incompleto** — **incomplete**

adj[ĩŋ.kõm.'plɛ.to]

Pero como ha mencionado, está incompleto. -But as you pointed out, it's incomplete.

6677 **acechar** — **stalk**

vb
[a.se.'tʃar]

Luke lo contrató para acechar a tu madre.
-Luke hired him to stalk your mother.

6678 **castellano** — **Spanish; Castilian Spanish**

adj; m
[kas.te.'ja.no]

Olvidé como lo dicen en castellano.
-I forget how they say it in Spanish.

6679 **duna** — **dune**

f
['du.na]

Estoy seguro de que nuestro hijo estará detrás de esa duna.
-I'm sure your son's on the other side of that dune.

6680 **termómetro** — **thermometer**

m
[tɛr.'mo.mɛ.tro]

El termómetro registró menos diez la noche pasada.
-The thermometer registered minus ten last night.

6681 **intromisión** — **meddling**

f
[ĩn.tro.mi.'sjõn]

Espero que no te moleste mi intromisión.
-I hope you don't mind my meddling.

6682 **tirante** — **tense**

adj
[ti.'rãn.te]

La situación en ese lugar era visiblemente tirante.
-The situation there was visibly tense.

6683 **consistente** — **consistent**

adj
[kõn.sis.'tẽn.te]

Es consistente con todos sus síntomas.
-It's consistent with all of her symptoms.

6684 **metralleta** — **submachine gun**

f
[mɛ.tra.'jɛ.ta]

Deme su metralleta y cargadores, soldado.
-Give me your submachine gun and clips, private.

6685 **reo** — **prisoner**

m
['re.o]

En cuanto entregue al reo volveré.
-As soon as I deliver the prisoner I'll return.

6686 **sombrilla** — **parasol**

f
[sõm.'bri.ja]

Esta sombrilla es más que una declaración de moda.
-This parasol's more than just a fashion statement.

6687 **complejidad** — **complexity**

f
[kõm.ple.xi.'ðað]

Debemos tratar de reducir su complejidad.
-We have to try to reduce its complexity.

6688 **calcio** — **calcium**

m
['kal.sjo]

Tiré mucho jugo de naranja con calcio.
-I have thrown back a lot of orange juice with calcium.

6689 **leucemia** — **leukemia**

f
[leu̯.ˈse.mja]

Mi hermana tuvo leucemia mientras crecimos.
-My sister had leukemia when I was growing up.

6690 encrucijada — crossroads

f
[ɛ̃ŋ.kru.si.ˈxa.ða]

Parece que estamos ante una encrucijada.
-It looks like we are at a crossroads.

6691 manifestar(se) — express; demonstrate, show up

vb; vbr
[ma.ni.fɛs.ˈtar]

China desea manifestar su agradecimiento a todos ellos.
-China wishes to express its thanks to all of them.

6692 áspero — rough

adj[ˈas.pɛ.ro]

El rostro de Tom está áspero porque debe afeitarse. -Tom's face feels rough because he needs to shave.

6693 activista — activist

m/f
[ak̚.ti.ˈβis.ta]

Fui un periodista activista desde muy joven.
-I was a journalist activist at an early age.

6694 lirio — lily

m
[ˈli.rjo]

Intentaremos crear una etiqueta para una limonada con sabor a lirio.
-We will try to create a label for a lemonade with a lily flavor.

6695 desvanecer(se) — fade

vb
[dɛs̠.βa.ne.ˈsɛr]

Es solo que no puede desvanecerse así en el aire.
-It just can't vanish into thin air.

6696 pereza — laziness

f
[pɛ.ˈre.sa]

La causa principal de su fracaso es la pereza.
-The primary cause of his failure is laziness.

6697 tramo — stretch

m
[ˈtra.mo]

Parece que decidieron nadar el último tramo.
-Looks like they decided to swim the last stretch.

6698 trébol — clover

m
[ˈtre.βol]

La flor oficial es el trébol rojo.
-The state flower is the red clover.

6699 desconcertado — bewildered

adj
[dɛs.kõn.sɛr.ˈta.ðo]

Lo cierto es, tío, que estaba confuso y ligeramente desconcertado.
-The truth is, mate, I was confused and slightly bewildered.

6700 eficacia — effectiveness

f
[e.fi.ˈka.sja]

Un año no bastará para determinar su eficacia.
-One year will not be enough to establish its effectiveness.

6701 ginecólogo — gynecologist

m
[xi.ne.ˈko.lo.ɣo]

Por cierto, soy un ginecólogo jubilado.
-By the way, I'm a retired gynecologist.

6702 atlas — atlas

m
[ˈat̚.las]

Había publicado un atlas detallado del cuerpo humano.
-He'd published a detailed atlas of the human body.

6703 detonar — detonate

vb
[dɛ.to.ˈnar]

Los misiles nucleares no van a detonar con el impacto.
-The nuke will not detonate at impact.

6704 barrido — sweep

m
[ba.ˈri.ðo]

Ese trabajo a menudo incluye el barrido de calles.
-Such labor often involves sweeping the streets.

6705 soprano — soprano

	m/f	Estaba muy orgulloso de mi voz de soprano.
	[so.ˈpra.no]	-I was so proud of my soprano voice.
6706	**perforar**	**drill**
	vb	Usted no necesita perforar tantos agujeros.
	[pɛr.fo.ˈrar]	-You don't need to drill so many holes.
6707	**implante**	**implant**
	m	Imagino que tendría algún tipo de implante quirúrgico.
	[ĩm.ˈplãn̯.te]	-I imagine he had some sort of surgical implant.
6708	**deseable**	**desirable**
	adj[de.se.ˈa.βle]	Sería deseable reducir estas diferencias políticas. -It would be desirable that these political differences were reduced.
6709	**madriguera**	**den**
	f	Ella ha estado en su madriguera todo el invierno.
	[ma.ðri.ˈɣɛ.ra]	-She has been in her den the whole winter.
6710	**chillar**	**yell**
	vb	Un detenido comenzó a chillar.
	[ʧi.ˈjar]	-A prisoner began to yell.
6711	**extremidad**	**limb**
	f	La pérdida de alguna extremidad es común entre los sobrevivientes.
	[ɛks.tre.mi.ˈðað]	-The loss of a limb is common among those who survive.
6712	**apresurar(se)**	**hurry**
	vb	Bueno, estas cosas no se pueden apresurar.
	[a.pre.su.ˈrar]	-Well, you can't hurry these things.
6713	**aplazamiento**	**postponement**
	m	Esta es la finalidad del aplazamiento.
	[ap̚.la.sa.ˈmjẽn̯.to]	-That is the aim of this postponement.
6714	**silueta**	**silhouette**
	f	Tienes que definirlo por la silueta.
	[si.ˈlwɛ.ta]	-You have to define it by the silhouette.
6715	**pulmonar**	**chest**
	adj	Una enfermedad pulmonar, todos lo saben.
	[pul.mo.ˈnar]	-Chest illness, they all know it.
6716	**aerosol**	**spray**
	m	No vendemos pinturas de aerosol o marcadores a menores.
	[a.ɛ.ro.ˈsol]	-We do not sell spray paint or markers to minors.
6717	**reconsiderar**	**reconsider**
	vb	Primero tenía que reconsiderar toda la situación.
	[re.kõn.si.ðɛ.ˈrar]	-I had to reconsider the whole situation first.
6718	**tecla**	**key**
	f	Use la tecla flecha abajo para desplazarse a través de los otros archivos y directorios.
	[ˈte.kla]	-Use the down arrow key to scroll through the other files and directories.
6719	**trompa**	**trunk, horn**
	f	La trompa del elefante es la herramienta perfecta para alcanzarlos.
	[ˈtrõm.pa]	-The elephant's trunk is the perfect tool for reaching it.
6720	**puntualidad**	**punctuality**
	f	Ya sabes lo importante que es la puntualidad para él.
	[pũn̯.twa.li.ˈðað]	-You know how important punctuality is to him.
6721	**liderar**	**lead**

	vb		Quisiera liderar a un pequeño equipo de hombres.
	[li.ðɛ.ˈrar]		-I would like to lead a small team of men.
6722	**lubricante**		**lubricant**
	m		Incluso podríamos encontrar un contenedor de lubricante ahí abajo.
	[lu.βri.ˈkã̠n.te]		-We may even find a container of lubricant down there.
6723	**colgante**		**hanging; pendant**
	adj; m		Vamos a necesitar ese colgante como evidencia.
	[kol.ˈɣã̠n.te]		-We're going to need that pendant for evidence.
6724	**órale**		**wow (LA), come on (LA)**
	int		¿Acaso te importa, hombre? ¡Órale!
	[ˈo.ra.le]		-Does it matter, man? Come on!
6725	**gel**		**gel**
	m		Deberías conseguirte uno de esos antifaces de gel refrigerante.
	[ˈxɛl]		-You should get one of those eye masks with the cooling gel in.
6726	**deleite**		**delight**
	m		Permíteme expresarte mi deleite por tu felicidad.
	[de.ˈlei̯.te]		-Allow me to express my delight over your happiness.
6727	**avecinarse**		**approach**
	vbr		Tienes que prepararte para lo que pueda avecinarse.
	[a.βe.si.ˈnar.se]		-You have to prepare for what might be coming.
6728	**abrumar**		**overwhelm**
	vb		Quiero decir, eso puede abrumar a cualquiera con ansiedad.
	[a.βru.ˈmar]		-I mean, that can overwhelm anyone with anxiety.
6729	**apoderar(se)**		**authorise; take over**
	vb; vbr		Se va a apoderar del programa.
	[a.po.ðɛ.ˈrar]		-She'll take over the show.
6730	**embarcación**		**embarkation**
	f		Quiero alquilar una embarcación en agosto.
	[ẽm.bar.ka.ˈsjõn]		-I want to hire a boat in August.
6731	**legislación**		**legislation**
	f		Ahora corresponde a los agricultores cumplir la legislación.
	[le.xiṣ.la.ˈsjõn]		-It is up to farmers to follow the legislation through.
6732	**incursión**		**incursion**
	f		En la incursión también murió un soldado.
	[ĩŋ.kur.ˈsjõn]		-A soldier has also been killed in the incursion.
6733	**fealdad**		**ugliness**
	f		Había suficiente fealdad en el mundo.
	[fe.al̠.ˈdað]		-There was enough ugliness in the world.
6734	**insólito**		**unheard of**
	adj		Es inusual, pero no insólito.
	[ĩn.ˈso.li.to]		-It's unusual, but not unheard of.
6735	**dictar**		**dictate**
	vb		Entonces estaremos en mejor posición para dictar términos.
	[dik̚.ˈtar]		-Then we'll be in a better position to dictate terms.
6736	**forro**		**lining, jacket**
	m		Está en el forro de tu vestido.
	[ˈfo.ro]		-It's in the lining of your dress.
6737	**verbo**		**verb**

	m	No tienes que conjugar el verbo.
	['bɛr.βo]	-You don't have to conjugate the verb.

6738 escudero — squire

m
[ɛs.ku.'ðɛ.ro]

Gracias por hacer de nuestro escudero.
-Thank you for being our squire.

6739 automovilístico — car

adj[au̯.to.mo.βi.'lis.ti.ko]

Somos conscientes de la sensibilidad del sector automovilístico. -We are aware of the sensitivities of the car sector.

6740 hereje — heretic

m/f
[ɛ.'re.xe]

Siempre olvido que es un hereje.
-I always forget that he is a heretic.

6741 reembolso — refund

m
[re.ẽm.'bol.so]

Los abogados no nos hicieron un reembolso.
-The lawyers didn't give us a refund.

6742 regar — water, spill

vb
[re.'ɣar]

David, debes regar estas plantas.
-David, you need to water these plants.

6743 lastre — ballast

m
['las.tre]

Iré arriba a revisar el lastre.
-I'm going upstairs to check the ballast.

6744 guardacostas — coastguard

m/f
[gwar.ða.'kos.tas]

Los servicios de guardacostas tienen como objetivo principal garantizar la seguridad marítima nacional.
-The main task of coastguard services is to ensure national maritime safety.

6745 paralítico — paralytic

m
[pa.ra.'li.ti.ko]

Todo mi lado derecho se está quedando paralítico.
-My whole right side is becoming paralytic.

6746 literario — literary

adj
[li.tɛ.'ra.rjo]

Hay un término literario para esa fanáticas.
-The literary world has a term for those fanatics.

6747 evolucionar — evolve

vb
[e.βo.lu.sjo.'nar]

Necesitamos tiempo para evolucionar y adaptarnos.
-We need time to evolve and to adapt.

6748 jeringa — syringe

f
[xɛ.'r̃ĩŋ.ga]

No utilice esta jeringa y elimínela adecuadamente.
-Do not use this syringe and dispose of it properly.

6749 balneario — spa

m
[bal.ne.'a.rjo]

Nunca había podido venir a un balneario.
-I've never been able to come to a spa.

6750 mezclado — mixed

adj
[mɛs.'kla.ðo]

Tiene ese aire de mérito mezclado con desesperación.
-She's got that air of entitlement mixed with desperation.

6751 convertible — convertible; convertible (LA)

adj; m
[kõm.bɛr.'ti.βle]

Un convertible como el que necesitamos.
-A convertible, like the one we need.

6752 vector — vector

m
[bek̚.'tor]

Espero un vector de su posición.
-Waiting to get a vector on his position.

6753 sostenido — sustained

adj
[sos.te.ˈni.ðo]

Precisará un esfuerzo sostenido y muy coordinado.
-It will require a sustained and very coordinated effort.

6754 impune — **unpunished**

adj[ĭm.ˈpu.ne]

La persona violenta queda prácticamente impune. -The violent person remains practically unpunished.

6755 enchufe — **wall socket**

m
[ɛ̃n̪.ˈʧu.fe]

No metas la lengua en el enchufe.
-Don't stick your tongue in the wall socket.

6756 naturalidad — **naturalness**

f
[na.tu.ra.li.ˈðað]

El secreto de su belleza es su naturalidad.
-The secret of her beauty is her naturalness.

6757 indulgencia — **indulgence**

f
[ĭn̪.dul.ˈxɛ̃n.sja]

Han engordado por nuestra indulgencia hacia ellos.
-They've grown fat off our indulgence of them.

6758 billón — **trillion**

num
[bi.ˈɟõn]

Tenemos este billón de horas al año.
-We've got this trillion hours a year.

6759 diestro — **right-handed, skilled**

adj
[ˈdjɛs.tro]

Soy diestro, pero he cogido la bola con la izquierda.
-I'm right-handed, but I caught the ball with my left.

6760 escote — **cleavage**

m
[ɛs.ˈko.te]

Esconderemos estas cosas en nuestro escote.
-We will hide this stuff in our cleavage.

6761 óptimo — **ideal**

adj
[ˈop̚.ti.mo]

Para nosotros este programa de trabajo sería el óptimo si se aprobará en su totalidad.
-We think that this programme of work would be ideal if it were adopted in full.

6762 jerarquía — **hierarchy**

f
[xɛ.rar.ˈki.a]

En los grupos se establece rápidamente una jerarquía definida.
-When kept in groups, a defined hierarchy is quickly established.

6763 cercar — **fence**

vb
[sɛr.ˈkar]

Afortunadamente ya terminé de cercar mi potrero.
-Fortunately, I finished my pasture fence.

6764 táctico — **tactical; tactician**

adj; m
[ˈtak̚.ti.ko]

Yo no recuerdo haber autorizado un simulacro táctico.
-I don't recall authorizing a tactical drill.

6765 matutino — **morning**

adj
[ma.tu.ˈti.no]

Estaba pensando que podríamos saltarnos el paseo matutino.
-I was thinking we could just skip the morning walk.

6766 veintitrés — **twenty-three**

num
[beĩn̪.ti.ˈtres]

En veintitrés años, jamás te he pedido nada.
-In twenty-three years, I have never asked you for a thing.

6767 banal — **banal**

adj
[ba.ˈnal]

La influenza sigue siendo una infección banal pero mortífera.
-Influenza remains a banal but deadly infection.

6768 ciudadanía — **citizenship**

f
[sju.ða.ða.ˈni.a]

La nacionalidad y la ciudadanía no son lo mismo.
-Nationality and citizenship are not the same thing.

6769 alentador — **encouraging**

adj[a.lẽn̪.ta.'ðor] El resto del panorama es mucho menos alentador. -The rest of the picture is much less encouraging.

6770 **inverso** **reverse**
adj
[ĩm.'bɛr.so]
El razonamiento inverso también es válido naturalmente.
-The opposite also applies of course.

6771 **empeñar(se)** **pawn; insist on**
vb; vbr
[ẽm.pe.'ɲar]
Tu padre perdió tanto que tuvo que empeñar todas sus pertenencias.
-Your dad lost so much, he had to pawn all of his valuables.

6772 **arce** **maple**
m
['ar.se]
Sé cómo distinguir un arce azucarero.
-I know how to tell a sugar maple.

6773 **fauna** **fauna, bunch of weirdos (coll)**
f
['fau̯.na]
Por ende, la fauna era extremadamente singular.
-The fauna was therefore extremely unique.

6774 **curro** **job (ES) (coll)**
m
['ku.ro]
Mi padre me ha conseguido un curro.
-My dad got me a job.

6775 **subdirector** **assistant manager**
m
[suβ.ði.rek̚.'tor]
Es la esposa de la subdirectora.
-She's the assistant manager's wife.

6776 **metano** **methane**
m
[mɛ.'ta.no]
Hay mucho metano naturalmente en nuestra atmósfera.
-There's lots of methane naturally in our atmosphere.

6777 **maternal** **maternal**
adj
[ma.tɛr.'nal]
Intentaré no ser demasiado maternal contigo.
-I'll try to not get too maternal on you.

6778 **estampida** **stampede**
f
[ɛs.tãm.'pi.ða]
Nuestra estampida empezará mañana al mediodía.
-Our stampede will start at high noon tomorrow.

6779 **confidencialidad** **confidentiality**
f
[kõɱ.fi.ðẽn.sja.li.'ðað]
Esa ley también garantiza el principio de confidencialidad.
-The principle of confidentiality is also guaranteed under the same Act.

6780 **rosada** **pink**
adj
[ro.'sa.ða]
La ciudad está construida con piedra rosada.
-The city is constructed of pink stone.

6781 **abstracto** **abstract**
adj
[aβs.'trak̚.to]
Ese proceso es absolutamente abstracto y muy inusual.
-That process is entirely abstract and very unusual.

6782 **mutilar** **mutilate**
vb
[mu.ti.'lar]
Se utilizaron puñales para mutilar los cuerpos.
-Daggers were used to mutilate the bodies.

6783 **repetido** **repeated**
adj
[re.pɛ.'ti.ðo]
Eso es algo que hemos repetido muchas veces.
-That is something we have repeated many times.

6784 **torero** **bullfighter**
m
[to.'rɛ.ro]
No me digas que es un torero.
-Don't tell me he's a bullfighter.

6785 **alegato** **plea**

m
[a.le.ˈɣa.to]

Permítame terminar haciendo un alegato especialmente enérgico a favor de una enmienda que yo mismo he propuesto.
-Allow me to finish by making a particularly strong plea in favor of an amendment that I myself have put forward.

6786 valeroso — **valiant**

adj
[ba.lɛ.ˈro.so]

Quería agradecerle por el valeroso esfuerzo de hoy.
-I wanted to thank you for your valiant effort today.

6787 lombriz — **earthworm**

f
[ˈlõm.bris]

A ella le gustó mi imitación de una lombriz de tierra.
-She liked my impression of an earthworm.

6788 relucir — **shine**

vb
[re.lu.ˈsir]

Es nuestro turno para relucir, sí.
-It's our time to shine, yes.

6789 decadente — **decadent**

adj
[de.ka.ˈðɛ̃n̪.te]

Todo lo decadente fomenta la revolución.
-Everything that is decadent speeds up the revolution.

6790 acorralar — **corral**

vb
[a.ko.ra.ˈlar]

Yo mismo he tratado de acorralar a estos animales.
-I have tried to corral these animals myself.

6791 moño — **bun**

m
[ˈmo.ɲo]

Tú deberías hacerte un moño en el pelo.
-You should tie your hair in a bun.

6792 financiación — **financing**

f
[fi.nãn.sja.ˈsjõn]

Ahora quisiera hablar brevemente de la financiación.
-I should now like to say a few words on financing.

6793 atropello — **hit-and-run**

m
[a.tro.ˈpe.jo]

Deja de actuar como si fueras una víctima de un atropello.
-Stop acting like you're some hit-and-run victim.

6794 erróneo — **wrong**

adj
[ɛ.ˈro.ne.o]

Queremos insistir en que ese planteamiento es erróneo.
-We wish to reiterate that this is the wrong approach.

6795 diversidad — **diversity**

f
[di.βɛr.si.ˈðað]

Hay mucha diversidad alrededor del mundo.
-There is so much diversity around the globe.

6796 crianza — **raising**

f
[ˈkrjãn.sa]

También presta apoyo a los padres en la crianza de sus hijos.
-It also gives support to parents in raising their children.

6797 compatible — **compatible**

adj
[kõm.pa.ˈti.βle]

Estuve analizando su sangre para encontrar un donante compatible.
-I was analyzing her blood chemistry to try to locate a compatible donor.

6798 teórico — **theoretical; theorist**

adj; m
[te.ˈo.ri.ko]

Esto requería un enfoque teórico y práctico.
-This required both a theoretical and a practical approach.

6799 diafragma — **diaphragm**

m
[dja.ˈfraɣ.ma]

Es la parte inferior del diafragma.
-It's the lower part of the diaphragm.

6800 improvisación — **improvisation**

f[ĩm.pro.βi.sa.ˈsjõn]

A veces me siento como si mi vida fuera una larga improvisación. -Sometimes I feel like my life is one long improvisation.

6801 harén — **harem**

m
[aˈrẽn]
He visto gente mejor dotada vigilando un harén.
-I've seen better-equipped men guarding a harem.

6802 castaña — chestnut

f
[kasˈta.ɲa]
La actividad económica principal en la zona es la producción de castaña.
-The principal economic activity in the area is chestnut production.

6803 elaborar — prepare

vb
[e.la.βoˈrar]
Son ellos quienes tienen que elaborar los programas.
-It is up to them to prepare the programmes.

6804 diva — diva

f
[ˈdi.βa]
Necesito saber cómo ser una diva.
-I need to figure out how to be a diva.

6805 turbulencia — turbulence

f
[tur.βuˈlẽn.sja]
Está llevándonos directo a la turbulencia.
-It's taking us right into the turbulence.

6806 proyectar — project

vb
[pro.jekˈtar]
Solo recuerda, lo más importante es proyectar confianza.
-Just remember, the most important thing is to project confidence.

6807 halo — halo

m
[ˈa.lo]
Está teniendo problemas con su halo.
-She's having a little trouble with her halo.

6808 contraer(se) — contract

vb
[kõn.traˈɛr]
Hay muchas más maneras de contraer mono.
-There are plenty of other ways to contract mono.

6809 estandarte — banner

m
[ɛs.tãnˈdar.te]
Yo llevo el sello y el estandarte.
-I carry the seal and the banner.

6810 emparedado — sandwich

m
[ẽm.pa.reˈða.ðo]
No recibirás el resto de mi emparedado.
-You're not getting the rest of my sandwich.

6811 transcurso — course

m
[trãnsˈkur.so]
Puedo cambiar en el transcurso del día.
-I can change during the course of a day.

6812 narración — narration

f
[na.raˈsjõn]
Está ayudándome con la narración del documental.
-She's helping with the narration for the documentary.

6813 antisemitismo — anti-Semitism

m
[ãn.ti.se.miˈtiş.mo]
Mencionó además el persistente problema del antisemitismo.
-It also referred to the continuing problem of anti-Semitism.

6814 cósmico — cosmic

adj
[ˈkoş.mi.ko]
Hay un balance cósmico natural en el universo.
-There is a natural cosmic balance in the universe.

6815 gótico — Gothic; Goth

adj; m
[ˈgo.ti.ko]
Creo que es gótico o algo.
-I think he's goth or something.

6816 maqueta — mockup

f[maˈkɛ.ta]
¿No le gusto la maqueta? -He didn't like the mockup?

6817 consentir — allow

vb
[kõn.sẽnˈtir]
No podemos consentir esto bajo ninguna circunstancia.
-We cannot allow this under any circumstances.

6818	**semejanza**	**likeness**
	f	Creo que tiene una semejanza estupenda.
	[se.me.ˈxãn.sa]	-I think it's a stunning likeness.
6819	**carcajada**	**loud laugh**
	f	Ella no pudo evitar estallar en una carcajada.
	[kar.ka.ˈxa.ða]	-She couldn't help bursting into laughter.
6820	**grato**	**agreeable**
	adj	Un perro rabioso sería un alumno más grato.
	[ˈgra.to]	-A rabid dog would be a more agreeable pupil.
6821	**llamativo**	**flashy**
	adj	Es un poco llamativo para mí.
	[ʎa.ma.ˈti.βo]	-It's a little flashy for me.
6822	**administrativo**	**administrative**
	adj	Tengo otra sugerencia de carácter más administrativo.
	[að.mi.nis.tra.ˈti.βo]	-I have another suggestion of a more administrative nature.
6823	**suela**	**sole**
	f	Hay un residuo aceitoso en la suela.
	[ˈswe.la]	-There's an oily residue on the sole.
6824	**organizador**	**organizer**
	m	El organizador del show lloraba ante la cámara.
	[or.ɣa.ni.sa.ˈðor]	-The organizer of the show was crying on camera.
6825	**vitalidad**	**vitality**
	f	Quería a alguien con más vitalidad.
	[bi.ta.li.ˈðað]	-He wanted somebody with more vitality.
6826	**potable**	**potable**
	adj	Queremos acceso a agua limpia y potable.
	[po.ˈta.βle]	-We want access to safe and potable water.
6827	**énfasis**	**emphasis**
	m	Puso mucho énfasis en este punto.
	[ˈẽɱ.fa.sis]	-He put great emphasis on this point.
6828	**partidario**	**in favour of; supporter**
	adj; m	Tú has sido un gran partidario.
	[par.ti.ˈða.rjo]	-You've been a big supporter.
6829	**coreografía**	**choreography**
	f	No sabe nada de la coreografía.
	[ko.re.o.ɣra.ˈfi.a]	-He doesn't know any of the choreography.
6830	**sucesivo**	**successive**
	adj	Preparará a un plan de trabajo para cada año sucesivo.
	[su.se.ˈsi.βo]	-Prepare a work plan for each successive year.
6831	**acorazado**	**armoured**
	m	Y yo soy un oso acorazado.
	[a.ko.ra.ˈsa.ðo]	-And I am an armored bear.
6832	**recolectar**	**gather**
	vb[re.ko.lek.ˈtar]	Podemos recolectar información sobre nuestro entorno. -We are able to gather information about our environment.
6833	**anchoa**	**anchovy**
	f	Una anchoa es suficiente para mí.
	[ãn̪.ˈʧo.a]	-One anchovy is plenty for me.
6834	**cavidad**	**cavity**

f
[ka.βi.ˈðað]
Es una reacción para proteger esa cavidad.
-It's a natural response to protect that cavity.

6835 infracción — **infraction**
f
[ĩm̩.frak.ˈsjõn]
El oficial superior fue declarado culpable de infracción en el servicio.
-The superior military officer was found guilty of a service infraction.

6836 terrorífico — **terrifying**
adj
[tɛ.ro.ˈri.fi.ko]
Puedo convertirlo en algo aún más horrible y terrorífico.
-I could turn him into something even more horrible and terrifying.

6837 renegar — **disown**
vb
[re.ne.ˈɣar]
¿Puedes renegar de una hermana?
-Can you disown a sibling?

6838 sensatez — **good judgement**
f
[sẽn.ˈsa.tes]
Es crucial que prevalezcan la sensatez, la visión y el liderazgo.
-It is crucial that wisdom, foresight, and leadership prevail.

6839 cazo — **pot**
m
[ˈka.so]
Podría prepararle un cazo de frijoles.
-I could fix you a pot of beans.

6840 ultimátum — **ultimatum**
m
[ul̩.ti.ˈma.tũm]
Creo que quería darle un ultimátum.
-I think that she wanted to give him an ultimatum.

6841 facción — **faction**
f
[fak.ˈsjõn]
No sé nada de ninguna facción.
-I don't know anything about a faction.

6842 veintiuno — **twenty-one**
num
[bei̯n.ˈtju.no]
Mi hermana tiene veintiuna casas.
-My sister has twenty-one houses.

6843 tejer — **weave**
vb
[te.ˈxɛr]
Todavía necesitas a aprender a tejer.
-You still need to learn how to weave.

6844 boa — **boa**
f
[ˈbo.a]
Trabajaba con 20 víboras venenosas y una boa no venenosa.
-He worked with 20 poisonous snakes and a non-poisonous boa.

6845 evadir — **avoid**
vb
[e.βa.ˈðir]
Ellos no pueden evadir el tráfico.
-They can't avoid the traffic.

6846 ahumar — **smoke up**
vb
[a.u.ˈmar]
También se utilizan para ahumar carne, pescado y productos lácteos.
-They are also used to smoke meat, fish and dairy products.

6847 carisma — **charisma**
m
[ka.ˈriṣ.ma]
Necesitamos un guitarrista con un poco de carisma.
-We need a guitarist with a bit of charisma.

6848 repisa — **shelf**
f[re.ˈpi.sa]
Él tomó un libro de la repisa. -He took a book off the shelf.

6849 indonesio — **Indonesian; Indonesian person**
adj; m
[ĩn.do.ˈne.sjo]
La verificación no reveló indicios que hicieran dudar del origen indonesio o malayo declarado.
-The verification did not reveal indications to put in question the declared Indonesian or Malaysian origin.

6850 alabanza — **praise**

	f		Por último, ofrecemos una plegaria en alabanza a nuestro Señor.
	[a.la.ˈβãn.sa]		-Finally, we offer a prayer in praise of our Lord.
6851	**prismáticos**	**binoculars**	
	m		No, solo estoy probando estos prismáticos nuevos.
	[priṣ.ˈma.ti.kos]		-No, I'm just trying out these new binoculars.
6852	**forrar(se)**	**cover; get rich**	
	vb; vbr		Me voy a forrar esta noche.
	[fo.ˈrar]		-I'm going to get rich tonight.
6853	**acreedor**	**deserving of; creditor**	
	adj; m		Esta evaluación tiene que hacerse utilizando el criterio del acreedor privado.
	[a.kre.e.ˈðor]		-This assessment has to be done using the private creditor test.
6854	**antojarse**	**fancy, feel like**	
	vbr		Se me antoja comer tarta.
	[ãn̪.to.ˈxar.se]		-I feel like eating cake.
6855	**arrasar**	**devastate**	
	vb		Esto podría arrasar el pueblo.
	[a.ra.ˈsar]		-This could devastate the town.
6856	**herradura**	**horseshoe**	
	f		Sigo diciendo que deberíamos usar una herradura.
	[ɛ.ra.ˈðu.ra]		-I still say we should use a horseshoe.
6857	**buzo**	**scuba diver**	
	m		No, eso no sería un buzo.
	[ˈbu.so]		-No, that wouldn't be a scuba diver.
6858	**desagradar**	**displease**	
	vb		Lamento hasta qué punto debo desagradar a su majestad.
	[de.sa.ɣra.ˈðar]		-I am sick to think how much I must displease Your Grace.
6859	**inversionista**	**investor**	
	m/f		También puedo conseguirte un inversionista nuevo.
	[ĩm.bɛr.sjo.ˈnis.ta]		-I can also get you a new investor.
6860	**kárate**	**karate**	
	m		Formo parte del club de kárate.
	[ˈka.ra.te]		-I belong to the karate club.
6861	**nicotina**	**nicotine**	
	f		El médico volvió a encontrarme nicotina en la orina.
	[ni.ko.ˈti.na]		-The doctor found nicotine in my urine again.
6862	**dorsal**	**dorsal**	
	adj		Tiene una raya fina negra en su aleta dorsal.
	[dor.ˈsal]		-He's got a thin, black stripe on his dorsal fin.
6863	**pedestal**	**pedestal**	
	m[pe.ðɛs.ˈtal]		Estoy subiendo al pedestal, Jeff. -I'm getting on the pedestal, jeff.
6864	**virilidad**	**virility**	
	f		Pero no estoy seguro de tu virilidad.
	[bi.ri.li.ˈðað]		-But I'm not sure about your virility.
6865	**estimado**	**appreciated; estimation, dear**	
	adj; m		Nuestro estimado hijo llegará enseguida.
	[ɛs.ti.ˈma.ðo]		-Our dear son will be arriving shortly.
6866	**desistir**	**desist**	
	vb		Ahora debería desistir y esta asamblea debería rechazar esta directiva.
	[de.sis.ˈtir]		-It should desist now, and this assembly should reject this directive.

6867 consultor
adj; m
[kõn.sul̪.ˈtor]

advisory; consultant
Soy un consultor para el departamento de policía.
-I am a consultant for the police department.

6868 actualización
f
[ak̚.twa.li.sa.ˈsjõn]

update
No hay necesidad de una actualización.
-There isn't any need for an update.

6869 tifón
m
[ti.ˈfõn]

typhoon
El tifón arrancó la mayor parte del muelle.
-The typhoon tore off most of the dock.

6870 estruendo
m
[ɛs.ˈtrwɛ̃n̪.do]

racket
Eso debería hacer un gran estruendo.
-That ought to make quite a racket.

6871 perjudicar
vb
[pɛr.xu.ði.ˈkar]

damage
Las decisiones erróneas pueden perjudicar seriamente el procedimiento.
-The wrong decisions can seriously damage the procedure.

6872 astronomía
f
[as.tro.no.ˈmi.a]

astronomy
En China aprendí química y astronomía.
-In China, I learned chemistry and astronomy.

6873 romanticismo
m
[ro.mãn̪.ti.ˈsis̪.mo]

romanticism
Es un escenario repleto de romanticismo que combina influencias italianas y francesas.
-It is a setting replete with romanticism, combining Italian and French influences.

6874 acierto
m
[a.ˈsjɛr.to]

right answer, wise decision
¿Deberíamos cuestionar el acierto de la ampliación?
-Should we call into question the wisdom of enlargement?

6875 nefasto
adj
[ne.ˈfas.to]

nefarious
Los mercenarios desempeñan un papel especialmente nefasto en los conflictos de la subregión.
-Mercenaries play a particularly nefarious role in conflicts in the subregion.

6876 carburador
m
[kar.βu.ra.ˈðor]

carburetor
Está relacionado con algo del carburador.
-It has something to do with the carburetor.

6877 viable
adj
[ˈbja.βle]

viable
En este momento no hay ninguna otra perspectiva viable.
-At this point, there's no other viable perspective.

6878 intoxicación
f
[ĩn̪.tok.si.ka.ˈsjõn]

intoxication
Eso es intoxicación, estoy seguro.
-That is some intoxication, I am sure.

6879 aptitud
f
[ap̚.ti.ˈtuð]

ability
Que el conocimiento y la aptitud sean los factores imperantes.
-Let knowledge and ability be the prevailing factors.

6880 dominación
f
[do.mi.na.ˈsjõn]

domination
Disfruta con el control y la dominación.
-He gets off on the control and the domination.

6881 colon
m
[ˈko.lõn]

colon
Necesitamos ver su colon funcionando.
-We need to see his colon at work.

6882 arsénico

arsenic

m
[ar.ˈse.ni.ko]

Nunca encontramos la procedencia del arsénico.
-We never found the source of the arsenic.

6883 condominio — **condominium**

m
[kõn̪.do.ˈmi.njo]

Tom compró un condominio cerca del lago.
-Tom bought a condominium near the lake.

6884 reproductor — **reproductive; DVD player**

adj; m
[re.pro.ðuk̚.ˈtor]

La organización también donó un reproductor de DVD.
-The organization also donated a DVD player.

6885 macizo — **solid**

adj
[ma.ˈsi.so]

Esto es un muro macizo de piedra y arena.
-This is a solid wall of stone and sand.

6886 perplejo — **perplexed**

adj
[pɛr.ˈple.xo]

Me admitió que su éxito lo tenía perplejo.
-And he admitted to me that he was perplexed by their success.

6887 consola — **console**

f
[kõn.ˈso.la]

Vigila la consola mientras intento arreglar esto.
-Keep your eye on the console while I try to fix this.

6888 aflojar — **loosen**

vb
[a.flo.ˈxar]

Quizás debería aflojarte esto un poquito.
-Maybe I should loosen this a bit for you.

6889 amparo — **protection**

m
[ãm.ˈpa.ro]

El incumplimiento de un auto de amparo constituye un acto punible.
-Breach of a protection order is a punishable offense.

6890 diferenciar — **differentiate**

vb
[di.fɛ.rɛ̃n.ˈsjar]

Por consiguiente, conviene diferenciar la naturaleza y el alcance de ambos conceptos.
-Consequently, it is necessary to differentiate the nature and scope of both concepts.

6891 neurosis — **neurosis**

f
[neu̯.ˈro.sis]

Y eso fue el shock final que determinó su neurosis.
-And that was the final shock that sealed your neurosis.

6892 neo — **neo**

pfx[ˈne.o]

Uno de los errores de los gobiernos neoliberales fue los cobros en las escuelas públicas. -One of the errors of the neo-liberal governments were the charges in public schools.

6893 imprevisible — **unpredictable**

adj
[ĩm.pre.βi.ˈsi.βle]

Busco a una mujer que sea imprevisible.
-I'm looking for a woman who is unpredictable.

6894 epilepsia — **epilepsy**

f
[e.pi.ˈlɛp.sja]

La epilepsia explicaría por qué no vio nada.
-The epilepsy would explain why she didn't see anything.

6895 desodorante — **deodorant**

m
[de.so.ðo.ˈrãn̪.te]

Estoy probando un desodorante natural para la tienda.
-I'm trying out this natural deodorant for the store.

6896 estallido — **explosion**

m
[ɛs.ta.ˈji.ðo]

Causará un estallido en la flota.
-It'll cause an explosion in the fleet.

6897 seiscientos — **six hundred**

num
[sei̯s.ˈsjẽn̪.tos]

Hoy lo puedo vender por seiscientos.
-I could sell it today for six hundred.

6898	**limbo**	**limbo**
	m	Están perdidos en un limbo de incertidumbre y desilusión.
	[ˈlĩm.bo]	-They are lost in a limbo of uncertainty and disappointment.

6899	**secuaz**	**minion**
	m	Le has fallado a la sociedad como secuaz.
	[ˈse.kwas]	-You have failed society as a minion.

6900	**aversión**	**aversion**
	f	Esto es lo que se conoce como terapia de aversión.
	[a.βɛrˈsjõn]	-This is what is known as aversion therapy.

6901	**quilate**	**carat**
	m	El quilate es una medida de peso, no el tamaño.
	[kiˈla.te]	-The carat is a measurement of weight, not size.

6902	**conjeturar**	**conjecture**
	vb	Pero conjeturar no nos va a ayudar.
	[kõŋ.xɛ.tuˈrar]	-But conjecture won't help us.

6903	**remolino**	**swirl**
	m	Pero esa es la belleza del remolino.
	[re.mo.ˈli.no]	-But that's the beauty of the swirl.

6904	**remediar**	**remedy**
	vb	Siempre será mejor prevenir que remediar.
	[re.me.ˈðjar]	-It will always be better to prevent than to remedy.

6905	**durazno**	**peach**
	m	El principal cultivo es el durazno.
	[du.ˈras̺.no]	-The main fruit crop is peach.

6906	**néctar**	**nectar**
	m	Solo quiero probar el néctar, muchachos.
	[ˈnek̚.tar]	-I just want to taste some nectar, guys.

6907	**nutriente**	**nutritious; nutrient**
	adj; m[nu.ˈtrjẽn̪.te]	El nitrógeno es un nutriente esencial en la naturaleza. -Nitrogen is an essential nutrient in nature.

6908	**estrechar(se)**	**narrow, hug; get smaller**
	vb; vbr	Eso debería ayudar a estrechar el círculo.
	[ɛs.tre.ˈtʃar]	-That should help narrow it down.

6909	**dócil**	**docile**
	adj	Estás consciente, pero te has vuelto completamente dócil.
	[ˈdo.sil]	-You're conscious, but you've been rendered completely docile.

6910	**corsé**	**corset**
	m	Una mujer realmente hermosa no necesita corsé.
	[kor.ˈse]	-A truly beautiful woman does not need a corset.

6911	**tentativa**	**attempt**
	f	Me preocupa cualquier tentativa de prejuzgar esta cuestión.
	[tẽn̪.ta.ˈti.βa]	-I am very concerned at any attempt to prejudge this issue.

6912	**intervalo**	**interval**
	m	Por lo tanto, habrá un corto intervalo.
	[ĩn̪.tɛr.ˈβa.lo]	-Therefore, there will be a short interval.

6913	**incorregible**	**incorrigible**
	adj	A mí me parece que este niño es absolutamente incorregible.
	[ĩŋ.ko.re.ˈxi.βle]	-It seems to me that this child is absolutely incorrigible.

| 6914 | **galope** | **gallop** |

m
[ga.ˈlo.pe]

Es el fin de tu galope.
-That's the end of your gallop.

6915 importación

importation

f
[ĩm.por.ta.ˈsjõn]

Se ha prohibido la importación de pájaros domésticos.
-A ban has been put in place in respect of the importation of pet birds.

6916 tendero

shopkeeper

m
[tẽn̪.ˈdɛ.ɾo]

Con esa mentalidad de tendero estamos condenados al fracaso.
-With that shopkeeper mentality, we are doomed to fail.

6917 payasada

charade

f
[pa.ja.ˈsa.ða]

Coincido con usted con respecto a esta payasada.
-I quite agree with your attitude toward this charade.

6918 ubicar(se)

locate, find

vb
[u.βi.ˈkar]

Ahora estoy tratando de ubicar el teléfono.
-I'm trying to locate the handset now.

6919 desinfectante

disinfectant; disinfectant

adj; m
[de.sĩn̪.fekˈ.ˈtã̃n̪.te]

Encontré residuos de desinfectante bajo sus uñas.
-I found residue from a disinfectant under her nails.

6920 comerciar

trade

vb
[ko.mɛr.ˈsjar]

Si quieres comerciar, hazte socio.
-If you want to trade, become a member.

6921 transcripción

transcription

f
[trãns.krip.ˈsjõn]

Incluso ha proporcionado una transcripción en braille del Corán.
-It had even provided a transcription of the Koran in Braille.

6922 latitud

latitude

f
[la.ti.ˈtuð]

En los mapas se debería indicar claramente la latitud y la longitud.
-Latitude and longitude should be clearly marked on maps.

6923 densidad

density

f[dẽn.si.ˈðað]

Cada medio de transporte público requiere una densidad mínima para resultar rentable. -Each mode of public transport requires a minimum density to be economic.

6924 vereda

path

f
[bɛ.ˈre.ða]

Vamos por esta vereda, Gertrude.
-Let's take the little path, Gertrude.

6925 reposar

rest

vb
[re.po.ˈsar]

Vamos a descansar un rato aquí.
-We will rest for a few moments here.

6926 apóstol

apostle

m
[a.ˈpos.tol]

Algunas personas piensan que era la apóstol número 13.
-Some people think she was the 13th apostle.

6927 insultante

insulting

adj
[ĩn.sul̪.ˈtã̃n̪.te]

Siento que piense que es insultante.
-I'm sorry you think it's insulting.

6928 incrementar

increase

vb
[ĩŋ.kre.mẽn̪.ˈtar]

Debemos incrementar nuestra capacidad de prevención colectiva.
-We need to increase our capacity for collective prevention.

6929 impulsar

boost, inspire

vb
[ĩm.pul.ˈsar]

Unos impuestos bien gastados pueden impulsar la productividad de una economía.
-If taxes are spent well, they can boost an economy's productivity.

6930 mechón

lock

	m	Pregúntale sobre el mechón de pelo.
	[me.ˈʧõn]	-Ask him about the lock of hair.

6931 **incierto** — **uncertain**

adj

[ĩn.ˈsjɛr.to]

El camino hacia la paz sigue siendo incierto.
-The path towards peace is still uncertain.

6932 **conspirador** — **conspirer**

m

[kõns.pi.ra.ˈðor]

Yo soy un antiguo conspirador.
-I am a former conspirer.

6933 **formato** — **format**

m

[for.ˈma.to]

Seleccione el formato que desee aplicar.
-Select the formatting that you want to apply.

6934 **confinamiento** — **confinement**

m

[kõɱ.fi.na.ˈmjẽn̪.to]

Su confinamiento continuo está causando estragos psicológicos en él.
-His continued confinement is wreaking psychological havoc on him.

6935 **emisario** — **emissary**

m

[e.mi.ˈsa.rjo]

El emisario debe venir a por la tercera caja.
-This emissary must be coming for the third box.

6936 **gotear** — **drip**

vb

[go.te.ˈar]

¿Tu ojo va a gotear cada vez que parpadees?
-Is your eye going to drip every time you blink?

6937 **indigente** — **indigent**

m

[ĩn.di.ˈxẽn̪.te]

Le dieron su llave a un indigente después del suceso.
-They gave their key to an indigent after the event.

6938 **feminista** — **feminist; feminist**

adj; m/f[fe.mi.ˈnis.ta]

Por ejemplo, la crítica feminista realizó una significativa contribución a la comprensión de los derechos humanos. -For example, feminist criticism made a significant contribution to a greater understanding of human rights.

6939 **ámbito** — **field**

m

[ˈãm.bi.to]

También participé en varias investigaciones públicas en este ámbito.
-I also took part in several public inquiries in this field.

6940 **neurona** — **neuron**

f

[neu̯.ˈro.na]

Esto es una neurona real ampliada diez mil veces.
-Here is an actual neuron, magnified ten thousand times.

6941 **pupila** — **pupil**

f

[pu.ˈpi.la]

Su pupila izquierda no está bien.
-His left pupil's not good.

6942 **quimioterapia** — **chemotherapy**

f

[ki.mjo.te.ˈra.pja]

Teníamos grandes esperanzas cuando inició su quimioterapia.
-We had high hopes when she began her chemotherapy.

6943 **antipático** — **unpleasant**

adj

[ãn̪.ˈti.pa.ti.ko]

No creo que fuera muy antipático en clase.
-I don't think I was actively unpleasant in class.

6944 **talco** — **talc**

m

[ˈtal.ko]

Todos nuestro bocadillos saben a polvos de talco y naftalina.
-All our sandwiches taste like talcum powder and mothballs.

6945 **encarar** — **confront**

vb

[ẽŋ.ka.ˈrar]

Debemos encarar la amenaza que plantea la división cultural y religiosa a través de la adopción de medidas concretas.
-We need to confront the threat of cultural and religious division with concrete action.

6946 arrebatar — **snatch**
vb
[a.re.βa.ˈtar]
En circunstancias como esta, la mayoría de las personas contratan a un detective privado para arrebatar al niño de nuevo.
-In circumstances like this, most people hire a private detective to snatch the child back.

6947 comprobación — **verification**
f
[kõm.pro.βa.ˈsjõn]
Dicha comprobación deberá hacerse por medio de la documentación migratoria en vigor.
-Such verification must be carried out using the migration documentation in force.

6948 infamia — **infamy**
f
[ĩɱ.ˈfa.mja]
La infamia caerá sobre tu nombre.
-Your name will go down in infamy.

6949 bohemio — **bohemian**
adj
[bo.ˈe.mjo]
No sé si soy un bohemio revolucionario.
-I don't know if I am a Bohemian revolutionary.

6950 éxodo — **exodus**
m
[ˈɛk.so.ðo]
En los dos últimos años se ha producido un éxodo de periodistas.
-In the past two years, there has been an exodus of journalists.

6951 bazar — **bazaar**
m[ba.ˈsar]
Probablemente la hizo alguien del bazar. -It's probably made by somebody down in the bazaar.

6952 hormiguero — **anthill**
m
[or.mi.ˈɣɛ.ro]
Quizás atacar el hormiguero era imposible.
-Maybe the attack against the anthill was impossible.

6953 tabú — **taboo**
adj
[ta.ˈβu]
Definitivamente hay un tabú contra eso.
-There's definitely a taboo against that.

6954 memorizar — **memorize**
vb
[me.mo.ri.ˈsar]
No tienes que memorizar un diccionario para tener un buen conocimiento de una lengua.
-You don't need to memorize a dictionary to have good knowledge of a language.

6955 concentrado — **concentrated**
m
[kõn.sɛ̃n.ˈtra.ðo]
Necesitas mantenerte concentrado hasta que esto termine.
-You need to stay focused until this is done.

6956 cundir — **spread, go well**
vb
[kũn.ˈdir]
Este ataque, indudablemente, ha hecho cundir el pánico y el temor.
-This attack, undoubtedly, also caused panic and fear.

6957 sumisión — **submission**
f
[su.mi.ˈsjõn]
Nos inclinaremos, como símbolo de sumisión.
-As a sign of submission, we are going to bow.

6958 intendente — **intendant**
m/f
[ĩn.tɛ̃n.ˈdɛ̃n.te]
El intendente también estaba alabando tu trabajo.
-The intendant was praising your work, too.

6959 sanguinario — **bloodthirsty**
adj
[sãŋ.gi.ˈna.rjo]
Es un monstruo sanguinario con ojos de ángel.
-She is a bloodthirsty monster with the eyes of an angel.

6960 neto — **net**
adj
[ˈnɛ.to]
El beneficio neto está en relación con el capital imponible.
-The net profit is set in relation to the taxable capital.

6961 difamación — **defamation**
f
[di.fa.ma.ˈsjõn]
Las únicas limitaciones son las encaminadas a impedir la difamación de otros y las obscenidades.
-The only restrictions are those to prevent defamation of others and obscenity.

6962 constitucional — **constitutional**
adj
[kõns.ti.tu.sjo.ˈnal]
Eso dependería del sistema constitucional vigente.
-That would depend on the constitutional system at issue.

6963 monarca — **monarch**
m/f
[mo.ˈnar.ka]
Prometo ser un monarca amable y generoso.
-I promise to be a kind and generous monarch.

6964 decapitar — **behead**
vb
[de.ka.pi.ˈtar]
Puede decapitar a tu enemigo de un solo golpe.
-It can behead your enemy in one stroke.

6965 cosechar — **harvest**
vb
[ko.se.ˈtʃar]
Podré alquilar las máquinas y cosechar.
-I will be able to harvest and rent the machines.

6966 tribal — **tribal**
adj
[tri.ˈβal]
Estamos buscando un pequeño asentamiento tribal.
-We're looking for a small tribal settlement.

6967 patriótico — **patriotic**
adj
[pa.ˈtrjo.ti.ko]
No sé si me siento muy patriótico.
-I don't know if I'm feeling all that patriotic.

6968 enderezar(se) — **straighten**
vb
[ẽṉ.dɛ.re.ˈsar]
Mire, podría enderezar al chico.
-Look, I could straighten the kid out.

6969 recargar — **recharge**
vb
[re.kar.ˈɣar]
Quizás no tuvieron tiempo suficiente para recargarlo.
-Perhaps they haven't had enough time to recharge it.

6970 inseguridad — **insecurity**
f
[ĩn.se.ɣu.ri.ˈðað]
Vivimos en un período de gran inseguridad.
-We are living in a period of great insecurity.

6971 transfusión — **transfusion**
f
[trãns.fu.ˈsjõn]
Esta mañana rechazó la transfusión de sangre.
-She refused a blood transfusion this morning.

6972 inimaginable — **unimaginable**
adj
[i.ni.ma.xi.ˈna.βle]
Fue un desastre de escala inimaginable.
-It was a disaster on an unimaginable scale.

6973 averiar — **break down**
vb
[a.βɛ.ˈrjar]
Algo se averiará en esta nave pronto.
-Something will break down on this boat soon.

6974 cabezón — **stubborn**
adj
[ka.βe.ˈsõn]
Ya sabes lo cabezón que es.
-You know how stubborn he is.

6975 higo — **fig**
m
[ˈi.ɣo]
Según recuerdo, usted solía adorar mi pastel de higo.
-As I recall, you used to adore my fig pie.

6976 combustión — **combustion**
f
[kõm.bus.ˈtjõn]
La combustión de combustibles fósiles acelera el efecto invernadero que afecta al clima en todo el mundo.

-Combustion of fossil fuels accelerates the greenhouse effect which affects climate across the globe.

6977	**judía**	**bean**
	m	Intentaba coger una judía con la paja.
	[xu.ˈði.a]	-I was trying to pick up a bean with the straw.
6978	**castor**	**beaver**
	m	Eso es lo mejor para un castor.
	[kas.ˈtor]	-That's the best thing for a beaver.
6979	**coeficiente**	**coefficient**
	m	Podemos determinar su coeficiente de crianza.
	[ko.e.fi.ˈsjẽn.te]	-We can determine his inbreeding coefficient.
6980	**materno**	**maternal**
	adj	Mi abuelo materno fue un asesino.
	[ma.ˈtɛr.no]	-My maternal grandfather was a murderer.
6981	**abogacía**	**legal profession**
	f [a.βo.ɣa.ˈsi.a]	No existe discriminación contra los hombres que ejercen la abogacía. -There is no discrimination against men engaged in the legal profession.
6982	**alcoholismo**	**alcoholism**
	m	Gracias a mí, tienes una predisposición genética al alcoholismo.
	[al.ko.o.ˈlis̪.mo]	-Thanks to me, you have a genetic predisposition to alcoholism.
6983	**aeronave**	**aircraft**
	f	Perder una aeronave podría entenderse como mala suerte.
	[a.ɛ.ro.ˈna.βe]	-To lose one aircraft may be regarded as a misfortune.
6984	**repugnar**	**disgust**
	vb	Ella estaba repugnada con su presencia.
	[re.puɣ.ˈnar]	-She was disgusted at his persistence.
6985	**adversidad**	**adversity**
	f	Deseamos compartir contigo la adversidad del destino.
	[að.βɛr.si.ˈðað]	-We wish to share with you the adversity of fate.
6986	**productivo**	**productive**
	adj	Sabíamos que iba a ser más productivo.
	[pro.ðuk̚.ˈti.βo]	-We knew it was going to be more productive.
6987	**hincha**	**fan**
	m/f	Un hincha fue disparado y cuatro policías terminaron heridos.
	[ˈĩn.tʃa]	-A fan was shot and four policemen got hurt.
6988	**novecientos**	**nine hundred**
	num	En China hay novecientos millones de personas empleadas en el sector agrícola.
	[no.βe.ˈsjẽn.tos]	-China has nine hundred million people employed in agriculture.
6989	**impedimento**	**impediment**
	m	No considero mi miopía como un impedimento.
	[ĩm.pe.ði.ˈmẽn.to]	-I don't consider my myopia as an impediment.
6990	**absorber**	**absorb**
	vb	Tengo el poder de absorber energía.
	[aβ.sor.ˈβɛr]	-I've got the power to absorb energy.
6991	**descomponer(se)**	**break down; slump**
	vb; vbr	Se organizó para descomponer su imprenta.
	[dɛs.kõm.po.ˈnɛr]	-It arranged for the press to break down.
6992	**franja**	**stripe, time zone**

f
['frãŋ.xa]
Hay una con una franja roja.
-There's one with a red stripe.

6993 **pitón** **python**
f
[pi.'tõn]
Mi compañera se encargará de la pitón.
-My partner will take care of the python.

6994 **temporizador** **timer**
m
[tẽm.po.ri.sa.'ðor]
Walter, necesito que eches un vistazo a este temporizador.
-Walter, I need you to take a look at this timer.

6995 **óptico** **optical; optician**
adj; m
['op̚.ti.ko]
Me gustaría realizar un diagnóstico óptico.
-I'd like to run an optical diagnostic.

6996 **pardo** **brown**
adj
['par.ðo]
Era un caballo pardo, mamá.
-It was a brown horse, mommy.

6997 **plus** **bonus**
m
['plus]
Mientras estemos secos, es un plus.
-As long as we can stay dry, that's a bonus.

6998 **lóbulo** **lobe**
m
['lo.βu.lo]
Extirpé un trozo del lóbulo superior.
-I excised a chunk of the superior lobe.

6999 **rehusar** **refuse**
vb
[re.u.'sar]
No estaba en posición de rehusar.
-I wasn't in a position to refuse.

7000 **inflexible** **inflexible**
adj
[ĩɱ.flɛk.'si.βle]
Describiría su posición al respecto como inflexible.
-I would describe his position on this as inflexible.

7001 **mejicano** **Mexican; Mexican person**
adj; m
[me.xi.'ka.no]
Te convertiste en un guapo muchachito mejicano.
-You've turned into a handsome little Mexican boy.

7002 **loma** **hill**
f
['lo.ma]
Está sobre la loma, bajando por el muelle.
-It's over the hill, down by the pier.

7003 **relevancia** **relevance**
f
[re.le.'βãn.sja]
No tiene relevancia para nada.
-It has no relevance to anything.

7004 **informativo** **informative; news bulletin**
adj; m
[ĩɱ.for.ma.'ti.βo]
Bien, esto ha sido informativo.
-Okay, well, this has been informative.

7005 **intocable** **untouchable**
adj
[ĩn̪.to.'ka.βle]
Ningún hombre es intocable, Olivia.
-No man is untouchable, Olivia.

7006 **interestatal** **interstate**
adj
[ĩn̪.tɛ.rɛs.ta.'tal]
Lo puedes ver mientras conduces por la carretera interestatal.
-You can see it as you drive by on the interstate highway.

7007 **filtración** **filtration**
f
[fil̪.tra.'sjõn]
El líquido resultante debe tratarse separando las partículas recogidas mediante sedimentación o filtración.
-The resulting liquid has to be treated by separating the collected dust by sedimentation or filtration.

7008 **intencional** **intentional**

	adj	Según sus notas, fue intencional.
	[ĩn̪.tẽn.sjo.ˈnal]	-According to your notes, this was intentional.
7009	**conservación**	**conservation**
	f	Le facilitamos la conservación de sus cigarros.
	[kõn.sɛr.βa.ˈsjõn]	-We facilitate him the conservation of his cigars.
7010	**exterminio**	**extermination**
	m	No hay necesidad de retrasar su exterminio.
	[ɛks.tɛr.ˈmi.njo]	-There is no need for the delay in their extermination.
7011	**desobedecer**	**disobey**
	vb	Tienes derecho a desobedecer la ley.
	[de.so.βe.ðe.ˈsɛr]	-You have a right to disobey the law.
7012	**convulsión**	**convulsion**
	f[kõm.bul.ˈsjõn]	Entonces los regimientos deben estar preparados para tal convulsión. -Then the regiments must be prepared for this convulsion.
7013	**pronunciado**	**pronounced**
	adj	El crecimiento fue más pronunciado en los países en desarrollo.
	[pro.nũn.ˈsja.ðo]	-Growth was most pronounced in developing countries.
7014	**fonda**	**inn**
	f	En esta época del año mi fonda siempre está vacía.
	[ˈfõn̪.da]	-At this time of year, my inn is always empty.
7015	**dominical**	**Sunday; Sunday magazine**
	adj; m	Lo leí en el suplemento dominical.
	[do.mi.ni.ˈkal]	-I read about it in the Sunday supplement.
7016	**enfocar**	**focus**
	vb	Pienso que todos deberíamos enfocarnos positivamente nuestro trabajo.
	[ẽɱ.fo.ˈkar]	-I think we should all focus on positivity in our work.
7017	**liceo**	**high school (LA)**
	m	Aquí hay una para ti, viene del liceo.
	[li.ˈse.o]	-Here's one for you, from the high school.
7018	**cerrajero**	**locksmith**
	m	Tendremos que llamar a un cerrajero.
	[sɛ.ra.ˈxɛ.ro]	-We will have to call in a locksmith.
7019	**mimar**	**pamper**
	vb	Tienes que mimar tu delicado estómago.
	[mi.ˈmar]	-You've got to pamper that delicate stomach of yours.
7020	**postor**	**bidder**
	m	Esperemos que no tengan otro postor.
	[pos.ˈtor]	-Let's hope they don't have another bidder.
7021	**incesto**	**incest**
	m	También hace frente al problema del incesto.
	[ĩn.ˈsɛs.to]	-It also addresses the issue of incest.
7022	**obsesivo**	**obsessive**
	adj	Eres un caso patológico de comportamiento obsesivo.
	[oβ.se.ˈsi.βo]	-You're like a case study in obsessive behavior.
7023	**hámster**	**hamster**
	m	Estaba ahorrando para comprar un hámster.
	[ˈãms.tɛr]	-I was saving up to buy a hamster.
7024	**bisexual**	**bisexual; bisexual**

adj; m/f   ¿Cómo te sientes siendo bisexual?
[bi.sɛk.ˈswal]   -How do you feel about being bisexual?

7025 defraudar   **disappoint**

vb   Vaya, siento defraudar a vuestros lectores.
[de.fraṵ.ˈðar]   -Well, I'm sorry to disappoint your readers.

7026 asir(se)   **grab**

vb   Deben asir su presa por la cola mientras evitan sus mandíbulas chasqueantes.
[a.ˈsir]   -They need to grab their prey by the tail while avoiding its snapping jaws.

7027 serenata   **serenade**

f   Los niños empezaron a darnos una serenata.
[sɛ.re.ˈna.ta]   -The band of children began to serenade us.

7028 deducción   **deduction**

f   Permítame felicitarle por su brillante deducción.
[de.ðuk.ˈsjõn]   -Let me congratulate you on your brilliant deduction.

7029 parodiar   **parody**

vb   Prefieren parodiar e ironizar a denunciar y dar testimonio, con la intención de
[pa.ro.ˈðjar]   exponer sus preocupaciones sociales y criticar estereotipos.
    -They prefer parody and irony to denounce and testimony, in order to exhibit their social concerns and criticize stereotypes.

7030 callejón   **alley**

m   Podrías haberme disparado en el callejón.
[ka.je.ˈxõn]   -You could have shot me in that alley.

7031 vertebral   **vertebral**

adj   Puede que tengas una fractura vertebral.
[bɛr.te.ˈβral]   -You might have a vertebral fracture.

7032 proletariado   **proletariat**

m   Te enseñaremos la dictadura del proletariado.
[pro.lɛ.ta.ˈrja.ðo]   -We'll show you the dictatorship of the proletariat.

7033 conformar(se)   **shape; resign yourself**

vb; vbr   Los resultados de la cumbre se utilizan para contribuir a conformar la futura
[kõɱ.for.ˈmar]   agenda de políticas gubernamentales.
    -The summit outcomes are used to help shape the Government's future policy agenda.

7034 clavel   **carnation**

m   Siga al hombre del clavel verde.
[kla.ˈβɛl]   -Follow the man with the green carnation.

7035 aguijón   **sting**

m   La avispa ha perdido su aguijón.
[a.ɣi.ˈxõn]   -The wasp has lost its sting.

7036 aceleración   **acceleration**

f   Ahora vamos a probar la aceleración.
[a.se.lɛ.ra.ˈsjõn]   -Now we're going to test the acceleration.

7037 falsificar   **falsify**

vb   Incluso llegué a falsificar el informe.
[fal.si.fi.ˈkar]   -I even went so far as to falsify the report.

7038 desperdicio   **waste**

m   Es un desperdicio que todos escribamos nuestro ensayo.
[dɛs.pɛr.ˈði.sjo]   -It's a waste for all of us to write our paper.

7039 igualar   **equalize**

	vb [i.ɣwa.ˈlar]	Hace mucho que la República está resuelta a igualar las oportunidades para sus ciudadanos con discapacidad. -The Republic has long been determined to equalize opportunities for its citizens with disabilities.
7040	**fábula** f [ˈfa.βu.la]	**fable** No creo que esto sea una fábula o una alegoría. -I don't think this is a fable or even an allegory.
7041	**secador** m [se.ka.ˈðor]	**hairdryer** Un secador cayó en la bañera. -A hairdryer fell into the bathtub.
7042	**sórdido** adj [ˈsor.ði.ðo]	**sordid** No puede creerse lo sórdidos que son. -You can't believe how sordid they are.
7043	**discapacitar** vb [dis.ka.pa.si.ˈtar]	**incapacitate** Estos cartuchos puede incapacitar un objetivo en segundos. -These cartridges can incapacitate a target in seconds.
7044	**beige** adj [ˈbei̯.xe]	**beige** Dijiste que llevaba un suéter beige. -You said he was wearing a beige sweater.
7045	**policíaco** adj [po.li.ˈsi.a.ko]	**police** Solo vivías para el trabajo policíaco. -All you ever lived for was police work.
7046	**estantería** f [ɛs.tãn̪.ˈtɛ.ri.a]	**bookcase** He visto una huella de zapato sangrienta junto a la estantería. -I noticed a bloody shoeprint by the bookcase.
7047	**proximidad** f [prok.si.mi.ˈðað]	**proximity** Somos conscientes de la proximidad del parque. -We're aware of the proximity to the park.
7048	**grosería** f [gro.sɛ.ˈri.a]	**rudeness** Se especializó en grosería en la facultad. -He majored in crudeness at med school.
7049	**perturbador** adj [pɛr.tur.βa.ˈðor]	**disturbing** Les advierto que lo pueden encontrar perturbador. -I warn you that you may find it disturbing.
7050	**digerir** vb [di.xɛ.ˈrir]	**digest** Tardaré en poder digerir lo detallado de su respuesta. -I will take time to digest the detail in your answer.
7051	**tolerante** adj [to.lɛ.ˈrãn̪.te]	**tolerant** También ayudará a crear una sociedad más acogedora y tolerante. -It will also help create a gentler, more tolerant society.
7052	**atacante** adj; m/f [a.ta.ˈkãn̪.te]	**combative; attacker** Nuestro atacante creyó que alguien de aquí le había robado. -Our attacker believed somebody here robbed him.
7053	**deserción** f [de.sɛr.ˈsjõn]	**desertion** Ha pedido el divorcio acusándola de deserción. -He's filed divorce papers accusing her of desertion.
7054	**asomar(se)** vb [a.so.ˈmar]	**show** No podré asomar la cara por allí de nuevo. -I can't ever show my face there again.
7055	**corromper**	**corrupt**

	vb	
	[ko.rõm.ˈpɛr]	

¡Están intentando corromper a nuestros hijos!
-They're trying to corrupt our children!

7056 tenaz — **tenacious**
adj
[ˈte.nas]

Debe ser muy tenaz para haber sobrevivido en ese lugar tanto tiempo.
-You must be tenacious to have survived that place so long.

7057 vegetación — **vegetation**
f
[be.xɛ.ta.ˈsjõn]

Significa que no habrá mucha vegetación.
-It means there won't be much vegetation.

7058 tripulante — **crew member**
m/f
[tri.pu.ˈlã̪n.te]

Parece que tenemos un tripulante adicional.
-It seems that we have an extra crew member.

7059 mobiliario — **furniture**
m
[mo.βi.ˈlja.rjo]

Últimamente no tengo suficiente mobiliario.
-Lately, I don't have enough furniture.

7060 abastecimiento — **supply**
m
[a.βas.te.si.ˈmjẽ̪n.to]

Los funcionarios competentes están esforzándose por regularizar el abastecimiento.
-The officials concerned are making every effort to regularize this supply.

7061 chorizo — **chorizo**
m
[ʧo.ˈri.so]

No hay pan para tanto chorizo.
-There is not enough bread for so much chorizo.

7062 espabilar(se) — **snap out of it**
vb
[ɛs.pa.βi.ˈlar]

Venga, que tienes que espabilarte.
-Come on, you have to snap out of it.

7063 cuneta — **ditch**
f
[ku.ˈnɛ.ta]

No quiero dejarlo en una cuneta.
-I don't want to leave him in a ditch.

7064 pelusa — **fluff**
f
[pe.ˈlu.sa]

Te está dejando la pelusa en los pantalones.
-Her fluff's coming off on your trousers.

7065 calculadora — **calculator**
f
[kal.ku.la.ˈðo.ra]

Esta calculadora te ayudará a descubrirlo.
-This calculator will help you figure it out.

7066 estresante — **stressful**
adj
[ɛs.tre.ˈsã̪n.te]

Tienes una vida muy importante y estresante.
-You have an important, stressful life.

7067 silo — **silo**
m
[ˈsi.lo]

Alguien trató de piratear un silo nuclear.
-Someone was trying to hack a nuclear silo.

7068 pimiento — **pepper**
m
[pi.ˈmjẽ̪n.to]

Era el pimiento más picante del mundo.
-It was the world's hottest pepper.

7069 vaina — **scabbard, pod**
f
[ˈbai̯.na]

Dame esa vaina para el entablillado.
-Give me that scabbard for the splint.

7070 metabolismo — **metabolism**
m
[mɛ.ta.βo.ˈliṣ.mo]

Tengo el metabolismo de una maratonista.
-I have the metabolism of a marathon runner.

7071 ferroviario — **railway; railwayman**

adj; m Han adoptado medidas para promover el sector ferroviario.
[fɛ.ro.ˈβja.rjo] -They adopted measures to promote the railway sector.

7072 solista   **soloist**

m/f Pero todavía no soy un solista.
[so.ˈlis.ta] -But I'm not yet a soloist.

7073 plancton   **plankton**

m[ˈplãŋk.tõn] Pero peces mucho más grandes también se alimentan de plancton. -But much bigger fish also feed on the plankton.

7074 yogur   **yogurt**

m Tenemos una máquina de yogur congelado y un trampolín.
[ɟʝo.ˈɣur] -We have a frozen yogurt machine and a trampoline.

7075 testosterona   **testosterone**

f Básicamente estaba ebrio con su propia testosterona.
[tɛs.tos.tɛ.ˈro.na] -But he was basically drunk on his own testosterone.

7076 infraestructura   **infrastructure**

f En muchas zonas, la infraestructura pública está en estado de abandono.
[ĩɱ.fra.ɛs.truk̚.ˈtu.ra] -In many areas, public infrastructure is in a state of decay.

7077 rumba   **rumba**

f Me resulta muy emocionante que fueras profesor de rumba.
[ˈrũm.ba] -I find it quite exciting that you were a rumba teacher.

7078 objetar   **object**

vb No puedo no objetar cuando pregunta indebidamente.
[oβ.xɛ.ˈtar] -I can't object when you phrase questions improperly.

7079 simbolizar   **symbolize**

vb El arzobispo ha simbolizado la bendición de la Iglesia.
[sĩm.bo.li.ˈsar] -The archbishop has symbolized the church's blessing.

7080 tapete   **rug**

m Esta Navidad recibirás mayormente cosas para la casa, como un nuevo tapete.
[ta.ˈpɛ.te] -This Christmas you're getting mostly stuff for the house, like a new rug.

7081 bebedor   **heavy drinker (coll); drinker**

adj; m Se volvió un asiduo bebedor de champán.
[be.βe.ˈðor] -He became a steady champagne drinker.

7082 migaja   **crumb**

f El hombre es una migaja en el universo.
[mi.ˈɣa.xa] -Man is a crumb in the universe.

7083 indignación   **indignation**

f Mucha gente está sintiendo esa indignación.
[ĩn̪.diɣ.na.ˈsjõn] -A lot of people are feeling that indignation.

7084 confort   **comfort**

m El único confort para mí es su felicidad.
[kõɱ.ˈfort] -The only comfort for me is her happiness.

7085 moderación   **moderation**

f Están aprendiendo moderación para que puedan vivir pasando desapercibidos.
[mo.ðɛ.ra.ˈsjõn] -They're learning moderation so they can live under the radar.

7086 nabo   **turnip**

m No se puede sacar espinaca de un nabo.
[ˈna.βo] -You can't get spinach out of a turnip.

7087 microbio   **microbe**

	m	No saben si es un virus o un microbio.
	[mi.ˈkro.βjo]	-They don't know if it's a virus or a microbe.
7088	**colombiano**	**Colombian; Colombian person**
	adj; m[ko.lõm.ˈbja.no]	El pueblo colombiano se ha alzado frente a la adversidad. -The Colombian people have risen against adversity.
7089	**secretaría**	**secretary's office**
	f	Los formularios de ingreso están disponibles en la secretaría.
	[se.krɛ.ta.ˈri.a]	-Application forms are available in the secretary's office.
7090	**hospedar**	**host**
	vb	Ninguno de ellos podía hospedar los escarabajos.
	[os.pe.ˈðar]	-None of them could host the beetles.
7091	**espárrago**	**asparagus**
	m	El espárrago me pareció demasiado insípido.
	[ɛs.ˈpa.ra.ɣo]	-I thought the asparagus was way under seasoned.
7092	**caricatura**	**caricature**
	f	La libertad de expresión se está convirtiendo en una caricatura.
	[ka.ri.ka.ˈtu.ra]	-Freedom of expression is becoming a caricature.
7093	**viril**	**virile**
	adj	Eres la manifestación viril de lo divino.
	[bi.ˈril]	-You are a virile manifestation of the divine.
7094	**apio**	**celery**
	m	Debería servirla con vodka y apio.
	[ˈa.pjo]	-You should serve it with vodka and celery.
7095	**detallado**	**detailed**
	adj	Pronto presentaremos un ofrecimiento concreto y detallado.
	[dɛ.ta.ˈja.ðo]	-We will soon submit a concrete and detailed bid.
7096	**perforación**	**drilling**
	f	Usamos un método de perforación completamente diferente.
	[pɛr.fo.ra.ˈsjõn]	-We use a totally different method of drilling.
7097	**azteca**	**Aztec; Aztec person**
	adj; m	Suena como algún tipo de extraño ritual azteca.
	[as.ˈte.ka]	-It sounds like some kind of weird Aztec ritual.
7098	**segmento**	**segment**
	m	Tenemos que encontrar el cuarto segmento.
	[sɛɣ.ˈmẽn̪.to]	-We've got to find the fourth segment.
7099	**cilindro**	**cylinder**
	m	No sabía dónde estaba enterrado el cilindro.
	[si.ˈlĩn̪.dro]	-I didn't know where the cylinder was buried.
7100	**piadoso**	**compassionate**
	adj	Lo que estoy haciendo es piadoso.
	[pja.ˈðo.so]	-What I'm doing is compassionate.
7101	**honradez**	**honesty**
	f	Se considera una garantía de honradez.
	[õn.ˈra.ðes]	-It is regarded as a guarantee of honesty.
7102	**res**	**farm animal**
	f	Debería ir al supermercado para comprar algunos huesos de res.
	[ˈres]	-You should go to the supermarket to buy some beef bones.
7103	**estribo**	**stirrup**

	m		Coloca tu pie izquierdo en este estribo.
	[ɛs.ˈtri.βo]		-Get your left foot in that stirrup.
7104	**inhalar**		**inhale**
	vb[i.na.ˈlar]		Lo que harás es inhalar el humo y mantenerlo. -What you're going to do is inhale the smoke and hold it.
7105	**prevención**		**prevention**
	f		Por ello la prevención tiene un rol esencial.
	[pre.βɛ̃n.ˈsjõn]		-Prevention, therefore, has a crucial role to play.
7106	**clínico**		**clinical; doctor**
	adj; m		Pueden encontrarla en el edificio clínico.
	[ˈkli.ni.ko]		-You can find her in the clinical building.
7107	**incisión**		**incision**
	f		Ojalá no hubiese hecho la incisión.
	[ĩn.si.ˈsjõn]		-I wish I hadn't made that incision.
7108	**ámbar**		**amber**
	m		Sabemos que alguien fue sacado del ámbar.
	[ˈãm.bar]		-We know that someone was taken from the amber.
7109	**utopía**		**utopia**
	f		Toma mi mano. Los dos vamos a construir una utopía.
	[u.to.ˈpi.a]		-Take my hand. The two of us are going to construct a utopia.
7110	**ordeñar**		**milk**
	vb		He tenido que ordeñar una cabra para conseguirla.
	[or.ðe.ˈɲar]		-I had to milk a goat to get it.
7111	**geometría**		**geometry**
	f		Esa es nuestra lección de geometría del día.
	[xe.o.mɛ.ˈtri.a]		-There's our geometry lesson for the day.
7112	**copo**		**flake**
	m		Cada copo que cae en mi mano me recuerda a él.
	[ˈko.po]		-Each snowflake that falls into my palm, reminds me of him.
7113	**óseo**		**bone**
	adj		Todo el daño óseo que encontré hasta ahora es resultado del fuego.
	[ˈo.se.o]		-All the bone damage I've found so far is a result of the fire.
7114	**orificio**		**hole**
	m		El cirujano utilizará un láser para sellar permanentemente el orificio.
	[o.ri.ˈfi.sjo]		-The doctor will use a laser to permanently seal the hole.
7115	**notificación**		**notification**
	f		La notificación no proporcionaba información sobre el itinerario del envío.
	[no.ti.fi.ka.ˈsjõn]		-The notification did not provide information concerning the itinerary of the shipment.
7116	**esfumar(se)**		**fade**
	vb		Pero la fama puede esfumarse en un momento.
	[ɛs.fu.ˈmar]		-But reputations can vanish in a moment.
7117	**exterminar**		**exterminate**
	vb		El propósito era exterminar a todo un pueblo.
	[ɛks.tɛr.mi.ˈnar]		-It was to exterminate an entire people.
7118	**partitura**		**sheet music**
	f		Mira, significa mucho para él, esa partitura.
	[par.ti.ˈtu.ra]		-Look, it means a lot to him, that sheet music.
7119	**sonámbulo**		**sleepwalker; sleepwalker**
	adj; m[so.ˈnãm.bu.lo]		Mala idea despertar a un sonámbulo. -Bad idea to wake a sleepwalker.

7120 infelicidad — unhappiness
f
[ĩm.fe.li.si.ˈðað]
Me equivoqué al culparte de mi infelicidad.
-I was wrong to blame you for my unhappiness.

7121 centeno — rye
m
[sẽn.ˈte.no]
La roya también afecta a la cebada y el centeno.
-The rust also affects barley and rye.

7122 armisticio — armistice
m
[ar.mis.ˈti.sjo]
No aspiran a conseguir un armisticio con el mundo civilizado.
-They do not seek an armistice with the civilized world.

7123 acomodar — accommodate
vb
[a.ko.mo.ˈðar]
Hicimos lo posible para acomodar su conducta.
-We did the best we could to accommodate his behavior.

7124 petrolero — oil tanker
m
[pɛ.tro.ˈlɛ.ro]
No es fácil negociar la compra de un petrolero.
-It's not easy to negotiate an oil tanker purchase.

7125 remitente — sender
m/f
[re.mi.ˈtẽn.te]
Tanto el remitente como el receptor deben estar familiarizados con la estructura de los datos.
-Both sender and receiver must be familiar with the structure of the data.

7126 contundente — convincing
adj
[kõn.tũn.ˈdẽn.te]
No puedes ser tan contundente, Jeremiah.
-You can't be so blunt, Jeremiah.

7127 euforia — euphoria
f
[eu̯.ˈfo.rja]
Podría estar padeciendo una forma de euforia falsa.
-You could be suffering from a form of false euphoria.

7128 restablecer — reestablish
vb
[rɛs.ta.βle.ˈsɛr]
Creí que querías restablecer nuestro vínculo.
-I thought you wanted to reestablish our bond.

7129 digestión — digestion
f
[di.xɛs.ˈtjõn]
Esta medicina promueve una buena digestión y una salud duradera del aparato digestivo.
-This medicine promotes good digestion and the sustained health of the digestive tract.

7130 lacrimógeno — tear
adj
[la.kri.ˈmo.xe.no]
Nos rociaron gas lacrimógeno, me rompí la nariz.
-We all got tear-gassed, I broke my nose.

7131 mormón — Mormon
m
[mor.ˈmõn]
Después de todo, la poligamia es un problema mormón.
-I mean, after all, polygamy is a Mormon problem.

7132 eslogan — slogan
m
[ɛs̞.ˈlo.ɣãn]
Nuestro eslogan lo resume todo: "Sabemos cómo te sientes".
-Our slogan sums it all up: "We know how you feel".

7133 falsedad — falseness
f
[fal.se.ˈðað]
Notó cierta falsedad en mi entusiasmo.
-He sensed a certain falseness in my enthusiasm.

7134 desmontar — disassemble
vb[dɛs̞.mõn.ˈtar]
También pueden montar y desmontar fácilmente sus infraestructuras. -They can also assemble and disassemble their infrastructure with ease.

7135 variación — variation

f

[ba.rja.ˈsjõn]

No hubo una variación significativa en los tipos de iniciativas conjuntas.
-There was no significant variation of types of joint initiatives.

7136 **desobediencia**　　　　**disobedience**

f

[de.so.βe.ˈðjɛ̃n.sja]

Están dispuestos a perdonarte por tu desobediencia.
-They are ready to forgive you for your disobedience.

7137 **suprimir**　　　　**suppress**

vb

[su.pri.ˈmir]

Solo puedes suprimir tu naturaleza durante un tiempo.
-You can only suppress your real nature for so long.

7138 **reclamación**　　　　**complaint**

f

[re.kla.ma.ˈsjõn]

Tengo que pedirte que firmes esta reclamación contra aquellos tres soldados.
-I'll have to ask you to sign this complaint against those three soldiers.

7139 **codificar**　　　　**encode**

vb

[ko.ði.fi.ˈkar]

Ayudó a codificar los documentos originales del gobierno.
-He helped encode the original government documents.

7140 **estafar**　　　　**swindle**

vb

[ɛs.ta.ˈfar]

Él y sus socios trataron de estafar a un muchacho.
-He and his partners tried to swindle a guy.

7141 **taburete**　　　　**stool**

m

[ta.βu.ˈrɛ.te]

Lo encontré en el taburete de un bar.
-I found it on a barstool.

7142 **recreación**　　　　**recreation**

f

[re.kre.a.ˈsjõn]

El hombre tiene un sentido pobre de la recreación.
-The man has a poor sense of recreation.

7143 **intrépido**　　　　**intrepid**

adj

[ĩn̪.ˈtre.pi.ðo]

Son las aventuras de un intrépido doctor.
-They are the adventures of an intrepid doctor.

7144 **parachoques**　　　　**bumper**

m

[pa.ra.ˈʧo.kes]

Pondré una cinta amarilla en mi parachoques.
-I will put a yellow ribbon on my bumper.

7145 **compuerta**　　　　**gate**

f

[kõm.ˈpwɛr.ta]

El pistón está diseñado para operar automáticamente la compuerta.
-The piston is designed to operate the gate automatically.

7146 **centrar**　　　　**centre**

vb

[sɛ̃n̪.ˈtrar]

Seleccione el texto que desee centrar en la página.
-Select the text that you want to center on the page.

7147 **tallo**　　　　**stem**

m

[ˈta.jo]

El tallo y las grandes hojas tienen los nervios grandes y rojizos.
-The stem and leaves are large reddish veins.

7148 **sedante**　　　　**sedative; sedative**

adj; m

[se.ˈðã̪n.te]

Llamaré y pediré un fuerte sedante.
-I'll call and order a strong sedative.

7149 **gruta**　　　　**cave**

f

[ˈgru.ta]

Para evitarlo dormiré contigo en esta gruta.
-To prevent this I will sleep with you in this cave.

7150 **rumano**　　　　**Romanian; Romanian person**

adj; m

[ru.ˈma.no]

El mercader era un marino rumano.
-The merchant was a Romanian sailor.

7151 **picadura**　　　　**sting**

f
[pi.ka.ˈðu.ra]
Es una mala reacción a la picadura.
-It's a bad reaction to the sting.

7152 pre
pfx
[ˈpre]
pre
Un módulo de prefacturación también está disponible.
-A pre invoice module is also available.

7153 soberanía
f
[so.βɛ.ra.ˈni.a]
sovereignty
En la ausencia de justicia, ¿qué es soberanía sino robo organizado?
-In the absence of justice, what is sovereignty but organized robbery?

7154 decidido
adj
[de.si.ˈði.ðo]
determined
Estoy decidido a realizar este plan.
-I am determined to carry out this plan.

7155 murmullo
m
[mur.ˈmu.ʝo]
babbling
Podría escuchar el murmullo de un arroyo y oír una canción que pudiera entender.
-I could listen to a babbling brook and hear a song that I could understand.

7156 acrobacia
f
[a.kro.ˈβa.sja]
stunt
Esta acrobacia costó 50 millones de dólares.
-This stunt cost $50 million.

7157 atlético
adj
[at̪.ˈlɛ.ti.ko]
athletic
Ninguno de los hombres desaparecidos es particularmente atlético.
-None of these missing men are particularly athletic.

7158 rábano
m
[ˈra.βa.no]
radish
Serviremos carne con rábano picante luego.
-We're serving roast beef with horseradish later.

7159 extradición
f
[ɛks.tra.ði.ˈsjõn]
extradition
Letonia ha implementado un doble sistema de extradición.
-A two-tier system on extradition has been put in place in Latvia.

7160 boutique
f
[boṷ.ˈti.ke]
boutique
El hotel pertenece a la categoría de los hoteles boutique temáticos.
-The Hotel falls into the category of themed boutique hotels.

7161 bicarbonato
m
[bi.kar.βo.ˈna.to]
bicarbonate
Tendrías que tomar bicarbonato con eso.
-You'd have to take bicarbonate with that one.

7162 subsidio
m
[suβ.ˈsi.ðjo]
subsidy
El subsidio familiar dura tres años.
-The family subsidy is payable for three years.

7163 proveniente
adj
[pro.βe.ˈnjẽn̪.te]
coming from
Esperamos que escuchen el mensaje de indignación y determinación proveniente de la comunidad internacional.
-We hope that they will heed the message of indignation and determination coming from the international community.

7164 almendra
f[al.ˈmẽn̪.dra]
almond
Toma un almendra, está cruda. -Have an almond, they're raw.

7165 derivado
adj; m
[dɛ.ri.ˈβa.ðo]
derived; derivative
Un derivado es un contrato que permite reducir el riesgo.
-A derivative is a contract that allows one to reduce risk.

7166 fertilizante
adj; m
[fɛr.ti.li.ˈsãn̪.te]
fertilizing; fertilizer
Se utiliza como valiosa fuente de fertilizante.
-It's used as a valuable source of fertilizer.

7167 raqueta
racket

	f	
	[ra.ˈkɛ.ta]	Intento jugar con la misma raqueta. -I try to play with the same racket.
7168	**detergente**	**detergent; detergent**
	adj; m	¿Estás intentando sobornarme con detergente?
	[dɛ.tɛr.ˈxɛ̃n.te]	-Are you trying to bribe me with laundry detergent?
7169	**servidumbre**	**servants**
	f	Por principios nunca chismorreo con la servidumbre.
	[sɛr.βi.ˈðũm.bre]	-I make a point never to gossip with servants.
7170	**mercante**	**merchant**
	m/f	Encontramos esta tarjeta de marino mercante en él.
	[mɛr.ˈkã̃n.te]	-We found this merchant seaman's card on him.
7171	**detentar**	**hold**
	vb	En el mundo actual ningún país puede detentar un monopolio de ninguna
	[dɛ.tɛ̃n.ˈtar]	clase en la resolución de conflictos.
		-In the present-day world, no country can hold a monopoly on any kind of
		conflict-resolution effort.
7172	**cloro**	**chlorine**
	m	Pero si le pones cloro, las algas morirán.
	[ˈklo.ro]	-But if you put chlorine in, the algae will die.
7173	**tónico**	**tonic**
	m	Quiero preguntarte si necesitas este tónico.
	[ˈto.ni.ko]	-I want to ask if you need this tonic.
7174	**vibrar**	**vibrate**
	vb	Trata de hacer vibrar la tabla del juego.
	[bi.ˈβrar]	-Try to vibrate the game board.
7175	**vendar**	**bandage**
	vb	Ayúdame a vendar al pobre niño.
	[bɛ̃n.ˈdar]	-Help me bandage the poor kid.
7176	**desafiante**	**challenging**
	adj	Intentemos algo un poco más desafiante.
	[de.sa.ˈfjã̃n.te]	-Let's try something a little more challenging.
7177	**becerro**	**calf**
	m	Primero quiero que encuentres el becerro.
	[be.ˈsɛ.ro]	-I want you to find the calf first.
7178	**mitin**	**rally**
	m	No sabía que estábamos en un mitin político.
	[ˈmi.tĩn]	-I didn't realize we were meeting at a political rally.
7179	**catarro**	**cold**
	m[ka.ˈta.ro]	El catarro no suele presentar fiebre alta. -The cold does not usually present a
		high fever.
7180	**lacayo**	**servant**
	m	El tratado te convierte en lacayo del Imperio británico.
	[la.ˈka.jo]	-This treaty makes you a servant of the British Empire.
7181	**bañador**	**swimsuit**
	m	Vamos a comprarte un bañador nuevo.
	[ba.ɲa.ˈðor]	-We're getting you a new swimsuit.
7182	**torbellino**	**whirlwind**
	m	El último día fue un verdadero torbellino.
	[tor.βe.ˈʝi.no]	-The final day was a whirlwind.
7183	**velar**	**look after**

	vb	
	[be.ˈlar]	

vb
[be.ˈlar]
Nosotros tenemos que velar por ella.
-We have to look after her.

7184 déficit — **deficit**
m
[ˈde.fi.sit]
También sería el último recurso en caso de déficit.
-It would also be the last resort in the case of a deficit.

7185 convenio — **agreement**
m
[kõm.ˈbe.njo]
Dicho convenio incluye también el apoyo a niños migrantes.
-The agreement also provides support for migrant children.

7186 desviación — **detour**
f
[dɛs̪.βja.ˈsjõn]
Se trata de una desviación y una distracción.
-It is a detour and a distraction.

7187 avivar — **fuel**
vb
[a.βi.ˈβar]
Una menor carga administrativa puede avivar el dinamismo económico.
-A lighter administrative burden can fuel economic dynamism.

7188 climático — **weather**
adj
[kli.ˈma.ti.ko]
Este boletín climático acaba de llegar.
-This weather bulletin just came off the wire.

7189 súbito — **sudden**
adj
[ˈsu.βi.to]
Ha habido un súbito cambio de plan.
-There was a sudden change of plan.

7190 espejismo — **illusion**
m
[ɛs.pe.ˈxis̪.mo]
Puede que... solo sea un espejismo.
-Maybe... it's an illusion.

7191 tentáculo — **tentacle**
m
[tẽn̪.ˈta.ku.lo]
Este tentáculo confirmó mis sospechas.
-This tentacle confirmed my suspicions.

7192 desleal — **disloyal**
adj
[dɛs̪.le.ˈal]
No pretendo parecer desleal pero él aceptaba demasiado.
-I don't mean to sound disloyal but he accepted too much.

7193 existente — **existing**
adj
[ɛk.sis.ˈtẽn̪.te]
Hay margen para cambiar y mejorar el sistema existente.
-There is scope for change and improvement of the existing system.

7194 oleada — **wave**
f
[o.le.ˈa.ða]
Detecto otra oleada de naves enemigas.
-I'm detecting another wave of enemy.

7195 saquear — **sack**
vb[sa.ke.ˈar]
Es hora de saquear para esta familia. -It's time for this family to sack up.

7196 estimular — **stimulate**
vb
[ɛs.ti.mu.ˈlar]
Bien, necesitamos estimular el riego sanguíneo.
-Well, we need to stimulate the blood flow.

7197 sien — **temple**
f
[ˈsjẽn]
Hay un golpe en su sien.
-There's a bruise on her temple.

7198 chocante — **shocking**
adj
[ʧo.ˈkãn̪.te]
Francamente, encuentro todo esto bastante chocante.
-Frankly, I find the whole affair rather shocking.

7199 impertinencia — **impertinence**
f
[ĩm.pɛr.ti.ˈnẽn.sja]
Discutiremos tu impertinencia luego, jovencita.
-We'll discuss your impertinence later, young lady.

7200 **recesión**   recession

f

[re.se.ˈsjõn]

La economía española parece estar entrando en recesión.
-The Spanish economy appears to be going into recession.

7201 **halago**   praise

m

[a.ˈla.ɣo]

Finalmente tengo algo digno de su halago.
-I finally have something worthy of her praise.

7202 **zas**   pow, bang

int

[ˈsas]

Sales fuera de la línea, ¡y zas!
-You step out of line, and pow!

7203 **perseverancia**   perseverance

f

[pɛr.se.βɛ.ˈrãn.sja]

Ganaste gracias a tu devoción y perseverancia.
-You've won because of your devotion and perseverance.

7204 **rebanada**   slice

f

[re.βa.ˈna.ða]

Toma la barra de pan y córtate una rebanada.
-Take the loaf of bread and cut yourself a slice.

7205 **motivar**   motivate

vb

[mo.ti.ˈβar]

La campaña tenía dos objetivos: informar y motivar.
-The campaign had two objectives: to inform and to motivate.

7206 **magnificar**   magnify

vb

[maɣ.ni.fi.ˈkar]

Todo lo que hace es magnificar tu debilidad.
-All it does is magnify your weakness.

7207 **avestruz**   ostrich

m

[a.ˈβɛs.trus]

La paloma y el avestruz son ambos pájaros; uno puede volar y el otro no.
-The pigeon and the ostrich are both birds; one can fly and the other cannot.

7208 **agonizar**   agonize

vb

[a.ɣo.ni.ˈsar]

Harry, no puedes agonizar sobre esto por más tiempo.
-Harry, you can't agonize over this any longer.

7209 **despreocupado**   carefree

adj

[dɛs.pre.o.ku.ˈpa.ðo]

Él estaba eufórico, despreocupado, vivo.
-He was elated, carefree, alive.

7210 **matinal**   morning

adj

[ma.ti.ˈnal]

Vamos a empezar nuestra reunión matinal.
-We're about to have our morning gathering.

7211 **polen**   pollen

m

[ˈpo.lẽn]

Hay mucho polen en el aire de Londres.
-There's a lot of pollen in this London air.

7212 **indiscreto**   indiscreet

adj

[ĩn̪.dis.ˈkrɛ.to]

Perdone, no quería ser indiscreto.
-Sorry, I did not want to be indiscreet.

7213 **desconfiado**   suspicious

adj

[dɛs.kõɱ.ˈfja.ðo]

Yo no diría que fuera desconfiado.
-I wouldn't say that I was suspicious.

7214 **pacificar**   pacify

vb

[pa.si.fi.ˈkar]

El propósito de mi viaje es pacificar a la gente.
-The purpose of my journey is to pacify the people.

7215 **desertar**   desert

vb

[de.sɛr.ˈtar]

Querías desertar pero temías avergonzar a tu viejo.
-You wanted to desert but feared shaming your old man.

7216 **dependencia**   dependence

f

[de.pẽn̪.ˈdẽn.sja]

No existe dependencia económica en sus vínculos familiares.

-There is no financial dependence involved in his family ties.

7217 **sintonía** **tuning**

f

[sĩn̪.ˈto.ni.a]

La sintonía es la clave de todas las transmisiones de radio y televisión.

-Tuning is the key to all radio and television transmission.

7218 **piratería** **piracy**

f

[pi.ra.tɛ.ˈri.a]

Condenamos cualquier acto de piratería, sin duda.

-We condemn any act of piracy, without a doubt.

7219 **carroña** **carrion**

f

[ka.ˈro.ɲa]

Le he dejado una carta, está en la carroña.

-I left him a letter, it's in the carrion.

7220 **vandalismo** **vandalism**

m

[bãn̪.da.ˈliṣ.mo]

Bueno, comenzó simplemente como vandalismo.

-Well, it started out as simple vandalism.

7221 **icono** **icon**

m

[i.ˈko.no]

Necesitamos un nuevo icono de Navidad.

-We need a new icon for Christmas.

7222 **virar** **turn**

vb

[bi.ˈrar]

No tienes claro el concepto de virar.

-You are unclear on the whole turning concept.

7223 **repercusión** **impact**

f

[re.pɛr.ku.ˈsjõn]

Está teniendo repercusión entre los ciudadanos.

-It is making an impact with the citizens.

7224 **tajo** **cut, work (coll)**

m

[ˈta.xo]

Bueno, quizás todo el dinero vino del tajo de alguien más.

-Well, maybe all the money came from someone else's cut.

7225 **funcional** **functional**

adj

[fũn.sjo.ˈnal]

Creo que simplemente intenta seguir siendo funcional.

-I think he's just trying to stay functional.

7226 **preceder** **go before**

vb

[pre.se.ˈðɛr]

Pero la reforma debe aprender de la experiencia y no preceder a ella.

-But reform should be instructed by experience, not precede it.

7227 **cobija** **blanket (LA)**

f

[ko.ˈβi.xa]

¿Podemos tomar una cobija para Patricia?

-Can we get a blanket for Patricia?

7228 **prolongar** **extend**

vb

[pro.lõŋ.ˈgar]

No queremos prolongar tu estancia aquí.

-We don't want to extend your stay here.

7229 **extracto** **extract**

m

[ɛks.ˈtrak̚.to]

Añade una cucharada de extracto de coco.

-Add one tablespoon coconut extract.

7230 **exportación** **exportation**

f

[ɛks.por.ta.ˈsjõn]

Se ha iniciado gradualmente la exportación de películas.

-Film exportation has been gradually undertaken.

7231 **lluvioso** **rainy**

adj

[ʎ ju.ˈβjo.so]

El clima lluvioso perduró por diez días consecutivos.

-The rainy weather lasted for ten days straight.

7232 **naciente** **rising**

adj
[na.ˈsjẽ̞n.te]

Como se esperaría de la estrella naciente del club de béisbol.
-As you'd expect from the rising star of the baseball club.

7233 titulado — **graduate**

m
[ti.tu.ˈla.ðo]

El gobierno se ha propuesto conseguir que en cada casa haya un titulado universitario.
-The government has pledged to ensure that every household will have a university graduate.

7234 alteración — **alteration**

f
[al̪.tɛ.ra.ˈsjõn]

El dolor lleva a la alteración de la psique.
-Pain leads to alteration of the psyche.

7235 impactar — **impact**

vb
[ĩm.pak̚.ˈtar]

Su luz se apagó al impactar en el suelo.
-Its light was extinguished on impact with the ground.

7236 ortodoxo — **orthodox**

adj
[or.to.ˈðok.so]

Ella acudió al templo ortodoxo.
-She went to the orthodox temple.

7237 duradero — **durable**

adj
[du.ra.ˈðɛ.ro]

Estos libros deberán imprimirse en un material duradero.
-Such books are required to be of a durable material.

7238 regocijo — **delight**

m
[re.ɣo.ˈsi.xo]

Esto no lo digo con ningún regocijo.
-I do not say that with any delight.

7239 metralla — **shrapnel**

f
[mɛ.ˈtra.ja]

Quitemos el resto de la metralla.
-Let's get the rest of this shrapnel.

7240 ancestral — **ancestral**

adj
[ãn.sɛs.ˈtral]

Tu espada ancestral podría perderse conmigo.
-Your ancestral sword might be lost with me.

7241 bruma — **mist**

f
[ˈbru.ma]

Debe seguir perdido en la bruma.
-He must still be missing in the mist.

7242 cinismo — **cynicism**

m[si.ˈniṣ.mo]

Ante tanta hipocresía y cinismo, preferimos abstenernos. -Faced with so much hypocrisy and cynicism, we prefer to abstain.

7243 desterrar — **exile**

vb
[dɛs.tɛ.ˈrar]

Voy a exiliar a tu familia.
-I will exile your family.

7244 tuerto — **blind in one eye**

adj
[ˈtwɛr.to]

Estoy buscando a un chico tuerto llamado Bruno.
-I'm looking for a one-eyed boy named Bruno.

7245 montículo — **mound**

m
[mõn̪.ˈti.ku.lo]

Disparó desde ahí detrás del montículo.
-He fired from over there behind the mound.

7246 ultrajar — **outrage**

vb
[ul̪.tra.ˈxar]

¿Cómo te atreves a ultrajar a mi persona?
-How dare you indulge this outrage on my person?

7247 competitivo — **competitive**

adj
[kõm.pɛ.ti.ˈti.βo]

Nuestro objetivo es dar el mejor servicio al precio más competitivo.
-Our goal is to give the highest services at a competitive price.

7248 inmundicia — **filth**

f
[ĩm.mũ̯n.ˈdi.sja]

Sin importar qué hagamos, esta inmundicia nos manchará.
-No matter what we do, we'll be tarred with this filth.

7249 incontrolable — **uncontrollable**

adj
[ĩŋ.kõ̯n.tro.ˈla.βle]

Pero entonces, de pronto, se volvió incontrolable.
-But then, suddenly, she became uncontrollable.

7250 capota — **hood**

f
[ka.ˈpo.ta]

Lo olvidaste en la capota del auto.
-You left it on the hood of your car.

7251 confiscar — **confiscate**

vb
[kõ̯m.fis.ˈkar]

Tenemos autorización para confiscar todo material pertinente.
-We've been authorized to confiscate all relevant materials.

7252 regulación — **regulation**

f
[re.ɣu.la.ˈsjõn]

Pueden hacerlo porque la regulación es optativa.
-They can do this as the regulation is optional.

7253 rectitud — **straightness**

f
[rek̚.ti.ˈtuð]

Estamos preparados para reconocer tu rectitud.
-We're prepared to grant you your righteousness.

7254 hartar(se) — **get on the nerves of; get sick of**

vb; vbr
[ar.ˈtar]

Creo que nos vamos a hartar de ella.
-I think we're going to get sick of her.

7255 fusilar — **shoot**

vb
[fu.si.ˈlar]

Soy yo al que van a fusilar.
-I'm the guy they're going to shoot.

7256 botar — **bounce, throw out (LA) (coll)**

vb
[bo.ˈtar]

Vete a botar tu pelota a otra parte.
-Go bounce your ball somewhere else.

7257 nudista — **nudist; nudist**

adj; m/f
[nu.ˈðis.ta]

Tom y Mary fueron a un club nudista.
-Tom and Mary went to a nudist club.

7258 logo — **logo (coll); ist**

m; sfx[ˈlo.ɣo]

Es el logo de la Universidad de Bradbury. -It's the Bradbury University logo.

7259 sarpullido — **rash**

m
[sar.pu.ˈʝi.ðo]

Ese alcohol no le provocó el sarpullido.
-That booze did not give him the rash.

7260 atasco — **jam, obstacle**

m
[a.ˈtas.ko]

Parece que tenemos un atasco en el aparcamiento.
-It seems we've got a traffic jam in the parking lot.

7261 nitrógeno — **nitrogen**

m
[ni.ˈtro.xe.no]

Entonces de ahí obtenemos nuestro nitrógeno.
-So that's where we get our nitrogen from.

7262 elevación — **elevation**

f
[e.le.βa.ˈsjõn]

Estaríamos más seguros a mayor elevación.
-We'd be safer at a higher elevation.

7263 clero — **clergy**

m
[ˈklɛ.ro]

El clero de ambas confesiones a menudo era hostigado y encarcelado.
-Clergy of both denominations were frequently harassed and faced with imprisonment.

7264 fresno — **ash**

	m		Está hecho de madera de fresno.
	['fɾɛ.ʂno]		-It's made of ash wood.
7265	**fractura**		**fracture**
	f		Creemos que tiene una fractura espinal.
	[fɾak̚.'tu.ɾa]		-We believe that he has a spinal fracture.
7266	**espantar**		**frighten, shoo away**
	vb		Vas a espantar mis peces.
	[ɛs.pãn̪.'taɾ]		-You will frighten my fish.
7267	**cinto**		**belt**
	m		No me voy a sacar este cinto.
	['sĩn̪.to]		-I'm not taking off this belt.
7268	**moraleja**		**moral of a fable**
	f		La moraleja de este cuento es clara.
	[mo.ɾa.'le.xa]		-The moral of this tale is clear.
7269	**imprudencia**		**carelessness**
	f		Y su imprudencia se lo quitó.
	[ĩm.pɾu.'ðɛ̃n.sja]		-And his carelessness took it from her.
7270	**campanario**		**bell tower**
	m		El campanario se hizo para épocas de guerra.
	[kãm.pa.'na.ɾjo]		-The bell tower was made for times of war.
7271	**vitrina**		**display cabinet**
	f		¿Por qué pone esa vitrina en el hall de entrada?
	[bi.'tri.na]		-Why does she put that display cabinet in the entrance hall?
7272	**viña**		**vineyard**
	f		Quiero una parte de la viña.
	['bi.ɲa]		-I want a share of the vineyard.
7273	**maltratar**		**abuse**
	vb		Nadie quiere maltratar a los niños.
	[mal̪.tɾa.'taɾ]		-None of us want to abuse children.
7274	**pasivo**		**passive; retiree**
	adj; m		El experimento requiere que el sujeto sea completamente pasivo.
	[pa.'si.βo]		-The experiment requires that the subject be completely passive.
7275	**veintisiete**		**twenty-seven**
	num		Se celebran veintisiete elecciones nacionales en situaciones muy diversas.
	[bei̯n.ti.'sjɛ.te]		-Twenty-seven national elections take place in a variety of different situations.
7276	**bíblico**		**biblical**
	adj		Jacob, tienes un nombre terriblemente bíblico.
	['bi.βli.ko]		-Jacob, you have a terribly biblical name.
7277	**pudor**		**modesty**
	m		Es un animal, pero también tiene pudor.
	[pu.'ðoɾ]		-He's an animal, but also he has some modesty.
7278	**flamenco**		**flamenco; flamingo**
	adj; m		Esta es la cuna del flamenco.
	[fla.'mɛ̃ŋ.ko]		-This is the birth home of flamenco.
7279	**cóndor**		**condor**
	m		A lo lejos sobrevuela un cóndor majestuoso.
	['kõn̪.doɾ]		-In the distance, a majestic condor is flying.
7280	**militante**		**militant; member, activist**

adj; m/f
[mi.li.ˈtãn̪.te]

Mi madre volvió a casarse con otro activista.
-My mother married again to another activist.

7281 caprichoso — **whimsical**

adj
[ka.pri.ˈʧo.so]

Soy caprichoso, pero nunca bromeo.
-I'm whimsical, but I never kid.

7282 pus — **pus**

m
[ˈpus]

Esto debería curar la inflamación, detener el pus.
-This should heal the inflammation, stop the pus.

7283 aliar — **unite**

adj
[a.ˈljar]

Debes aliar a tu tribu con los rebeldes.
-You must ally your tribe with the rebel forces.

7284 efectuar — **carry out**

vb
[e.fek̚.ˈtwar]

Podrá efectuar controles sobre el terreno.
-It may carry out verifications on the spot.

7285 aristocracia — **aristocracy**

f
[a.ris.to.ˈkra.sja]

Solo entre la aristocracia se encuentra gente así.
-You can only find people like that in the aristocracy.

7286 corcel — **steed**

m
[kor.ˈsɛl]

Fuiste un fiel y poderoso corcel.
-You were a faithful and mighty steed.

7287 veintiocho — **twenty-eight**

num
[bei̯n.ˈtjo.ʧo]

Sesenta y cuatro veces dos son ciento veintiocho.
-Sixty-four times two is one hundred twenty-eight.

7288 lavaplatos — **dishwasher**

m/f
[la.βap̚.ˈla.tos]

Está bien, seré el lavaplatos.
-All right, I'll be the dishwasher.

7289 sofocante — **suffocating**

adj[so.fo.ˈkãn̪.te]

La ironía de hoy es sofocante. -The irony of today is suffocating.

7290 melena — **mane**

f
[me.ˈle.na]

Necesito peinar esta negra melena enmarañada.
-I need to comb out this shaggy black mane.

7291 gendarme — **police officer**

m/f
[xẽn̪.ˈdar.me]

¡Será mejor que no toques al gendarme!
-You better not touch the policeman!

7292 presidir — **preside over**

vb
[pre.si.ˈðir]

Valoramos asimismo la oportunidad de presidir toda esta comunidad.
-We also value the opportunity to preside over this entire community.

7293 reproducir — **reproduce, copy**

vb
[re.pro.ðu.ˈsir]

También puede intentar reproducir fallos irreproducibles.
-You can also try to reproduce unreproducible bugs.

7294 potasio — **potassium**

m
[po.ˈta.sjo]

Necesitamos encontrar la causa de su bajo potasio.
-We need to find the cause of your low potassium.

7295 trazar — **trace**

vb
[tra.ˈsar]

Tiene que volver a trazar tus pasos.
-He has to get back to trace your steps.

7296 chimpancé — **chimpanzee**

m
[ʧĩm.pãn.ˈse]

Cada chimpancé tiene su propia personalidad.
-Every chimpanzee has his or her own personality.

| 7297 | **reproche** | **reproach** |

m

[re.ˈpro.ʧe]

Ese es un reproche de nuestro tiempo.
-This is a reproach of our times.

7298 **prosperar** **thrive**

vb

[pros.pɛ.ˈrar]

Si queremos prosperar, debes confiar en mí.
-If we want to thrive, you must trust me.

7299 **tesorero** **treasurer**

m

[te.so.ˈrɛ.ro]

Renuncié a mi posición como tesorero del club.
-I resigned from my position as club treasurer.

7300 **onza** **ounce**

f

[ˈõn.sa]

No venderé otra onza de tus cargamentos.
-I won't sell another ounce of your cargo.

7301 **oprimir** **oppress**

vb

[o.pri.ˈmir]

No pueden oprimir a la gente que ya no tiene miedo.
-You cannot oppress the people who are not afraid anymore.

7302 **esmalte** **nail polish, varnish**

m

[ɛş.ˈmal̪.te]

Tu esmalte no parece particularmente nuevo.
-Your nail polish doesn't look particularly new.

7303 **repaso** **review**

m

[re.ˈpa.so]

Quiero verte en la sesión de repaso de mañana.
-I want to see you at tomorrow's review session.

7304 **torpeza** **clumsiness**

f

[tor.ˈpe.sa]

No sé de donde sacaste tu torpeza.
-Can't think where you get your clumsiness from.

7305 **fervor** **fervor**

m[fɛr.ˈβor]

He moderado mi fervor con piedad. -I have tempered my fervor with piety.

7306 **pitillo** **cigarette**

m

[pi.ˈti.ʝo]

Y luego se encendió un pitillo.
-And then he lit a cigarette.

7307 **detección** **detection**

f

[dɛ.tɛk.ˈsjõn]

Puede utilizarse para la navegación y la detección.
-It can be used for navigation and detection.

7308 **coito** **intercourse**

m

[ˈkoi̯.to]

El coito y el parto pueden ser sumamente dolorosos y producir complicaciones.
-Sexual intercourse and childbirth may be extremely painful and result in complications.

7309 **nasal** **nasal**

adj

[na.ˈsal]

Acéptalo, tiene un problema nasal.
-Face it, he's got a nasal problem.

7310 **parámetro** **parameter**

m

[pa.ˈra.mɛ.tro]

Este parámetro no es aplicable aún a los vagones de mercancías.
-This parameter is not yet applicable to freight wagons.

7311 **emerger** **emerge**

vb

[e.mɛr.ˈxɛr]

Resulta que patrones complejos pueden emerger de ingredientes simples.
-It turns out that complex patterns can emerge from simple ingredients.

7312 **esparcir** **spread**

vb

[ɛs.par.ˈsir]

Pretende esparcir odiosas mentiras sobre mí.
-She intends to spread hateful lies about me.

7313	**movilización**	**mobilization**
	f	Está intentando provocar una movilización francesa.
	[mo.βi.li.sa.ˈsjõn]	-It's intended to provoke a French mobilization.

7314	**imparable**	**unstoppable**
	adj	Seríamos un equipo formidable, imparable.
	[ĩm.pa.ˈra.βle]	-We'd be a formidable team, unstoppable.

7315	**balar**	**bleat**
	vb	Si son separadas, empiezan a balar muy alto.
	[ba.ˈlar]	-If they are separated, they start to bleat loudly.

7316	**cortocircuito**	**short-circuit**
	m	Uno de estos sistemas detecta el cortocircuito y lo neutraliza.
	[kor.to.sir.ˈkwi.to]	-One of those systems detects the short-circuit and neutralizes it.

7317	**verificación**	**verification**
	f	Esta verificación concluirá antes del fin de 1999.
	[bɛ.ri.fi.ka.ˈsjõn]	-This verification will be concluded before the end of 1999.

7318	**destructivo**	**destructive**
	adj	Me pregunto cuál será más destructivo.
	[dɛs.truk̚.ˈti.βo]	-I wonder which one will be more destructive.

7319	**especular**	**speculate**
	vb	No quiero especular acerca de las causas y los efectos.
	[ɛs.pe.ku.ˈlar]	-I do not want to speculate about cause and effect.

| 7320 | **papelera** | **bin** |
| | f[pa.pe.ˈlɛ.ra] | Los funcionarios encontraron el espray de pimienta en una papelera cerca de la estación de metro. -Officers found the pepper spray in a bin near the underground station. |

7321	**palomar**	**dovecote**
	m	El palomar ha estado vacío durante años.
	[pa.lo.ˈmar]	-The dovecote has been empty for some years.

7322	**autenticidad**	**authenticity**
	f	De esta manera se garantiza la autenticidad del producto.
	[au̯.tẽn̪.ti.si.ˈðað]	-In this way, the authenticity of the product is guaranteed.

7323	**guardabosques**	**forest ranger**
	m/f	Como guardabosques, soy responsable de su seguridad.
	[gwar.ða.ˈβos.kes]	-As a forest ranger, I'm responsible for your safety.

7324	**derrota**	**defeat**
	f	Justo cuando pensaba que aceptaría la derrota...
	[dɛ.ˈro.ta]	-Just when he thought he would accept the defeat...

7325	**electromagnético**	**electromagnetic**
	adj	Otro rasgo distintivo de las armas nucleares es el impulso electromagnético.
	[e.lek̚.tro.may.ˈnɛ.ti.ko]	-Another feature distinctive to nuclear weapons is the electromagnetic pulse.

7326	**teología**	**theology**
	f	Si tuviera respuesta para todo, enseñaría teología en París.
	[te.o.lo.ˈxi.a]	-If I had the answers to everything, I'd be teaching theology in Paris.

7327	**patrullero**	**patrolman**
	m	Envíe a un patrullero a la casa de Logan.
	[pa.tru.ˈjɛ.ro]	-I sent a patrolman to Logan's house.

7328	**tuerca**	**screw**
	f	Tiene que tener una tuerca suelta.
	[ˈtwɛr.ka]	-She must have a screw loose.

| 7329 | **arrugar** | **wrinkle** |

arrugar
vb
[a.ru.ˈɣar]

wrinkle
Trata de no arrugar el vestido.
-Try not to wrinkle this dress.

7330 **blasfemo**
adj
[blas.ˈfe.mo]

blasphemous
Supongo que es horriblemente blasfemo decirlo aquí.
-I suppose it's terribly blasphemous to be saying that here.

7331 **lupa**
f
[ˈlu.pa]

magnifying glass
Observa su bolsillo con una lupa.
-Look at his pocket with a magnifying glass.

7332 **empresarial**
adj
[ẽm.pre.sa.ˈrjal]

corporate
El sector privado promoverá iniciativas de responsabilidad social empresarial.
-The private sector will promote corporate social responsibility initiatives.

7333 **plural**
m
[plu.ˈral]

plural
Suena mal cuando usas el plural.
-It sounds wrong when you use the plural.

7334 **con antelación**
adv
[kon ãn̪.te.la.ˈsjõn]

beforehand
Me presentaré con antelación para aprobar los preparativos.
-I will present myself beforehand, to approve the arrangements.

7335 **cuestionario**
m
[kwɛs.tjo.ˈna.rjo]

questionnaire
El texto se adjuntaría al cuestionario.
-The text would be attached to the questionnaire.

7336 **asedio**
m
[a.ˈse.ðjo]

siege
Eso nos da tiempo para prepararnos para un asedio.
-Which gives us time to prepare for a siege.

7337 **lucro**
m
[ˈlu.kro]

profit
La víctima también tendrá derecho a pedir indemnización por lucro cesante.
-The victim has a right to demand also the compensation of the unearned profit.

7338 **sepulcro**
m
[se.ˈpul.kro]

tomb
Es como una mujer levantándose del sepulcro.
-She is like a woman rising from a tomb.

7339 **larva**
f
[ˈlar.βa]

larva
Cada uno de estos nódulos tiene una larva.
-Each of these nodules contains a larva.

7340 **precoz**
adj
[ˈpre.kos]

precocious
Y no era precoz, sino moderadamente inteligente.
-I wasn't precocious, just moderately intelligent.

7341 **saqueo**
m
[sa.ˈke.o]

pillage
El saqueo de los bosques tropicales es un azote para nuestro planeta.
-The pillage of tropical forests is a scourge for our planet.

7342 **diagrama**
m
[dja.ˈɣra.ma]

diagram
El diagrama refleja la media de las edades.
-The diagram reflects the average ages.

7343 **proclamar**
vb
[pro.kla.ˈmar]

proclaim
Sin embargo, todavía es muy temprano para proclamar una victoria.
-It is too soon, however, to proclaim victory.

7344 **clemente**
adj
[kle.ˈmẽn̪.te]

merciful
Él será más clemente conmigo que con usted.
-He will be more merciful to me than to you.

7345 **deplorable**
adj
[dep̚.lo.ˈra.βle]
deplorable
No me importa cuánto te guste, deplorable criatura.
-I don't care how much you love it, you deplorable creature.

7346 **eminente**
adj
[e.mi.ˈnẽn̪.te]
eminent
El monumento se erigió en honor al eminente filósofo.
-The monument was erected in honor of the eminent philosopher.

7347 **portazo**
m
[por.ˈta.so]
slam
No fui yo el que dio un portazo.
-It wasn't me who slammed the door.

7348 **levadura**
f
[le.βa.ˈðu.ɾa]
yeast
Disuelve el extracto de levadura en 100 ml de agua.
-Dissolve the yeast extract in 100 ml water.

7349 **delirante**
adj
[de.li.ˈrãn̪.te]
delirious
Apuesto a que está un poco delirante.
-I bet he's pretty delirious.

7350 **plantear**
vb[plãn̪.te.ˈar]
pose
Dicho esto, quisiera plantear las siguientes preguntas. -Having said that, let me pose the following questions.

7351 **alcaldía**
f
[al.kal̪.ˈdi.a]
mayor's office
Encontrarás mi placa en la alcaldía.
-You'll find the badge down in the mayor's office.

7352 **nulo**
adj
[ˈnu.lo]
invalid
Naturalmente, los matrimonios forzados son ilegales y todo matrimonio contraído bajo tales condiciones se considera nulo.
-Of course, forced marriage was against the law, and any marriage contracted under such conditions would be considered invalid.

7353 **sobrecarga**
f
[so.βre.ˈkar.ɣa]
overload
Parece que estaba produciendo una sobrecarga.
-It appears it was building toward an overload.

7354 **limo**
m
[ˈli.mo]
mud
El aire huele a limo.
-The air smells of mud.

7355 **nordeste**
m
[nor.ˈðɛs.te]
north-east
Posteriormente hizo un giro y emprendió rumbo nordeste.
-It then turned and flew back to the north-east.

7356 **reelección**
f
[re.e.lɛk.ˈsjõn]
reelection
Perdió la reelección y finalmente se suicidó.
-He lost the reelection and eventually, he killed himself.

7357 **pesquero**
adj; m
[pɛs.ˈkɛ.ro]
fishing; fishing boat
Me recogió un barco pesquero francés.
-I got picked up by a French fishing boat.

7358 **sobrepasar**
vb
[so.βre.pa.ˈsar]
exceed
La duración total de período de aislamiento no debe sobrepasar las 48 horas.
-The total duration of isolation must not exceed 48 hours.

7359 **demoler**
vb
[de.mo.ˈlɛr]
demolish
Nos ordenaron demoler este edificio hoy.
-We were ordered to demolish this place by today.

7360 **integración**
f
[ĩn̪.te.ɣra.ˈsjõn]
integration
Parece existir más separación y partición que integración.
-There seems to be more separation and partition than integration.

7361	**rejilla**	**rack**
	f	Deja enfriar al pan sobre una rejilla.
	[re.ˈxi.ʝa]	-Leave the bread to cool on a rack.
7362	**enjambre**	**swarm**
	m	Un enjambre de avispones atacó a los adolescentes.
	[ẽɲ.ˈxãm.bre]	-A swarm of hornets attacked the teenagers.
7363	**prominente**	**prominent**
	adj	Era un escritor exitoso de una revista prominente.
	[pro.mi.ˈnẽn̪.te]	-I was a successful writer at a prominent magazine.
7364	**resguardo**	**receipt**
	m	Tenía un resguardo en su bolsillo.
	[rɛş.ˈɣwar.ðo]	-He had a receipt in his pocket.
7365	**intolerancia**	**intolerance**
	f[ĩn̪.to.lɛ.ˈrãn.sja]	Aquí la intolerancia no es tolerada. -Here, intolerance will not be tolerated.
7366	**arduo**	**arduous**
	adj	Fue un proceso arduo y prolongado.
	[ˈar.ðwo]	-It was a long and arduous process.
7367	**nominación**	**nomination**
	f	Humildemente te pido que aceptes mi nominación.
	[no.mi.na.ˈsjõn]	-I humbly ask you to accept my nomination.
7368	**tumulto**	**tumult**
	m	Ella dijo que le gustaba el tumulto.
	[tu.ˈmul̪.to]	-She said she liked the tumult.
7369	**pordiosero**	**beggar**
	m	No quiero parecer un pordiosero.
	[por.ðjo.ˈsɛ.ro]	-I don't want to look like a beggar.
7370	**escarlata**	**scarlet; scarlet**
	adj; m	Yo habría escogido la bufanda escarlata.
	[ɛs.kar.ˈla.ta]	-I would've gone with the scarlet scarf.
7371	**barullo**	**noise**
	m	El pingüino estaba haciendo el barullo.
	[ba.ˈru.ʝo]	-The penguin was making that noise.
7372	**ahuyentar**	**drive away**
	vb	Es un amuleto, para ahuyentar a los demonios.
	[a.u.ʝẽn̪.ˈtar]	-It's a charm, to drive away demons.
7373	**hacha**	**axe**
	f	No quería dejar su hacha atrás.
	[ˈa.tʃa]	-Didn't want to leave his ax behind.
7374	**regularidad**	**consistency**
	f	Me preocupaba mucho su regularidad con la medicación.
	[re.ɣu.la.ri.ˈðað]	-I had a lot of concerns with his consistency with the medication.
7375	**comandancia**	**headquarters**
	f	Es una orden de la comandancia.
	[ko.mãn̪.ˈdãn.sja]	-It's an order from headquarters.
7376	**apendicitis**	**appendicitis**
	f	Tenemos un caso de apendicitis aguda aquí.
	[a.pẽn̪.di.ˈsi.tis]	-We've got a case of acute appendicitis here.
7377	**ingenuidad**	**naivety**

f
[ĩŋ.xe.nwi.ˈðað]

Norma, su ingenuidad me asombra.
-Norma, your naivety amazes me.

7378 **bache**   **bump**

m
[ˈba.ʧe]

Nos hemos comido un pequeño bache del camino.
-We hit a little bump in the road.

7379 **monetario**   **monetary**

adj
[mo.nɛ.ˈta.rjo]

El régimen monetario tiene que encarar aún las nuevas cuestiones que surgen de una integración más profunda.
-The monetary regime still has to address new issues arising out of deeper integration.

7380 **aniquilación**   **annihilation**

f[a.ni.ki.la.ˈsjõn]

Esta sería una guerra de aniquilación. -This was to be a war of annihilation.

7381 **recibimiento**   **reception**

m
[re.si.βi.ˈmjẽn̯.to]

Si que se pone contenta de verme, no esperaba este recibimiento.
-You really look happy to see me, I wasn't expecting such reception.

7382 **medidor**   **measuring; meter**

adj; m
[me.ði.ˈðor]

La aguja va pegada a un médidor de presión.
-The needle is attached to a pressure meter.

7383 **glándula**   **gland**

f
[ˈglãn̯.du.la]

Necesitaba cirugía para extirpar su glándula suprarrenal derecha.
-He needed surgery to remove his right adrenal gland.

7384 **inadecuado**   **unsuitable**

adj
[i.na.ðe.ˈkwa.ðo]

Esta consideración confirma el carácter inadecuado del segundo enfoque.
-This finding confirms that the second approach is unsuitable.

7385 **monumental**   **monumental**

adj
[mo.nu.mẽn̯.ˈtal]

Inclusive el mínimo esfuerzo seria monumental para ella ahora mismo.
-Even the tiniest effort is monumental for her right now.

7386 **recluso**   **be in prison; prisoner**

adj; m
[re.ˈklu.so]

Los gastos corren por cuenta del recluso.
-The costs are required to be met by the prisoner.

7387 **estresar(se)**   **stress**

vb
[ɛs.tre.ˈsar]

No quiero estresar al cocodrilo más de lo debido.
-I don't want to stress the crocodile more than I have to.

7388 **parking**   **parking lot**

m
[par.ˈkĩŋ]

Tenemos una urgencia en el parking.
-We have a situation in the parking lot.

7389 **migración**   **migration**

f
[mi.ɣra.ˈsjõn]

La migración de personas calificadas presenta algunos aspectos positivos.
-The migration of skilled migrants has a number of positive aspects.

7390 **titanio**   **titanium**

m
[ti.ˈta.njo]

El titanio se prefiere generalmente porque es ligero y puede soportar altas presiones y temperaturas.
-Titanium is generally preferred because it's lightweight and can withstand high compression and temperature.

7391 **púbico**   **pubic**

adj
[ˈpu.βi.ko]

Junto con un pelo púbico femenino sin identificar.
-Along with an unidentified female pubic hair.

7392 **reprimir**   **suppress**

vb
[re.pri.ˈmir]

No debes reprimir tus sentimientos.
-You should not suppress your feelings.

7393	**procesamiento**	**prosecution**
	m	Así aumentarán las posibilidades de un procesamiento con éxito.
	[pro.se.sa.ˈmjẽn̪.to]	-In this way, the chances of a successful prosecution will be increased.
7394	**susurrar**	**whisper**
	vb	No tienes por qué susurrar, friki.
	[su.su.ˈrar]	-You don't have to whisper, weirdo.
7395	**inaudito**	**unheard-of**
	adj [i.nau̯.ˈði.to]	Lejos de ser algo inaudito, también podría funcionar en este caso. -Far from being unheard-of, it could work in this case too.
7396	**vigilia**	**vigil**
	f	Tal vez está cansada por la vigilia.
	[bi.ˈxi.lja]	-Perhaps you were tired from your vigil.
7397	**coordinar**	**coordinate**
	vb	También necesitamos coordinar mejor nuestra asistencia técnica.
	[ko.or.ði.ˈnar]	-We also need to coordinate our technical assistance better.
7398	**alineado**	**aligned**
	adj	Debes mantener tu futuro alineado correctamente.
	[a.li.ne.ˈa.ðo]	-You have to keep your future properly aligned.
7399	**involuntario**	**involuntary**
	adj	Tiene razón, es un reflejo involuntario.
	[ĩm.bo.lũn̪.ˈta.rjo]	-He's right, it's an involuntary reflex.
7400	**retornar**	**return**
	vb	La gente debe retornar a los hogares natales.
	[rɛ.tor.ˈnar]	-People must return to their homes.
7401	**séquito**	**entourage**
	m	Ha decidido unirse al séquito permanentemente.
	[ˈse.ki.to]	-He's decided to permanently join the entourage.
7402	**desolación**	**devastation**
	f	Hemos visto avances asimétricos en conflictos con trayectoria histórica de desolación y violencia.
	[de.so.la.ˈsjõn]	-We have seen uneven progress in conflicts with a history of devastation and violence.
7403	**devastar**	**devastate**
	vb	Hay muchas maneras de devastar una huerta.
	[de.βas.ˈtar]	-There are so many ways to devastate an orchard.
7404	**habitar**	**dwell**
	vb	Todos los animales y los seres humanos buscaban un lugar para habitar.
	[a.βi.ˈtar]	-All the animals and humans looked for a place to dwell.
7405	**estatuto**	**statute**
	m	Debería pasar el estatuto de limitaciones.
	[ɛs.ta.ˈtu.to]	-It must be past the statute of limitations.
7406	**extenso**	**extensive**
	adj	Le agradezco su extenso discurso ante el Parlamento.
	[ɛks.ˈtẽn.so]	-I thank him for his very extensive address to Parliament.
7407	**acumular**	**accumulate**
	vb	Se necesitan años para acumular tanta basura.
	[a.ku.mu.ˈlar]	-It must have taken years to accumulate this mess.
7408	**noviazgo**	**engagement**
	m	Vuestro noviazgo aún no es oficial.
	[no.ˈβjas̬.ɣo]	-Your engagement isn't official yet.

7409 **teñir**　　**dye**
vb
[te.ˈɲir]　　Puedes conservar tu vestido y teñir el resto.
　　-You can keep your outfit and dye the rest of it.

7410 **mota**　　**speck**
f[ˈmo.ta]　　Sabía que había vida en esta mota. -I knew there was life on this speck.

7411 **compulsivo**　　**compulsive**
adj
[kõm.pul.ˈsi.βo]　　Mi tío era compulsivo acerca de todas esas cosas.
　　-My uncle was compulsive about all that stuff.

7412 **cualificar**　　**qualify**
vb
[kwa.li.fi.ˈkar]　　Entonces, ¿esto se puede cualificar como iluminación ambiental?
　　-So, does this qualify as mood lighting?

7413 **cauteloso**　　**cautious**
adj
[kau̯.te.ˈlo.so]　　Y ahora necesitas ser aún más cauteloso.
　　-And now you need to be even more cautious.

7414 **predecesor**　　**predecessor**
m
[pre.ðe.se.ˈsor]　　También agradecemos la labor de su predecesor.
　　-We are also grateful to your predecessor for his efforts.

7415 **pensador**　　**thinker**
m
[pẽn.sa.ˈðor]　　Él es un pensador independiente.
　　-He is an independent thinker.

7416 **empleador**　　**employer**
m
[ẽm.ple.a.ˈðor]　　Todo empleador que infringe estas disposiciones es multado o sancionado.
　　-Any employer who violates these provisions is fined or subject to punishment.

7417 **granizo**　　**hail**
m
[gra.ˈni.so]　　Esa noche, una tormenta de granizo destruyó su auto.
　　-That night, a hail storm smashed his car.

7418 **succión**　　**suction**
f
[suk.ˈsjõn]　　Necesito mucha succión para poder ver esta arteria.
　　-I need lots of suction so I can see this artery.

7419 **fobia**　　**phobia**
f
[ˈfo.βja]　　La fobia social es diferente de la timidez.
　　-Social phobia is different from shyness.

7420 **tea**　　**torch**
f
[ˈte.a]　　Dale una tea para que pueda ver el camino.
　　-Give him a torch so he can see the road.

7421 **hostal**　　**hostel**
m
[os.ˈtal]　　Vine con algunas chicas del hostal.
　　-I came along with some girls from the hostel.

7422 **leproso**　　**leprous; leper**
adj; m
[le.ˈpro.so]　　Estaba empezando a sentirme como un leproso.
　　-I was beginning to feel like a leper.

7423 **inadmisible**　　**unacceptable**
adj
[i.nað.mi.ˈsi.βle]　　Es inadmisible, y quisiera una respuesta.
　　-It is unacceptable and I should like an answer.

7424 **tutela**　　**guardianship**
f
[tu.ˈte.la]　　No se pierde la tutela ni siquiera cuando los padres están separados.
　　-Guardianship is not lost even when parents are separated.

7425 **trote**　　**trot**

m
['tro.te]

Los caballos se mueven de tres maneras: Paso, trote y galope.
-Horses walk in three modes: Walk, trot and gallop.

7426 **constelación** **constellation**

f
[kõns.te.la.ˈsjõn]

Ahí arriba está la constelación de Orión.
-That up there's the constellation of Orion.

7427 **cigüeña** **stork**

f
[si.ˈɣwe.ɲa]

Si fueras mi hija, te enviaría de vuelta con la cigüeña.
-If you were my kid, I'd mail you back to the stork.

7428 **rivalidad** **rivalry**

f
[ri.βa.li.ˈðað]

El continente africano es un terreno de especial rivalidad.
-The African continent is a field of particular rivalry.

7429 **salvamento** **rescue**

m
[sal.βa.ˈmẽn̪.to]

Estas son las operaciones de búsqueda y salvamento hasta la fecha.
-These are the search and rescue operations to date.

7430 **conyugal** **conjugal**

adj
[kõn̪.ɟʝu.ˈɣal]

Me otorgó una visita conyugal con mi novia.
-He gave me a conjugal visit with my girlfriend.

7431 **desgraciar** **ruin**

vb
[dɛʂ.ɣra.ˈsjar]

No puedes dejar que una mala racha desgracie tu vida para siempre.
-You can't let a tough break ruin your whole life.

7432 **pretensión** **ambition**

f
[pɾɛ.tẽn.ˈsjõn]

Sabemos, sin embargo, que nuestra pretensión tiene algo de ilusorio.
-However, we know that our ambition is somewhat illusory.

7433 **florero** **vase**

m
[flo.ˈɾɛ.ro]

Quizás haya dejado algo de esa hierba en un florero.
-Maybe he left a little of that grass in a vase.

7434 **fastidioso** **annoying**

adj
[fas.ti.ˈðjo.so]

Recibió otra carta de ese hombre fastidioso.
-And you got another letter from that annoying man.

7435 **diantres** **damn it**

int
[ˈdjãn̪.tres]

Más lento, diantres, más lento.
-Slower, damn it, go slower.

7436 **lingote** **ingot**

m
[lĩŋ.ˈgo.te]

Dale un lingote para el Arzobispo.
-Give him an ingot for the Archbishop.

7437 **despeje** **clearance**

m
[dɛs.ˈpe.xe]

La misión de planificación examinó varias posibilidades de actividades de despeje de minas.
-The planning mission reviewed various options for mine clearance.

7438 **extraviar(se)** **misplace**

vb
[ɛks.tra.ˈβjar]

¿Tú cómo puedes extraviar 200 libras?
-How can you just misplace £200?

7439 **tedioso** **tedious**

adj
[te.ˈðjo.so]

Tengo que decir que fue un proceso tedioso.
-I must say, it was a tedious exercise.

7440 **madero** **log, cop (coll)**

m
[ma.ˈðɛ.ro]

Me encanta la emoción del grano floreciente, o el madero hendido.
-I love the thrill of the grain flourishing or the log splitting.

7441 **sabotear** **sabotage**

vb[sa.βo.te.ˈar]   No estoy intentando sabotear a la tribu. -I'm not trying to sabotage the tribe.

7442 ileso — **unhurt**

adj

[i.ˈle.so]

El conductor resultó ileso y consiguió escapar de la zona.
-The driver was unhurt and managed to escape from the area.

7443 dígito — **digit**

m

[ˈdi.xi.to]

Los valores posibles de dicho código consisten en un solo dígito.
-The possible values of that code consist of a single digit.

7444 machista — **sexist; sexist**

adj; m

[ma.ˈʧis.ta]

No digo que seas un monstruo machista.
-I'm not saying that you're a sexist monster.

7445 realismo — **realism**

m

[re.a.ˈliş.mo]

Así que intentamos incrementar el realismo.
-So, we try to increase the realism.

7446 recortar — **trim**

vb

[re.kor.ˈtar]

Recuerdo cuando solías recortar mi jardín.
-I remember when you used to trim my garden.

7447 humanitario — **humanitarian**

adj

[u.ma.ni.ˈta.rjo]

Nos espera un gran reto humanitario.
-There is a big humanitarian challenge ahead of us.

7448 martirio — **martyrdom**

m

[mar.ˈti.rjo]

Pero el martirio es diferente y peligroso.
-But martyrdom is different and dangerous.

7449 cubeta — **tray, bucket**

f

[ku.ˈβɛ.ta]

Voy por una cubeta de agua.
-I'll get a bucket of water.

7450 petardo — **firecracker**

m

[pɛ.ˈtar.ðo]

Imagínese un petardo en la palma de su mano.
-Imagine a firecracker in the palm of your hand.

7451 defectuoso — **defective**

adj

[de.fek.ˈtwo.so]

Llamarlo "defectuoso" no parece adecuado.
-Calling him "defective" does not seem suitable.

7452 rozar — **brush against**

vb

[ro.ˈsar]

Tus manos deberían rozarle accidentalmente.
-Your hands should brush him accidentally.

7453 bonificación — **bonus**

f

[bo.ni.fi.ka.ˈsjõn]

Pero así no conseguiría una bonificación.
-And that wouldn't get you a bonus.

7454 hervido — **boiled; casserole**

adj; m

[ɛr.ˈβi.ðo]

Hace dos semanas probé un huevo hervido.
-Two weeks ago, I tried a soft-boiled egg.

7455 turbio — **muddy**

adj

[ˈtur.βjo]

Bueno, es húmedo y turbio.
-Well, it's wet and muddy.

7456 recrear — **recreate**

vb

[re.kre.ˈar]

Todos estos años estaba intentando recrear una familia.
-All these years he was trying to recreate a family.

7457 dineral — **fortune**

m[di.nɛ.ˈral]

Te has gastado un dineral en los muebles. -You spent a fortune on furniture.

7458 acantilado — **steep; cliff**

adj; m Deberíamos buscar al otro lado del acantilado.
[a.kãn̪.ti.ˈla.ðo] -We should search the other side of the cliff.

7459 pavimento **pavement**

m Se golpeó muy duro con el pavimento.
[pa.βi.ˈmẽn̪.to] -He hit the pavement so hard.

7460 hurtar **steal**

vb Un funcionario intentó hurtar ocho bobinas de alambre de púas.
[ur.ˈtar] -A staff member attempted to steal eight bundles of concertina wire.

7461 lepra **leprosy**

f Ellos fueron quienes curaron mi lepra.
[ˈle.pra] -They were the ones who cured my leprosy.

7462 simplicidad **simplicity**

f Ello redundaría en mayor simplicidad y transparencia.
[sĩm.pli.si.ˈðað] -This will make for greater simplicity and transparency.

7463 pródigo **prodigal, generous**

adj Soy el hijo pródigo tratando de enmendarse.
[ˈpro.ði.ɣo] -I'm the prodigal son trying to make amends.

7464 sinónimo **synonym; synonymous**

adj; m Género no es sinónimo de mujer.
[si.ˈno.ni.mo] -Gender is not a synonym for "female".

7465 embrollar(se) **confuse**

vb Los efectos del mercado único no han hecho más que embrollar la cuestión.
[ẽm.bro.ˈjar] -The effect of the single market has been to confuse the issue.

7466 drástico **drastic**

adj Quizás quieras probar algo un poco menos drástico.
[ˈdras.ti.ko] -You might want to try something a little less drastic.

7467 miligramo **milligram**

m La dosis normal es alrededor de un miligramo.
[mi.li.ˈɣra.mo] -The normal dose is around one milligram.

7468 boliche **bowling, nightclub (LA)**

m Odiaría perder la bola de boliche de papá.
[bo.ˈli.tʃe] -I'd hate to lose my father's bowling ball.

7469 empatía **empathy**

f ¿Siente alguna empatía por él?
[ẽm.pa.ˈti.a] -Do you feel any empathy for him?

7470 interacción **interaction**

f Continuaremos apoyando esta interacción en el futuro.
[ĩn̪.te.rak.ˈsjõn] -We will continue to support such interaction in the future.

7471 yodo **iodine**

m También encontrarán varias tabletas de yodo en sus raciones semanales .
[ˈɟjo.ðo] -You will also find several iodine tablets in your weekly rations.

7472 enfurecer(se) **drive mad, enrage**

vb[ẽm.fu.re.ˈsɛr] Fingen ser tan compasivos, esforzándose en no enfurecer una pobre alma. -
They pretend to be so compassionate, trying hard not to enrage a poor soul.

7473 vocero **spokesman**

m Es el vocero de toda su industria.
[bo.ˈsɛ.ro] -He's the spokesman for his entire industry.

7474 evasivo **evasive**

adj
[e.βa.ˈsi.βo]

Y desecharlos como locos es igualmente evasivo.
-And to dismiss them as madmen is equally evasive.

7475 desdén — **disdain**

m
[dɛş.ˈðẽn]

Su desdén fue muy claro por la mirada que me dio.
-Your disdain was perfectly clear from the look you gave me.

7476 cegar — **blind**

vb
[se.ˈɣar]

Subiré un virus diseñado para cegar sus defensas.
-I will upload a virus that is designed to blind their defenses.

7477 variable — **variable**

f
[ba.ˈrja.βle]

Hay una variable que quiero aislar.
-I have a variable I'd like to isolate.

7478 cornisa — **cornice**

f
[kor.ˈni.sa]

Su cornisa está decorada con triglifos y metopas.
-The cornice is decorated with triglyphs and metopes.

7479 garrote — **stick**

m
[ga.ˈro.te]

No, pero soy buena con el garrote.
-No, but I'm good with a stick.

7480 mayúsculo — **tremendous**

adj
[ma.ˈjus.ku.lo]

Casi se convierte en un desastre mayúsculo.
-That was almost a major disaster.

7481 revertir — **revert**

vb
[re.βɛr.ˈtir]

Seleccione la revisión que desea revertir.
-Select the revision you wish to revert.

7482 reencuentro — **reencounter**

m
[re.ẽŋ.ˈkwẽn.tro]

Yo pensaba que esto era un reencuentro, no una entrevista de trabajo.
-I thought it was a reencounter, not a job interview.

7483 zodiaco — **zodiac**

m
[so.ˈðja.ko]

Para identificar los planetas hay que familiarizarse con las estrellas de zodiaco porque siguen la eclíptica.
-To identify planets it is necessary to get acquainted with the stars of the zodiac because they follow the ecliptic.

7484 premier — **premiere**

f
[pre.ˈmjɛr]

Debemos preparar la película para la premier.
-We must get the film ready for the premiere.

7485 elocuencia — **eloquence**

f
[e.lo.ˈkwẽn.sja]

La elocuencia política que muestra es realmente impresionante.
-Your political eloquence is very impressive indeed.

7486 franquicia — **franchise**

f
[frãŋ.ˈki.sja]

Estaba siendo expulsada de la franquicia.
-I was being pushed away from the franchise.

7487 embriaguez — **drunkenness**

f[ẽm.ˈbrja.ɣes]

La embriaguez no está en el vino. -Drunkenness isn't in the wine.

7488 cervecería — **brewery**

f
[sɛr.βe.sɛ.ˈri.a]

Estos departamentos pertenecían a la cervecería.
-These flats used to belong to the brewery.

7489 páramo — **wasteland**

m
[ˈpa.ra.mo]

El sur se transformó en un páramo.
-The south was turned into a wasteland.

7490 híbrido — **mix; hybrid**

adj; m

['i.βri.ðo]

Es un híbrido entre chinche y cucaracha.

-It's like a hybrid between a bedbug and a cockroach.

7491 **garbo** **grace**

m

['gar.βo]

Aunque sí que reaccioné con cierta cantidad de garbo bajo presión.

-Though I did react with a certain amount of grace under pressure.

7492 **patología** **pathology**

f

[pa.to.lo.'xi.a]

Porque has contribuido mucho a mi patología.

-Because you have contributed a lot to my pathology.

7493 **dimitir** **resign**

vb

[di.mi.'tir]

Pero eso significa que tendría que dimitir.

-But that means I'd have to resign.

7494 **patilla** **sideburn**

f

[pa.'ti.ʝa]

Está junto a tu patilla izquierda.

-It is by your left sideburn.

7495 **encía** **gum**

f

[ẽn.'si.a]

Este es una enfermedad de la encía.

-This one is a gum disease.

7496 **resorte** **spring**

m

[re.'sor.te]

La portilla tiene un resorte roto.

-There is a busted spring in the chute.

7497 **inaugural** **inaugural**

adj

[i.nau̯.ɣu.'ral]

No puedo llevarte al baile inaugural.

-I can't take you to the inaugural ball.

7498 **roedor** **rodent, mouse (coll)**

m

[ro.e.'ðor]

Hay un pequeño roedor mirándome mientras trabajo.

-There is a small rodent looking at me while I work.

7499 **forestal** **forest; ranger**

adj; m

[fo.rɛs.'tal]

No quiero iniciar otro incendio forestal.

-I don't want to start another forest fire.

7500 **implicación** **implication**

f

[ĩm.pli.ka.'sjõn]

Ignoraré la implicación de su pregunta, detective.

-I'll ignore the implication of your question, detective.

7501 **urgir** **press**

vb

[ur.'xir]

Hemos de urgir el restablecimiento de esta autonomía.

-We must press for the restoration of this autonomy.

7502 **chantajear** **blackmail**

vb

[ʧãn̪.ta.xe.'ar]

Quizás su siguiente movimiento es intentar chantajear al sheriff.

-Maybe his next move is to try to blackmail the sheriff.

7503 **bestial** **brutal**

adj[bɛs.'tjal]

Tengo una resaca bestial y se me revuelve el estómago. -I have a beastly hangover and my bowels are in a tumble.

7504 **renombre** **renown**

m

[re.'nõm.bre]

Ella es una violinista de cierto renombre.

-She's a violinist of some renown.

7505 **frenesí** **frenzy**

m

[fre.ne.'si]

Los tiburones están a punto de unirse al frenesí.

-Next to join the frenzy are the sharks.

7506 **heces** **dregs, feces**

fpl
Puedo llevar las heces yo sola.
['e.ses]
-I can transport the feces on my own.

7507 atletismo **athletics**
m
A mí no me interesaba el atletismo.
[at̪.lɛ.ˈtis̺.mo]
-I wasn't interested in athletics.

7508 zurrar **spank**
vb
Y te prometemos que nadie te volverá a zurrar otra vez.
[su.ˈrar]
-And we promise that no one will ever spank you again.

7509 finalista **finalist; finalist**
adj; m/f
Reciban a nuestro primer finalista.
[fi.na.ˈlis.ta]
-Please welcome our first finalist.

7510 alegar **claim**
vb
Podría alegar que las bombas salvaron vidas.
[a.le.ˈɣar]
-So you could claim the bombings saved lives.

7511 estrenar **use for the first time**
vb
Será duro, peligroso y una excelente oportunidad de estrenar mis nuevos
[ɛs.tre.ˈnar]
pantalones.
-It'll be tough, dangerous, and a perfect chance to premiere my new cargo
shorts.

7512 poro **pore**
m
Con cada poro de mi cuerpo, tengo miedo.
[ˈpo.ro]
-With every pore of my body, I'm scared.

7513 indignante **outrageous**
adj
Lo que está ocurriendo aquí es, sencillamente, indignante.
[ĩn.diɣ.ˈnãn̪.te]
-What is happening here is simply outrageous.

7514 catastrófico **catastrophic**
adj
Sería un evento catastrófico para el planeta.
[ka.tas.ˈtro.fi.ko]
-It would be a catastrophic event for the planet.

7515 canino **canine; canine tooth**
adj; m
Creo que es un diente canino.
[ka.ˈni.no]
-I think it's a canine tooth.

7516 dote **dowry**
f
Guárdalo como parte de tu dote.
[ˈdo.te]
-Keep it as a portion of your dowry.

7517 radial **radio; circular saw**
adj; f
Nuevamente recibo el sonido radial, señor.
[ra.ˈðjal]
-I'm getting that radio sound again, sir.

7518 podio **podium**
m[ˈpo.ðjo]
Todos los candidatos se sentaron en el podio. -All candidates were seated at
the podium.

7519 relevar **relieve, substitute**
vb
Tocar un instrumento puede relevar mucho estrés.
[re.le.ˈβar]
-Playing an instrument can relieve a lot of stress.

7520 burócrata **bureaucrat**
m/f
Soy simplemente un burócrata del sistema.
[bu.ˈro.kra.ta]
-I am merely a bureaucrat of the system.

7521 intermitente **intermittent; blinker**
adj; m
Parece que se trata de un problema intermitente.
[ĩn.tɛr.mi.ˈtẽn̪.te]
-It seems to be an intermittent problem.

7522 helio **helium**

	m	El helio resuena de otra forma en mis cuerdas vocales.
	['e.ljo]	-The helium resonates differently with my vocal chords.
7523	**elixir**	**elixir**
	m	Este café debe ser un elixir de la juventud.
	[e.lik.'sir]	-This cafe must be my elixir of youth.
7524	**autonomía**	**autonomy**
	f	Se habla mucho sobre la autonomía personal.
	[au̯.to.no.'mi.a]	-Now, we hear a lot of talk about personal autonomy.
7525	**furor**	**fury**
	m	El furor de los cielos puede atacar en cualquier momento.
	[fu.'ror]	-The fury of heaven may strike at any moment.

Argentine slang

Adjectives

Rank	Spanish-PoS	Translation(s)
5007	numeroso-adj	numerous
5013	experimental-adj	experimental
5018	heroico-adj	heroic
5022	hebreo-adj; m	Hebrew; Jew
5025	nato-adj	born
5029	incompetente-adj	incompetent
5035	significativo-adj	significant
5041	académico-adj; m	academic; academic
5043	regional-adj	regional
5052	transparente-adj	transparent
5053	intolerable-adj	unbearable
5055	húngaro-adj; m	Hungarian; Hungarian person
5056	escandaloso-adj	scandalous
5057	imperdonable-adj	unforgivable
5059	vertical-adj	vertical
5062	frecuente-adj	frequent
5073	irracional-adj	irrational
5081	latino-adj; m	Latin; Latino
5082	inmóvil-adj	immobile
5088	repleto-adj	full
5094	gringo-adj; m	gringo; gringo (coll), foreigner (LA) (coll)
5102	odioso-adj	odious
5108	fluido-m; adj; adv	fluid; free-flowing; fluently
5117	menudo-adj	small
5118	continental-adj	continental
5120	casual-adj	chance
5126	mutante-adj; m/f	mutating; mutant
5136	llorón-adj; m	whiny; crybaby
5137	errado-adj	wrong
5168	inmune-adj	immune
5179	entusiasta-m; adj	fan; enthusiastic
5184	apto-adj	suitable
5186	zurdo-adj; m	left-handed; left-handed person
5187	inolvidable-adj	unforgettable
5192	excesivo-adj	excessive
5197	genético-adj	genetic
5199	obligatorio-adj	mandatory
5203	extravagante-adj	extravagant
5207	provisional-adj	provisional
5209	filipino-adj; m	Philippine; Philippine person
5210	impermeable-m; adj	weatherproof; waterproof
5212	ocasional-adj	occasional
5218	excéntrico-adj; m	eccentric; eccentric person
5222	rastreador-adj; m	tracking; tracker
5224	desempleado-adj; m	unemployed; unemployed person
5226	asiático-adj; m	Asian; Asian person
5228	consiguiente-adj	consequent
5237	inseguro-adj	unsafe, insecure
5243	fugaz-adj	brief
5247	impredecible-adj	unpredictable
5249	gigantesco-adj	gigantic
5263	gradual-adj	gradual
5264	desconectado-adj	disconnected
5266	racial-adj	racial
5267	venenoso-adj	poisonous
5272	mezquino-adj	mean
5274	aislado-adj	isolated
5279	solemne-adj	solemn
5280	belga-adj; m	Belgian; Belgian person
5281	temible-adj	fearsome
5289	amateur-adj	amateur
5292	válido-adj	valid
5295	reconfortante-adj	heartwarming
5296	serbio-adj; m	Serbian; Serb
5299	locomotora-f; adj	locomotive; locomotor
5305	anal-adj	anal
5307	doméstico-adj	domestic
5315	genuino-adj	genuine
5317	obediente-adj	obedient
5321	accesorio-m; adj	accessory; secondary
5327	costoso-adj	expensive
5332	miniatura-f; adj	miniature; miniature
5334	aterrorizado-adj	terrified
5335	sombrío-adj	somber
5336	favorable-adj	favorable
5343	devoto-m; adj	devotee; devout
5345	idéntico-adj	identical

5348	**pionero**-*adj; m*	pioneering; pioneer
5354	**cacharro**-*adj; m*	junky; wreck
5359	**estéril**-*adj*	sterile
5365	**electoral**-*adj*	electoral
5366	**sanguíneo**-*adj*	sanguine
5367	**carnal**-*adj*	carnal
5380	**penoso**-*adj*	pitiful, embarrassing
5389	**abundante**-*adj*	abundant
5393	**biológico**-*adj*	biological
5394	**irreal**-*adj*	unreal
5401	**tirado**-*adj*	stranded
5403	**mercenario**-*m; adj*	mercenary; mercenary
5415	**crónico**-*adj*	chronic
5416	**manifiesto**-*m; adj*	manifest; evident
5426	**rabioso**-*adj*	rabid
5427	**ilustre**-*adj*	illustrious
5428	**matador**-*m; adj*	matador; deadly
5429	**singular**-*m; adj*	special; unique
5430	**sirio**-*adj; m*	Syrian; Syrian
5433	**patente**-*f; adj*	clear; patent
5435	**obsceno**-*adj*	obscene
5436	**credencial**-*f; adj*	identity document; accrediting
5438	**deshonesto**-*adj*	dishonest
5440	**chuleta**-*f; adj*	chop; sassy (coll)
5442	**paralelo**-*m; adj*	parallel; parallel
5444	**comunitario**-*adj*	communal
5455	**decisivo**-*adj*	decisive
5460	**calamar**-*adj; m*	dummy; squid
5473	**inválido**-*adj; m*	invalid; disabled person
5474	**competente**-*adj*	competent
5475	**realista**-*m; adj*	realist; realistic
5476	**cuadrilátero**-*m; adj*	ring; four-sided
5482	**satisfactorio**-*adj*	satisfactory
5483	**detenido**-*adj; m*	stopped, arrested; prisoner
5490	**cubano**-*adj; m*	Cuban; Cuban person
5491	**oliva**-*adj; f*	olive; olive
5493	**bondadoso**-*adj*	kind
5497	**inquietante**-*adj*	disturbing
5498	**escalofriante**-*adj*	spooky
5500	**lujoso**-*adj*	luxurious
5504	**colectivo**-*adj; m*	collective; group
5505	**calzado**-*adj; m*	wearing shoes; footwear
5517	**deslumbrante**-*adj*	dazzling
5518	**carguero**-*adj; m*	freight; freighter
5525	**placentero**-*adj*	pleasurable
5526	**gráfico**-*adj*	graphic
5529	**dependiente**-*adj; m*	dependent; shop assistant
5534	**fértil**-*adj*	fertile
5535	**semanal**-*adj*	weekly
5541	**característico**-*adj*	characteristic
5542	**psíquico**-*adj*	psychic
5543	**facial**-*adj*	facial
5546	**canario**-*adj; m*	from the Canary Islands, canary yellow; Canary Islander, canary
5552	**insensato**-*adj; m*	foolish; foolish
5553	**elemental**-*adj*	elementary
5554	**desordenado**-*adj*	disorganized
5562	**bosnio**-*adj; m*	Bosnian; Bosnian person
5565	**indigno**-*adj*	unworthy
5567	**dotado**-*adj*	gifted
5569	**problemático**-*adj*	problematic
5570	**externo**-*adj*	external
5574	**indudable**-*adj*	undeniable
5575	**flotante**-*adj*	floating
5579	**lechero**-*adj; m*	milk; milkman
5590	**genital**-*adj*	genital
5601	**erótico**-*adj*	erotic
5604	**supuesto**-*adj; m*	supposed; case
5605	**referente a**-*adj*	regarding
5607	**inmobiliaria**-*adj; f*	real-estate; real state agency
5609	**vegetariano**-*adj*	vegetarian
5611	**sonoro**-*adj*	loud
5614	**invasor**-*m; adj*	invader; invading
5616	**chic**-*adj*	chic
5617	**ligado**-*adj*	bound
5618	**participante**-*m/f; adj*	participant; participating
5621	**descontento**-*adj; m*	discontented; displeasure
5627	**memorable**-*adj*	memorable
5632	**magnético**-*adj*	magnetic

5637	**senil**-*adj*	senile	5798	**deportista**-*adj; m/f*	sporty; athlete
5645	**cafetero**-*adj*	fond of coffee	5803	**ingrato**-*adj*	ungrateful
5649	**jorobado**-*adj; m*	hunched; hunchback	5805	**espeso**-*adj*	thick
5653	**enfermizo**-*adj*	sickly	5809	**protestante**-*adj*	Protestant
5655	**democrático**-*adj*	democratic	5810	**místico**-*adj; m*	mystic; mystic
5656	**burgués**-*adj; m*	middle-class; rich person	5813	**gratuito**-*adj*	free, uncalled for
5658	**sádico**-*adj; m*	sadistic; sadist	5816	**antibiótico**-*adj; m*	antibiotic; antibiotic
5662	**medieval**-*adj*	medieval	5817	**siciliano**-*adj; m*	Sicilian; Sicilian person
5666	**abominable**-*adj*	abominable	5820	**inmaduro**-*adj*	immature, unripe
5667	**suroeste**-*adj*	southwest	5821	**soso**-*adj*	dull, boring
5675	**vasto**-*adj*	vast	5823	**estático**-*adj*	static
5681	**danés**-*adj; m*	Danish; Danish person	5827	**poético**-*adj*	poetic
5683	**instantáneo**-*adj*	instant	5829	**tóxico**-*adj*	toxic
5689	**depredador**-*adj; m*	predatory; predator	5832	**indefinido**-*adj*	indefinite
5690	**silvestre**-*adj*	wild	5837	**auditorio**-*adj; m*	hearing; auditorium
5691	**imponente**-*adj*	imposing	5840	**próspero**-*adj*	prosperous
5692	**brasileño**-*adj; m*	Brazilian; Brazilian person	5843	**aventurero**-*adj; m*	adventurous; adventurer
5693	**intermedio**-*adj; m*	intermediate; intermission	5844	**armónico**-*adj*	harmonious
5701	**rígido**-*adj*	rigid	5847	**impulsivo**-*adj*	impulsive
5703	**brusco**-*adj*	abrupt	5849	**impreso**-*adj; m*	printed; flyer
5704	**competidor**-*adj; m*	competitor; competitor	5852	**rural**-*adj*	rural
5708	**fabricante**-*adj; m*	manufacturing; manufacturer	5861	**inmobiliario**-*adj*	real-estate
5712	**diminuto**-*adj*	tiny	5867	**australiano**-*adj; m*	Australian; Australian person
5728	**componente**-*adj; m*	built in; component	5872	**susceptible**-*adj*	susceptible
5737	**infalible**-*adj*	infallible	5874	**socialista**-*adj*	socialist
5751	**innumerable**-*adj*	innumerable	5877	**mamífero**-*m; adj*	mammal; mammal
5758	**alerta**-*f; adj; adv*	alarm; alert; on the alert	5880	**milagroso**-*adj*	miraculous
5761	**decepcionante**-*adj*	disappointing	5888	**virtual**-*adj*	virtual
5762	**urbano**-*adj*	urban	5898	**liviano**-*adj*	light
5763	**iraquí**-*adj; m*	Iraqi; Iraqi person	5903	**fiable**-*adj*	trustworthy
5772	**pelotudo**-*adj; m*	slow, dumb (LA) (coll); young adult (LA)	5904	**vocal**-*adj; f*	vocal; vowel
5773	**ajeno**-*adj*	somebody else's	5914	**gubernamental**-*adj*	governmental
5774	**conquistador**-*m; adj*	conqueror, Casanova; seductive	5915	**irregular**-*adj*	irregular
			5918	**estético**-*adj*	cosmetic
			5919	**ultra**-*pfx; adj; m/f*	over; ultra; extremist
5780	**calmo**-*adj*	calm	5922	**considerado**-*adj*	considerate
5788	**inhumano**-*adj*	inhumane	5923	**vicioso**-*adj*	depraved, vicious
			5927	**cantor**-*adj; m*	singing; singer
			5930	**jugoso**-*adj*	juicy

5931	**olímpico**-*adj; m*	Olympian; Olympian
5933	**aéreo**-*adj*	aerial
5936	**limpiador**-*adj; m*	cleaning; wiper (LA)
5940	**artillero**-*adj; m*	artillery; artilleryman
5946	**mensual**-*adj*	monthly
5947	**preocupante**-*adj*	alarming
5952	**inservible**-*adj*	unusable
5953	**sobresaliente**-*adj; m*	protruding; outstanding
5955	**exótico**-*adj*	exotic
5958	**prematuro**-*adj*	premature
5962	**diversos**-*adj*	various
5967	**cosmético**-*adj; m*	cosmetic; cosmetic
5969	**vikingo**-*adj; m*	Viking; Viking
5971	**cochino**-*adj; m*	dirty; pig
5988	**luminoso**-*adj*	bright
5990	**restante**-*adj*	remaining
6000	**navideño**-*adj*	Christmas
6006	**mestizo**-*adj; m*	racially mixed; mixed race
6009	**temeroso**-*adj*	afraid
6011	**sangrado**-*adj*	bleed
6013	**incógnito**-*adj; m*	incognito; incognito
6015	**indígena**-*adj; m*	native; native person
6017	**articular**-*adj; vb*	joint; articulate
6021	**capricornio**-*adj*	Capricorn
6035	**galante**-*adj*	gallant
6042	**apasionante**-*adj*	thrilling
6044	**ocular**-*adj; m*	eye; lens
6045	**borroso**-*adj*	blurred
6048	**revuelto**-*adj; m*	messy; scrambled eggs
6050	**grotesco**-*adj*	hideous
6052	**ateo**-*adj; m*	atheistic; atheist
6054	**impactante**-*adj*	stunning
6055	**tenebroso**-*adj*	gloomy
6059	**preferible**-*adj*	preferable
6069	**misionero**-*adj; m*	missionary; missionary
6072	**ladera**-*adj; f*	lateral; hillside
6077	**educativo**-*adj*	educational
6085	**temerario**-*adj*	reckless
6095	**vietnamita**-*adj; m/f*	Vietnamese; Vietnamese person
6100	**repulsivo**-*adj*	repulsive
6109	**farmacéutico**-*adj; m*	pharmaceutical; pharmacist
6113	**muscular**-*adj*	muscular
6115	**psicótico**-*adj*	psychotic
6117	**constructor**-*adj; m*	building; builder
6119	**apacible**-*adj*	gentle
6122	**contrabandista**-*adj; m*	contraband; smuggler
6123	**corporativo**-*adj*	corporate
6126	**turístico**-*adj*	tourist
6136	**trivial**-*adj*	trivial
6138	**platino**-*adj; m*	platinum; platinum
6148	**persistente**-*adj*	persistent
6153	**imparcial**-*adj*	impartial
6158	**computador**-*adj; m*	computer; computer (LA)
6160	**dirigente**-*m/f; adj*	leader; leading
6163	**inexplicable**-*adj*	inexplicable
6164	**aturdido**-*adj*	confused
6168	**desastroso**-*adj*	disastrous
6175	**orgánico**-*adj*	organic
6177	**devastador**-*adj*	devastating
6182	**terrenal**-*adj*	earthly
6185	**clandestino**-*adj*	clandestine
6201	**codicioso**-*adj*	greedy
6204	**expuesto**-*adj*	exposed
6213	**molecular**-*adj*	molecular
6214	**abdominal**-*adj; f*	abdominal; crunch
6215	**espontáneo**-*adj*	spontaneous
6216	**paisano**-*adj; m*	from the same place; civilian
6225	**averiado**-*adj*	broken down
6227	**apretado**-*adj*	cramped
6231	**inclinado**-*adj*	inclined
6236	**idealista**-*adj; m*	idealistic; idealist
6239	**irritable**-*adj*	irritable
6240	**indulgente**-*adj*	indulgent
6243	**anarquista**-*m/f; adj*	anarchist; anarchist
6244	**ágil**-*adj*	agile
6245	**colosal**-*adj*	colossal
6250	**asegurador**-*adj; m*	insurance; insurer
6254	**derrotado**-*adj*	defeated

6255	**agrícola**-*adj*	agricultural
6261	**maligno**-*adj*	malign
6262	**horizontal**-*adj*	horizontal
6263	**vano**-*adj*	futile
6265	**detestable**-*adj*	despicable
6267	**benéfico**-*adj*	charity
6276	**robusto**-*adj*	robust
6279	**retórico**-*adj*	rhetorical
6286	**regresivo**-*adj*	regressive
6287	**erudito**-*adj; m*	expert; erudite person
6290	**horrendo**-*adj*	horrendous
6291	**traicionero**-*adj*	treacherous
6293	**balístico**-*adj*	ballistic
6294	**tranquilizante**-*adj; m*	reassuring; tranquilizer
6328	**presuntuoso**-*adj*	conceited
6334	**colonial**-*adj*	colonial
6339	**rentable**-*adj*	profitable
6346	**estéreo**-*adj; m*	stereo; stereo
6347	**mellizo**-*adj; m*	twin; twin
6348	**influyente**-*adj*	influential
6354	**cinematográfico**-*adj*	cinematographic
6360	**cuántico**-*adj*	quantum
6362	**hablador**-*adj*	talkative
6363	**ronco**-*adj*	hoarse
6369	**mediano**-*adj*	medium-sized
6375	**especializado**-*adj*	specialized
6380	**incomparable**-*adj*	incomparable
6384	**sanitario**-*m; adj*	bathroom; sanitary
6388	**incomprensible**-*adj*	incomprehensible
6389	**impensable**-*adj*	unthinkable
6396	**fotográfico**-*adj*	photographic
6397	**verbal**-*adj*	verbal
6398	**respetuoso**-*adj*	respectful
6399	**perspicaz**-*adj*	keen
6402	**gobernante**-*adj; m*	ruling; leader
6407	**fusible**-*adj; m*	fusible; fuse
6416	**dudoso**-*adj*	dubious
6417	**meteorológico**-*adj*	meteorological
6419	**victorioso**-*adj*	victorious
6424	**cotidiano**-*adj*	daily, routine
6428	**debido**-*adj*	properly
6429	**alimenticio**-*adj*	food
6441	**comanche**-*adj; m/f*	Comanche; Comanche Indian
6449	**propulsor**-*adj; m*	propellant; promoter
6450	**acuático**-*adj*	aquatic
6454	**llano**-*adj*	flat
6457	**fastidiado**-*adj*	fed up, broken (ES)
6461	**ambiental**-*adj*	environmental
6462	**desconcertante**-*adj*	upsetting
6465	**emotivo**-*adj*	emotional
6468	**cooperativo**-*adj*	cooperative
6476	**arterial**-*adj*	arterial
6478	**benefactor**-*adj; m*	benevolent; benefactor
6479	**melancólico**-*adj*	melancholic
6488	**concursante**-*adj; m/f*	competing; contestant
6490	**gratificante**-*adj*	gratifying
6496	**denso**-*adj*	thick
6502	**mojado**-*adj*	wet
6504	**extremista**-*adj; m/f*	extreme; extremist
6513	**unánime**-*adj*	unanimous
6515	**auricular**-*adj; m*	auricular; headset
6528	**incondicional**-*adj; m/f*	unconditional; stalwart
6531	**desapercibido**-*adj*	unnoticed
6536	**insaciable**-*adj*	insatiable
6537	**capitular**-*vb; adj*	capitulate; town hall
6543	**escéptico**-*adj; m*	skeptic; skeptic
6544	**controlador**-*adj; m*	controlling; controller
6545	**inoportuno**-*adj*	inopportune
6549	**lácteo**-*adj; m*	dairy; lactose
6551	**guerrillero**-*adj; m*	guerrilla; guerrilla
6552	**extraoficial**-*adj*	unofficial
6556	**imprescindible**-*adj*	essential
6557	**multimillonario**-*adj*	multimillionaire
6558	**inseparable**-*adj*	inseparable
6566	**integral**-*adj*	comprehensive
6569	**colaborador**-*adj; m*	cooperative; contributor, co-worker
6572	**elocuente**-*adj*	eloquent
6575	**dinámico**-*adj*	dynamic

6578	**descompuesto**-*adj*	broken down	6692	**áspero**-*adj*	rough
6581	**impenetrable**-*adj*	impenetrable	6699	**desconcertado**-*adj*	bewildered
6586	**publicitario**-*adj; m*	advertising; publicist	6708	**deseable**-*adj*	desirable
			6715	**pulmonar**-*adj*	chest
6588	**alarmante**-*adj*	alarming	6723	**colgante**-*adj; m*	hanging; pendant
6589	**ruin**-*adj*	despicable	6734	**insólito**-*adj*	unheard of
6591	**accesible**-*adj*	accessible	6739	**automovilístico**-*adj*	car
6593	**checo**-*adj; m*	Czech; Czech person	6746	**literario**-*adj*	literary
6595	**incurable**-*adj*	incurable	6750	**mezclado**-*adj*	mixed
6597	**incontable**-*adj*	countless	6751	**convertible**-*adj; m*	convertible; convertible (LA)
6598	**dichoso**-*adj*	happy			
6599	**adoptivo**-*adj*	adoptive	6753	**sostenido**-*adj*	sustained
6602	**andante**-*adj*	walking	6754	**impune**-*adj*	unpunished
6603	**aritmético**-*adj; m*	arithmetic; arithmetician	6759	**diestro**-*adj*	right-handed, skilled
6604	**electo**-*adj; m*	elected; elected member	6761	**óptimo**-*adj*	ideal
			6764	**táctico**-*adj; m*	tactical; tactician
6610	**sureño**-*adj; m*	southern; southerner	6765	**matutino**-*adj*	morning
			6767	**banal**-*adj*	banal
6612	**descalzo**-*adj*	barefoot	6769	**alentador**-*adj*	encouraging
6613	**baboso**-*adj*	slimy	6770	**inverso**-*adj*	reverse
6617	**excusado**-*adj; m*	superfluous; restroom	6777	**maternal**-*adj*	maternal
6618	**primordial**-*adj*	primary	6780	**rosada**-*adj*	pink
6620	**predecible**-*adj*	predictable	6781	**abstracto**-*adj*	abstract
6632	**metropolitano**-*adj; m*	urban; subway	6783	**repetido**-*adj*	repeated
			6786	**valeroso**-*adj*	valiant
6635	**agresor**-*adj; m*	attacking; attacker	6789	**decadente**-*adj*	decadent
6641	**virtuoso**-*adj; m*	virtuous; virtuoso	6794	**erróneo**-*adj*	wrong
6645	**escurridizo**-*adj*	evasive, slippery	6797	**compatible**-*adj*	compatible
6646	**perjudicial**-*adj*	harmful	6798	**teórico**-*adj; m*	theoretical; theorist
6647	**deforme**-*adj*	misshapen			
6652	**insistente**-*adj*	insistent	6814	**cósmico**-*adj*	cosmic
6653	**festivo**-*adj*	festive, holiday	6815	**gótico**-*adj; m*	Gothic; Goth
6654	**soberbio**-*adj*	proud	6820	**grato**-*adj*	agreeable
6657	**escaso**-*adj*	lacking	6821	**llamativo**-*adj*	flashy
6658	**indirecto**-*adj*	indirect	6822	**administrativo**-*adj*	administrative
6666	**impar**-*adj*	odd	6826	**potable**-*adj*	potable
6670	**coherente**-*adj*	coherent	6828	**partidario**-*adj; m*	in favour of; supporter
6672	**simbólico**-*adj*	symbolic			
6673	**ilimitado**-*adj*	unlimited	6830	**sucesivo**-*adj*	successive
6674	**residencial**-*adj*	residential	6836	**terrorífico**-*adj*	terrifying
6676	**incompleto**-*adj*	incomplete	6849	**indonesio**-*adj; m*	Indonesian; Indonesian person
6678	**castellano**-*adj; m*	Spanish; Castilian Spanish	6853	**acreedor**-*adj; m*	deserving of; creditor
6682	**tirante**-*adj*	tense	6862	**dorsal**-*adj*	dorsal
6683	**consistente**-*adj*	consistent			

6865	**estimado**-*adj; m*	appreciated; estimation, dear
6867	**consultor**-*adj; m*	advisory; consultant
6875	**nefasto**-*adj*	nefarious
6877	**viable**-*adj*	viable
6884	**reproductor**-*adj; m*	reproductive; DVD player
6885	**macizo**-*adj*	solid
6886	**perplejo**-*adj*	perplexed
6893	**imprevisible**-*adj*	unpredictable
6907	**nutriente**-*adj; m*	nutritious; nutrient
6909	**dócil**-*adj*	docile
6913	**incorregible**-*adj*	incorrigible
6919	**desinfectante**-*adj; m*	disinfectant; disinfectant
6927	**insultante**-*adj*	insulting
6931	**incierto**-*adj*	uncertain
6938	**feminista**-*adj; m/f*	feminist; feminist
6943	**antipático**-*adj*	unpleasant
6949	**bohemio**-*adj*	bohemian
6953	**tabú**-*adj*	taboo
6959	**sanguinario**-*adj*	bloodthirsty
6960	**neto**-*adj*	net
6962	**constitucional**-*adj*	constitutional
6966	**tribal**-*adj*	tribal
6967	**patriótico**-*adj*	patriotic
6972	**inimaginable**-*adj*	unimaginable
6974	**cabezón**-*adj*	stubborn
6980	**materno**-*adj*	maternal
6986	**productivo**-*adj*	productive
6995	**óptico**-*adj; m*	optical; optician
6996	**pardo**-*adj*	brown
7000	**inflexible**-*adj*	inflexible
7001	**mejicano**-*adj; m*	Mexican; Mexican person
7004	**informativo**-*adj; m*	informative; news bulletin
7005	**intocable**-*adj*	untouchable
7006	**interestatal**-*adj*	interstate
7008	**intencional**-*adj*	intentional
7013	**pronunciado**-*adj*	pronounced
7015	**dominical**-*adj; m*	Sunday; Sunday magazine
7022	**obsesivo**-*adj*	obsessive
7024	**bisexual**-*adj; m/f*	bisexual; bisexual
7031	**vertebral**-*adj*	vertebral
7042	**sórdido**-*adj*	sordid
7044	**beige**-*adj*	beige
7045	**policíaco**-*adj*	police
7049	**perturbador**-*adj*	disturbing
7051	**tolerante**-*adj*	tolerant
7052	**atacante**-*adj; m/f*	combative; attacker
7056	**tenaz**-*adj*	tenacious
7066	**estresante**-*adj*	stressful
7071	**ferroviario**-*adj; m*	railway; railwayman
7081	**bebedor**-*adj; m*	heavy drinker (coll); drinker
7088	**colombiano**-*adj; m*	Colombian; Colombian person
7093	**viril**-*adj*	virile
7095	**detallado**-*adj*	detailed
7097	**azteca**-*adj; m*	Aztec; Aztec person
7100	**piadoso**-*adj*	compassionate
7106	**clínico**-*adj; m*	clinical; doctor
7113	**óseo**-*adj*	bone
7119	**sonámbulo**-*adj; m*	sleepwalker; sleepwalker
7126	**contundente**-*adj*	convincing
7130	**lacrimógeno**-*adj*	tear
7143	**intrépido**-*adj*	intrepid
7148	**sedante**-*adj; m*	sedative; sedative
7150	**rumano**-*adj; m*	Romanian; Romanian person
7154	**decidido**-*adj*	determined
7157	**atlético**-*adj*	athletic
7163	**proveniente**-*adj*	coming from
7165	**derivado**-*adj; m*	derived; derivative
7166	**fertilizante**-*adj; m*	fertilizing; fertilizer
7168	**detergente**-*adj; m*	detergent; detergent
7176	**desafiante**-*adj*	challenging
7188	**climático**-*adj*	weather
7189	**súbito**-*adj*	sudden
7192	**desleal**-*adj*	disloyal
7193	**existente**-*adj*	existing
7198	**chocante**-*adj*	shocking
7209	**despreocupado**-*adj*	carefree
7210	**matinal**-*adj*	morning

7212	**indiscreto**-*adj*	indiscreet
7213	**desconfiado**-*adj*	suspicious
7225	**funcional**-*adj*	functional
7231	**lluvioso**-*adj*	rainy
7232	**naciente**-*adj*	rising
7236	**ortodoxo**-*adj*	orthodox
7237	**duradero**-*adj*	durable
7240	**ancestral**-*adj*	ancestral
7244	**tuerto**-*adj*	blind in one eye
7247	**competitivo**-*adj*	competitive
7249	**incontrolable**-*adj*	uncontrollable
7257	**nudista**-*adj; m/f*	nudist; nudist
7274	**pasivo**-*adj; m*	passive; retiree
7276	**bíblico**-*adj*	biblical
7278	**flamenco**-*adj; m*	flamenco; flamingo
7280	**militante**-*adj; m/f*	militant; member, activist
7281	**caprichoso**-*adj*	whimsical
7283	**aliar**-*adj*	unite
7289	**sofocante**-*adj*	suffocating
7309	**nasal**-*adj*	nasal
7314	**imparable**-*adj*	unstoppable
7318	**destructivo**-*adj*	destructive
7325	**electromagnético**-*adj*	electromagnetic
7330	**blasfemo**-*adj*	blasphemous
7332	**empresarial**-*adj*	corporate
7340	**precoz**-*adj*	precocious
7344	**clemente**-*adj*	merciful
7345	**deplorable**-*adj*	deplorable
7346	**eminente**-*adj*	eminent
7349	**delirante**-*adj*	delirious
7352	**nulo**-*adj*	invalid
7357	**pesquero**-*adj; m*	fishing; fishing boat
7363	**prominente**-*adj*	prominent
7366	**arduo**-*adj*	arduous
7370	**escarlata**-*adj; m*	scarlet; scarlet
7379	**monetario**-*adj*	monetary
7382	**medidor**-*adj; m*	measuring; meter
7384	**inadecuado**-*adj*	unsuitable
7385	**monumental**-*adj*	monumental
7386	**recluso**-*adj; m*	be in prison; prisoner
7391	**púbico**-*adj*	pubic
7395	**inaudito**-*adj*	unheard-of
7398	**alineado**-*adj*	aligned
7399	**involuntario**-*adj*	involuntary
7406	**extenso**-*adj*	extensive
7411	**compulsivo**-*adj*	compulsive
7413	**cauteloso**-*adj*	cautious
7422	**leproso**-*adj; m*	leprous; leper
7423	**inadmisible**-*adj*	unacceptable
7430	**conyugal**-*adj*	conjugal
7434	**fastidioso**-*adj*	annoying
7439	**tedioso**-*adj*	tedious
7442	**ileso**-*adj*	unhurt
7444	**machista**-*adj; m*	sexist; sexist
7447	**humanitario**-*adj*	humanitarian
7451	**defectuoso**-*adj*	defective
7454	**hervido**-*adj; m*	boiled; casserole
7455	**turbio**-*adj*	muddy
7458	**acantilado**-*adj; m*	steep; cliff
7463	**pródigo**-*adj*	prodigal, generous
7464	**sinónimo**-*adj; m*	synonym; synonymous
7466	**drástico**-*adj*	drastic
7474	**evasivo**-*adj*	evasive
7480	**mayúsculo**-*adj*	tremendous
7490	**híbrido**-*adj; m*	mix; hybrid
7497	**inaugural**-*adj*	inaugural
7499	**forestal**-*adj; m*	forest; ranger
7503	**bestial**-*adj*	brutal
7509	**finalista**-*adj; m/f*	finalist; finalist
7513	**indignante**-*adj*	outrageous
7514	**catastrófico**-*adj*	catastrophic
7515	**canino**-*adj; m*	canine; canine tooth
7517	**radial**-*adj; f*	radio; circular saw
7521	**intermitente**-*adj; m*	intermittent; blinker

Adverbs

Rank	Spanish-PoS	Translation(s)
5048	**antaño**-*adv*	formerly
5108	**fluido**-*m; adj; adv*	fluid; free-flowing; fluently
5230	**por doquier**-*adv*	all over the place
5593	**de antemano**-*adv*	beforehand
5646	**anteayer**-*adv*	day before yesterday
5758	**alerta**-*f; adj; adv*	alarm; alert; on the alert
5893	**allende**-*adv*	on the other side
5900	**viceversa**-*adv*	vice versa
5981	**entretanto**-*adv*	meanwhile
6125	**adrede**-*adv*	intentionally
7334	**con antelación**-*adv*	beforehand

Nouns

Rank	Spanish-PoS	Translation(s)
5001	**indicio**-*m*	indication
5002	**piña**-*f*	pineapple
5004	**trayecto**-*m*	journey
5005	**linaje**-*m*	lineage
5006	**manantial**-*m*	spring
5008	**negligencia**-*f*	negligence
5009	**coyote**-*m*	coyote
5011	**fulano**-*m*	some guy (coll)
5012	**milenio**-*m*	millennium
5015	**analista**-*m/f*	analyst
5016	**hermosura**-*f*	beauty
5017	**erupción**-*f*	eruption
5019	**marfil**-*m*	ivory
5020	**malaria**-*f*	malaria
5021	**precipicio**-*m*	cliff
5022	**hebreo**-*adj; m*	Hebrew; Jew
5023	**hipnosis**-*f*	hypnosis
5024	**persiana**-*f*	blind
5026	**parabrisas**-*m*	windshield
5027	**demencia**-*f*	dementia
5030	**cuchilla**-*f*	blade
5032	**receptor**-*m*	recipient
5033	**socialismo**-*m*	socialism
5036	**sonda**-*f*	catheter
5038	**despertador**-*m*	alarm clock
5039	**cactus**-*m*	cactus
5041	**académico**-*adj; m*	academic; academic
5044	**candado**-*m*	padlock
5045	**musa**-*f*	muse
5050	**sacramento**-*m*	sacrament
5051	**arruga**-*f*	wrinkle
5054	**pronóstico**-*m*	prediction
5055	**húngaro**-*adj; m*	Hungarian; Hungarian person
5058	**francotirador**-*m*	sniper
5060	**camionero**-*m*	truck driver
5063	**ecuación**-*f*	equation
5064	**guisante**-*m*	pea
5065	**maternidad**-*f*	maternity
5067	**receso**-*m*	break
5068	**higiene**-*f*	hygiene
5069	**negación**-*f*	denial
5070	**lomo**-*m*	loin
5071	**opresión**-*f*	oppression
5072	**reducción**-*f*	reduction
5074	**gentileza**-*f*	gentleness
5076	**comino**-*m*	cumin
5078	**principiante**-*m/f*	beginner
5079	**pantera**-*f*	panther
5080	**cava**-*m*	cava
5081	**latino**-*adj; m*	Latin; Latino
5083	**empujón**-*m*	push
5084	**travesía**-*f*	voyage
5085	**élite**-*f*	elite
5086	**resplandor**-*m*	brightness
5087	**simulacro**-*m*	drill
5089	**escasez**-*f*	shortage
5090	**festín**-*m*	feast
5091	**indiferencia**-*f*	indifference
5092	**bollo**-*m*	bread roll, sweet bun
5093	**pinza**-*f*	clothespin
5094	**gringo**-*adj; m*	gringo; gringo (coll), foreigner (LA) (coll)
5095	**marioneta**-*f*	puppet
5096	**colono**-*m*	settler, tenant farmer
5097	**subconsciente**-*m*	subconscious
5098	**pera**-*f*	pear
5099	**azafata**-*f*	flight attendant
5100	**intriga**-*f*	scheme
5101	**procurador**-*m*	attorney
5103	**arrepentimiento**-*m*	remorse
5104	**dictador**-*m*	dictator
5105	**falsificación**-*f*	counterfeit
5106	**galán**-*m*	handsome man
5107	**trimestre**-*m*	trimester
5108	**fluido**-*m; adj; adv*	fluid; free-flowing; fluently
5109	**expansión**-*f*	expansion
5110	**bulto**-*m*	lump
5111	**redención**-*f*	redemption
5112	**delicia**-*f*	delight
5113	**supervisión**-*f*	supervision
5114	**ahogo**-*m*	distress, difficulty breathing
5115	**descaro**-*m*	impertinence
5116	**repetición**-*f*	repetition

5119	**llanta**-*f*	tire	
5122	**soplo**-*m*	breeze, breath	
5123	**plátano**-*m*	banana	
5124	**mentón**-*m*	chin	
5125	**mordisco**-*m*	bite	
5126	**mutante**-*adj; m/f*	mutating; mutant	
5127	**apretón**-*m*	squeeze	
5128	**gaseosa**-*f*	soda	
5130	**costura**-*f*	seam, needlework	
5131	**albóndiga**-*f*	meatball	
5132	**intestino**-*m*	intestine	
5133	**imprenta**-*f*	printing	
5134	**preliminar**-*m*	preliminary	
5135	**cristianismo**-*m*	Christianity	
5136	**llorón**-*adj; m*	whiny; crybaby	
5139	**suavidad**-*f*	softness	
5141	**gozo**-*m*	joy	
5142	**vigor**-*m*	vigor	
5143	**jeque**-*m*	sheik	
5144	**tuberculosis**-*f*	tuberculosis	
5145	**cloaca**-*f*	sewer	
5146	**gueto**-*m*	ghetto	
5147	**uranio**-*m*	uranium	
5148	**audio**-*sm*	audio	
5149	**mandamiento**-*m*	commandment	
5150	**modestia**-*f*	modesty	
5151	**recipiente**-*m*	container	
5152	**sanidad**-*f*	health service	
5154	**imán**-*m*	magnet	
5155	**micro**-*m*	mic, minibus	
5157	**borrador**-*m*	draft, rubber	
5158	**dominó**-*m*	dominoes	
5159	**carnero**-*m*	ram	
5160	**patrimonio**-*m*	heritage, wealth	
5161	**cobardía**-*f*	cowardice	
5162	**suplente**-*m*	substitute	
5163	**estabilidad**-*f*	stability	
5164	**pose**-*f*	pose	
5165	**recluta**-*m/f*	recruit	
5166	**geografía**-*f*	geography	
5167	**caloría**-*f*	calorie	
5169	**palma**-*f*	palm	
5170	**litera**-*f*	bunk	
5171	**potro**-*m*	colt	
5173	**fundador**-*m*	founder	
5174	**germen**-*m*	germ	

5175	**combatiente**-*m*	fighter
5176	**fascismo**-*m*	fascism
5177	**votante**-*m*	voter
5178	**ombligo**-*m*	belly button
5179	**entusiasta**-*m; adj*	fan; enthusiastic
5180	**jarabe**-*m*	syrup
5181	**acertijo**-*m*	riddle
5182	**prohibición**-*f*	prohibition
5183	**hectárea**-*f*	hectare
5185	**rector**-*m*	dean
5186	**zurdo**-*adj; m*	left-handed; left-handed person
5188	**adulterio**-*m*	adultery
5189	**vinagre**-*m*	vinegar
5190	**sequía**-*f*	drought
5193	**protegido**-*m*	protegé
5194	**octava**-*f*	octave
5195	**invernadero**-*m*	greenhouse
5196	**transacción**-*f*	transaction
5198	**venado**-*m*	deer
5200	**lápida**-*f*	tombstone
5201	**delegado**-*m*	delegate
5202	**biografía**-*f*	biography
5205	**guionista**-*m/f*	screenwriter
5206	**zumbido**-*m*	buzz
5209	**filipino**-*adj; m*	Philippine; Philippine person
5210	**impermeable**-*m; adj*	weatherproof; waterproof
5211	**párroco**-*m*	parish priest
5213	**juzgado**-*m*	court
5214	**jaqueca**-*f*	migraine
5216	**aspirador**-*m*	vacuum
5217	**asignación**-*f*	assignment
5218	**excéntrico**-*adj; m*	eccentric; eccentric person
5219	**disparate**-*m*	folly
5220	**mezquita**-*f*	mosque
5221	**barricada**-*f*	barricade
5222	**rastreador**-*adj; m*	tracking; tracker
5224	**desempleado**-*adj; m*	unemployed; unemployed person
5225	**vanguardia**-*f*	avant-garde, vanguard
5226	**asiático**-*adj; m*	Asian; Asian person
5229	**aguardiente**-*m*	moonshine

5232	**coleccionista**-*m/f*	collector
5233	**eclipse**-*m*	eclipse
5234	**enfrentamiento**-*m*	confrontation
5235	**meteoro**-*m*	meteor
5238	**alergia**-*f*	allergy
5239	**golosina**-*f*	candy
5240	**abad**-*m*	abbot
5241	**calavera**-*f*	skull
5244	**ruiseñor**-*m*	nightingale
5245	**cerrojo**-*m*	bolt
5246	**andén**-*m*	platform
5248	**túnica**-*f*	tunic
5250	**compartimiento**-*m*	compartment
5254	**sartén**-*f*	frying pan
5255	**recepcionista**-*m/f*	receptionist
5256	**clérigo**-*m*	cleric
5257	**descuido**-*m*	carelessness
5258	**insomnio**-*m*	insomnia
5259	**seriedad**-*f*	seriousness
5262	**valija**-*f*	suitcase
5268	**adaptación**-*f*	adaptation
5270	**dimisión**-*f*	resignation
5271	**decadencia**-*f*	decline
5273	**hazaña**-*f*	feat
5275	**temblor**-*m*	tremor
5276	**admisión**-*f*	admission
5277	**ama de casa**-*f*	housewife
5278	**reliquia**-*f*	relic
5280	**belga**-*adj; m*	Belgian; Belgian person
5284	**monto**-*m*	sum
5285	**bombón**-*m*	chocolate, beauty (coll)
5286	**conducto**-*m*	channel
5288	**extracción**-*f*	extraction
5291	**latido**-*m*	beat
5294	**trasto**-*m*	piece of junk
5296	**serbio**-*adj; m*	Serbian; Serb
5297	**hipo**-*m*	hiccup
5299	**locomotora**-*f; adj*	locomotive; locomotor
5300	**aplicación**-*f*	application
5301	**meditación**-*f*	meditation
5302	**médula**-*f*	marrow
5303	**reproducción**-*f*	reproduction
5304	**link**-*m*	link
5306	**amargura**-*f*	bitterness
5308	**preparado**-*m*	qualified
5309	**tiza**-*f*	chalk
5310	**egoísmo**-*m*	selfishness
5311	**melón**-*m*	melon
5312	**porvenir**-*m*	future
5313	**bacalao**-*m*	cod
5314	**resentimiento**-*m*	resentment
5316	**dardo**-*m*	dart
5320	**astucia**-*f*	cunning
5321	**accesorio**-*m; adj*	accessory; secondary
5322	**demandante**-*m/f*	plaintiff
5324	**totalidad**-*f*	entirety
5325	**explotación**-*f*	exploitation
5326	**guillotina**-*f*	guillotine
5328	**anticipo**-*m*	advance
5329	**prudencia**-*f*	caution
5330	**borrachera**-*f*	drunkenness
5331	**bufete**-*m*	firm of lawyers
5332	**miniatura**-*f; adj*	miniature; miniature
5333	**reencarnación**-*f*	reincarnation
5337	**sudeste**-*m*	southeast
5338	**sinfonía**-*f*	symphony
5339	**espiral**-*f*	spiral
5341	**maratón**-*m*	marathon
5342	**animación**-*f*	animation
5343	**devoto**-*m; adj*	devotee; devout
5347	**barranco**-*m*	cliff
5348	**pionero**-*adj; m*	pioneering; pioneer
5349	**esgrima**-*f*	fencing
5350	**tarro**-*m*	jar
5351	**lanzador**-*m*	pitcher
5352	**visón**-*m*	mink
5353	**hobby**-*m*	hobby
5354	**cacharro**-*adj; m*	junky; wreck
5358	**muralla**-*f*	wall
5360	**chusma**-*f*	rabble
5361	**pepino**-*m*	cucumber
5362	**beneficencia**-*f*	charity
5363	**anotación**-*f*	annotation
5364	**eficiencia**-*f*	efficiency
5371	**mecha**-*f*	wick
5372	**amazona**-*f*	amazon
5373	**reclutamiento**-*m*	recruitment
5375	**solidaridad**-*f*	solidarity

5376	subida-*f*	rise
5377	trastorno-*m*	disorder
5378	magnitud-*f*	magnitude
5379	dique-*m*	dike
5382	distinción-*f*	distinction
5383	nómina-*f*	salary
5384	úlcera-*f*	ulcer
5385	espagueti-*m*	spaghetti
5387	publicación-*f*	publication
5390	inventor-*m*	inventor
5391	semáforo-*m*	traffic light
5392	tocador-*m*	dressing table
5397	sandalia-*f*	sandal
5399	platillo-*m*	plate
5400	despensa-*f*	pantry
5402	fango-*m*	mud
5403	mercenario-*m; adj*	mercenary; mercenary
5404	ensueño-*m*	fantasy
5408	rendimiento-*m*	performance
5410	conserva-*f*	canned food
5411	agricultor-*m*	farmer
5413	alfiler-*m*	pin
5414	exactitud-*f*	accuracy
5416	manifiesto-*m; adj*	manifest; evident
5418	abrazo-*m*	hug
5421	introducción-*f*	introduction
5422	guitarrista-*m/f*	guitarist
5424	afirmación-*f*	affirmation
5425	psiquiatría-*f*	psychiatry
5428	matador-*m; adj*	matador; deadly
5429	singular-*m; adj*	special; unique
5430	sirio-*adj; m*	Syrian; Syrian
5431	puntuación-*f*	punctuation
5432	clientela-*f*	clientele
5433	patente-*f; adj*	clear; patent
5434	copiloto-*m/f*	copilot
5436	credencial-*f; adj*	identity document; accrediting
5439	melancolía-*f*	melancholy
5440	chuleta-*f; adj*	chop; sassy (coll)
5442	paralelo-*m; adj*	parallel; parallel
5443	malta-*f*	malt
5445	avatar-*m*	avatar
5446	foca-*f*	seal
5447	mercadería-*f*	merchandise

5449	apunte-*m*	note
5450	vajilla-*f*	tableware
5451	preferencia-*f*	preference
5452	hostilidad-*f*	hostility
5453	congregación-*f*	congregation
5454	manifestante-*m/f*	demonstrator
5457	colmillo-*m*	fang
5458	gallinero-*m*	henhouse
5459	equipamiento-*m*	equipment
5460	calamar-*adj; m*	dummy; squid
5463	arteria-*f*	artery
5464	citación-*f*	citation
5465	ventura-*f*	fortune
5466	coronación-*f*	coronation
5467	recital-*m*	recital
5468	frustración-*f*	frustration
5469	corresponsal-*m/f*	correspondent
5470	hipocresía-*f*	hypocrisy
5471	gremio-*m*	guild, union
5472	ente-*m*	entity
5473	inválido-*adj; m*	invalid; disabled person
5475	realista-*m; adj*	realist; realistic
5476	cuadrilátero-*m; adj*	ring; four-sided
5477	contradicción-*f*	contradiction
5478	estatus-*m*	status
5479	apagón-*m*	blackout
5480	naipe-*m*	playing card
5481	blasfemia-*f*	blasphemy
5483	detenido-*adj; m*	stopped, arrested; prisoner
5484	esquema-*m*	diagram
5485	conteo-*m*	count
5486	defunción-*f*	death
5487	reclamo-*m*	decoy
5488	dentadura-*f*	dentures
5489	madurez-*f*	maturity
5490	cubano-*adj; m*	Cuban; Cuban person
5491	oliva-*adj; f*	olive; olive
5494	patinaje-*m*	skating
5495	encuesta-*f*	survey
5501	seguimiento-*m*	tracking
5502	anatomía-*f*	anatomy
5503	hallazgo-*m*	discovery
5504	colectivo-*adj; m*	collective; group

5505	**calzado**-*adj; m*	wearing shoes; footwear
5506	**alfabeto**-*m*	alphabet
5507	**abanico**-*m*	fan, variety
5508	**desventaja**-*f*	disadvantage
5509	**cascabel**-*m*	bell
5510	**realización**-*f*	realization
5511	**porte**-*m*	demeanor
5512	**vestimenta**-*f*	clothing
5513	**mástil**-*m*	mast
5514	**cabellera**-*f*	hair
5515	**parálisis**-*f*	paralysis
5518	**carguero**-*adj; m*	freight; freighter
5519	**vídeojuego**-*m*	vídeo game
5520	**azufre**-*m*	sulfur
5521	**firmeza**-*f*	firmness
5522	**capellán**-*m*	chaplain
5523	**fabricación**-*f*	manufacturing
5524	**indicación**-*f*	indication
5528	**adorno**-*m*	ornament
5529	**dependiente**-*adj; m*	dependent; shop assistant
5531	**caimán**-*m*	caiman
5536	**magnate**-*m*	tycoon
5538	**indemnización**-*f*	compensation
5539	**avería**-*f*	breakdown
5540	**porra**-*f*	nightstick
5544	**delirio**-*m*	delirium
5545	**heladera**-*f*	refrigerator
5546	**canario**-*adj; m*	from the Canary Islands, canary yellow; Canary Islander, canary
5547	**barbaridad**-*f*	atrocity
5548	**ideología**-*f*	ideology
5549	**radiador**-*m*	radiator
5550	**testimonio**-*m*	testimony
5551	**altavoz**-*m*	speaker
5552	**insensato**-*adj; m*	foolish; foolish
5555	**traductor**-*m*	translator
5556	**meñique**-*m*	little finger
5557	**tirón**-*m*	pull
5558	**restricción**-*f*	restriction
5559	**melocotón**-*m*	peach
5561	**fatiga**-*f*	fatigue
5562	**bosnio**-*adj; m*	Bosnian; Bosnian person

5563	**carril**-*m*	lane
5564	**centinela**-*m/f*	sentinel
5566	**superioridad**-*f*	superiority
5568	**buceo**-*m*	diving
5571	**mililitro**-*m*	milliliter
5572	**debut**-*m*	debut
5573	**serenidad**-*f*	calm
5576	**rotación**-*f*	rotation
5577	**creatividad**-*f*	creativity
5579	**lechero**-*adj; m*	milk; milkman
5580	**provocación**-*f*	provocation
5582	**relevo**-*m*	replacement
5584	**estadía**-*f*	stay
5585	**coste**-*m*	cost
5586	**aerolínea**-*f*	airline
5587	**torrente**-*m*	torrent
5589	**Sor**-*f*	Sister
5592	**inclinación**-*f*	inclination
5594	**proporción**-*f*	proportion
5595	**represión**-*f*	repression
5597	**bisabuelo**-*m*	great-grandfather
5599	**suspenso**-*m*	failing grade, suspense (LA)
5602	**mazo**-*m*	mallet
5604	**supuesto**-*adj; m*	supposed; case
5606	**botiquín**-*m*	first-aid kit
5607	**inmobiliaria**-*adj; f*	real-estate; real state agency
5608	**puma**-*m*	puma
5610	**bautizo**-*m*	baptism
5612	**naufragio**-*m*	shipwreck
5613	**estela**-*f*	wake
5614	**invasor**-*m; adj*	invader; invading
5615	**coordinación**-*f*	coordination
5618	**participante**-*m/f; adj*	participant; participating
5619	**carpeta**-*f*	folder
5620	**violinista**-*m/f*	violinist
5621	**descontento**-*adj; m*	discontented; displeasure
5622	**nadador**-*m*	swimmer
5623	**microscopio**-*m*	microscope
5625	**demolición**-*f*	demolition
5626	**levantamiento**-*m*	uprising
5630	**agitación**-*f*	agitation
5631	**buscador**-*m*	searcher
5634	**balanza**-*f*	scales

5636	**inversor-***m*	investor
5638	**racismo-***m*	racism
5639	**arpa-***f*	harp
5640	**pico-***m*	pick, peak, small amount
5641	**vallar-***vb; m*	fence; fenced enclosure
5642	**cese-***m*	cessation
5644	**olimpiada-***f*	Olympics
5647	**amnistía-***f*	amnesty
5648	**bambú-***m*	bamboo
5649	**jorobado-***adj; m*	hunched; hunchback
5650	**excavación-***f*	excavation
5651	**eslabón-***m*	link
5652	**llanura-***f*	plain
5654	**notario-***m*	public notary
5656	**burgués-***adj; m*	middle-class; rich person
5658	**sádico-***adj; m*	sadistic; sadist
5659	**aceptación-***f*	acceptance
5660	**minoría-***f*	minority
5661	**tentador-***m*	tempting
5663	**matriz-***f*	womb
5668	**incapacidad-***f*	inability
5669	**galón-***m*	gallon
5670	**desdichado-***m*	unhappy
5671	**rito-***m*	rite
5673	**destello-***m*	flash, sparkle
5676	**allanamiento-***m*	flattening, forced entry
5677	**proyectil-***m*	projectile
5679	**limitación-***f*	limitation
5681	**danés-***adj; m*	Danish; Danish person
5682	**inquisición-***f*	inquisition
5684	**casilla-***f*	box
5685	**ómnibus-***m*	bus
5688	**cúpula-***f*	dome, leadership
5689	**depredador-***adj; m*	predatory; predator
5692	**brasileño-***adj; m*	Brazilian; Brazilian person
5693	**intermedio-***adj; m*	intermediate; intermission
5694	**cono-***m*	cone
5695	**escáner-***m*	scanner
5698	**infante-***m/f*	infant
5699	**descubierto-***m*	uncovered
5704	**competidor-***adj; m*	competitor; competitor
5706	**portavoz-***m/f*	spokesperson
5708	**fabricante-***adj; m*	manufacturing; manufacturer
5709	**abstinencia-***f*	withdrawal
5710	**razonamiento-***m*	reasoning
5711	**recordatorio-***m*	reminder
5713	**cosmos-***m*	cosmos
5715	**corneta-***f; m/f*	cornet; cornet player
5717	**viruela-***f*	smallpox
5719	**mitología-***f*	mythology
5721	**impaciencia-***f*	impatience
5722	**dúo-***m*	pair
5723	**inflación-***f*	inflation
5724	**exorcismo-***m*	exorcism
5725	**currículum-***m*	curriculum
5727	**incienso-***m*	incense
5728	**componente-***adj; m*	built in; component
5729	**orador-***m*	public speaker
5730	**aviador-***m*	pilot
5731	**verja-***f*	fence
5732	**lucio-***m*	pike
5733	**clasificación-***f*	classification
5734	**medusa-***f*	jellyfish
5735	**sífilis-***f*	syphilis
5736	**cráter-***m*	crater
5738	**lamento-***m*	lament
5739	**tapadera-***f*	cover
5741	**caverna-***f*	cavern
5742	**incertidumbre-***f*	uncertainty
5744	**ordenanza-***f*	ordinance
5745	**patriotismo-***m*	patriotism
5747	**concesión-***f*	concession
5748	**cesto-***m*	basket
5750	**proteína-***f*	protein
5752	**sudoeste-***m*	south-west
5753	**aristócrata-***m/f*	aristocrat
5754	**duración-***f*	length of time
5755	**maquinista-***m/f*	machinist
5756	**vega-***f*	meadow
5757	**pintada-***f*	graffiti
5758	**alerta-***f; adj; adv*	alarm; alert; on the alert

5759	**canela**-*f*	cinnamon
5760	**colmena**-*f*	hive
5763	**iraquí**-*adj; m*	Iraqi; Iraqi person
5764	**extorsión**-*f*	extortion
5765	**procesión**-*f*	procession
5766	**crepúsculo**-*m*	twilight
5767	**azote**-*m*	scourge, spank
5768	**patrocinador**-*m*	sponsor
5769	**cacahuete**-*m*	peanut
5770	**eliminación**-*f*	elimination
5771	**colisión**-*f*	collision
5772	**pelotudo**-*adj; m*	slow, dumb (LA) (coll); young adult (LA)
5774	**conquistador**-*m; adj*	conqueror, Casanova; seductive
5775	**chal**-*m*	shawl
5777	**feto**-*m*	fetus
5783	**electricista**-*m/f*	electrician
5784	**sandía**-*f*	watermelon
5785	**milímetro**-*m*	millimeter
5786	**simulación**-*f*	simulation
5787	**génesis**-*f*	origin
5794	**hipódromo**-*m*	racecourse
5796	**caño**-*m*	pipe
5798	**deportista**-*adj; m/f*	sporty; athlete
5799	**lapicero**-*m*	pencil
5804	**desempeño**-*m*	performance
5806	**cuadrante**-*m*	quadrant
5808	**manipulación**-*f*	handling
5810	**místico**-*adj; m*	mystic; mystic
5811	**fascinación**-*f*	fascination
5812	**cresta**-*f*	crest
5814	**diabetes**-*f*	diabetes
5815	**camuflaje**-*m*	camouflage
5816	**antibiótico**-*adj; m*	antibiotic; antibiotic
5817	**siciliano**-*adj; m*	Sicilian; Sicilian person
5818	**masturbación**-*f*	masturbation
5822	**coalición**-*f*	coalition
5824	**gorrión**-*m*	sparrow
5825	**avalancha**-*f*	avalanche
5830	**desecho**-*m*	waste
5833	**cerro**-*m*	hill
5834	**clic**-*m*	click
5835	**disfrute**-*m*	enjoyment
5836	**anomalía**-*f*	anomaly
5837	**auditorio**-*adj; m*	hearing; auditorium
5839	**ansia**-*f*	craving
5841	**víveres**-*mpl*	supplies
5842	**mercader**-*m/f*	merchant
5843	**aventurero**-*adj; m*	adventurous; adventurer
5846	**pasarela**-*f*	walkway
5849	**impreso**-*adj; m*	printed; flyer
5850	**pío**-*m*	tweet
5851	**molde**-*m*	mould
5853	**travesura**-*f*	mischief
5856	**chapa**-*f*	sheet
5858	**cáscara**-*f*	shell
5859	**furgón**-*m*	van
5860	**historieta**-*f*	cartoon strip
5862	**ocaso**-*m*	sunset
5863	**concepción**-*f*	conception
5865	**despliegue**-*m*	deployment
5866	**gerencia**-*f*	management
5867	**australiano**-*adj; m*	Australian; Australian person
5869	**elogio**-*m*	compliment
5870	**ceguera**-*f*	blindness
5871	**iniciación**-*f*	initiation
5875	**urna**-*f*	vase
5876	**tapón**-*m*	plug, cover
5877	**mamífero**-*m; adj*	mammal; mammal
5878	**desacato**-*m*	contempt
5879	**monopolio**-*m*	monopoly
5881	**alineación**-*f*	line-up
5882	**contratista**-*m/f*	contractor
5885	**muela**-*f*	molar
5886	**bautismo**-*m*	baptism
5887	**cañería**-*f*	pipe
5889	**arete**-*m*	earring
5890	**gamba**-*f*	prawn
5891	**aura**-*f*	aura
5892	**fumador**-*m*	smoker
5894	**busto**-*m*	bust
5896	**despedida**-*f*	farewell
5899	**abdomen**-*m*	abdomen
5901	**bacteria**-*f*	bacterium
5902	**cajero**-*m*	cashier, cash point
5904	**vocal**-*adj; f*	vocal; vowel

5905	**aceituna**-*f*	olive
5906	**rascacielos**-*m*	skyscraper
5908	**rubí**-*m*	ruby
5909	**asombro**-*m*	astonishment
5910	**castidad**-*f*	chastity
5911	**cantera**-*f*	quarry
5913	**cripta**-*f*	crypt
5916	**caricia**-*f*	caress
5917	**ortografía**-*f*	orthography
5919	**ultra**-*pfx; adj; m/f*	over; ultra; extremist
5920	**desilusión**-*f*	disappointment
5921	**excremento**-*m*	excrement
5924	**perfume**-*m*	perfume
5925	**sanguijuela**-*f*	leech
5926	**adolescencia**-*f*	adolescence
5927	**cantor**-*adj; m*	singing; singer
5929	**contribuyente**-*m/f*	taxpayer
5931	**olímpico**-*adj; m*	Olympian; Olympian
5932	**prodigio**-*m*	wonder
5935	**vello**-*m*	fuzz
5936	**limpiador**-*adj; m*	cleaning; wiper (LA)
5937	**réplica**-*f*	replica
5938	**exigencia**-*f*	demand
5939	**teclado**-*m*	keyboard
5940	**artillero**-*adj; m*	artillery; artilleryman
5941	**contención**-*f*	containment
5944	**monarquía**-*f*	monarchy
5945	**bateador**-*m*	batter
5948	**mosquetero**-*m*	musketeer
5949	**manojo**-*m*	handful
5950	**fragancia**-*f*	fragrance
5951	**estímulo**-*m*	stimulus, incentive
5953	**sobresaliente**-*adj; m*	protruding; outstanding
5954	**itinerario**-*m*	itinerary
5956	**cliché**-*m*	cliche
5959	**purgatorio**-*m*	purgatory
5960	**fraile**-*m*	friar
5961	**abono**-*m*	fertilizer
5963	**pedazo**-*m*	chunk
5964	**cetro**-*m*	scepter
5965	**cupón**-*m*	coupon
5967	**cosmético**-*adj; m*	cosmetic; cosmetic
5968	**chacal**-*m*	jackal
5969	**vikingo**-*adj; m*	Viking; Viking
5970	**bombilla**-*f*	bulb
5971	**cochino**-*adj; m*	dirty; pig
5972	**Alpes**-*mpl*	Alps
5973	**pretendiente**-*m*	suitor
5974	**abertura**-*f*	opening
5975	**interrogación**-*f*	interrogation
5977	**susurro**-*m*	whisper
5978	**peregrino**-*m*	pilgrim
5979	**nacionalidad**-*f*	nationality
5984	**constancia**-*f*	persistence
5989	**lino**-*m*	linen
5995	**genocidio**-*m*	genocide
5996	**penetración**-*f*	penetration
5997	**intelecto**-*m*	intellect
5998	**anulación**-*f*	annulment
6002	**guardarropa**-*m*	wardrobe
6003	**maniquí**-*m*	mannequin
6004	**barrote**-*m*	bar
6005	**cuchara**-*f*	spoon
6006	**mestizo**-*adj; m*	racially mixed; mixed race
6007	**intermediario**-*m*	intermediary
6008	**brote**-*m*	outbreak
6010	**aproximación**-*f*	approximation
6012	**hélice**-*f*	propeller
6013	**incógnito**-*adj; m*	incognito; incognito
6014	**almeja**-*f*	clam, pussy (coll)
6015	**indígena**-*adj; m*	native; native person
6016	**reforma**-*f*	reform
6018	**voltio**-*m*	volt
6019	**cláusula**-*f*	clause
6020	**óxido**-*m*	rust
6022	**vértigo**-*m*	vertigo
6023	**atrocidad**-*f*	atrocity
6024	**gama**-*f*	range
6025	**complicidad**-*f*	involvement
6027	**intrigante**-*m*	intriguing
6029	**tardanza**-*f*	delay
6030	**burguesía**-*f*	the middle-class
6031	**apareamiento**-*m*	mating
6033	**rebote**-*m*	bounce
6034	**mutación**-*f*	mutation
6036	**arrastre**-*m*	dragging

6037	**follón**-*m*	racket
6038	**jerga**-*f*	slang
6039	**cumplimiento**-*m*	compliance
6040	**aleta**-*f*	fin
6041	**párpado**-*m*	eyelid
6043	**desconfianza**-*f*	distrust
6044	**ocular**-*adj; m*	eye; lens
6046	**burocracia**-*f*	bureaucracy
6047	**machete**-*m*	machete
6048	**revuelto**-*adj; m*	messy; scrambled eggs
6049	**antojo**-*m*	whim
6052	**ateo**-*adj; m*	atheistic; atheist
6053	**sarcasmo**-*m*	sarcasm
6056	**pestaña**-*f*	eyelash
6057	**trenza**-*f*	braid
6058	**encierro**-*m*	confinement
6060	**contraste**-*m*	contrast
6061	**reflexión**-*f*	reflection
6063	**macarrones**-*mpl*	macaroni
6064	**requisito**-*m*	requirement
6065	**mira**-*f*	sight
6066	**conservatorio**-*m*	conservatory
6068	**hormigón**-*m*	concrete
6069	**misionero**-*adj; m*	missionary; missionary
6071	**merienda**-*f*	afternoon snack
6072	**ladera**-*adj; f*	lateral; hillside
6074	**credo**-*m*	creed
6075	**torso**-*m*	torso
6076	**esquizofrenia**-*f*	schizophrenia
6078	**átomo**-*m*	atom
6080	**entidad**-*f*	organization
6081	**corrida**-*f*	bullfight
6082	**cianuro**-*m*	cyanide
6083	**inquietud**-*f*	restlessness
6084	**memorial**-*m*	memorial
6086	**especulación**-*f*	speculation
6087	**narrador**-*m*	narrator
6089	**chelín**-*m*	shilling
6090	**reconciliación**-*f*	reconciliation
6091	**calamidad**-*f*	calamity
6093	**lienzo**-*m*	canvas
6095	**vietnamita**-*adj; m/f*	Vietnamese; Vietnamese person
6096	**ciruela**-*f*	plum
6097	**velero**-*m*	sailing boat
6098	**barraca**-*f*	hut
6099	**gaviota**-*f*	seagull
6101	**malestar**-*m*	discomfort
6102	**granito**-*m*	granite
6103	**mantel**-*m*	tablecloth
6104	**pinchazo**-*m*	prick, pinch
6106	**refrán**-*m*	saying
6109	**farmacéutico**-*adj; m*	pharmaceutical; pharmacist
6111	**aspirante**-*m/f*	candidate
6114	**guita**-*f*	money (coll)
6116	**sucesión**-*f*	succession
6117	**constructor**-*adj; m*	building; builder
6120	**audacia**-*f*	audacity
6121	**visibilidad**-*f*	visibility
6122	**contrabandista**-*adj; m*	contraband; smuggler
6124	**pibe**-*m*	boy (coll)
6127	**asfixia**-*f*	suffocation
6129	**jardinería**-*f*	gardening
6130	**moco**-*m*	mucus
6131	**pendejada**-*f*	bullshit (LA) (coll)
6132	**sucursal**-*f*	branch
6134	**indulto**-*m*	pardon
6138	**platino**-*adj; m*	platinum; platinum
6139	**rigor**-*m*	exactitude, rigour
6140	**banjo**-*m*	banjo
6141	**cineasta**-*m/f*	filmmaker
6142	**intrusión**-*f*	intrusion
6143	**distribuidor**-*m*	distributor
6144	**transportador**-*m*	transporter
6145	**envenenamiento**-*m*	poisoning
6146	**bayoneta**-*f*	bayonet
6147	**asta**-*f*	horn
6149	**presagio**-*m*	omen
6150	**ardor**-*m*	burning sensation
6151	**iceberg**-*m*	iceberg
6152	**cerámica**-*f*	ceramic
6154	**estuche**-*m*	case
6155	**cebra**-*f*	zebra
6157	**vejiga**-*f*	bladder
6158	**computador**-*adj; m*	computer; computer (LA)
6159	**optimismo**-*m*	optimism
6160	**dirigente**-*m/f; adj*	leader; leading
6162	**metrópoli**-*f*	metropolis

6165	maestría-*f*	mastery
6166	dureza-*f*	hardness
6167	estragos-*mpl*	havoc
6169	espécimen-*m*	specimen
6170	fracción-*f*	fraction
6172	discriminación-*f*	discrimination
6173	proyector-*m*	projector
6174	paleta-*f*	palette, lollipop
6176	nirvana-*m*	nirvana
6179	represalia-*f*	reprisal
6180	aseo-*m*	bathroom
6181	arquero-*m*	archer
6183	confrontación-*f*	confrontation
6184	predicción-*f*	prediction
6187	paño-*m*	cloth
6188	barcaza-*f*	barge
6189	elenco-*m*	cast
6190	caparazón-*m*	shell
6191	clítoris-*m*	clitoris
6192	evasión-*f*	evasion
6193	zapatero-*m*	shoemaker
6194	acecho-*m*	stalking
6195	computación-*f*	computer studies (LA)
6197	restauración-*f*	restoration
6198	recámara-*f*	chamber
6200	maleza-*f*	undergrowth
6202	diplomacia-*f*	diplomacy
6205	paradoja-*f*	paradox
6207	concejo-*m*	council
6208	ceño-*m*	frown
6209	tribuna-*f*	stand
6211	artritis-*f*	arthritis
6212	paracaidista-*m/f*	parachutist
6214	abdominal-*adj; f*	abdominal; crunch
6216	paisano-*adj; m*	from the same place; civilian
6218	fósil-*m*	fossil
6219	cacao-*m*	cocoa
6221	municipio-*m*	municipality
6222	nombramiento-*m*	appointment
6226	cisterna-*f*	tanker
6228	caseta-*f*	hut
6229	diluvio-*m*	downpour
6230	textura-*f*	texture
6233	consumidor-*m*	consumer
6235	vendaje-*m*	bandage
6236	idealista-*adj; m*	idealistic; idealist
6237	redactor-*m*	editor
6238	cabecera-*f*	headboard
6241	conveniencia-*f*	advantage
6242	calentador-*m*	water heater
6243	anarquista-*m/f; adj*	anarchist; anarchist
6247	titán-*m*	titan
6249	orquídea-*f*	orchid
6250	asegurador-*adj; m*	insurance; insurer
6251	vizconde-*m*	viscount
6252	oyente-*m/f*	listener
6253	ampolla-*f*	vial, blister
6256	cafeína-*f*	caffeine
6257	insulina-*f*	insulin
6258	detonación-*f*	detonation
6259	guerrilla-*f*	guerrilla
6266	presentador-*m*	presenter
6268	columpio-*m*	swing
6269	damasco-*m*	apricot
6270	nodriza-*f*	nursemaid
6274	desembarco-*m*	landing
6275	silbido-*m*	whistle
6277	júbilo-*m*	joy
6278	gramática-*f*	grammar
6280	descomposición-*f*	decomposition
6281	indigestión-*f*	indigestion
6282	anécdota-*f*	anecdote
6283	contratiempo-*m*	setback
6284	incompetencia-*f*	incompetence
6285	tenor-*m*	tenor
6287	erudito-*adj; m*	expert; erudite person
6288	novelista-*m/f*	novelist
6289	espanto-*m*	terror
6292	miga-*f*	crumb
6294	tranquilizante-*adj; m*	reassuring; tranquilizer
6295	álamo-*m*	poplar
6298	intersección-*f*	intersection
6300	telégrafo-*m*	telegraph
6301	cordial-*m*	cordial
6302	expulsión-*f*	expulsion
6303	cáliz-*m*	goblet
6304	camarógrafo-*m*	cameraman

6305	escaparate-*m*	closet (LA), shop window
6306	calambre-*m*	cramp
6307	molécula-*f*	molecule
6309	oasis-*m*	oasis
6310	muleta-*f*	crutch
6311	sauce-*m*	willow
6312	pileta-*f*	basil (LA), pool (LA)
6313	resonancia-*f*	resonance
6314	expectativa-*f*	expectation
6315	mambo-*m*	mambo, issue (LA)
6317	absolución-*f*	absolution
6318	sureste-*m*	southeast
6319	audiencia-*f*	hearing
6321	fusilamiento-*m*	execution by firing squad
6322	cuarteto-*m*	quartet
6323	alubia-*f*	bean
6324	adquisición-*f*	acquisition
6325	pandillero-*m*	member of a gang
6326	propulsión-*f*	propulsion
6327	fiasco-*m*	fiasco
6329	carrete-*m*	reel
6330	reptil-*m*	reptile
6331	neblina-*f*	mist
6333	joroba-*f*	hump
6336	adoración-*f*	adoration
6337	informática-*f*	computing
6338	espinaca-*f*	spinach
6340	chalet-*m*	cottage
6341	planificación-*f*	planning
6342	vicario-*m*	vicar
6344	arándano-*m*	blueberry
6346	estéreo-*adj; m*	stereo; stereo
6347	mellizo-*adj; m*	twin; twin
6349	escultor-*m*	sculptor
6350	joyero-*m*	jeweller, jewellery box
6351	liquidación-*f*	settlement
6352	repertorio-*m*	repertoire
6353	clarinete-*m; m/f*	clarinet; clarinettist
6357	huerta-*f*	vegetable garden
6358	lavadero-*m*	sink, laundry room
6359	hemisferio-*m*	hemisphere
6361	derramamiento-*m*	shedding
6365	atraso-*m*	backwardness
6366	vigía-*m/f*	lookout
6367	modificación-*f*	modification
6368	pique-*m*	pique
6370	drenaje-*m*	drainage
6372	fertilidad-*f*	fertility
6373	destornillador-*m*	screwdriver
6374	prefectura-*f*	prefecture
6376	continuidad-*f*	continuity
6377	alcoba-*f*	bedroom
6378	primogénito-*m*	firstborn
6379	acordeón-*m*	accordion
6381	persuasión-*f*	persuasion
6382	coliseo-*m*	coliseum
6383	agresividad-*f*	aggressiveness
6384	sanitario-*m; adj*	bathroom; sanitary
6385	frigorífico-*m*	refrigerator
6386	curación-*f*	healing
6392	obstrucción-*f*	obstruction
6393	diésel-*m*	diesel
6394	pulmonía-*f*	pneumonia
6395	bisturí-*m*	scalpel
6400	herpes-*m*	herpes
6402	gobernante-*adj; m*	ruling; leader
6403	ecuador-*m*	equator
6405	trámite-*m*	process
6406	gabardina-*f*	raincoat
6407	fusible-*adj; m*	fusible; fuse
6408	glaciar-*m*	glacier
6409	historiador-*m*	historian
6411	asfalto-*m*	asphalt
6412	lujo-*m*	luxury
6413	península-*f*	peninsula
6414	indicador-*m*	indicator
6415	pedal-*m*	pedal
6418	leñador-*m*	woodcutter
6420	revuelo-*m*	stir
6423	mortero-*m*	mortar
6425	incremento-*m*	increase
6426	apéndice-*m*	appendix
6427	registrador-*m*	registrar
6430	cojín-*m*	cushion
6431	confidente-*m*	confidant
6432	agotamiento-*m*	exhaustion
6435	aeródromo-*m*	aerodrome
6436	sarampión-*m*	measles
6438	usuario-*m*	user
6439	éter-*m*	ether

6441	**comanche**-*adj; m/f*	Comanche; Comanche Indian
6443	**enciclopedia**-*f*	encyclopedia
6444	**arqueólogo**-*m*	archaeologist
6447	**recaudación**-*f*	collection
6448	**pubertad**-*f*	puberty
6449	**propulsor**-*adj; m*	propellant; promoter
6452	**penicilina**-*f*	penicillin
6453	**capitolio**-*m*	Capitol
6455	**estampilla**-*f*	stamp (LA), seal (ES)
6456	**mechero**-*m*	lighter
6458	**malla**-*f*	mesh
6459	**publicista**-*m/f*	publicist
6460	**seta**-*f*	mushroom
6464	**anticipación**-*f*	in advance
6466	**tejar**-*vb; m*	tile; tile factory
6467	**faena**-*f*	chore
6469	**viga**-*f*	beam
6470	**duplicado**-*m*	duplicate
6472	**repollo**-*m*	cabbage
6473	**sepultura**-*f*	burial
6474	**crucifijo**-*m*	crucifix
6478	**benefactor**-*adj; m*	benevolent; benefactor
6481	**observatorio**-*m*	observatory
6482	**portafolio**-*m*	portfolio
6483	**colecta**-*f*	collection
6485	**seducción**-*f*	seduction
6486	**hachís**-*m*	hash
6487	**odisea**-*f*	odyssey
6488	**concursante**-*adj; m/f*	competing; contestant
6489	**clon**-*m*	clone
6491	**gestión**-*f*	paperwork, management
6492	**pleito**-*m*	lawsuit
6493	**aspiración**-*f*	breathing, aspiration
6494	**arado**-*m*	plow
6495	**calidez**-*f*	warmth
6498	**radiografía**-*f*	radiography
6499	**hojalata**-*f*	tin
6500	**primicia**-*f*	scoop
6501	**dialecto**-*m*	dialect
6503	**conducción**-*f*	driving
6504	**extremista**-*adj; m/f*	extreme; extremist
6505	**mortalidad**-*f*	mortality
6507	**exageración**-*f*	exaggeration
6508	**heroísmo**-*m*	heroism
6509	**cochera**-*f*	garage (LA), depot
6510	**fundamento**-*m*	foundation
6512	**vertedero**-*m*	garbage dump
6514	**paladar**-*m*	palate
6515	**auricular**-*adj; m*	auricular; headset
6516	**carrusel**-*m*	carousel
6517	**sorteo**-*m*	raffle
6518	**asteroide**-*m*	asteroid
6521	**timidez**-*f*	shyness
6523	**clímax**-*m*	climax
6524	**comarca**-*f*	region
6525	**hambruna**-*f*	famine
6526	**meca**-*f*	mecca
6527	**chorro**-*m*	stream
6528	**incondicional**-*adj; m/f*	unconditional; stalwart
6529	**marisco**-*m*	shellfish
6530	**ribera**-*f*	riverbank
6532	**psicosis**-*f*	psychosis
6533	**hepatitis**-*f*	hepatitis
6534	**flan**-*m*	flan
6535	**afición**-*f*	hobby, fans
6539	**mora**-*f*	blackberry
6540	**turba**-*f*	mob
6541	**controversia**-*f*	controversy
6542	**justificación**-*f*	justification
6543	**escéptico**-*adj; m*	skeptic; skeptic
6544	**controlador**-*adj; m*	controlling; controller
6547	**futbolista**-*m/f*	football player
6548	**arqueología**-*f*	archeology
6549	**lácteo**-*adj; m*	dairy; lactose
6550	**ciénaga**-*f*	swamp
6551	**guerrillero**-*adj; m*	guerrilla; guerrilla
6554	**renovación**-*f*	renovation
6555	**puñalada**-*f*	stab
6559	**tocadiscos**-*m*	record player
6560	**emblema**-*m*	emblem
6562	**pastelería**-*f*	patisserie
6563	**descendencia**-*f*	offspring
6565	**próstata**-*f*	prostate
6567	**cuesta**-*f*	slope

6569	**colaborador**-*adj; m*	cooperative; contributor, co-worker
6570	**stock**-*m*	stock
6571	**contramaestre**-*m*	boatswain
6574	**fijación**-*f*	fixation
6577	**plutonio**-*m*	plutonium
6580	**astro**-*m*	star
6583	**paternidad**-*f*	paternity
6584	**candidatura**-*f*	candidacy
6585	**tifus**-*m*	typhus
6586	**publicitario**-*adj; m*	advertising; publicist
6587	**astillero**-*m*	shipyard
6590	**delincuencia**-*f*	delinquency
6593	**checo**-*adj; m*	Czech; Czech person
6594	**hábitat**-*m*	habitat
6596	**confederación**-*f*	confederation
6600	**canica**-*f*	marble
6601	**confín**-*m*	border
6603	**aritmético**-*adj; m*	arithmetic; arithmetician
6604	**electo**-*adj; m*	elected; elected member
6605	**dióxido**-*m*	dioxide
6606	**colesterol**-*m*	cholesterol
6608	**cautiverio**-*m*	captivity
6609	**diámetro**-*m*	diameter
6610	**sureño**-*adj; m*	southern; southerner
6611	**caucho**-*m*	rubber
6616	**incentivo**-*m*	incentive
6617	**excusado**-*adj; m*	superfluous; restroom
6621	**conversión**-*f*	conversion
6622	**monedero**-*m*	purse
6623	**viñedo**-*m*	vineyard
6624	**malicia**-*f*	malice
6625	**resfrío**-*m*	cold
6626	**terrateniente**-*m/f*	landowner
6627	**voltaje**-*m*	voltage
6628	**panfleto**-*m*	pamphlet
6630	**jazmín**-*m*	jasmine
6631	**faja**-*f*	sash
6632	**metropolitano**-*adj; m*	urban; subway
6633	**peaje**-*m*	toll
6634	**herejía**-*f*	heresy
6635	**agresor**-*adj; m*	attacking; attacker
6636	**contracción**-*f*	contraction
6638	**cautela**-*f*	caution
6640	**ozono**-*m*	ozone
6641	**virtuoso**-*adj; m*	virtuous; virtuoso
6642	**bordado**-*m*	embroidery
6643	**promotor**-*m*	promoter
6644	**pichón**-*m*	squab
6649	**hamaca**-*f*	hammock
6651	**pincel**-*m*	paint brush
6655	**ráfaga**-*f*	burst
6656	**alquitrán**-*m*	tar
6659	**avispa**-*f*	wasp
6660	**contraataque**-*m*	counterattack
6661	**ofrecimiento**-*m*	offer
6662	**compostura**-*f*	composure
6663	**calumnia**-*f*	slander
6664	**saga**-*f*	saga
6667	**pantufla**-*f*	slipper
6668	**impotencia**-*f*	impotence
6669	**devolución**-*f*	refund
6671	**albañil**-*m/f*	builder
6678	**castellano**-*adj; m*	Spanish; Castilian Spanish
6679	**duna**-*f*	dune
6680	**termómetro**-*m*	thermometer
6681	**intromisión**-*f*	meddling
6684	**metralleta**-*f*	submachine gun
6685	**reo**-*m*	prisoner
6686	**sombrilla**-*f*	parasol
6687	**complejidad**-*f*	complexity
6688	**calcio**-*m*	calcium
6689	**leucemia**-*f*	leukemia
6690	**encrucijada**-*f*	crossroads
6693	**activista**-*m/f*	activist
6694	**lirio**-*m*	lily
6696	**pereza**-*f*	laziness
6697	**tramo**-*m*	stretch
6698	**trébol**-*m*	clover
6700	**eficacia**-*f*	effectiveness
6701	**ginecólogo**-*m*	gynecologist
6702	**atlas**-*m*	atlas
6704	**barrido**-*m*	sweep
6705	**soprano**-*m/f*	soprano
6707	**implante**-*m*	implant

6709	**madriguera**-*f*	den
6711	**extremidad**-*f*	limb
6713	**aplazamiento**-*m*	postponement
6714	**silueta**-*f*	silhouette
6716	**aerosol**-*m*	spray
6718	**tecla**-*f*	key
6719	**trompa**-*f*	trunk, horn
6720	**puntualidad**-*f*	punctuality
6722	**lubricante**-*m*	lubricant
6723	**colgante**-*adj; m*	hanging; pendant
6725	**gel**-*m*	gel
6726	**deleite**-*m*	delight
6730	**embarcación**-*f*	embarkation
6731	**legislación**-*f*	legislation
6732	**incursión**-*f*	incursion
6733	**fealdad**-*f*	ugliness
6736	**forro**-*m*	lining, jacket
6737	**verbo**-*m*	verb
6738	**escudero**-*m*	squire
6740	**hereje**-*m/f*	heretic
6741	**reembolso**-*m*	refund
6743	**lastre**-*m*	ballast
6744	**guardacostas**-*m/f*	coastguard
6745	**paralítico**-*m*	paralytic
6748	**jeringa**-*f*	syringe
6749	**balneario**-*m*	spa
6751	**convertible**-*adj; m*	convertible; convertible (LA)
6752	**vector**-*m*	vector
6755	**enchufe**-*m*	wall socket
6756	**naturalidad**-*f*	naturalness
6757	**indulgencia**-*f*	indulgence
6760	**escote**-*m*	cleavage
6762	**jerarquía**-*f*	hierarchy
6764	**táctico**-*adj; m*	tactical; tactician
6768	**ciudadanía**-*f*	citizenship
6772	**arce**-*m*	maple
6773	**fauna**-*f*	fauna, bunch of weirdos (coll)
6774	**curro**-*m*	job (ES) (coll)
6775	**subdirector**-*m*	assistant manager
6776	**metano**-*m*	methane
6778	**estampida**-*f*	stampede
6779	**confidencialidad**-*f*	confidentiality
6784	**torero**-*m*	bullfighter
6785	**alegato**-*m*	plea
6787	**lombriz**-*f*	earthworm
6791	**moño**-*m*	bun
6792	**financiación**-*f*	financing
6793	**atropello**-*m*	hit-and-run
6795	**diversidad**-*f*	diversity
6796	**crianza**-*f*	raising
6798	**teórico**-*adj; m*	theoretical; theorist
6799	**diafragma**-*m*	diaphragm
6800	**improvisación**-*f*	improvisation
6801	**harén**-*m*	harem
6802	**castaña**-*f*	chestnut
6804	**diva**-*f*	diva
6805	**turbulencia**-*f*	turbulence
6807	**halo**-*m*	halo
6809	**estandarte**-*m*	banner
6810	**emparedado**-*m*	sandwich
6811	**transcurso**-*m*	course
6812	**narración**-*f*	narration
6813	**antisemitismo**-*m*	anti-Semitism
6815	**gótico**-*adj; m*	Gothic; Goth
6816	**maqueta**-*f*	mockup
6818	**semejanza**-*f*	likeness
6819	**carcajada**-*f*	loud laugh
6823	**suela**-*f*	sole
6824	**organizador**-*m*	organizer
6825	**vitalidad**-*f*	vitality
6827	**énfasis**-*m*	emphasis
6828	**partidario**-*adj; m*	in favour of; supporter
6829	**coreografía**-*f*	choreography
6831	**acorazado**-*m*	armoured
6833	**anchoa**-*f*	anchovy
6834	**cavidad**-*f*	cavity
6835	**infracción**-*f*	infraction
6838	**sensatez**-*f*	good judgement
6839	**cazo**-*m*	pot
6840	**ultimátum**-*m*	ultimatum
6841	**facción**-*f*	faction
6844	**boa**-*f*	boa
6847	**carisma**-*m*	charisma
6848	**repisa**-*f*	shelf
6849	**indonesio**-*adj; m*	Indonesian; Indonesian person
6850	**alabanza**-*f*	praise
6851	**prismáticos**-*m*	binoculars

6853	**acreedor**-*adj; m*	deserving of; creditor
6856	**herradura**-*f*	horseshoe
6857	**buzo**-*m*	scuba diver
6859	**inversionista**-*m/f*	investor
6860	**kárate**-*m*	karate
6861	**nicotina**-*f*	nicotine
6863	**pedestal**-*m*	pedestal
6864	**virilidad**-*f*	virility
6865	**estimado**-*adj; m*	appreciated; estimation, dear
6867	**consultor**-*adj; m*	advisory; consultant
6868	**actualización**-*f*	update
6869	**tifón**-*m*	typhoon
6870	**estruendo**-*m*	racket
6872	**astronomía**-*f*	astronomy
6873	**romanticismo**-*m*	romanticism
6874	**acierto**-*m*	right answer, wise decision
6876	**carburador**-*m*	carburetor
6878	**intoxicación**-*f*	intoxication
6879	**aptitud**-*f*	ability
6880	**dominación**-*f*	domination
6881	**colon**-*m*	colon
6882	**arsénico**-*m*	arsenic
6883	**condominio**-*m*	condominium
6884	**reproductor**-*adj; m*	reproductive; DVD player
6887	**consola**-*f*	console
6889	**amparo**-*m*	protection
6891	**neurosis**-*f*	neurosis
6894	**epilepsia**-*f*	epilepsy
6895	**desodorante**-*m*	deodorant
6896	**estallido**-*m*	explosion
6898	**limbo**-*m*	limbo
6899	**secuaz**-*m*	minion
6900	**aversión**-*f*	aversion
6901	**quilate**-*m*	carat
6903	**remolino**-*m*	swirl
6905	**durazno**-*m*	peach
6906	**néctar**-*m*	nectar
6907	**nutriente**-*adj; m*	nutritious; nutrient
6910	**corsé**-*m*	corset
6911	**tentativa**-*f*	attempt
6912	**intervalo**-*m*	interval
6914	**galope**-*m*	gallop
6915	**importación**-*f*	importation
6916	**tendero**-*m*	shopkeeper
6917	**payasada**-*f*	charade
6919	**desinfectante**-*adj; m*	disinfectant; disinfectant
6921	**transcripción**-*f*	transcription
6922	**latitud**-*f*	latitude
6923	**densidad**-*f*	density
6924	**vereda**-*f*	path
6926	**apóstol**-*m*	apostle
6930	**mechón**-*m*	lock
6932	**conspirador**-*m*	conspirer
6933	**formato**-*m*	format
6934	**confinamiento**-*m*	confinement
6935	**emisario**-*m*	emissary
6937	**indigente**-*m*	indigent
6938	**feminista**-*adj; m/f*	feminist; feminist
6939	**ámbito**-*m*	field
6940	**neurona**-*f*	neuron
6941	**pupila**-*f*	pupil
6942	**quimioterapia**-*f*	chemotherapy
6944	**talco**-*m*	talc
6947	**comprobación**-*f*	verification
6948	**infamia**-*f*	infamy
6950	**éxodo**-*m*	exodus
6951	**bazar**-*m*	bazaar
6952	**hormiguero**-*m*	anthill
6955	**concentrado**-*m*	concentrated
6957	**sumisión**-*f*	submission
6958	**intendente**-*m/f*	intendant
6961	**difamación**-*f*	defamation
6963	**monarca**-*m/f*	monarch
6970	**inseguridad**-*f*	insecurity
6971	**transfusión**-*f*	transfusion
6975	**higo**-*m*	fig
6976	**combustión**-*f*	combustion
6977	**judía**-*m*	bean
6978	**castor**-*m*	beaver
6979	**coeficiente**-*m*	coefficient
6981	**abogacía**-*f*	legal profession
6982	**alcoholismo**-*m*	alcoholism
6983	**aeronave**-*f*	aircraft
6985	**adversidad**-*f*	adversity
6987	**hincha**-*m/f*	fan
6989	**impedimento**-*m*	impediment
6992	**franja**-*f*	stripe, time zone

6993	**pitón**-*f*	python	
6994	**temporizador**-*m*	timer	
6995	**óptico**-*adj; m*	optical; optician	
6997	**plus**-*m*	bonus	
6998	**lóbulo**-*m*	lobe	
7001	**mejicano**-*adj; m*	Mexican; Mexican person	

N	Word	Meaning	N	Word	Meaning
6993	**pitón**-*f*	python	7065	**calculadora**-*f*	calculator
6994	**temporizador**-*m*	timer	7067	**silo**-*m*	silo
6995	**óptico**-*adj; m*	optical; optician	7068	**pimiento**-*m*	pepper
6997	**plus**-*m*	bonus	7069	**vaina**-*f*	scabbard, pod
6998	**lóbulo**-*m*	lobe	7070	**metabolismo**-*m*	metabolism
7001	**mejicano**-*adj; m*	Mexican; Mexican person	7071	**ferroviario**-*adj; m*	railway; railwayman
7002	**loma**-*f*	hill	7072	**solista**-*m/f*	soloist
7003	**relevancia**-*f*	relevance	7073	**plancton**-*m*	plankton
7004	**informativo**-*adj; m*	informative; news bulletin	7074	**yogur**-*m*	yogurt
7007	**filtración**-*f*	filtration	7075	**testosterona**-*f*	testosterone
7009	**conservación**-*f*	conservation	7076	**infraestructura**-*f*	infrastructure
7010	**exterminio**-*m*	extermination	7077	**rumba**-*f*	rumba
7012	**convulsión**-*f*	convulsion	7080	**tapete**-*m*	rug
7014	**fonda**-*f*	inn	7081	**bebedor**-*adj; m*	heavy drinker (coll); drinker
7015	**dominical**-*adj; m*	Sunday; Sunday magazine	7082	**migaja**-*f*	crumb
7017	**liceo**-*m*	high school (LA)	7083	**indignación**-*f*	indignation
7018	**cerrajero**-*m*	locksmith	7084	**confort**-*m*	comfort
7020	**postor**-*m*	bidder	7085	**moderación**-*f*	moderation
7021	**incesto**-*m*	incest	7086	**nabo**-*m*	turnip
7023	**hámster**-*m*	hamster	7087	**microbio**-*m*	microbe
7024	**bisexual**-*adj; m/f*	bisexual; bisexual	7088	**colombiano**-*adj; m*	Colombian; Colombian person
7027	**serenata**-*f*	serenade	7089	**secretaría**-*f*	secretary's office
7028	**deducción**-*f*	deduction	7091	**espárrago**-*m*	asparagus
7030	**callejón**-*m*	alley	7092	**caricatura**-*f*	caricature
7032	**proletariado**-*m*	proletariat	7094	**apio**-*m*	celery
7034	**clavel**-*m*	carnation	7096	**perforación**-*f*	drilling
7035	**aguijón**-*m*	sting	7097	**azteca**-*adj; m*	Aztec; Aztec person
7036	**aceleración**-*f*	acceleration	7098	**segmento**-*m*	segment
7038	**desperdicio**-*m*	waste	7099	**cilindro**-*m*	cylinder
7040	**fábula**-*f*	fable	7101	**honradez**-*f*	honesty
7041	**secador**-*m*	hairdryer	7102	**res**-*f*	farm animal
7046	**estantería**-*f*	bookcase	7103	**estribo**-*m*	stirrup
7047	**proximidad**-*f*	proximity	7105	**prevención**-*f*	prevention
7048	**grosería**-*f*	rudeness	7106	**clínico**-*adj; m*	clinical; doctor
7052	**atacante**-*adj; m/f*	combative; attacker	7107	**incisión**-*f*	incision
7053	**deserción**-*f*	desertion	7108	**ámbar**-*m*	amber
7057	**vegetación**-*f*	vegetation	7109	**utopía**-*f*	utopia
7058	**tripulante**-*m/f*	crew member	7111	**geometría**-*f*	geometry
7059	**mobiliario**-*m*	furniture	7112	**copo**-*m*	flake
7060	**abastecimiento**-*m*	supply	7114	**orificio**-*m*	hole
7061	**chorizo**-*m*	chorizo	7115	**notificación**-*f*	notification
7063	**cuneta**-*f*	ditch	7118	**partitura**-*f*	sheet music
7064	**pelusa**-*f*	fluff			

7119	**sonámbulo**-*adj; m*	sleepwalker; sleepwalker
7120	**infelicidad**-*f*	unhappiness
7121	**centeno**-*m*	rye
7122	**armisticio**-*m*	armistice
7124	**petrolero**-*m*	oil tanker
7125	**remitente**-*m/f*	sender
7127	**euforia**-*f*	euphoria
7129	**digestión**-*f*	digestion
7131	**mormón**-*m*	Mormon
7132	**eslogan**-*m*	slogan
7133	**falsedad**-*f*	falseness
7135	**variación**-*f*	variation
7136	**desobediencia**-*f*	disobedience
7138	**reclamación**-*f*	complaint
7141	**taburete**-*m*	stool
7142	**recreación**-*f*	recreation
7144	**parachoques**-*m*	bumper
7145	**compuerta**-*f*	gate
7147	**tallo**-*m*	stem
7148	**sedante**-*adj; m*	sedative; sedative
7149	**gruta**-*f*	cave
7150	**rumano**-*adj; m*	Romanian; Romanian person
7151	**picadura**-*f*	sting
7153	**soberanía**-*f*	sovereignty
7155	**murmullo**-*m*	babbling
7156	**acrobacia**-*f*	stunt
7158	**rábano**-*m*	radish
7159	**extradición**-*f*	extradition
7160	**boutique**-*f*	boutique
7161	**bicarbonato**-*m*	bicarbonate
7162	**subsidio**-*m*	subsidy
7164	**almendra**-*f*	almond
7165	**derivado**-*adj; m*	derived; derivative
7166	**fertilizante**-*adj; m*	fertilizing; fertilizer
7167	**raqueta**-*f*	racket
7168	**detergente**-*adj; m*	detergent; detergent
7169	**servidumbre**-*f*	servants
7170	**mercante**-*m/f*	merchant
7172	**cloro**-*m*	chlorine
7173	**tónico**-*m*	tonic
7177	**becerro**-*m*	calf
7178	**mitin**-*m*	rally
7179	**catarro**-*m*	cold
7180	**lacayo**-*m*	servant
7181	**bañador**-*m*	swimsuit
7182	**torbellino**-*m*	whirlwind
7184	**déficit**-*m*	deficit
7185	**convenio**-*m*	agreement
7186	**desviación**-*f*	detour
7190	**espejismo**-*m*	illusion
7191	**tentáculo**-*m*	tentacle
7194	**oleada**-*f*	wave
7197	**sien**-*f*	temple
7199	**impertinencia**-*f*	impertinence
7200	**recesión**-*f*	recession
7201	**halago**-*m*	praise
7203	**perseverancia**-*f*	perseverance
7204	**rebanada**-*f*	slice
7207	**avestruz**-*m*	ostrich
7211	**polen**-*m*	pollen
7216	**dependencia**-*f*	dependence
7217	**sintonía**-*f*	tuning
7218	**piratería**-*f*	piracy
7219	**carroña**-*f*	carrion
7220	**vandalismo**-*m*	vandalism
7221	**icono**-*m*	icon
7223	**repercusión**-*f*	impact
7224	**tajo**-*m*	cut, work (coll)
7227	**cobija**-*f*	blanket (LA)
7229	**extracto**-*m*	extract
7230	**exportación**-*f*	exportation
7233	**titulado**-*m*	graduate
7234	**alteración**-*f*	alteration
7238	**regocijo**-*m*	delight
7239	**metralla**-*f*	shrapnel
7241	**bruma**-*f*	mist
7242	**cinismo**-*m*	cynicism
7245	**montículo**-*m*	mound
7248	**inmundicia**-*f*	filth
7250	**capota**-*f*	hood
7252	**regulación**-*f*	regulation
7253	**rectitud**-*f*	straightness
7257	**nudista**-*adj; m/f*	nudist; nudist
7258	**logo**-*m; sfx*	logo (coll); ist
7259	**sarpullido**-*m*	rash
7260	**atasco**-*m*	jam, obstacle
7261	**nitrógeno**-*m*	nitrogen
7262	**elevación**-*f*	elevation
7263	**clero**-*m*	clergy
7264	**fresno**-*m*	ash

7265	**fractura**-*f*	fracture
7267	**cinto**-*m*	belt
7268	**moraleja**-*f*	moral of a fable
7269	**imprudencia**-*f*	carelessness
7270	**campanario**-*m*	bell tower
7271	**vitrina**-*f*	display cabinet
7272	**viña**-*f*	vineyard
7274	**pasivo**-*adj; m*	passive; retiree
7277	**pudor**-*m*	modesty
7278	**flamenco**-*adj; m*	flamenco; flamingo
7279	**cóndor**-*m*	condor
7280	**militante**-*adj; m/f*	militant; member, activist
7282	**pus**-*m*	pus
7285	**aristocracia**-*f*	aristocracy
7286	**corcel**-*m*	steed
7288	**lavaplatos**-*m/f*	dishwasher
7290	**melena**-*f*	mane
7291	**gendarme**-*m/f*	police officer
7294	**potasio**-*m*	potassium
7296	**chimpancé**-*m*	chimpanzee
7297	**reproche**-*m*	reproach
7299	**tesorero**-*m*	treasurer
7300	**onza**-*f*	ounce
7302	**esmalte**-*m*	nail polish, varnish
7303	**repaso**-*m*	review
7304	**torpeza**-*f*	clumsiness
7305	**fervor**-*m*	fervor
7306	**pitillo**-*m*	cigarette
7307	**detección**-*f*	detection
7308	**coito**-*m*	intercourse
7310	**parámetro**-*m*	parameter
7313	**movilización**-*f*	mobilization
7316	**cortocircuito**-*m*	short-circuit
7317	**verificación**-*f*	verification
7320	**papelera**-*f*	bin
7321	**palomar**-*m*	dovecote
7322	**autenticidad**-*f*	authenticity
7323	**guardabosques**-*m/f*	forest ranger
7324	**derrota**-*f*	defeat
7326	**teología**-*f*	theology
7327	**patrullero**-*m*	patrolman
7328	**tuerca**-*f*	screw
7331	**lupa**-*f*	magnifying glass
7333	**plural**-*m*	plural
7335	**cuestionario**-*m*	questionnaire
7336	**asedio**-*m*	siege
7337	**lucro**-*m*	profit
7338	**sepulcro**-*m*	tomb
7339	**larva**-*f*	larva
7341	**saqueo**-*m*	pillage
7342	**diagrama**-*m*	diagram
7347	**portazo**-*m*	slam
7348	**levadura**-*f*	yeast
7351	**alcaldía**-*f*	mayor's office
7353	**sobrecarga**-*f*	overload
7354	**limo**-*m*	mud
7355	**nordeste**-*m*	north-east
7356	**reelección**-*f*	reelection
7357	**pesquero**-*adj; m*	fishing; fishing boat
7360	**integración**-*f*	integration
7361	**rejilla**-*f*	rack
7362	**enjambre**-*m*	swarm
7364	**resguardo**-*m*	receipt
7365	**intolerancia**-*f*	intolerance
7367	**nominación**-*f*	nomination
7368	**tumulto**-*m*	tumult
7369	**pordiosero**-*m*	beggar
7370	**escarlata**-*adj; m*	scarlet; scarlet
7371	**barullo**-*m*	noise
7373	**hacha**-*f*	axe
7374	**regularidad**-*f*	consistency
7375	**comandancia**-*f*	headquarters
7376	**apendicitis**-*f*	appendicitis
7377	**ingenuidad**-*f*	naivety
7378	**bache**-*m*	bump
7380	**aniquilación**-*f*	annihilation
7381	**recibimiento**-*m*	reception
7382	**medidor**-*adj; m*	measuring; meter
7383	**glándula**-*f*	gland
7386	**recluso**-*adj; m*	be in prison; prisoner
7388	**parking**-*m*	parking lot
7389	**migración**-*f*	migration
7390	**titanio**-*m*	titanium
7393	**procesamiento**-*m*	prosecution
7396	**vigilia**-*f*	vigil
7401	**séquito**-*m*	entourage
7402	**desolación**-*f*	devastation
7405	**estatuto**-*m*	statute

7408	**noviazgo**-*m*	engagement
7410	**mota**-*f*	speck
7414	**predecesor**-*m*	predecessor
7415	**pensador**-*m*	thinker
7416	**empleador**-*m*	employer
7417	**granizo**-*m*	hail
7418	**succión**-*f*	suction
7419	**fobia**-*f*	phobia
7420	**tea**-*f*	torch
7421	**hostal**-*m*	hostel
7422	**leproso**-*adj; m*	leprous; leper
7424	**tutela**-*f*	guardianship
7425	**trote**-*m*	trot
7426	**constelación**-*f*	constellation
7427	**cigüeña**-*f*	stork
7428	**rivalidad**-*f*	rivalry
7429	**salvamento**-*m*	rescue
7432	**pretensión**-*f*	ambition
7433	**florero**-*m*	vase
7436	**lingote**-*m*	ingot
7437	**despeje**-*m*	clearance
7440	**madero**-*m*	log, cop (coll)
7443	**dígito**-*m*	digit
7444	**machista**-*adj; m*	sexist; sexist
7445	**realismo**-*m*	realism
7448	**martirio**-*m*	martyrdom
7449	**cubeta**-*f*	tray, bucket
7450	**petardo**-*m*	firecracker
7453	**bonificación**-*f*	bonus
7454	**hervido**-*adj; m*	boiled; casserole
7457	**dineral**-*m*	fortune
7458	**acantilado**-*adj; m*	steep; cliff
7459	**pavimento**-*m*	pavement
7461	**lepra**-*f*	leprosy
7462	**simplicidad**-*f*	simplicity
7464	**sinónimo**-*adj; m*	synonym; synonymous
7467	**miligramo**-*m*	milligram
7468	**boliche**-*m*	bowling, nightclub (LA)
7469	**empatía**-*f*	empathy
7470	**interacción**-*f*	interaction
7471	**yodo**-*m*	iodine
7473	**vocero**-*m*	spokesman
7475	**desdén**-*m*	disdain
7477	**variable**-*f*	variable
7478	**cornisa**-*f*	cornice
7479	**garrote**-*m*	stick
7482	**reencuentro**-*m*	reencounter
7483	**zodiaco**-*m*	zodiac
7484	**premier**-*f*	premiere
7485	**elocuencia**-*f*	eloquence
7486	**franquicia**-*f*	franchise
7487	**embriaguez**-*f*	drunkenness
7488	**cervecería**-*f*	brewery
7489	**páramo**-*m*	wasteland
7490	**híbrido**-*adj; m*	mix; hybrid
7491	**garbo**-*m*	grace
7492	**patología**-*f*	pathology
7494	**patilla**-*f*	sideburn
7495	**encía**-*f*	gum
7496	**resorte**-*m*	spring
7498	**roedor**-*m*	rodent, mouse (coll)
7499	**forestal**-*adj; m*	forest; ranger
7500	**implicación**-*f*	implication
7504	**renombre**-*m*	renown
7505	**frenesí**-*m*	frenzy
7506	**heces**-*fpl*	dregs, feces
7507	**atletismo**-*m*	athletics
7509	**finalista**-*adj; m/f*	finalist; finalist
7512	**poro**-*m*	pore
7515	**canino**-*adj; m*	canine; canine tooth
7516	**dote**-*f*	dowry
7517	**radial**-*adj; f*	radio; circular saw
7518	**podio**-*m*	podium
7520	**burócrata**-*m/f*	bureaucrat
7521	**intermitente**-*adj; m*	intermittent; blinker
7522	**helio**-*m*	helium
7523	**elixir**-*m*	elixir
7524	**autonomía**-*f*	autonomy
7525	**furor**-*m*	fury

Numerals

Rank	Spanish-*PoS*	Translation(s)
5290	**diecinueve**-*num*	nineteen
5356	**veinticuatro**-*num*	twenty-four
5496	**centenar**-*num*	hundred
5680	**veintidós**-*num*	twenty-two
6520	**cuatrocientos**-*num*	four hundred
6758	**billón**-*num*	trillion
6766	**veintitrés**-*num*	twenty-three
6842	**veintiuno**-*num*	twenty-one
6897	**seiscientos**-*num*	six hundred
6988	**novecientos**-*num*	nine hundred
7275	**veintisiete**-*num*	twenty-seven
7287	**veintiocho**-*num*	twenty-eight

Verbs

Rank	Spanish-PoS	Translation(s)
5003	**reclutar**-*vb*	recruit
5010	**presenciar**-*vb*	witness
5014	**encarcelar**-*vb*	imprison
5028	**poblar**-*vb*	populate
5031	**imitar**-*vb*	imitate
5034	**donar**-*vb*	donate
5037	**extraer**-*vb*	extract
5040	**telefonear**-*vb*	call
5042	**asombrar(se)**-*vb*	amaze
5046	**captar**-*vb*	capture
5047	**reinar**-*vb*	reign
5049	**difundir**-*vb*	spread
5061	**revivir**-*vb*	revive
5066	**prender**-*vb*	fasten, light
5075	**detectar**-*vb*	detect
5077	**preciar(se)**-*vb; vbr*	value; pride yourself in
5121	**trepar**-*vb*	climb
5129	**familiarizar(se)**-*vb*	become familiar with
5138	**residir**-*vb*	reside
5140	**censurar**-*vb*	censor
5153	**apuñalar**-*vb*	stab
5156	**presumir**-*vb*	presume
5172	**sacudir(se)**-*vb; vbr*	shake; get rid off
5191	**orar**-*vb*	pray, make a speech
5204	**introducir(se)**-*vb*	introduce
5208	**merodear**-*vb*	lurk
5215	**progresar**-*vb*	progress
5223	**cabrear**-*vb*	piss off
5227	**complicar(se)**-*vb*	complicate
5231	**entretener(se)**-*vb*	entertain
5236	**emitir**-*vb*	broadcast
5242	**estirar(se)**-*vb*	stretch
5251	**contemplar**-*vb*	contemplate, take into account
5252	**repasar**-*vb*	check
5253	**gozar**-*vb*	enjoy
5260	**concluir**-*vb*	conclude
5261	**contribuir**-*vb*	contribute
5265	**oscurecer**-*vb*	get dark
5269	**comentar**-*vb*	discuss, mention
5282	**sorber**-*vb*	slurp
5283	**concordar**-*vb*	agree
5287	**recomendar**-*vb*	recommend
5293	**bombardear**-*vb*	bomb
5298	**blindar**-*vb*	armor
5318	**liquidar**-*vb*	finish, eliminate
5319	**finalizar**-*vb*	conclude
5323	**rellenar**-*vb*	fill
5340	**denegar**-*vb*	deny
5344	**mediar**-*vb*	mediate
5346	**financiar**-*vb*	finance
5355	**improvisar**-*vb*	improvise
5357	**barrer**-*vb*	sweep
5368	**ampliar**-*vb*	enlarge
5369	**pudrir(se)**-*vb*	rot
5370	**conmover**-*vb*	move
5374	**vaciar**-*vb*	empty
5381	**restaurar**-*vb*	restore
5386	**incendiar**-*vb*	burn down
5388	**evaluar**-*vb*	evaluate
5395	**podar**-*vb*	prune
5396	**proseguir**-*vb*	continue
5398	**fundar**-*vb*	found
5405	**sustituir**-*vb*	replace
5406	**jalar**-*vb*	pull
5407	**generar**-*vb*	generate
5409	**incomodar**-*vb*	make uncomfortable
5412	**trastornar**-*vb*	drive mad
5417	**calificar**-*vb*	mark
5419	**afligir(se)**-*vb*	grieve, suffer from
5420	**encadenar**-*vb*	chain
5423	**pelar**-*vb*	peel
5437	**inspeccionar**-*vb*	inspect
5441	**entregar(se)**-*vb*	deliver
5448	**aspirar**-*vb*	inhale
5456	**imprimir**-*vb*	print
5461	**jubilar(se)**-*vb; vbr*	get rid of; retire
5462	**fascinar**-*vb*	fascinate
5492	**fastidiar(se)**-*vb; vbr*	annoy; put up with
5499	**tapar**-*vb*	cover
5516	**boxear**-*vb*	box
5527	**abatir(se)**-*vb; vbr*	take down; fold up, become depressed
5530	**rizar**-*vb*	curl
5532	**desaguar**-*vb*	drain
5533	**bañar(se)**-*vb*	bathe
5537	**barajar**-*vb*	shuffle

5560	**restringir**-*vb*	restrict
5578	**convocar**-*vb*	summon
5581	**remar**-*vb*	row
5583	**prescindir**-*vb*	get by without
5588	**heredar**-*vb*	inherit
5591	**designar**-*vb*	appoint
5596	**equivocarse**-*vbr*	be wrong
5598	**derretir**-*vb*	melt
5600	**taladrar**-*vb*	drill
5603	**sanar**-*vb*	heal
5624	**inclinar(se)**-*vb; vbr*	bend, persuade; bow, tend toward
5628	**resbalar(se)**-*vb*	slip
5629	**florecer**-*vb*	bloom
5633	**equipar(se)**-*vb*	equip
5635	**nevar**-*vb*	snow
5641	**vallar**-*vb; m*	fence; fenced enclosure
5643	**saldar**-*vb*	pay off
5657	**afilar(se)**-*vb; vbr*	sharpen; become thin
5664	**recaudar**-*vb*	collect
5665	**fundir(se)**-*vb; vbr*	melt; melt, burn out
5672	**ladrar**-*vb*	bark
5674	**excavar**-*vb*	dig
5678	**atorar(se)**-*vb; vbr*	obstruct; get tongue-tied
5686	**refinar**-*vb*	refine
5687	**fregar**-*vb*	wash
5696	**licenciar(se)**-*vb; vbr*	award a degree, license; get a degree
5697	**nublar(se)**-*vb*	cloud
5700	**desembarcar(se)**-*vb; vbr*	unload; disembark
5702	**delatar**-*vb*	betray
5705	**secar(se)**-*vb*	dry
5707	**hinchar(se)**-*vb; vbr*	swell; stuff yourself
5714	**compadecer**-*vb*	pity
5716	**crucificar**-*vb*	crucify
5718	**deslizar(se)**-*vb*	slip, sneak
5720	**guisar**-*vb*	stew
5726	**cocer**-*vb*	boil
5740	**aparcar**-*vb*	park
5743	**sembrar**-*vb*	sow
5746	**saborear**-*vb*	savor

5749	**enfriar(se)**-*vb; vbr*	cool; get cold, catch a cold
5776	**cortejar**-*vb*	court
5778	**pilotar**-*vb*	pilot
5779	**sustentar(se)**-*vb*	sustain, support
5781	**combinar**-*vb*	combine
5782	**fugarse**-*vbr*	break out
5789	**astillar**-*vb*	splinter
5790	**predicar**-*vb*	preach
5791	**promover**-*vb*	promote
5792	**halagar**-*vb*	flatter
5793	**adecuar(se)**-*vb*	adjust
5795	**danzar**-*vb*	dance
5797	**felicitar**-*vb*	congratulate
5800	**engordar**-*vb*	gain weight
5801	**apelar**-*vb*	appeal
5802	**favorecer**-*vb*	favour
5807	**clasificar(se)**-*vb; vbr*	classify; win a place
5819	**aterrorizar(se)**-*vb*	terrorise
5826	**posponer**-*vb*	postpone
5828	**asar**-*vb*	roast
5831	**sobornar**-*vb*	bribe
5838	**resucitar**-*vb*	resurrect
5845	**deducir**-*vb*	deduce
5854	**despreciar**-*vb*	despise
5855	**entristecer(se)**-*vb*	sadden
5857	**percibir**-*vb*	perceive
5864	**proveer**-*vb*	supply
5868	**preñar**-*vb*	impregnate
5873	**seleccionar**-*vb*	select
5883	**osar**-*vb*	dare
5884	**renovar**-*vb*	renew
5895	**acoger(se)**-*vb; vbr*	accept, take in; find shelter
5897	**situar(se)**-*vb*	place
5907	**procesar**-*vb*	process
5912	**implorar**-*vb*	implore
5928	**contaminar**-*vb*	contaminate
5934	**certificar**-*vb*	certify
5942	**deletrear**-*vb*	spell out
5943	**otorgar**-*vb*	award
5957	**minar**-*vb*	mine
5966	**disminuir**-*vb*	decrease
5976	**premeditar**-*vb*	premeditate
5980	**azotar**-*vb*	whip
5982	**tentar**-*vb*	tempt

5983	**reforzar**-*vb*	strengthen
5985	**emprender**-*vb*	undertake
5986	**desolar**-*vb*	devastate
5987	**rumorearse**-*vbr*	be rumoured
5991	**desviar(se)**-*vb*	divert
5992	**conllevar**-*vb*	entail
5993	**oxidar(se)**-*vb*	rust
5994	**tropezar(se)**-*vb*	stumble
5999	**inundar**-*vb*	flood
6001	**demorar(se)**-*vb; vbr*	delay; arrive late
6017	**articular**-*adj; vb*	joint; articulate
6026	**precipitar(se)**-*vb*	hurry
6028	**proporcionar**-*vb*	provide
6032	**modificar**-*vb*	modify
6051	**sujetar**-*vb*	hold
6062	**recitar**-*vb*	recite
6067	**voltear(se)**-*vb*	turn around
6070	**influir**-*vb*	influence
6073	**estorbar**-*vb*	obstruct
6079	**infiltrar**-*vb*	infiltrate
6088	**irritar(se)**-*vb*	irritate
6092	**remover**-*vb*	stir, remove
6094	**aterrar**-*vb*	terrify
6105	**desilusionar(se)**-*vb*	let down
6107	**administrar**-*vb*	manage
6108	**revelar(se)**-*vb*	reveal
6110	**esforzarse**-*vbr*	make an effort
6112	**recobrar(se)**-*vb*	recover
6118	**retomar**-*vb*	resume
6128	**meditar**-*vb*	meditate
6133	**renacer**-*vb*	revive
6135	**consumir**-*vb*	consume
6137	**aparentar**-*vb*	feign
6156	**resentirse**-*vbr*	feel resentful
6161	**liar(se)**-*vb; vbr*	mishandle (ES), roll; get embroiled
6171	**tajar**-*vb*	cut
6178	**aportar**-*vb*	contribute
6186	**precisar**-*vb*	require, specify
6196	**irrumpir**-*vb*	burst in
6199	**someter**-*vb*	submit
6203	**silbar**-*vb*	whistle
6206	**absolver**-*vb*	absolve
6210	**radiografiar**-*vb*	X-ray
6217	**traficar**-*vb*	traffic
6220	**rehacer**-*vb*	redo
6223	**embrujar**-*vb*	bewitch
6224	**padecer**-*vb*	suffer
6232	**destacar**-*vb*	stand out
6234	**capacitar**-*vb*	train
6246	**atormentar**-*vb*	torment
6248	**constituir**-*vb*	constitute
6260	**concebir**-*vb*	conceive
6264	**chistar**-*vb*	talk back, make a sound
6271	**distraer(se)**-*vb*	distract
6272	**persuadir**-*vb*	persuade
6273	**amarrar**-*vb*	tie
6296	**domar**-*vb*	tame
6297	**derrumbar(se)**-*vb*	demolish, break down
6299	**consolar**-*vb*	comfort
6308	**simular**-*vb*	pretend
6316	**restar**-*vb*	deduct
6320	**interponer(se)**-*vb; vbr*	interject; intervene
6332	**equivaler**-*vb*	be equal to
6335	**regentar**-*vb*	manage
6343	**adaptar(se)**-*vb*	adapt
6345	**coronar**-*vb*	crown
6355	**derrocar**-*vb*	overthrow
6356	**valorar**-*vb*	value
6364	**ansiar**-*vb*	yearn
6371	**desconectar**-*vb*	disconnect
6387	**bautizar**-*vb*	baptize
6390	**beneficiar**-*vb*	benefit
6391	**enmascarar**-*vb*	mask
6401	**reñir**-*vb*	tell off, fight
6404	**detallar**-*vb*	detail
6410	**pulir**-*vb*	polish
6421	**arrepentirse**-*vbr*	regret
6422	**helar**-*vb*	freeze
6433	**anticipar(se)**-*vb*	anticipate
6434	**condecorar**-*vb*	decorate
6437	**depositar**-*vb*	deposit
6440	**pinchar**-*vb*	poke, inject
6442	**trabar(se)**-*vb; vbr*	lock, start up; get tangled up
6445	**implantar**-*vb*	implant
6446	**expandir**-*vb*	expand, spread
6451	**rugir**-*vb*	roar
6463	**oxigenar(se)**-*vb; vbr*	oxygenate; get fresh air

6466	**tejar**-*vb; m*	tile; tile factory
6471	**desactivar**-*vb*	deactivate
6475	**interceptar**-*vb*	intercept
6477	**intimidar**-*vb*	intimidate
6480	**acariciar**-*vb*	caress
6484	**devorar**-*vb*	devour
6497	**convivir**-*vb*	live together with
6506	**izar**-*vb*	hoist
6511	**supervisar**-*vb*	supervise
6519	**estrangular**-*vb*	strangle
6522	**recompensar**-*vb*	reward
6537	**capitular**-*vb; adj*	capitulate; town hall
6538	**trinar**-*vb*	chirp, be very angry
6546	**descartar**-*vb*	discard
6553	**enredar(se)**-*vb*	tangle, confuse, mess with (ES)
6561	**disimular**-*vb*	disguise
6564	**sumergir(se)**-*vb*	immerse
6568	**postrar(se)**-*vb*	prostrate
6573	**coleccionar**-*vb*	collect
6576	**turbar**-*vb*	disturb
6579	**fortalecer**-*vb*	strengthen
6582	**conjurar**-*vb*	conjure
6592	**facilitar**-*vb*	facilitate
6607	**angustiar(se)**-*vb*	upset
6614	**esquivar**-*vb*	dodge
6615	**sumar**-*vb*	add
6619	**privilegiar**-*vb*	grant a privilege to
6629	**alardear**-*vb*	boast
6637	**raptar**-*vb*	kidnap
6639	**distribuir**-*vb*	distribute
6648	**eludir**-*vb*	avoid
6650	**acosar**-*vb*	harass
6665	**toser**-*vb*	cough
6675	**aplaudir**-*vb*	applaud
6677	**acechar**-*vb*	stalk
6691	**manifestar(se)**-*vb; vbr*	express; demonstrate, show up
6695	**desvanecer(se)**-*vb*	fade
6703	**detonar**-*vb*	detonate
6706	**perforar**-*vb*	drill
6710	**chillar**-*vb*	yell
6712	**apresurar(se)**-*vb*	hurry
6717	**reconsiderar**-*vb*	reconsider
6721	**liderar**-*vb*	lead
6727	**avecinarse**-*vbr*	approach
6728	**abrumar**-*vb*	overwhelm
6729	**apoderar(se)**-*vb; vbr*	authorise; take over
6735	**dictar**-*vb*	dictate
6742	**regar**-*vb*	water, spill
6747	**evolucionar**-*vb*	evolve
6763	**cercar**-*vb*	fence
6771	**empeñar(se)**-*vb; vbr*	pawn; insist on
6782	**mutilar**-*vb*	mutilate
6788	**relucir**-*vb*	shine
6790	**acorralar**-*vb*	corral
6803	**elaborar**-*vb*	prepare
6806	**proyectar**-*vb*	project
6808	**contraer(se)**-*vb*	contract
6817	**consentir**-*vb*	allow
6832	**recolectar**-*vb*	gather
6837	**renegar**-*vb*	disown
6843	**tejer**-*vb*	weave
6845	**evadir**-*vb*	avoid
6846	**ahumar**-*vb*	smoke up
6852	**forrar(se)**-*vb; vbr*	cover; get rich
6854	**antojarse**-*vbr*	fancy, feel like
6855	**arrasar**-*vb*	devastate
6858	**desagradar**-*vb*	displease
6866	**desistir**-*vb*	desist
6871	**perjudicar**-*vb*	damage
6888	**aflojar**-*vb*	loosen
6890	**diferenciar**-*vb*	differentiate
6902	**conjeturar**-*vb*	conjecture
6904	**remediar**-*vb*	remedy
6908	**estrechar(se)**-*vb; vbr*	narrow, hug; get smaller
6918	**ubicar(se)**-*vb*	locate, find
6920	**comerciar**-*vb*	trade
6925	**reposar**-*vb*	rest
6928	**incrementar**-*vb*	increase
6929	**impulsar**-*vb*	boost, inspire
6936	**gotear**-*vb*	drip
6945	**encarar**-*vb*	confront
6946	**arrebatar**-*vb*	snatch
6954	**memorizar**-*vb*	memorize
6956	**cundir**-*vb*	spread, go well
6964	**decapitar**-*vb*	behead
6965	**cosechar**-*vb*	harvest

6968	**enderezar(se)**-*vb*	straighten
6969	**recargar**-*vb*	recharge
6973	**averiar**-*vb*	break down
6984	**repugnar**-*vb*	disgust
6990	**absorber**-*vb*	absorb
6991	**descomponer(se)**-*vb; vbr*	break down; slump
6999	**rehusar**-*vb*	refuse
7011	**desobedecer**-*vb*	disobey
7016	**enfocar**-*vb*	focus
7019	**mimar**-*vb*	pamper
7025	**defraudar**-*vb*	disappoint
7026	**asir(se)**-*vb*	grab
7029	**parodiar**-*vb*	parody
7033	**conformar(se)**-*vb; vbr*	shape; resign yourself
7037	**falsificar**-*vb*	falsify
7039	**igualar**-*vb*	equalize
7043	**discapacitar**-*vb*	incapacitate
7050	**digerir**-*vb*	digest
7054	**asomar(se)**-*vb*	show
7055	**corromper**-*vb*	corrupt
7062	**espabilar(se)**-*vb*	snap out of it
7078	**objetar**-*vb*	object
7079	**simbolizar**-*vb*	symbolize
7090	**hospedar**-*vb*	host
7104	**inhalar**-*vb*	inhale
7110	**ordeñar**-*vb*	milk
7116	**esfumar(se)**-*vb*	fade
7117	**exterminar**-*vb*	exterminate
7123	**acomodar**-*vb*	accommodate
7128	**restablecer**-*vb*	reestablish
7134	**desmontar**-*vb*	disassemble
7137	**suprimir**-*vb*	suppress
7139	**codificar**-*vb*	encode
7140	**estafar**-*vb*	swindle
7146	**centrar**-*vb*	centre
7171	**detentar**-*vb*	hold
7174	**vibrar**-*vb*	vibrate
7175	**vendar**-*vb*	bandage
7183	**velar**-*vb*	look after
7187	**avivar**-*vb*	fuel
7195	**saquear**-*vb*	sack
7196	**estimular**-*vb*	stimulate
7205	**motivar**-*vb*	motivate
7206	**magnificar**-*vb*	magnify
7208	**agonizar**-*vb*	agonize

7214	**pacificar**-*vb*	pacify
7215	**desertar**-*vb*	desert
7222	**virar**-*vb*	turn
7226	**preceder**-*vb*	go before
7228	**prolongar**-*vb*	extend
7235	**impactar**-*vb*	impact
7243	**desterrar**-*vb*	exile
7246	**ultrajar**-*vb*	outrage
7251	**confiscar**-*vb*	confiscate
7254	**hartar(se)**-*vb; vbr*	get on the nerves of; get sick of
7255	**fusilar**-*vb*	shoot
7256	**botar**-*vb*	bounce, throw out (LA) (coll)
7266	**espantar**-*vb*	frighten, shoo away
7273	**maltratar**-*vb*	abuse
7284	**efectuar**-*vb*	carry out
7292	**presidir**-*vb*	preside over
7293	**reproducir**-*vb*	reproduce, copy
7295	**trazar**-*vb*	trace
7298	**prosperar**-*vb*	thrive
7301	**oprimir**-*vb*	oppress
7311	**emerger**-*vb*	emerge
7312	**esparcir**-*vb*	spread
7315	**balar**-*vb*	bleat
7319	**especular**-*vb*	speculate
7329	**arrugar**-*vb*	wrinkle
7343	**proclamar**-*vb*	proclaim
7350	**plantear**-*vb*	pose
7358	**sobrepasar**-*vb*	exceed
7359	**demoler**-*vb*	demolish
7372	**ahuyentar**-*vb*	drive away
7387	**estresar(se)**-*vb*	stress
7392	**reprimir**-*vb*	suppress
7394	**susurrar**-*vb*	whisper
7397	**coordinar**-*vb*	coordinate
7400	**retornar**-*vb*	return
7403	**devastar**-*vb*	devastate
7404	**habitar**-*vb*	dwell
7407	**acumular**-*vb*	accumulate
7409	**teñir**-*vb*	dye
7412	**cualificar**-*vb*	qualify
7431	**desgraciar**-*vb*	ruin
7438	**extraviar(se)**-*vb*	misplace
7441	**sabotear**-*vb*	sabotage
7446	**recortar**-*vb*	trim

7452	**rozar**-*vb*	brush against
7456	**recrear**-*vb*	recreate
7460	**hurtar**-*vb*	steal
7465	**embrollar(se)**-*vb*	confuse
7472	**enfurecer(se)**-*vb*	drive mad, enrage
7476	**cegar**-*vb*	blind
7481	**revertir**-*vb*	revert
7493	**dimitir**-*vb*	resign
7501	**urgir**-*vb*	press
7502	**chantajear**-*vb*	blackmail
7508	**zurrar**-*vb*	spank
7510	**alegar**-*vb*	claim
7511	**estrenar**-*vb*	use for the first time
7519	**relevar**-*vb*	relieve, substitute

Alphabetical Order

Rank	Spanish-*PoS*	Translation(s)

A

Rank	Spanish-*PoS*	Translation(s)
5240	**abad**-*m*	abbot
5507	**abanico**-*m*	fan, variety
7060	**abastecimiento**-*m*	supply
5527	**abatir(se)**-*vb; vbr*	take down; fold up, become depressed
5899	**abdomen**-*m*	abdomen
6214	**abdominal**-*adj; f*	abdominal; crunch
5974	**abertura**-*f*	opening
6981	**abogacía**-*f*	legal profession
5666	**abominable**-*adj*	abominable
5961	**abono**-*m*	fertilizer
5418	**abrazo**-*m*	hug
6728	**abrumar**-*vb*	overwhelm
6317	**absolución**-*f*	absolution
6206	**absolver**-*vb*	absolve
6990	**absorber**-*vb*	absorb
5709	**abstinencia**-*f*	withdrawal
6781	**abstracto**-*adj*	abstract
5389	**abundante**-*adj*	abundant
5041	**académico**-*adj; m*	academic; academic
7458	**acantilado**-*adj; m*	steep; cliff
6480	**acariciar**-*vb*	caress
6591	**accesible**-*adj*	accessible
5321	**accesorio**-*m; adj*	accessory; secondary
6677	**acechar**-*vb*	stalk
6194	**acecho**-*m*	stalking
5905	**aceituna**-*f*	olive
7036	**aceleración**-*f*	acceleration
5659	**aceptación**-*f*	acceptance
5181	**acertijo**-*m*	riddle
6874	**acierto**-*m*	right answer, wise decision
5895	**acoger(se)**-*vb; vbr*	accept, take in; find shelter
7123	**acomodar**-*vb*	accommodate
6831	**acorazado**-*m*	armoured
6379	**acordeón**-*m*	accordion
6790	**acorralar**-*vb*	corral
6650	**acosar**-*vb*	harass
6853	**acreedor**-*adj; m*	deserving of; creditor
7156	**acrobacia**-*f*	stunt
6693	**activista**-*m/f*	activist
6868	**actualización**-*f*	update
6450	**acuático**-*adj*	aquatic
7407	**acumular**-*vb*	accumulate
5268	**adaptación**-*f*	adaptation
6343	**adaptar(se)**-*vb*	adapt
5793	**adecuar(se)**-*vb*	adjust
6107	**administrar**-*vb*	manage
6822	**administrativo**-*adj*	administrative
5276	**admisión**-*f*	admission
5926	**adolescencia**-*f*	adolescence
6599	**adoptivo**-*adj*	adoptive
6336	**adoración**-*f*	adoration
5528	**adorno**-*m*	ornament
6324	**adquisición**-*f*	acquisition
6125	**adrede**-*adv*	intentionally
5188	**adulterio**-*m*	adultery
6985	**adversidad**-*f*	adversity
5933	**aéreo**-*adj*	aerial
6435	**aeródromo**-*m*	aerodrome
5586	**aerolínea**-*f*	airline
6983	**aeronave**-*f*	aircraft
6716	**aerosol**-*m*	spray
6535	**afición**-*f*	hobby, fans
5657	**afilar(se)**-*vb; vbr*	sharpen; become thin
5424	**afirmación**-*f*	affirmation
5419	**afligir(se)**-*vb*	grieve, suffer from
6888	**aflojar**-*vb*	loosen
6244	**ágil**-*adj*	agile
5630	**agitación**-*f*	agitation
7208	**agonizar**-*vb*	agonize
6432	**agotamiento**-*m*	exhaustion
6383	**agresividad**-*f*	aggressiveness
6635	**agresor**-*adj; m*	attacking; attacker
6255	**agrícola**-*adj*	agricultural
5411	**agricultor**-*m*	farmer
5229	**aguardiente**-*m*	moonshine
7035	**aguijón**-*m*	sting

5114	ahogo-*m*	distress, difficulty breathing	6889	amparo-*m*	protection
6846	ahumar-*vb*	smoke up	5368	ampliar-*vb*	enlarge
7372	ahuyentar-*vb*	drive away	6253	ampolla-*f*	vial, blister
5274	aislado-*adj*	isolated	5305	anal-*adj*	anal
5773	ajeno-*adj*	somebody else's	5015	analista-*m/f*	analyst
6850	alabanza-*f*	praise	6243	anarquista-*m/f; adj*	anarchist; anarchist
6295	álamo-*m*	poplar	5502	anatomía-*f*	anatomy
6629	alardear-*vb*	boast	7240	ancestral-*adj*	ancestral
6588	alarmante-*adj*	alarming	6833	anchoa-*f*	anchovy
6671	albañil-*m/f*	builder	6602	andante-*adj*	walking
5131	albóndiga-*f*	meatball	5246	andén-*m*	platform
7351	alcaldía-*f*	mayor's office	6282	anécdota-*f*	anecdote
6377	alcoba-*f*	bedroom	6607	angustiar(se)-*vb*	upset
6982	alcoholismo-*m*	alcoholism	5342	animación-*f*	animation
7510	alegar-*vb*	claim	7380	aniquilación-*f*	annihilation
6785	alegato-*m*	plea	5836	anomalía-*f*	anomaly
6769	alentador-*adj*	encouraging	5363	anotación-*f*	annotation
5238	alergia-*f*	allergy	5839	ansia-*f*	craving
5758	alerta-*f; adj; adv*	alarm; alert; on the alert	6364	ansiar-*vb*	yearn
			5048	antaño-*adv*	formerly
6040	aleta-*f*	fin	5646	anteayer-*adv*	day before yesterday
5506	alfabeto-*m*	alphabet			
5413	alfiler-*m*	pin	5816	antibiótico-*adj; m*	antibiotic; antibiotic
7283	aliar-*adj*	unite			
6429	alimenticio-*adj*	food	6464	anticipación-*f*	in advance
5881	alineación-*f*	line-up	6433	anticipar(se)-*vb*	anticipate
7398	alineado-*adj*	aligned	5328	anticipo-*m*	advance
5676	allanamiento-*m*	flattening, forced entry	6943	antipático-*adj*	unpleasant
			5848	anti-*pfx*	anti
5893	allende-*adv*	on the other side	6813	antisemitismo-*m*	anti-Semitism
6014	almeja-*f*	clam, pussy (coll)	6854	antojarse-*vbr*	fancy, feel like
7164	almendra-*f*	almond	6049	antojo-*m*	whim
5972	Alpes-*mpl*	Alps	5998	anulación-*f*	annulment
6656	alquitrán-*m*	tar	6119	apacible-*adj*	gentle
5551	altavoz-*m*	speaker	5479	apagón-*m*	blackout
7234	alteración-*f*	alteration	5740	aparcar-*vb*	park
6323	alubia-*f*	bean	6031	apareamiento-*m*	mating
5277	ama de casa-*f*	housewife	6137	aparentar-*vb*	feign
5306	amargura-*f*	bitterness	6042	apasionante-*adj*	thrilling
6273	amarrar-*vb*	tie	5801	apelar-*vb*	appeal
5289	amateur-*adj*	amateur	6426	apéndice-*m*	appendix
5372	amazona-*f*	amazon	7376	apendicitis-*f*	appendicitis
7108	ámbar-*m*	amber	7094	apio-*m*	celery
6461	ambiental-*adj*	environmental	6675	aplaudir-*vb*	applaud
6939	ámbito-*m*	field	6713	aplazamiento-*m*	postponement
5647	amnistía-*f*	amnesty	5300	aplicación-*f*	application

6729	**apoderar(se)**-*vb; vbr*	authorise; take over
6178	**aportar**-*vb*	contribute
6926	**apóstol**-*m*	apostle
6712	**apresurar(se)**-*vb*	hurry
6227	**apretado**-*adj*	cramped
5127	**apretón**-*m*	squeeze
6010	**aproximación**-*f*	approximation
6879	**aptitud**-*f*	ability
5184	**apto**-*adj*	suitable
5153	**apuñalar**-*vb*	stab
5449	**apunte**-*m*	note
6494	**arado**-*m*	plow
6344	**arándano**-*m*	blueberry
6772	**arce**-*m*	maple
6150	**ardor**-*m*	burning sensation
7366	**arduo**-*adj*	arduous
5889	**arete**-*m*	earring
7285	**aristocracia**-*f*	aristocracy
5753	**aristócrata**-*m/f*	aristocrat
6603	**aritmético**-*adj; m*	arithmetic; arithmetician
7122	**armisticio**-*m*	armistice
5844	**armónico**-*adj*	harmonious
5639	**arpa**-*f*	harp
6548	**arqueología**-*f*	archeology
6444	**arqueólogo**-*m*	archaeologist
6181	**arquero**-*m*	archer
6855	**arrasar**-*vb*	devastate
6036	**arrastre**-*m*	dragging
6946	**arrebatar**-*vb*	snatch
5103	**arrepentimiento**-*m*	remorse
6421	**arrepentirse**-*vbr*	regret
5051	**arruga**-*f*	wrinkle
7329	**arrugar**-*vb*	wrinkle
6882	**arsénico**-*m*	arsenic
5463	**arteria**-*f*	artery
6476	**arterial**-*adj*	arterial
6017	**articular**-*adj; vb*	joint; articulate
5940	**artillero**-*adj; m*	artillery; artilleryman
6211	**artritis**-*f*	arthritis
5828	**asar**-*vb*	roast
7336	**asedio**-*m*	siege
6250	**asegurador**-*adj; m*	insurance; insurer
6180	**aseo**-*m*	bathroom
6411	**asfalto**-*m*	asphalt
6127	**asfixia**-*f*	suffocation
5226	**asiático**-*adj; m*	Asian; Asian person
5217	**asignación**-*f*	assignment
7026	**asir(se)**-*vb*	grab
7054	**asomar(se)**-*vb*	show
5042	**asombrar(se)**-*vb*	amaze
5909	**asombro**-*m*	astonishment
6692	**áspero**-*adj*	rough
6493	**aspiración**-*f*	breathing, aspiration
5216	**aspirador**-*m*	vacuum
6111	**aspirante**-*m/f*	candidate
5448	**aspirar**-*vb*	inhale
6147	**asta**-*f*	horn
6518	**asteroide**-*m*	asteroid
5789	**astillar**-*vb*	splinter
6587	**astillero**-*m*	shipyard
6580	**astro**-*m*	star
6872	**astronomía**-*f*	astronomy
5320	**astucia**-*f*	cunning
7052	**atacante**-*adj; m/f*	combative; attacker
7260	**atasco**-*m*	jam, obstacle
6052	**ateo**-*adj; m*	atheistic; atheist
6094	**aterrar**-*vb*	terrify
5334	**aterrorizado**-*adj*	terrified
5819	**aterrorizar(se)**-*vb*	terrorise
6702	**atlas**-*m*	atlas
7157	**atlético**-*adj*	athletic
7507	**atletismo**-*m*	athletics
6078	**átomo**-*m*	atom
5678	**atorar(se)**-*vb; vbr*	obstruct; get tongue-tied
6246	**atormentar**-*vb*	torment
6365	**atraso**-*m*	backwardness
6023	**atrocidad**-*f*	atrocity
6793	**atropello**-*m*	hit-and-run
6164	**aturdido**-*adj*	confused
6120	**audacia**-*f*	audacity
6319	**audiencia**-*f*	hearing
5148	**audio**-*sm*	audio
5837	**auditorio**-*adj; m*	hearing; auditorium
5891	**aura**-*f*	aura

6515	**auricular**-*adj; m*	auricular; headset
5867	**australiano**-*adj; m*	Australian; Australian person
7322	**autenticidad**-*f*	authenticity
6739	**automovilístico**-*adj*	car
7524	**autonomía**-*f*	autonomy
5825	**avalancha**-*f*	avalanche
5445	**avatar**-*m*	avatar
6727	**avecinarse**-*vbr*	approach
5843	**aventurero**-*adj; m*	adventurous; adventurer
6225	**averiado**-*adj*	broken down
5539	**avería**-*f*	breakdown
6973	**averiar**-*vb*	break down
6900	**aversión**-*f*	aversion
7207	**avestruz**-*m*	ostrich
5730	**aviador**-*m*	pilot
6659	**avispa**-*f*	wasp
7187	**avivar**-*vb*	fuel
5099	**azafata**-*f*	flight attendant
5980	**azotar**-*vb*	whip
5767	**azote**-*m*	scourge, spank
7097	**azteca**-*adj; m*	Aztec; Aztec person
5520	**azufre**-*m*	sulfur

B

6613	**baboso**-*adj*	slimy
5313	**bacalao**-*m*	cod
7378	**bache**-*m*	bump
5901	**bacteria**-*f*	bacterium
5634	**balanza**-*f*	scales
7315	**balar**-*vb*	bleat
6293	**balístico**-*adj*	ballistic
6749	**balneario**-*m*	spa
5648	**bambú**-*m*	bamboo
7181	**bañador**-*m*	swimsuit
6767	**banal**-*adj*	banal
5533	**bañar(se)**-*vb*	bathe
6140	**banjo**-*m*	banjo
5537	**barajar**-*vb*	shuffle
5547	**barbaridad**-*f*	atrocity
6188	**barcaza**-*f*	barge
6098	**barraca**-*f*	hut

5347	**barranco**-*m*	cliff
5357	**barrer**-*vb*	sweep
5221	**barricada**-*f*	barricade
6704	**barrido**-*m*	sweep
6004	**barrote**-*m*	bar
7371	**barullo**-*m*	noise
5945	**bateador**-*m*	batter
5886	**bautismo**-*m*	baptism
6387	**bautizar**-*vb*	baptize
5610	**bautizo**-*m*	baptism
6146	**bayoneta**-*f*	bayonet
6951	**bazar**-*m*	bazaar
7081	**bebedor**-*adj; m*	heavy drinker (coll); drinker
7177	**becerro**-*m*	calf
7044	**beige**-*adj*	beige
5280	**belga**-*adj; m*	Belgian; Belgian person
6478	**benefactor**-*adj; m*	benevolent; benefactor
5362	**beneficencia**-*f*	charity
6390	**beneficiar**-*vb*	benefit
6267	**benéfico**-*adj*	charity
7503	**bestial**-*adj*	brutal
7276	**bíblico**-*adj*	biblical
7161	**bicarbonato**-*m*	bicarbonate
6758	**billón**-*num*	trillion
5202	**biografía**-*f*	biography
5393	**biológico**-*adj*	biological
5597	**bisabuelo**-*m*	great-grandfather
7024	**bisexual**-*adj; m/f*	bisexual; bisexual
6395	**bisturí**-*m*	scalpel
5481	**blasfemia**-*f*	blasphemy
7330	**blasfemo**-*adj*	blasphemous
5298	**blindar**-*vb*	armor
6844	**boa**-*f*	boa
6949	**bohemio**-*adj*	bohemian
7468	**boliche**-*m*	bowling, nightclub (LA)
5092	**bollo**-*m*	bread roll, sweet bun
5293	**bombardear**-*vb*	bomb
5970	**bombilla**-*f*	bulb
5285	**bombón**-*m*	chocolate, beauty (coll)
5493	**bondadoso**-*adj*	kind
7453	**bonificación**-*f*	bonus

6642	**bordado**-*m*	embroidery
5330	**borrachera**-*f*	drunkenness
5157	**borrador**-*m*	draft, rubber
6045	**borroso**-*adj*	blurred
5562	**bosnio**-*adj; m*	Bosnian; Bosnian person
7256	**botar**-*vb*	bounce, throw out (LA) (coll)
5606	**botiquín**-*m*	first-aid kit
7160	**boutique**-*f*	boutique
5516	**boxear**-*vb*	box
5692	**brasileño**-*adj; m*	Brazilian; Brazilian person
6008	**brote**-*m*	outbreak
7241	**bruma**-*f*	mist
5703	**brusco**-*adj*	abrupt
5568	**buceo**-*m*	diving
5331	**bufete**-*m*	firm of lawyers
5110	**bulto**-*m*	lump
5656	**burgués**-*adj; m*	middle-class; rich person
6030	**burguesía**-*f*	the middle-class
6046	**burocracia**-*f*	bureaucracy
7520	**burócrata**-*m/f*	bureaucrat
5631	**buscador**-*m*	searcher
5894	**busto**-*m*	bust
6857	**buzo**-*m*	scuba diver

C

6238	**cabecera**-*f*	headboard
5514	**cabellera**-*f*	hair
6974	**cabezón**-*adj*	stubborn
5223	**cabrear**-*vb*	piss off
5769	**cacahuete**-*m*	peanut
6219	**cacao**-*m*	cocoa
5354	**cacharro**-*adj; m*	junky; wreck
5039	**cactus**-*m*	cactus
6256	**cafeína**-*f*	caffeine
5645	**cafetero**-*adj*	fond of coffee
5531	**caimán**-*m*	caiman
5902	**cajero**-*m*	cashier, cash point
5460	**calamar**-*adj; m*	dummy; squid
6306	**calambre**-*m*	cramp
6091	**calamidad**-*f*	calamity
5241	**calavera**-*f*	skull

6688	**calcio**-*m*	calcium
7065	**calculadora**-*f*	calculator
6242	**calentador**-*m*	water heater
6495	**calidez**-*f*	warmth
5417	**calificar**-*vb*	mark
6303	**cáliz**-*m*	goblet
7030	**callejón**-*m*	alley
5780	**calmo**-*adj*	calm
5167	**caloría**-*f*	calorie
6663	**calumnia**-*f*	slander
5505	**calzado**-*adj; m*	wearing shoes; footwear
6304	**camarógrafo**-*m*	cameraman
5060	**camionero**-*m*	truck driver
7270	**campanario**-*m*	bell tower
5815	**camuflaje**-*m*	camouflage
5546	**canario**-*adj; m*	from the Canary Islands, canary yellow; Canary Islander, canary
5044	**candado**-*m*	padlock
6584	**candidatura**-*f*	candidacy
5759	**canela**-*f*	cinnamon
5887	**cañería**-*f*	pipe
6600	**canica**-*f*	marble
7515	**canino**-*adj; m*	canine; canine tooth
5796	**caño**-*m*	pipe
5911	**cantera**-*f*	quarry
5927	**cantor**-*adj; m*	singing; singer
6234	**capacitar**-*vb*	train
6190	**caparazón**-*m*	shell
5522	**capellán**-*m*	chaplain
6453	**capitolio**-*m*	Capitol
6537	**capitular**-*vb; adj*	capitulate; town hall
7250	**capota**-*f*	hood
7281	**caprichoso**-*adj*	whimsical
6021	**capricornio**-*adj*	Capricorn
5046	**captar**-*vb*	capture
5541	**característico**-*adj*	characteristic
6876	**carburador**-*m*	carburetor
6819	**carcajada**-*f*	loud laugh
5518	**carguero**-*adj; m*	freight; freighter
7092	**caricatura**-*f*	caricature
5916	**caricia**-*f*	caress
6847	**carisma**-*m*	charisma

5367	**carnal**-*adj*	carnal		5968	**chacal**-*m*	jackal
5159	**carnero**-*m*	ram		6340	**chalet**-*m*	cottage
5619	**carpeta**-*f*	folder		5775	**chal**-*m*	shawl
6329	**carrete**-*m*	reel		7502	**chantajear**-*vb*	blackmail
5563	**carril**-*m*	lane		5856	**chapa**-*f*	sheet
7219	**carroña**-*f*	carrion		6593	**checo**-*adj; m*	Czech; Czech person
6516	**carrusel**-*m*	carousel		6089	**chelín**-*m*	shilling
5509	**cascabel**-*m*	bell		5616	**chic**-*adj*	chic
5858	**cáscara**-*f*	shell		6710	**chillar**-*vb*	yell
6228	**caseta**-*f*	hut		7296	**chimpancé**-*m*	chimpanzee
5684	**casilla**-*f*	box		6264	**chistar**-*vb*	talk back, make a sound
6802	**castaña**-*f*	chestnut		7198	**chocante**-*adj*	shocking
6678	**castellano**-*adj; m*	Spanish; Castilian Spanish		7061	**chorizo**-*m*	chorizo
5910	**castidad**-*f*	chastity		6527	**chorro**-*m*	stream
6978	**castor**-*m*	beaver		5440	**chuleta**-*f; adj*	chop; sassy (coll)
5120	**casual**-*adj*	chance		5360	**chusma**-*f*	rabble
7179	**catarro**-*m*	cold		6082	**cianuro**-*m*	cyanide
7514	**catastrófico**-*adj*	catastrophic		6550	**ciénaga**-*f*	swamp
6611	**caucho**-*m*	rubber		7427	**cigüeña**-*f*	stork
6638	**cautela**-*f*	caution		7099	**cilindro**-*m*	cylinder
7413	**cauteloso**-*adj*	cautious		6141	**cineasta**-*m/f*	filmmaker
6608	**cautiverio**-*m*	captivity		6354	**cinematográfico**-*adj*	cinematographic
5080	**cava**-*m*	cava		7242	**cinismo**-*m*	cynicism
5741	**caverna**-*f*	cavern		7267	**cinto**-*m*	belt
6834	**cavidad**-*f*	cavity		6096	**ciruela**-*f*	plum
6839	**cazo**-*m*	pot		6226	**cisterna**-*f*	tanker
6155	**cebra**-*f*	zebra		5464	**citación**-*f*	citation
7476	**cegar**-*vb*	blind		6768	**ciudadanía**-*f*	citizenship
5870	**ceguera**-*f*	blindness		6185	**clandestino**-*adj*	clandestine
6208	**ceño**-*m*	frown		6353	**clarinete**-*m; m/f*	clarinet; clarinettist
5140	**censurar**-*vb*	censor		5733	**clasificación**-*f*	classification
5496	**centenar**-*num*	hundred		5807	**clasificar(se)**-*vb; vbr*	classify; win a place
7121	**centeno**-*m*	rye		6019	**cláusula**-*f*	clause
5564	**centinela**-*m/f*	sentinel		7034	**clavel**-*m*	carnation
7146	**centrar**-*vb*	centre		7344	**clemente**-*adj*	merciful
6152	**cerámica**-*f*	ceramic		5256	**clérigo**-*m*	cleric
6763	**cercar**-*vb*	fence		7263	**clero**-*m*	clergy
7018	**cerrajero**-*m*	locksmith		5956	**cliché**-*m*	cliche
5245	**cerrojo**-*m*	bolt		5834	**clic**-*m*	click
5833	**cerro**-*m*	hill		5432	**clientela**-*f*	clientele
5934	**certificar**-*vb*	certify		7188	**climático**-*adj*	weather
7488	**cervecería**-*f*	brewery		6523	**clímax**-*m*	climax
5642	**cese**-*m*	cessation				
5748	**cesto**-*m*	basket				
5964	**cetro**-*m*	scepter				

7106	**clínico**-*adj; m*	clinical; doctor
6191	**clítoris**-*m*	clitoris
5145	**cloaca**-*f*	sewer
6489	**clon**-*m*	clone
7172	**cloro**-*m*	chlorine
5822	**coalición**-*f*	coalition
5161	**cobardía**-*f*	cowardice
7227	**cobija**-*f*	blanket (LA)
5726	**cocer**-*vb*	boil
6509	**cochera**-*f*	garage (LA), depot
5971	**cochino**-*adj; m*	dirty; pig
6201	**codicioso**-*adj*	greedy
7139	**codificar**-*vb*	encode
6979	**coeficiente**-*m*	coefficient
6670	**coherente**-*adj*	coherent
7308	**coito**-*m*	intercourse
6430	**cojín**-*m*	cushion
6569	**colaborador**-*adj; m*	cooperative; contributor, co-worker
6573	**coleccionar**-*vb*	collect
5232	**coleccionista**-*m/f*	collector
6483	**colecta**-*f*	collection
5504	**colectivo**-*adj; m*	collective; group
6606	**colesterol**-*m*	cholesterol
6723	**colgante**-*adj; m*	hanging; pendant
6382	**coliseo**-*m*	coliseum
5771	**colisión**-*f*	collision
5760	**colmena**-*f*	hive
5457	**colmillo**-*m*	fang
7088	**colombiano**-*adj; m*	Colombian; Colombian person
6334	**colonial**-*adj*	colonial
6881	**colon**-*m*	colon
5096	**colono**-*m*	settler, tenant farmer
6245	**colosal**-*adj*	colossal
6268	**columpio**-*m*	swing
6441	**comanche**-*adj; m/f*	Comanche; Comanche Indian
7375	**comandancia**-*f*	headquarters
6524	**comarca**-*f*	region
5175	**combatiente**-*m*	fighter
5781	**combinar**-*vb*	combine
6976	**combustión**-*f*	combustion

5269	**comentar**-*vb*	discuss, mention
6920	**comerciar**-*vb*	trade
5076	**comino**-*m*	cumin
5714	**compadecer**-*vb*	pity
5250	**compartimiento**-*m*	compartment
6797	**compatible**-*adj*	compatible
5474	**competente**-*adj*	competent
5704	**competidor**-*adj; m*	competitor; competitor
7247	**competitivo**-*adj*	competitive
6687	**complejidad**-*f*	complexity
5227	**complicar(se)**-*vb*	complicate
6025	**complicidad**-*f*	involvement
5728	**componente**-*adj; m*	built in; component
6662	**compostura**-*f*	composure
6947	**comprobación**-*f*	verification
7145	**compuerta**-*f*	gate
7411	**compulsivo**-*adj*	compulsive
6195	**computación**-*f*	computer studies (LA)
6158	**computador**-*adj; m*	computer; computer (LA)
5444	**comunitario**-*adj*	communal
7334	**con antelación**-*adv*	beforehand
6260	**concebir**-*vb*	conceive
6207	**concejo**-*m*	council
6955	**concentrado**-*m*	concentrated
5863	**concepción**-*f*	conception
5747	**concesión**-*f*	concession
5260	**concluir**-*vb*	conclude
5283	**concordar**-*vb*	agree
6488	**concursante**-*adj; m/f*	competing; contestant
6434	**condecorar**-*vb*	decorate
6883	**condominio**-*m*	condominium
7279	**cóndor**-*m*	condor
6503	**conducción**-*f*	driving
5286	**conducto**-*m*	channel
6596	**confederación**-*f*	confederation
6779	**confidencialidad**-*f*	confidentiality
6431	**confidente**-*m*	confidant
6934	**confinamiento**-*m*	confinement
6601	**confín**-*m*	border
7251	**confiscar**-*vb*	confiscate

7033	**conformar(se)**-*vb; vbr*	shape; resign yourself
7084	**confort**-*m*	comfort
6183	**confrontación**-*f*	confrontation
5453	**congregación**-*f*	congregation
6902	**conjeturar**-*vb*	conjecture
6582	**conjurar**-*vb*	conjure
5992	**conllevar**-*vb*	entail
5370	**conmover**-*vb*	move
5694	**cono**-*m*	cone
5774	**conquistador**-*m; adj*	conqueror, Casanova; seductive
6817	**consentir**-*vb*	allow
7009	**conservación**-*f*	conservation
5410	**conserva**-*f*	canned food
6066	**conservatorio**-*m*	conservatory
5922	**considerado**-*adj*	considerate
5228	**consiguiente**-*adj*	consequent
6683	**consistente**-*adj*	consistent
6887	**consola**-*f*	console
6299	**consolar**-*vb*	comfort
6932	**conspirador**-*m*	conspirer
5984	**constancia**-*f*	persistence
7426	**constelación**-*f*	constellation
6962	**constitucional**-*adj*	constitutional
6248	**constituir**-*vb*	constitute
6117	**constructor**-*adj; m*	building; builder
6867	**consultor**-*adj; m*	advisory; consultant
6233	**consumidor**-*m*	consumer
6135	**consumir**-*vb*	consume
5928	**contaminar**-*vb*	contaminate
5251	**contemplar**-*vb*	contemplate, take into account
5941	**contención**-*f*	containment
5485	**conteo**-*m*	count
5118	**continental**-*adj*	continental
6376	**continuidad**-*f*	continuity
6660	**contraataque**-*m*	counterattack
6122	**contrabandista**-*adj; m*	contraband; smuggler
6636	**contracción**-*f*	contraction
5477	**contradicción**-*f*	contradiction
6808	**contraer(se)**-*vb*	contract
6571	**contramaestre**-*m*	boatswain
6060	**contraste**-*m*	contrast
6283	**contratiempo**-*m*	setback
5882	**contratista**-*m/f*	contractor
5261	**contribuir**-*vb*	contribute
5929	**contribuyente**-*m/f*	taxpayer
6544	**controlador**-*adj; m*	controlling; controller
6541	**controversia**-*f*	controversy
7126	**contundente**-*adj*	convincing
6241	**conveniencia**-*f*	advantage
7185	**convenio**-*m*	agreement
6621	**conversión**-*f*	conversion
6751	**convertible**-*adj; m*	convertible; convertible (LA)
6497	**convivir**-*vb*	live together with
5578	**convocar**-*vb*	summon
7012	**convulsión**-*f*	convulsion
7430	**conyugal**-*adj*	conjugal
6468	**cooperativo**-*adj*	cooperative
5615	**coordinación**-*f*	coordination
7397	**coordinar**-*vb*	coordinate
5434	**copiloto**-*m/f*	copilot
7112	**copo**-*m*	flake
7286	**corcel**-*m*	steed
6301	**cordial**-*m*	cordial
6829	**coreografía**-*f*	choreography
5715	**corneta**-*f; m/f*	cornet; cornet player
7478	**cornisa**-*f*	cornice
5466	**coronación**-*f*	coronation
6345	**coronar**-*vb*	crown
6123	**corporativo**-*adj*	corporate
5469	**corresponsal**-*m/f*	correspondent
6081	**corrida**-*f*	bullfight
7055	**corromper**-*vb*	corrupt
6910	**corsé**-*m*	corset
5776	**cortejar**-*vb*	court
7316	**cortocircuito**-*m*	short-circuit
6965	**cosechar**-*vb*	harvest
5967	**cosmético**-*adj; m*	cosmetic; cosmetic
6814	**cósmico**-*adj*	cosmic
5713	**cosmos**-*m*	cosmos
5585	**coste**-*m*	cost
5327	**costoso**-*adj*	expensive

5130	**costura**-*f*	seam, needlework
6424	**cotidiano**-*adj*	daily, routine
5009	**coyote**-*m*	coyote
5736	**cráter**-*m*	crater
5577	**creatividad**-*f*	creativity
5436	**credencial**-*f; adj*	identity document; accrediting
6074	**credo**-*m*	creed
5766	**crepúsculo**-*m*	twilight
5812	**cresta**-*f*	crest
6796	**crianza**-*f*	raising
5913	**cripta**-*f*	crypt
5135	**cristianismo**-*m*	Christianity
5415	**crónico**-*adj*	chronic
5716	**crucificar**-*vb*	crucify
6474	**crucifijo**-*m*	crucifix
5806	**cuadrante**-*m*	quadrant
5476	**cuadrilátero**-*m; adj*	ring; four-sided
7412	**cualificar**-*vb*	qualify
6360	**cuántico**-*adj*	quantum
6322	**cuarteto**-*m*	quartet
6520	**cuatrocientos**-*num*	four hundred
5490	**cubano**-*adj; m*	Cuban; Cuban person
7449	**cubeta**-*f*	tray, bucket
6005	**cuchara**-*f*	spoon
5030	**cuchilla**-*f*	blade
6567	**cuesta**-*f*	slope
7335	**cuestionario**-*m*	questionnaire
6039	**cumplimiento**-*m*	compliance
6956	**cundir**-*vb*	spread, go well
7063	**cuneta**-*f*	ditch
5965	**cupón**-*m*	coupon
5688	**cúpula**-*f*	dome, leadership
6386	**curación**-*f*	healing
5725	**currículum**-*m*	curriculum
6774	**curro**-*m*	job (ES) (coll)

D

6269	**damasco**-*m*	apricot
5681	**danés**-*adj; m*	Danish; Danish person
5795	**danzar**-*vb*	dance
5316	**dardo**-*m*	dart
5593	**de antemano**-*adv*	beforehand
6428	**debido**-*adj*	properly
5572	**debut**-*m*	debut
5271	**decadencia**-*f*	decline
6789	**decadente**-*adj*	decadent
6964	**decapitar**-*vb*	behead
5761	**decepcionante**-*adj*	disappointing
7154	**decidido**-*adj*	determined
5455	**decisivo**-*adj*	decisive
7028	**deducción**-*f*	deduction
5845	**deducir**-*vb*	deduce
7451	**defectuoso**-*adj*	defective
7184	**déficit**-*m*	deficit
6647	**deforme**-*adj*	misshapen
7025	**defraudar**-*vb*	disappoint
5486	**defunción**-*f*	death
5702	**delatar**-*vb*	betray
5201	**delegado**-*m*	delegate
6726	**deleite**-*m*	delight
5942	**deletrear**-*vb*	spell out
5112	**delicia**-*f*	delight
6590	**delincuencia**-*f*	delinquency
7349	**delirante**-*adj*	delirious
5544	**delirio**-*m*	delirium
5322	**demandante**-*m/f*	plaintiff
5027	**demencia**-*f*	dementia
5655	**democrático**-*adj*	democratic
7359	**demoler**-*vb*	demolish
5625	**demolición**-*f*	demolition
6001	**demorar(se)**-*vb; vbr*	delay; arrive late
5340	**denegar**-*vb*	deny
6923	**densidad**-*f*	density
6496	**denso**-*adj*	thick
5488	**dentadura**-*f*	dentures
7216	**dependencia**-*f*	dependence
5529	**dependiente**-*adj; m*	dependent; shop assistant
7345	**deplorable**-*adj*	deplorable
5798	**deportista**-*adj; m/f*	sporty; athlete
6437	**depositar**-*vb*	deposit
5689	**depredador**-*adj; m*	predatory; predator

7165	**derivado**-*adj; m*	derived; derivative
6361	**derramamiento**-*m*	shedding
5598	**derretir**-*vb*	melt
6355	**derrocar**-*vb*	overthrow
6254	**derrotado**-*adj*	defeated
7324	**derrota**-*f*	defeat
6297	**derrumbar(se)**-*vb*	demolish, break down
5878	**desacato**-*m*	contempt
6471	**desactivar**-*vb*	deactivate
7176	**desafiante**-*adj*	challenging
6858	**desagradar**-*vb*	displease
5532	**desaguar**-*vb*	drain
6531	**desapercibido**-*adj*	unnoticed
6168	**desastroso**-*adj*	disastrous
6612	**descalzo**-*adj*	barefoot
5115	**descaro**-*m*	impertinence
6546	**descartar**-*vb*	discard
6563	**descendencia**-*f*	offspring
6991	**descomponer(se)**-*vb; vbr*	break down; slump
6280	**descomposición**-*f*	decomposition
6578	**descompuesto**-*adj*	broken down
6699	**desconcertado**-*adj*	bewildered
6462	**desconcertante**-*adj*	upsetting
5264	**desconectado**-*adj*	disconnected
6371	**desconectar**-*vb*	disconnect
7213	**desconfiado**-*adj*	suspicious
6043	**desconfianza**-*f*	distrust
5621	**descontento**-*adj; m*	discontented; displeasure
5699	**descubierto**-*m*	uncovered
5257	**descuido**-*m*	carelessness
7475	**desdén**-*m*	disdain
5670	**desdichado**-*m*	unhappy
6708	**deseable**-*adj*	desirable
5830	**desecho**-*m*	waste
5700	**desembarcar(se)**-*vb; vbr*	unload; disembark
6274	**desembarco**-*m*	landing
5804	**desempeño**-*m*	performance

5224	**desempleado**-*adj; m*	unemployed; unemployed person
7053	**deserción**-*f*	desertion
7215	**desertar**-*vb*	desert
7431	**desgraciar**-*vb*	ruin
5438	**deshonesto**-*adj*	dishonest
5591	**designar**-*vb*	appoint
6105	**desilusionar(se)**-*vb*	let down
5920	**desilusión**-*f*	disappointment
6919	**desinfectante**-*adj; m*	disinfectant; disinfectant
6866	**desistir**-*vb*	desist
7192	**desleal**-*adj*	disloyal
5718	**deslizar(se)**-*vb*	slip, sneak
5517	**deslumbrante**-*adj*	dazzling
7134	**desmontar**-*vb*	disassemble
7011	**desobedecer**-*vb*	disobey
7136	**desobediencia**-*f*	disobedience
6895	**desodorante**-*m*	deodorant
7402	**desolación**-*f*	devastation
5986	**desolar**-*vb*	devastate
5554	**desordenado**-*adj*	disorganized
5896	**despedida**-*f*	farewell
7437	**despeje**-*m*	clearance
5400	**despensa**-*f*	pantry
7038	**desperdicio**-*m*	waste
5038	**despertador**-*m*	alarm clock
5865	**despliegue**-*m*	deployment
5854	**despreciar**-*vb*	despise
7209	**despreocupado**-*adj*	carefree
6232	**destacar**-*vb*	stand out
5673	**destello**-*m*	flash, sparkle
7243	**desterrar**-*vb*	exile
6373	**destornillador**-*m*	screwdriver
7318	**destructivo**-*adj*	destructive
6695	**desvanecer(se)**-*vb*	fade
5508	**desventaja**-*f*	disadvantage
7186	**desviación**-*f*	detour
5991	**desviar(se)**-*vb*	divert
7095	**detallado**-*adj*	detailed
6404	**detallar**-*vb*	detail
7307	**detección**-*f*	detection
5075	**detectar**-*vb*	detect

5483	**detenido**-*adj; m*	stopped, arrested; prisoner
7171	**detentar**-*vb*	hold
7168	**detergente**-*adj; m*	detergent; detergent
6265	**detestable**-*adj*	despicable
6258	**detonación**-*f*	detonation
6703	**detonar**-*vb*	detonate
6177	**devastador**-*adj*	devastating
7403	**devastar**-*vb*	devastate
6669	**devolución**-*f*	refund
6484	**devorar**-*vb*	devour
5343	**devoto**-*m; adj*	devotee; devout
5814	**diabetes**-*f*	diabetes
6799	**diafragma**-*m*	diaphragm
7342	**diagrama**-*m*	diagram
6501	**dialecto**-*m*	dialect
6609	**diámetro**-*m*	diameter
7435	**diantres**-*int*	damn it
6598	**dichoso**-*adj*	happy
5104	**dictador**-*m*	dictator
6735	**dictar**-*vb*	dictate
5290	**diecinueve**-*num*	nineteen
6393	**diésel**-*m*	diesel
6759	**diestro**-*adj*	right-handed, skilled
6961	**difamación**-*f*	defamation
6890	**diferenciar**-*vb*	differentiate
5049	**difundir**-*vb*	spread
7050	**digerir**-*vb*	digest
7129	**digestión**-*f*	digestion
7443	**dígito**-*m*	digit
6229	**diluvio**-*m*	downpour
5712	**diminuto**-*adj*	tiny
5270	**dimisión**-*f*	resignation
7493	**dimitir**-*vb*	resign
6575	**dinámico**-*adj*	dynamic
7457	**dineral**-*m*	fortune
6605	**dióxido**-*m*	dioxide
6202	**diplomacia**-*f*	diplomacy
5379	**dique**-*m*	dike
6160	**dirigente**-*m/f; adj*	leader; leading
7043	**discapacitar**-*vb*	incapacitate
6172	**discriminación**-*f*	discrimination
5835	**disfrute**-*m*	enjoyment
6561	**disimular**-*vb*	disguise
5966	**disminuir**-*vb*	decrease
5219	**disparate**-*m*	folly
5382	**distinción**-*f*	distinction
6271	**distraer(se)**-*vb*	distract
6143	**distribuidor**-*m*	distributor
6639	**distribuir**-*vb*	distribute
6804	**diva**-*f*	diva
6795	**diversidad**-*f*	diversity
5962	**diversos**-*adj*	various
6909	**dócil**-*adj*	docile
6296	**domar**-*vb*	tame
5307	**doméstico**-*adj*	domestic
6880	**dominación**-*f*	domination
7015	**dominical**-*adj; m*	Sunday; Sunday magazine
5158	**dominó**-*m*	dominoes
5034	**donar**-*vb*	donate
6862	**dorsal**-*adj*	dorsal
5567	**dotado**-*adj*	gifted
7516	**dote**-*f*	dowry
7466	**drástico**-*adj*	drastic
6370	**drenaje**-*m*	drainage
6416	**dudoso**-*adj*	dubious
6679	**duna**-*f*	dune
5722	**dúo**-*m*	pair
6470	**duplicado**-*m*	duplicate
5754	**duración**-*f*	length of time
7237	**duradero**-*adj*	durable
6905	**durazno**-*m*	peach
6166	**dureza**-*f*	hardness

E

5233	**eclipse**-*m*	eclipse
5063	**ecuación**-*f*	equation
6403	**ecuador**-*m*	equator
6077	**educativo**-*adj*	educational
7284	**efectuar**-*vb*	carry out
6700	**eficacia**-*f*	effectiveness
5364	**eficiencia**-*f*	efficiency
5310	**egoísmo**-*m*	selfishness
6803	**elaborar**-*vb*	prepare
6604	**electo**-*adj; m*	elected; elected member
5365	**electoral**-*adj*	electoral
5783	**electricista**-*m/f*	electrician

7325	**electromagnético-**_adj_	electromagnetic	
5553	**elemental-**_adj_	elementary	
6189	**elenco-**_m_	cast	
7262	**elevación-**_f_	elevation	
5770	**eliminación-**_f_	elimination	
5085	**élite-**_f_	elite	
7523	**elixir-**_m_	elixir	
7485	**elocuencia-**_f_	eloquence	
6572	**elocuente-**_adj_	eloquent	
5869	**elogio-**_m_	compliment	
6648	**eludir-**_vb_	avoid	
6730	**embarcación-**_f_	embarkation	
6560	**emblema-**_m_	emblem	
7487	**embriaguez-**_f_	drunkenness	
7465	**embrollar(se)-**_vb_	confuse	
6223	**embrujar-**_vb_	bewitch	
7311	**emerger-**_vb_	emerge	
7346	**eminente-**_adj_	eminent	
6935	**emisario-**_m_	emissary	
5236	**emitir-**_vb_	broadcast	
6465	**emotivo-**_adj_	emotional	
6810	**emparedado-**_m_	sandwich	
7469	**empatía-**_f_	empathy	
6771	**empeñar(se)-**_vb; vbr_	pawn; insist on	
7416	**empleador-**_m_	employer	
5985	**emprender-**_vb_	undertake	
7332	**empresarial-**_adj_	corporate	
5083	**empujón-**_m_	push	
5420	**encadenar-**_vb_	chain	
6945	**encarar-**_vb_	confront	
5014	**encarcelar-**_vb_	imprison	
6755	**enchufe-**_m_	wall socket	
7495	**encía-**_f_	gum	
6443	**enciclopedia-**_f_	encyclopedia	
6058	**encierro-**_m_	confinement	
6690	**encrucijada-**_f_	crossroads	
5495	**encuesta-**_f_	survey	
6968	**enderezar(se)-**_vb_	straighten	
6827	**énfasis-**_m_	emphasis	
5653	**enfermizo-**_adj_	sickly	
7016	**enfocar-**_vb_	focus	
5234	**enfrentamiento-**_m_	confrontation	
5749	**enfriar(se)-**_vb; vbr_	cool; get cold, catch a cold	

7472	**enfurecer(se)-**_vb_	drive mad, enrage
5800	**engordar-**_vb_	gain weight
7362	**enjambre-**_m_	swarm
6391	**enmascarar-**_vb_	mask
6553	**enredar(se)-**_vb_	tangle, confuse, mess with (ES)
5404	**ensueño-**_m_	fantasy
5472	**ente-**_m_	entity
6080	**entidad-**_f_	organization
5441	**entregar(se)-**_vb_	deliver
5981	**entretanto-**_adv_	meanwhile
5231	**entretener(se)-**_vb_	entertain
5855	**entristecer(se)-**_vb_	sadden
5179	**entusiasta-**_m; adj_	fan; enthusiastic
6145	**envenenamiento-**_m_	poisoning
6894	**epilepsia-**_f_	epilepsy
5459	**equipamiento-**_m_	equipment
5633	**equipar(se)-**_vb_	equip
6332	**equivaler-**_vb_	be equal to
5596	**equivocarse-**_vbr_	be wrong
5601	**erótico-**_adj_	erotic
5137	**errado-**_adj_	wrong
6794	**erróneo-**_adj_	wrong
6287	**erudito-**_adj; m_	expert; erudite person
5017	**erupción-**_f_	eruption
5498	**escalofriante-**_adj_	spooky
5056	**escandaloso-**_adj_	scandalous
5695	**escáner-**_m_	scanner
6305	**escaparate-**_m_	closet (LA), shop window
7370	**escarlata-**_adj; m_	scarlet; scarlet
5089	**escasez-**_f_	shortage
6657	**escaso-**_adj_	lacking
6543	**escéptico-**_adj; m_	skeptic; skeptic
6760	**escote-**_m_	cleavage
6738	**escudero-**_m_	squire
6349	**escultor-**_m_	sculptor
6645	**escurridizo-**_adj_	evasive, slippery
6110	**esforzarse-**_vbr_	make an effort
7116	**esfumar(se)-**_vb_	fade
5349	**esgrima-**_f_	fencing
5651	**eslabón-**_m_	link
7132	**eslogan-**_m_	slogan

7302	**esmalte**-*m*	nail polish, varnish
7062	**espabilar(se)**-*vb*	snap out of it
5385	**espagueti**-*m*	spaghetti
7266	**espantar**-*vb*	frighten, shoo away
6289	**espanto**-*m*	terror
7312	**esparcir**-*vb*	spread
7091	**espárrago**-*m*	asparagus
6375	**especializado**-*adj*	specialized
6169	**espécimen**-*m*	specimen
6086	**especulación**-*f*	speculation
7319	**especular**-*vb*	speculate
7190	**espejismo**-*m*	illusion
5805	**espeso**-*adj*	thick
6338	**espinaca**-*f*	spinach
5339	**espiral**-*f*	spiral
6215	**espontáneo**-*adj*	spontaneous
5484	**esquema**-*m*	diagram
6614	**esquivar**-*vb*	dodge
6076	**esquizofrenia**-*f*	schizophrenia
5163	**estabilidad**-*f*	stability
5584	**estadía**-*f*	stay
7140	**estafar**-*vb*	swindle
6896	**estallido**-*m*	explosion
6778	**estampida**-*f*	stampede
6455	**estampilla**-*f*	stamp (LA), seal (ES)
6809	**estandarte**-*m*	banner
7046	**estantería**-*f*	bookcase
5823	**estático**-*adj*	static
5478	**estatus**-*m*	status
7405	**estatuto**-*m*	statute
5613	**estela**-*f*	wake
6346	**estéreo**-*adj; m*	stereo; stereo
5359	**estéril**-*adj*	sterile
5918	**estético**-*adj*	cosmetic
6865	**estimado**-*adj; m*	appreciated; estimation, dear
7196	**estimular**-*vb*	stimulate
5951	**estímulo**-*m*	stimulus, incentive
5242	**estirar(se)**-*vb*	stretch
6073	**estorbar**-*vb*	obstruct
6167	**estragos**-*mpl*	havoc
6519	**estrangular**-*vb*	strangle

6908	**estrechar(se)**-*vb; vbr*	narrow, hug; get smaller
7511	**estrenar**-*vb*	use for the first time
7066	**estresante**-*adj*	stressful
7387	**estresar(se)**-*vb*	stress
7103	**estribo**-*m*	stirrup
6870	**estruendo**-*m*	racket
6154	**estuche**-*m*	case
6439	**éter**-*m*	ether
7127	**euforia**-*f*	euphoria
6845	**evadir**-*vb*	avoid
5388	**evaluar**-*vb*	evaluate
6192	**evasión**-*f*	evasion
7474	**evasivo**-*adj*	evasive
6747	**evolucionar**-*vb*	evolve
5414	**exactitud**-*f*	accuracy
6507	**exageración**-*f*	exaggeration
5650	**excavación**-*f*	excavation
5674	**excavar**-*vb*	dig
5218	**excéntrico**-*adj; m*	eccentric; eccentric person
5192	**excesivo**-*adj*	excessive
5921	**excremento**-*m*	excrement
6617	**excusado**-*adj; m*	superfluous; restroom
5938	**exigencia**-*f*	demand
7193	**existente**-*adj*	existing
6950	**éxodo**-*m*	exodus
5724	**exorcismo**-*m*	exorcism
5955	**exótico**-*adj*	exotic
6446	**expandir**-*vb*	expand, spread
5109	**expansión**-*f*	expansion
6314	**expectativa**-*f*	expectation
5013	**experimental**-*adj*	experimental
5325	**explotación**-*f*	exploitation
7230	**exportación**-*f*	exportation
6204	**expuesto**-*adj*	exposed
6302	**expulsión**-*f*	expulsion
7406	**extenso**-*adj*	extensive
7117	**exterminar**-*vb*	exterminate
7010	**exterminio**-*m*	extermination
5570	**externo**-*adj*	external
5764	**extorsión**-*f*	extortion
5288	**extracción**-*f*	extraction
7229	**extracto**-*m*	extract
7159	**extradición**-*f*	extradition

5037	**extraer**-*vb*	extract
6552	**extraoficial**-*adj*	unofficial
5203	**extravagante**-*adj*	extravagant
7438	**extraviar(se)**-*vb*	misplace
6711	**extremidad**-*f*	limb
6504	**extremista**-*adj; m/f*	extreme; extremist

F

5523	**fabricación**-*f*	manufacturing
5708	**fabricante**-*adj; m*	manufacturing; manufacturer
7040	**fábula**-*f*	fable
6841	**facción**-*f*	faction
5543	**facial**-*adj*	facial
6592	**facilitar**-*vb*	facilitate
6467	**faena**-*f*	chore
6631	**faja**-*f*	sash
7133	**falsedad**-*f*	falseness
5105	**falsificación**-*f*	counterfeit
7037	**falsificar**-*vb*	falsify
5129	**familiarizar(se)**-*vb*	become familiar with
5402	**fango**-*m*	mud
6109	**farmacéutico**-*adj; m*	pharmaceutical; pharmacist
5811	**fascinación**-*f*	fascination
5462	**fascinar**-*vb*	fascinate
5176	**fascismo**-*m*	fascism
6457	**fastidiado**-*adj*	fed up, broken (ES)
5492	**fastidiar(se)**-*vb; vbr*	annoy; put up with
7434	**fastidioso**-*adj*	annoying
5561	**fatiga**-*f*	fatigue
6773	**fauna**-*f*	fauna, bunch of weirdos (coll)
5336	**favorable**-*adj*	favorable
5802	**favorecer**-*vb*	favour
6733	**fealdad**-*f*	ugliness
5797	**felicitar**-*vb*	congratulate
6938	**feminista**-*adj; m/f*	feminist; feminist
7071	**ferroviario**-*adj; m*	railway; railwayman
5534	**fértil**-*adj*	fertile
6372	**fertilidad**-*f*	fertility

7166	**fertilizante**-*adj; m*	fertilizing; fertilizer
7305	**fervor**-*m*	fervor
5090	**festín**-*m*	feast
6653	**festivo**-*adj*	festive, holiday
5777	**feto**-*m*	fetus
5903	**fiable**-*adj*	trustworthy
6327	**fiasco**-*m*	fiasco
6574	**fijación**-*f*	fixation
5209	**filipino**-*adj; m*	Philippine; Philippine person
7007	**filtración**-*f*	filtration
7509	**finalista**-*adj; m/f*	finalist; finalist
5319	**finalizar**-*vb*	conclude
6792	**financiación**-*f*	financing
5346	**financiar**-*vb*	finance
5521	**firmeza**-*f*	firmness
7278	**flamenco**-*adj; m*	flamenco; flamingo
6534	**flan**-*m*	flan
5629	**florecer**-*vb*	bloom
7433	**florero**-*m*	vase
5575	**flotante**-*adj*	floating
5108	**fluido**-*m; adj; adv*	fluid; free-flowing; fluently
7419	**fobia**-*f*	phobia
5446	**foca**-*f*	seal
6037	**follón**-*m*	racket
7014	**fonda**-*f*	inn
7499	**forestal**-*adj; m*	forest; ranger
6933	**formato**-*m*	format
6852	**forrar(se)**-*vb; vbr*	cover; get rich
6736	**forro**-*m*	lining, jacket
6579	**fortalecer**-*vb*	strengthen
6218	**fósil**-*m*	fossil
6396	**fotográfico**-*adj*	photographic
6170	**fracción**-*f*	fraction
7265	**fractura**-*f*	fracture
5950	**fragancia**-*f*	fragrance
5960	**fraile**-*m*	friar
5058	**francotirador**-*m*	sniper
6992	**franja**-*f*	stripe, time zone
7486	**franquicia**-*f*	franchise
5062	**frecuente**-*adj*	frequent
5687	**fregar**-*vb*	wash
7505	**frenesí**-*m*	frenzy
7264	**fresno**-*m*	ash

6385	**frigorífico**-*m*	refrigerator
5468	**frustración**-*f*	frustration
5782	**fugarse**-*vbr*	break out
5243	**fugaz**-*adj*	brief
5011	**fulano**-*m*	some guy (coll)
5892	**fumador**-*m*	smoker
7225	**funcional**-*adj*	functional
5173	**fundador**-*m*	founder
6510	**fundamento**-*m*	foundation
5398	**fundar**-*vb*	found
5665	**fundir(se)**-*vb; vbr*	melt; melt, burn out
5859	**furgón**-*m*	van
7525	**furor**-*m*	fury
6407	**fusible**-*adj; m*	fusible; fuse
6321	**fusilamiento**-*m*	execution by firing squad
7255	**fusilar**-*vb*	shoot
6547	**futbolista**-*m/f*	football player

G

6406	**gabardina**-*f*	raincoat
5106	**galán**-*m*	handsome man
6035	**galante**-*adj*	gallant
5458	**gallinero**-*m*	henhouse
5669	**galón**-*m*	gallon
6914	**galope**-*m*	gallop
6024	**gama**-*f*	range
5890	**gamba**-*f*	prawn
7491	**garbo**-*m*	grace
7479	**garrote**-*m*	stick
5128	**gaseosa**-*f*	soda
6099	**gaviota**-*f*	seagull
6725	**gel**-*m*	gel
7291	**gendarme**-*m/f*	police officer
5407	**generar**-*vb*	generate
5787	**génesis**-*f*	origin
5197	**genético**-*adj*	genetic
5590	**genital**-*adj*	genital
5995	**genocidio**-*m*	genocide
5074	**gentileza**-*f*	gentleness
5315	**genuino**-*adj*	genuine
5166	**geografía**-*f*	geography
7111	**geometría**-*f*	geometry
5866	**gerencia**-*f*	management

5174	**germen**-*m*	germ
6491	**gestión**-*f*	paperwork, management
5249	**gigantesco**-*adj*	gigantic
6701	**ginecólogo**-*m*	gynecologist
6408	**glaciar**-*m*	glacier
7383	**glándula**-*f*	gland
6402	**gobernante**-*adj; m*	ruling; leader
5239	**golosina**-*f*	candy
5824	**gorrión**-*m*	sparrow
6936	**gotear**-*vb*	drip
6815	**gótico**-*adj; m*	Gothic; Goth
5253	**gozar**-*vb*	enjoy
5141	**gozo**-*m*	joy
5263	**gradual**-*adj*	gradual
5526	**gráfico**-*adj*	graphic
6278	**gramática**-*f*	grammar
6102	**granito**-*m*	granite
7417	**granizo**-*m*	hail
6490	**gratificante**-*adj*	gratifying
6820	**grato**-*adj*	agreeable
5813	**gratuito**-*adj*	free, uncalled for
5471	**gremio**-*m*	guild, union
5094	**gringo**-*adj; m*	gringo; gringo (coll), foreigner (LA) (coll)
7048	**grosería**-*f*	rudeness
6050	**grotesco**-*adj*	hideous
7149	**gruta**-*f*	cave
7323	**guardabosques**-*m/f*	forest ranger
6744	**guardacostas**-*m/f*	coastguard
6002	**guardarropa**-*m*	wardrobe
5914	**gubernamental**-*adj*	governmental
6259	**guerrilla**-*f*	guerrilla
6551	**guerrillero**-*adj; m*	guerrilla; guerrilla
5146	**gueto**-*m*	ghetto
5326	**guillotina**-*f*	guillotine
5205	**guionista**-*m/f*	screenwriter
5064	**guisante**-*m*	pea
5720	**guisar**-*vb*	stew
6114	**guita**-*f*	money (coll)
5422	**guitarrista**-*m/f*	guitarist

H

7404	**habitar**-*vb*	dwell	
6594	**hábitat**-*m*	habitat	
6362	**hablador**-*adj*	talkative	
7373	**hacha**-*f*	axe	
6486	**hachís**-*m*	hash	
5792	**halagar**-*vb*	flatter	
7201	**halago**-*m*	praise	
5503	**hallazgo**-*m*	discovery	
6807	**halo**-*m*	halo	
6649	**hamaca**-*f*	hammock	
6525	**hambruna**-*f*	famine	
7023	**hámster**-*m*	hamster	
6801	**harén**-*m*	harem	
7254	**hartar(se)**-*vb; vbr*	get on the nerves of; get sick of	
5273	**hazaña**-*f*	feat	
5022	**hebreo**-*adj; m*	Hebrew; Jew	
7506	**heces**-*fpl*	dregs, feces	
5183	**hectárea**-*f*	hectare	
5545	**heladera**-*f*	refrigerator	
6422	**helar**-*vb*	freeze	
6012	**hélice**-*f*	propeller	
7522	**helio**-*m*	helium	
6359	**hemisferio**-*m*	hemisphere	
6533	**hepatitis**-*f*	hepatitis	
5588	**heredar**-*vb*	inherit	
6740	**hereje**-*m/f*	heretic	
6634	**herejía**-*f*	heresy	
5016	**hermosura**-*f*	beauty	
5018	**heroico**-*adj*	heroic	
6508	**heroísmo**-*m*	heroism	
6400	**herpes**-*m*	herpes	
6856	**herradura**-*f*	horseshoe	
7454	**hervido**-*adj; m*	boiled; casserole	
7490	**híbrido**-*adj; m*	mix; hybrid	
5068	**higiene**-*f*	hygiene	
6975	**higo**-*m*	fig	
6987	**hincha**-*m/f*	fan	
5707	**hinchar(se)**-*vb; vbr*	swell; stuff yourself	
5023	**hipnosis**-*f*	hypnosis	
5470	**hipocresía**-*f*	hypocrisy	
5794	**hipódromo**-*m*	racecourse	
5297	**hipo**-*m*	hiccup	
6409	**historiador**-*m*	historian	

5860	**historieta**-*f*	cartoon strip	
5353	**hobby**-*m*	hobby	
6499	**hojalata**-*f*	tin	
7101	**honradez**-*f*	honesty	
6262	**horizontal**-*adj*	horizontal	
6068	**hormigón**-*m*	concrete	
6952	**hormiguero**-*m*	anthill	
6290	**horrendo**-*adj*	horrendous	
7090	**hospedar**-*vb*	host	
7421	**hostal**-*m*	hostel	
5452	**hostilidad**-*f*	hostility	
6357	**huerta**-*f*	vegetable garden	
7447	**humanitario**-*adj*	humanitarian	
5055	**húngaro**-*adj; m*	Hungarian; Hungarian person	
7460	**hurtar**-*vb*	steal	

I

6151	**iceberg**-*m*	iceberg	
7221	**icono**-*m*	icon	
6236	**idealista**-*adj; m*	idealistic; idealist	
5345	**idéntico**-*adj*	identical	
5548	**ideología**-*f*	ideology	
7039	**igualar**-*vb*	equalize	
7442	**ileso**-*adj*	unhurt	
6673	**ilimitado**-*adj*	unlimited	
5427	**ilustre**-*adj*	illustrious	
5154	**imán**-*m*	magnet	
5031	**imitar**-*vb*	imitate	
5721	**impaciencia**-*f*	impatience	
6054	**impactante**-*adj*	stunning	
7235	**impactar**-*vb*	impact	
7314	**imparable**-*adj*	unstoppable	
6666	**impar**-*adj*	odd	
6153	**imparcial**-*adj*	impartial	
6989	**impedimento**-*m*	impediment	
6581	**impenetrable**-*adj*	impenetrable	
6389	**impensable**-*adj*	unthinkable	
5057	**imperdonable**-*adj*	unforgivable	
5210	**impermeable**-*m; adj*	weatherproof; waterproof	
7199	**impertinencia**-*f*	impertinence	
6445	**implantar**-*vb*	implant	
6707	**implante**-*m*	implant	
7500	**implicación**-*f*	implication	

5912	**implorar**-*vb*	implore
5691	**imponente**-*adj*	imposing
6915	**importación**-*f*	importation
6668	**impotencia**-*f*	impotence
5247	**impredecible**-*adj*	unpredictable
5133	**imprenta**-*f*	printing
6556	**imprescindible**-*adj*	essential
5849	**impreso**-*adj; m*	printed; flyer
6893	**imprevisible**-*adj*	unpredictable
5456	**imprimir**-*vb*	print
6800	**improvisación**-*f*	improvisation
5355	**improvisar**-*vb*	improvise
7269	**imprudencia**-*f*	carelessness
6929	**impulsar**-*vb*	boost, inspire
5847	**impulsivo**-*adj*	impulsive
6754	**impune**-*adj*	unpunished
7384	**inadecuado**-*adj*	unsuitable
7423	**inadmisible**-*adj*	unacceptable
7395	**inaudito**-*adj*	unheard-of
7497	**inaugural**-*adj*	inaugural
5668	**incapacidad**-*f*	inability
5386	**incendiar**-*vb*	burn down
6616	**incentivo**-*m*	incentive
5742	**incertidumbre**-*f*	uncertainty
7021	**incesto**-*m*	incest
5727	**incienso**-*m*	incense
6931	**incierto**-*adj*	uncertain
7107	**incisión**-*f*	incision
5592	**inclinación**-*f*	inclination
6231	**inclinado**-*adj*	inclined
5624	**inclinar(se)**-*vb; vbr*	bend, persuade; bow, tend toward
6013	**incógnito**-*adj; m*	incognito; incognito
5409	**incomodar**-*vb*	make uncomfortable
6380	**incomparable**-*adj*	incomparable
6284	**incompetencia**-*f*	incompetence
5029	**incompetente**-*adj*	incompetent
6676	**incompleto**-*adj*	incomplete
6388	**incomprensible**-*adj*	incomprehensible
6528	**incondicional**-*adj; m/f*	unconditional; stalwart
6597	**incontable**-*adj*	countless
7249	**incontrolable**-*adj*	uncontrollable
6913	**incorregible**-*adj*	incorrigible
6928	**incrementar**-*vb*	increase
6425	**incremento**-*m*	increase
6595	**incurable**-*adj*	incurable
6732	**incursión**-*f*	incursion
5832	**indefinido**-*adj*	indefinite
5538	**indemnización**-*f*	compensation
5524	**indicación**-*f*	indication
6414	**indicador**-*m*	indicator
5001	**indicio**-*m*	indication
5091	**indiferencia**-*f*	indifference
6015	**indígena**-*adj; m*	native; native person
6937	**indigente**-*m*	indigent
6281	**indigestión**-*f*	indigestion
7083	**indignación**-*f*	indignation
7513	**indignante**-*adj*	outrageous
5565	**indigno**-*adj*	unworthy
6658	**indirecto**-*adj*	indirect
7212	**indiscreto**-*adj*	indiscreet
6849	**indonesio**-*adj; m*	Indonesian; Indonesian person
5574	**indudable**-*adj*	undeniable
6757	**indulgencia**-*f*	indulgence
6240	**indulgente**-*adj*	indulgent
6134	**indulto**-*m*	pardon
6163	**inexplicable**-*adj*	inexplicable
5737	**infalible**-*adj*	infallible
6948	**infamia**-*f*	infamy
5698	**infante**-*m/f*	infant
7120	**infelicidad**-*f*	unhappiness
6079	**infiltrar**-*vb*	infiltrate
5723	**inflación**-*f*	inflation
7000	**inflexible**-*adj*	inflexible
6070	**influir**-*vb*	influence
6348	**influyente**-*adj*	influential
6337	**informática**-*f*	computing
7004	**informativo**-*adj; m*	informative; news bulletin
6835	**infracción**-*f*	infraction
7076	**infraestructura**-*f*	infrastructure
7377	**ingenuidad**-*f*	naivety
5803	**ingrato**-*adj*	ungrateful
7104	**inhalar**-*vb*	inhale
5788	**inhumano**-*adj*	inhumane
5871	**iniciación**-*f*	initiation

6972	inimaginable-*adj*	unimaginable
5820	inmaduro-*adj*	immature, unripe
5607	inmobiliaria-*adj; f*	real-estate; real state agency
5861	inmobiliario-*adj*	real-estate
5082	inmóvil-*adj*	immobile
7248	inmundicia-*f*	filth
5168	inmune-*adj*	immune
5751	innumerable-*adj*	innumerable
5187	inolvidable-*adj*	unforgettable
6545	inoportuno-*adj*	inopportune
5497	inquietante-*adj*	disturbing
6083	inquietud-*f*	restlessness
5682	inquisición-*f*	inquisition
6536	insaciable-*adj*	insatiable
6970	inseguridad-*f*	insecurity
5237	inseguro-*adj*	unsafe, insecure
5552	insensato-*adj; m*	foolish; foolish
6558	inseparable-*adj*	inseparable
5952	inservible-*adj*	unusable
6652	insistente-*adj*	insistent
6734	insólito-*adj*	unheard of
5258	insomnio-*m*	insomnia
5437	inspeccionar-*vb*	inspect
5683	instantáneo-*adj*	instant
6257	insulina-*f*	insulin
6927	insultante-*adj*	insulting
7360	integración-*f*	integration
6566	integral-*adj*	comprehensive
5997	intelecto-*m*	intellect
7008	intencional-*adj*	intentional
6958	intendente-*m/f*	intendant
7470	interacción-*f*	interaction
6475	interceptar-*vb*	intercept
7006	interestatal-*adj*	interstate
6007	intermediario-*m*	intermediary
5693	intermedio-*adj; m*	intermediate; intermission
7521	intermitente-*adj; m*	intermittent; blinker
6320	interponer(se)-*vb; vbr*	interject; intervene
5975	interrogación-*f*	interrogation
6298	intersección-*f*	intersection
6912	intervalo-*m*	interval
5132	intestino-*m*	intestine
6477	intimidar-*vb*	intimidate

7005	intocable-*adj*	untouchable
5053	intolerable-*adj*	unbearable
7365	intolerancia-*f*	intolerance
6878	intoxicación-*f*	intoxication
7143	intrépido-*adj*	intrepid
5100	intriga-*f*	scheme
6027	intrigante-*m*	intriguing
5421	introducción-*f*	introduction
5204	introducir(se)-*vb*	introduce
6681	intromisión-*f*	meddling
6142	intrusión-*f*	intrusion
5999	inundar-*vb*	flood
5473	inválido-*adj; m*	invalid; disabled person
5614	invasor-*m; adj*	invader; invading
5390	inventor-*m*	inventor
5195	invernadero-*m*	greenhouse
6859	inversionista-*m/f*	investor
6770	inverso-*adj*	reverse
5636	inversor-*m*	investor
7399	involuntario-*adj*	involuntary
5763	iraquí-*adj; m*	Iraqi; Iraqi person
5073	irracional-*adj*	irrational
5394	irreal-*adj*	unreal
5915	irregular-*adj*	irregular
6239	irritable-*adj*	irritable
6088	irritar(se)-*vb*	irritate
6196	irrumpir-*vb*	burst in
5954	itinerario-*m*	itinerary
6506	izar-*vb*	hoist

J

5406	jalar-*vb*	pull
5214	jaqueca-*f*	migraine
5180	jarabe-*m*	syrup
6129	jardinería-*f*	gardening
6630	jazmín-*m*	jasmine
5143	jeque-*m*	sheik
6762	jerarquía-*f*	hierarchy
6038	jerga-*f*	slang
6748	jeringa-*f*	syringe
5649	jorobado-*adj; m*	hunched; hunchback
6333	joroba-*f*	hump
6350	joyero-*m*	jeweller, jewellery box

5461	jubilar(se)-*vb; vbr*	get rid of; retire
6277	júbilo-*m*	joy
6977	judía-*m*	bean
5930	jugoso-*adj*	juicy
6542	justificación-*f*	justification
5213	juzgado-*m*	court

K

6860	kárate-*m*	karate

L

7180	lacayo-*m*	servant
7130	lacrimógeno-*adj*	tear
6549	lácteo-*adj; m*	dairy; lactose
6072	ladera-*adj; f*	lateral; hillside
5672	ladrar-*vb*	bark
5738	lamento-*m*	lament
5351	lanzador-*m*	pitcher
5799	lapicero-*m*	pencil
5200	lápida-*f*	tombstone
7339	larva-*f*	larva
6743	lastre-*m*	ballast
5291	latido-*m*	beat
5081	latino-*adj; m*	Latin; Latino
6922	latitud-*f*	latitude
6358	lavadero-*m*	sink, laundry room
7288	lavaplatos-*m/f*	dishwasher
5579	lechero-*adj; m*	milk; milkman
6731	legislación-*f*	legislation
6418	leñador-*m*	woodcutter
7461	lepra-*f*	leprosy
7422	leproso-*adj; m*	leprous; leper
6689	leucemia-*f*	leukemia
7348	levadura-*f*	yeast
5626	levantamiento-*m*	uprising
6161	liar(se)-*vb; vbr*	mishandle (ES), roll; get embroiled
5696	licenciar(se)-*vb; vbr*	award a degree, license; get a degree
7017	liceo-*m*	high school (LA)
6721	liderar-*vb*	lead
6093	lienzo-*m*	canvas

5617	ligado-*adj*	bound
6898	limbo-*m*	limbo
5679	limitación-*f*	limitation
7354	limo-*m*	mud
5936	limpiador-*adj; m*	cleaning; wiper (LA)
5005	linaje-*m*	lineage
7436	lingote-*m*	ingot
5304	link-*m*	link
5989	lino-*m*	linen
6351	liquidación-*f*	settlement
5318	liquidar-*vb*	finish, eliminate
6694	lirio-*m*	lily
5170	litera-*f*	bunk
6746	literario-*adj*	literary
5898	liviano-*adj*	light
6821	llamativo-*adj*	flashy
6454	llano-*adj*	flat
5119	llanta-*f*	tire
5652	llanura-*f*	plain
5136	llorón-*adj; m*	whiny; crybaby
7231	lluvioso-*adj*	rainy
6998	lóbulo-*m*	lobe
5299	locomotora-*f; adj*	locomotive; locomotor
7258	logo-*m; sfx*	logo (coll); ist
7002	loma-*f*	hill
6787	lombriz-*f*	earthworm
5070	lomo-*m*	loin
6722	lubricante-*m*	lubricant
5732	lucio-*m*	pike
7337	lucro-*m*	profit
6412	lujo-*m*	luxury
5500	lujoso-*adj*	luxurious
5988	luminoso-*adj*	bright
7331	lupa-*f*	magnifying glass

M

6063	macarrones-*mpl*	macaroni
6047	machete-*m*	machete
7444	machista-*adj; m*	sexist; sexist
6885	macizo-*adj*	solid
7440	madero-*m*	log, cop (coll)
6709	madriguera-*f*	den
5489	madurez-*f*	maturity

6165	**maestría**-*f*	mastery
5536	**magnate**-*m*	tycoon
5632	**magnético**-*adj*	magnetic
7206	**magnificar**-*vb*	magnify
5378	**magnitud**-*f*	magnitude
5020	**malaria**-*f*	malaria
6101	**malestar**-*m*	discomfort
6200	**maleza**-*f*	undergrowth
6624	**malicia**-*f*	malice
6261	**maligno**-*adj*	malign
6458	**malla**-*f*	mesh
5443	**malta**-*f*	malt
7273	**maltratar**-*vb*	abuse
6315	**mambo**-*m*	mambo, issue (LA)
5877	**mamífero**-*m; adj*	mammal; mammal
5006	**manantial**-*m*	spring
5149	**mandamiento**-*m*	commandment
5454	**manifestante**-*m/f*	demonstrator
6691	**manifestar(se)**-*vb; vbr*	express; demonstrate, show up
5416	**manifiesto**-*m; adj*	manifest; evident
5808	**manipulación**-*f*	handling
6003	**maniquí**-*m*	mannequin
5949	**manojo**-*m*	handful
6103	**mantel**-*m*	tablecloth
6816	**maqueta**-*f*	mockup
5755	**maquinista**-*m/f*	machinist
5341	**maratón**-*m*	marathon
5019	**marfil**-*m*	ivory
5095	**marioneta**-*f*	puppet
6529	**marisco**-*m*	shellfish
7448	**martirio**-*m*	martyrdom
5513	**mástil**-*m*	mast
5818	**masturbación**-*f*	masturbation
5428	**matador**-*m; adj*	matador; deadly
6777	**maternal**-*adj*	maternal
5065	**maternidad**-*f*	maternity
6980	**materno**-*adj*	maternal
7210	**matinal**-*adj*	morning
5663	**matriz**-*f*	womb
6765	**matutino**-*adj*	morning
7480	**mayúsculo**-*adj*	tremendous
5602	**mazo**-*m*	mallet
6526	**meca**-*f*	mecca

5371	**mecha**-*f*	wick
6456	**mechero**-*m*	lighter
6930	**mechón**-*m*	lock
6369	**mediano**-*adj*	medium-sized
5344	**mediar**-*vb*	mediate
7382	**medidor**-*adj; m*	measuring; meter
5662	**medieval**-*adj*	medieval
5301	**meditación**-*f*	meditation
6128	**meditar**-*vb*	meditate
5302	**médula**-*f*	marrow
5734	**medusa**-*f*	jellyfish
7001	**mejicano**-*adj; m*	Mexican; Mexican person
5439	**melancolía**-*f*	melancholy
6479	**melancólico**-*adj*	melancholic
7290	**melena**-*f*	mane
6347	**mellizo**-*adj; m*	twin; twin
5559	**melocotón**-*m*	peach
5311	**melón**-*m*	melon
5627	**memorable**-*adj*	memorable
6084	**memorial**-*m*	memorial
6954	**memorizar**-*vb*	memorize
5556	**meñique**-*m*	little finger
5946	**mensual**-*adj*	monthly
5124	**mentón**-*m*	chin
5117	**menudo**-*adj*	small
5447	**mercadería**-*f*	merchandise
5842	**mercader**-*m/f*	merchant
7170	**mercante**-*m/f*	merchant
5403	**mercenario**-*m; adj*	mercenary; mercenary
6071	**merienda**-*f*	afternoon snack
5208	**merodear**-*vb*	lurk
6006	**mestizo**-*adj; m*	racially mixed; mixed race
7070	**metabolismo**-*m*	metabolism
6776	**metano**-*m*	methane
6417	**meteorológico**-*adj*	meteorological
5235	**meteoro**-*m*	meteor
7239	**metralla**-*f*	shrapnel
6684	**metralleta**-*f*	submachine gun
6162	**metrópoli**-*f*	metropolis
6632	**metropolitano**-*adj; m*	urban; subway
6750	**mezclado**-*adj*	mixed
5272	**mezquino**-*adj*	mean

5220	**mezquita**-*f*	mosque
7087	**microbio**-*m*	microbe
5155	**micro**-*m*	mic, minibus
5623	**microscopio**-*m*	microscope
6292	**miga**-*f*	crumb
7082	**migaja**-*f*	crumb
7389	**migración**-*f*	migration
5880	**milagroso**-*adj*	miraculous
5012	**milenio**-*m*	millennium
7467	**miligramo**-*m*	milligram
5571	**mililitro**-*m*	milliliter
5785	**milímetro**-*m*	millimeter
7280	**militante**-*adj; m/f*	militant; member, activist
7019	**mimar**-*vb*	pamper
5957	**minar**-*vb*	mine
5332	**miniatura**-*f; adj*	miniature; miniature
5660	**minoría**-*f*	minority
6065	**mira**-*f*	sight
6069	**misionero**-*adj; m*	missionary; missionary
5810	**místico**-*adj; m*	mystic; mystic
7178	**mitin**-*m*	rally
5719	**mitología**-*f*	mythology
7059	**mobiliario**-*m*	furniture
6130	**moco**-*m*	mucus
7085	**moderación**-*f*	moderation
5150	**modestia**-*f*	modesty
6367	**modificación**-*f*	modification
6032	**modificar**-*vb*	modify
6502	**mojado**-*adj*	wet
5851	**molde**-*m*	mould
6307	**molécula**-*f*	molecule
6213	**molecular**-*adj*	molecular
6963	**monarca**-*m/f*	monarch
5944	**monarquía**-*f*	monarchy
6622	**monedero**-*m*	purse
7379	**monetario**-*adj*	monetary
6791	**moño**-*m*	bun
5879	**monopolio**-*m*	monopoly
7245	**montículo**-*m*	mound
5284	**monto**-*m*	sum
7385	**monumental**-*adj*	monumental
6539	**mora**-*f*	blackberry
7268	**moraleja**-*f*	moral of a fable
5125	**mordisco**-*m*	bite

7131	**mormón**-*m*	Mormon
6505	**mortalidad**-*f*	mortality
6423	**mortero**-*m*	mortar
5948	**mosquetero**-*m*	musketeer
7410	**mota**-*f*	speck
7205	**motivar**-*vb*	motivate
7313	**movilización**-*f*	mobilization
5885	**muela**-*f*	molar
6310	**muleta**-*f*	crutch
6557	**multimillonario**-*adj*	multimillionaire
6221	**municipio**-*m*	municipality
5358	**muralla**-*f*	wall
7155	**murmullo**-*m*	babbling
5045	**musa**-*f*	muse
6113	**muscular**-*adj*	muscular
6034	**mutación**-*f*	mutation
5126	**mutante**-*adj; m/f*	mutating; mutant
6782	**mutilar**-*vb*	mutilate

N

7086	**nabo**-*m*	turnip
7232	**naciente**-*adj*	rising
5979	**nacionalidad**-*f*	nationality
5622	**nadador**-*m*	swimmer
5480	**naipe**-*m*	playing card
6812	**narración**-*f*	narration
6087	**narrador**-*m*	narrator
7309	**nasal**-*adj*	nasal
5025	**nato**-*adj*	born
6756	**naturalidad**-*f*	naturalness
5612	**naufragio**-*m*	shipwreck
6000	**navideño**-*adj*	Christmas
6331	**neblina**-*f*	mist
6906	**néctar**-*m*	nectar
6875	**nefasto**-*adj*	nefarious
5069	**negación**-*f*	denial
5008	**negligencia**-*f*	negligence
6892	**neo**-*pfx*	neo
6960	**neto**-*adj*	net
6940	**neurona**-*f*	neuron
6891	**neurosis**-*f*	neurosis
5635	**nevar**-*vb*	snow
6861	**nicotina**-*f*	nicotine
6176	**nirvana**-*m*	nirvana

7261	**nitrógeno**-*m*	nitrogen
6270	**nodriza**-*f*	nursemaid
6222	**nombramiento**-*m*	appointment
7367	**nominación**-*f*	nomination
5383	**nómina**-*f*	salary
7355	**nordeste**-*m*	north-east
5654	**notario**-*m*	public notary
7115	**notificación**-*f*	notification
6988	**novecientos**-*num*	nine hundred
6288	**novelista**-*m/f*	novelist
7408	**noviazgo**-*m*	engagement
5697	**nublar(se)**-*vb*	cloud
7257	**nudista**-*adj; m/f*	nudist; nudist
7352	**nulo**-*adj*	invalid
5007	**numeroso**-*adj*	numerous
6907	**nutriente**-*adj; m*	nutritious; nutrient

O

6309	**oasis**-*m*	oasis
5317	**obediente**-*adj*	obedient
7078	**objetar**-*vb*	object
5199	**obligatorio**-*adj*	mandatory
5435	**obsceno**-*adj*	obscene
6481	**observatorio**-*m*	observatory
7022	**obsesivo**-*adj*	obsessive
6392	**obstrucción**-*f*	obstruction
5212	**ocasional**-*adj*	occasional
5862	**ocaso**-*m*	sunset
5194	**octava**-*f*	octave
6044	**ocular**-*adj; m*	eye; lens
5102	**odioso**-*adj*	odious
6487	**odisea**-*f*	odyssey
6661	**ofrecimiento**-*m*	offer
7194	**oleada**-*f*	wave
5644	**olimpiada**-*f*	Olympics
5931	**olímpico**-*adj; m*	Olympian; Olympian
5491	**oliva**-*adj; f*	olive; olive
5178	**ombligo**-*m*	belly button
5685	**ómnibus**-*m*	bus
7300	**onza**-*f*	ounce
5071	**opresión**-*f*	oppression
7301	**oprimir**-*vb*	oppress
6995	**óptico**-*adj; m*	optical; optician

6159	**optimismo**-*m*	optimism
6761	**óptimo**-*adj*	ideal
5729	**orador**-*m*	public speaker
6724	**órale**-*int*	wow (LA), come on (LA)
5191	**orar**-*vb*	pray, make a speech
5744	**ordenanza**-*f*	ordinance
7110	**ordeñar**-*vb*	milk
6175	**orgánico**-*adj*	organic
6824	**organizador**-*m*	organizer
7114	**orificio**-*m*	hole
6249	**orquídea**-*f*	orchid
7236	**ortodoxo**-*adj*	orthodox
5917	**ortografía**-*f*	orthography
5883	**osar**-*vb*	dare
5265	**oscurecer**-*vb*	get dark
7113	**óseo**-*adj*	bone
5943	**otorgar**-*vb*	award
5993	**oxidar(se)**-*vb*	rust
6020	**óxido**-*m*	rust
6463	**oxigenar(se)**-*vb; vbr*	oxygenate; get fresh air
6252	**oyente**-*m/f*	listener
6640	**ozono**-*m*	ozone

P

7214	**pacificar**-*vb*	pacify
6224	**padecer**-*vb*	suffer
6216	**paisano**-*adj; m*	from the same place; civilian
6514	**paladar**-*m*	palate
6174	**paleta**-*f*	palette, lollipop
5169	**palma**-*f*	palm
7321	**palomar**-*m*	dovecote
6325	**pandillero**-*m*	member of a gang
6628	**panfleto**-*m*	pamphlet
6187	**paño**-*m*	cloth
5079	**pantera**-*f*	panther
6667	**pantufla**-*f*	slipper
7320	**papelera**-*f*	bin
5026	**parabrisas**-*m*	windshield
6212	**paracaidista**-*m/f*	parachutist
7144	**parachoques**-*m*	bumper
6205	**paradoja**-*f*	paradox

5442	**paralelo**-*m; adj*	parallel; parallel
5515	**parálisis**-*f*	paralysis
6745	**paralítico**-*m*	paralytic
7310	**parámetro**-*m*	parameter
7489	**páramo**-*m*	wasteland
6996	**pardo**-*adj*	brown
7388	**parking**-*m*	parking lot
7029	**parodiar**-*vb*	parody
6041	**párpado**-*m*	eyelid
5211	**párroco**-*m*	parish priest
5618	**participante**-*m/f; adj*	participant; participating
6828	**partidario**-*adj; m*	in favour of; supporter
7118	**partitura**-*f*	sheet music
5846	**pasarela**-*f*	walkway
7274	**pasivo**-*adj; m*	passive; retiree
6562	**pastelería**-*f*	patisserie
5433	**patente**-*f; adj*	clear; patent
6583	**paternidad**-*f*	paternity
7494	**patilla**-*f*	sideburn
5494	**patinaje**-*m*	skating
7492	**patología**-*f*	pathology
5160	**patrimonio**-*m*	heritage, wealth
6967	**patriótico**-*adj*	patriotic
5745	**patriotismo**-*m*	patriotism
5768	**patrocinador**-*m*	sponsor
7327	**patrullero**-*m*	patrolman
7459	**pavimento**-*m*	pavement
6917	**payasada**-*f*	charade
6633	**peaje**-*m*	toll
6415	**pedal**-*m*	pedal
5963	**pedazo**-*m*	chunk
6863	**pedestal**-*m*	pedestal
5423	**pelar**-*vb*	peel
5772	**pelotudo**-*adj; m*	slow, dumb (LA) (coll); young adult (LA)
7064	**pelusa**-*f*	fluff
6131	**pendejada**-*f*	bullshit (LA) (coll)
5996	**penetración**-*f*	penetration
6452	**penicilina**-*f*	penicillin
6413	**península**-*f*	peninsula
5380	**penoso**-*adj*	pitiful, embarrassing
7415	**pensador**-*m*	thinker
5361	**pepino**-*m*	cucumber
5098	**pera**-*f*	pear
5857	**percibir**-*vb*	perceive
5978	**peregrino**-*m*	pilgrim
6696	**pereza**-*f*	laziness
7096	**perforación**-*f*	drilling
6706	**perforar**-*vb*	drill
5924	**perfume**-*m*	perfume
6871	**perjudicar**-*vb*	damage
6646	**perjudicial**-*adj*	harmful
6886	**perplejo**-*adj*	perplexed
7203	**perseverancia**-*f*	perseverance
5024	**persiana**-*f*	blind
6148	**persistente**-*adj*	persistent
6399	**perspicaz**-*adj*	keen
6272	**persuadir**-*vb*	persuade
6381	**persuasión**-*f*	persuasion
7049	**perturbador**-*adj*	disturbing
7357	**pesquero**-*adj; m*	fishing; fishing boat
6056	**pestaña**-*f*	eyelash
7450	**petardo**-*m*	firecracker
7124	**petrolero**-*m*	oil tanker
7100	**piadoso**-*adj*	compassionate
6124	**pibe**-*m*	boy (coll)
7151	**picadura**-*f*	sting
6644	**pichón**-*m*	squab
5640	**pico**-*m*	pick, peak, small amount
6312	**pileta**-*f*	basil (LA), pool (LA)
5778	**pilotar**-*vb*	pilot
7068	**pimiento**-*m*	pepper
5002	**piña**-*f*	pineapple
6651	**pincel**-*m*	paint brush
6440	**pinchar**-*vb*	poke, inject
6104	**pinchazo**-*m*	prick, pinch
5757	**pintada**-*f*	graffiti
5093	**pinza**-*f*	clothespin
5850	**pío**-*m*	tweet
5348	**pionero**-*adj; m*	pioneering; pioneer
6368	**pique**-*m*	pique
7218	**piratería**-*f*	piracy
7306	**pitillo**-*m*	cigarette
6993	**pitón**-*f*	python
5525	**placentero**-*adj*	pleasurable
7073	**plancton**-*m*	plankton

6341	**planificación**-*f*	planning	5134	**preliminar**-*m*	preliminary
7350	**plantear**-*vb*	pose	5958	**prematuro**-*adj*	premature
5123	**plátano**-*m*	banana	5976	**premeditar**-*vb*	premeditate
5399	**platillo**-*m*	plate	7484	**premier**-*f*	premiere
6138	**platino**-*adj; m*	platinum; platinum	5868	**preñar**-*vb*	impregnate
			5066	**prender**-*vb*	fasten, light
6492	**pleito**-*m*	lawsuit	5947	**preocupante**-*adj*	alarming
7333	**plural**-*m*	plural	5308	**preparado**-*m*	qualified
6997	**plus**-*m*	bonus	7152	**pre**-*pfx*	pre
6577	**plutonio**-*m*	plutonium	6149	**presagio**-*m*	omen
5028	**poblar**-*vb*	populate	5583	**prescindir**-*vb*	get by without
5395	**podar**-*vb*	prune	5010	**presenciar**-*vb*	witness
7518	**podio**-*m*	podium	6266	**presentador**-*m*	presenter
5827	**poético**-*adj*	poetic	7292	**presidir**-*vb*	preside over
7211	**polen**-*m*	pollen	5156	**presumir**-*vb*	presume
7045	**policíaco**-*adj*	police	6328	**presuntuoso**-*adj*	conceited
5230	**por doquier**-*adv*	all over the place	5973	**pretendiente**-*m*	suitor
7369	**pordiosero**-*m*	beggar	7432	**pretensión**-*f*	ambition
7512	**poro**-*m*	pore	7105	**prevención**-*f*	prevention
5540	**porra**-*f*	nightstick	6500	**primicia**-*f*	scoop
6482	**portafolio**-*m*	portfolio	6378	**primogénito**-*m*	firstborn
5706	**portavoz**-*m/f*	spokesperson	6618	**primordial**-*adj*	primary
7347	**portazo**-*m*	slam	5078	**principiante**-*m/f*	beginner
5511	**porte**-*m*	demeanor	6851	**prismáticos**-*m*	binoculars
5312	**porvenir**-*m*	future	6619	**privilegiar**-*vb*	grant a privilege to
5164	**pose**-*f*	pose			
5826	**posponer**-*vb*	postpone	5569	**problemático**-*adj*	problematic
7020	**postor**-*m*	bidder	7393	**procesamiento**-*m*	prosecution
6568	**postrar(se)**-*vb*	prostrate	5907	**procesar**-*vb*	process
6826	**potable**-*adj*	potable	5765	**procesión**-*f*	procession
7294	**potasio**-*m*	potassium	7343	**proclamar**-*vb*	proclaim
5171	**potro**-*m*	colt	5101	**procurador**-*m*	attorney
7226	**preceder**-*vb*	go before	5932	**prodigio**-*m*	wonder
5077	**preciar(se)**-*vb; vbr*	value; pride yourself in	7463	**pródigo**-*adj*	prodigal, generous
5021	**precipicio**-*m*	cliff	6986	**productivo**-*adj*	productive
6026	**precipitar(se)**-*vb*	hurry	5215	**progresar**-*vb*	progress
6186	**precisar**-*vb*	require, specify	5182	**prohibición**-*f*	prohibition
7340	**precoz**-*adj*	precocious	7032	**proletariado**-*m*	proletariat
7414	**predecesor**-*m*	predecessor	7228	**prolongar**-*vb*	extend
6620	**predecible**-*adj*	predictable	7363	**prominente**-*adj*	prominent
5790	**predicar**-*vb*	preach	6643	**promotor**-*m*	promoter
6184	**predicción**-*f*	prediction	5791	**promover**-*vb*	promote
6374	**prefectura**-*f*	prefecture	5054	**pronóstico**-*m*	prediction
5451	**preferencia**-*f*	preference	7013	**pronunciado**-*adj*	pronounced
6059	**preferible**-*adj*	preferable	6028	**proporcionar**-*vb*	provide

5594	**proporción**-*f*	proportion
6326	**propulsión**-*f*	propulsion
6449	**propulsor**-*adj; m*	propellant; promoter
5396	**proseguir**-*vb*	continue
7298	**prosperar**-*vb*	thrive
5840	**próspero**-*adj*	prosperous
6565	**próstata**-*f*	prostate
5193	**protegido**-*m*	protegé
5750	**proteína**-*f*	protein
5809	**protestante**-*adj*	Protestant
5864	**proveer**-*vb*	supply
7163	**proveniente**-*adj*	coming from
5207	**provisional**-*adj*	provisional
5580	**provocación**-*f*	provocation
7047	**proximidad**-*f*	proximity
6806	**proyectar**-*vb*	project
5677	**proyectil**-*m*	projectile
6173	**proyector**-*m*	projector
5329	**prudencia**-*f*	caution
6532	**psicosis**-*f*	psychosis
6115	**psicótico**-*adj*	psychotic
5425	**psiquiatría**-*f*	psychiatry
5542	**psíquico**-*adj*	psychic
6448	**pubertad**-*f*	puberty
7391	**púbico**-*adj*	pubic
5387	**publicación**-*f*	publication
6459	**publicista**-*m/f*	publicist
6586	**publicitario**-*adj; m*	advertising; publicist
7277	**pudor**-*m*	modesty
5369	**pudrir(se)**-*vb*	rot
6410	**pulir**-*vb*	polish
6715	**pulmonar**-*adj*	chest
6394	**pulmonía**-*f*	pneumonia
5608	**puma**-*m*	puma
6555	**puñalada**-*f*	stab
5431	**puntuación**-*f*	punctuation
6720	**puntualidad**-*f*	punctuality
6941	**pupila**-*f*	pupil
5959	**purgatorio**-*m*	purgatory
7282	**pus**-*m*	pus

Q

6901	**quilate**-*m*	carat

6942	**quimioterapia**-*f*	chemotherapy

R

7158	**rábano**-*m*	radish
5426	**rabioso**-*adj*	rabid
5266	**racial**-*adj*	racial
5638	**racismo**-*m*	racism
5549	**radiador**-*m*	radiator
7517	**radial**-*adj; f*	radio; circular saw
6498	**radiografía**-*f*	radiography
6210	**radiografiar**-*vb*	X-ray
6655	**ráfaga**-*f*	burst
6637	**raptar**-*vb*	kidnap
7167	**raqueta**-*f*	racket
5906	**rascacielos**-*m*	skyscraper
5222	**rastreador**-*adj; m*	tracking; tracker
5710	**razonamiento**-*m*	reasoning
7445	**realismo**-*m*	realism
5475	**realista**-*m; adj*	realist; realistic
5510	**realización**-*f*	realization
7204	**rebanada**-*f*	slice
6033	**rebote**-*m*	bounce
6198	**recámara**-*f*	chamber
6969	**recargar**-*vb*	recharge
6447	**recaudación**-*f*	collection
5664	**recaudar**-*vb*	collect
5255	**recepcionista**-*m/f*	receptionist
5032	**receptor**-*m*	recipient
7200	**recesión**-*f*	recession
5067	**receso**-*m*	break
7381	**recibimiento**-*m*	reception
5151	**recipiente**-*m*	container
5467	**recital**-*m*	recital
6062	**recitar**-*vb*	recite
7138	**reclamación**-*f*	complaint
5487	**reclamo**-*m*	decoy
7386	**recluso**-*adj; m*	be in prison; prisoner
5165	**recluta**-*m/f*	recruit
5373	**reclutamiento**-*m*	recruitment
5003	**reclutar**-*vb*	recruit
6112	**recobrar(se)**-*vb*	recover
6832	**recolectar**-*vb*	gather
5287	**recomendar**-*vb*	recommend

6522	**recompensar**-*vb*	reward	6092	**remover**-*vb*	stir, remove
6090	**reconciliación**-*f*	reconciliation	6133	**renacer**-*vb*	revive
5295	**reconfortante**-*adj*	heartwarming	5408	**rendimiento**-*m*	performance
6717	**reconsiderar**-*vb*	reconsider	6837	**renegar**-*vb*	disown
5711	**recordatorio**-*m*	reminder	6401	**reñir**-*vb*	tell off, fight
7446	**recortar**-*vb*	trim	7504	**renombre**-*m*	renown
7142	**recreación**-*f*	recreation	6554	**renovación**-*f*	renovation
7456	**recrear**-*vb*	recreate	5884	**renovar**-*vb*	renew
7253	**rectitud**-*f*	straightness	6339	**rentable**-*adj*	profitable
5185	**rector**-*m*	dean	6685	**reo**-*m*	prisoner
6237	**redactor**-*m*	editor	5252	**repasar**-*vb*	check
5111	**redención**-*f*	redemption	7303	**repaso**-*m*	review
5072	**reducción**-*f*	reduction	7223	**repercusión**-*f*	impact
7356	**reelección**-*f*	reelection	6352	**repertorio**-*m*	repertoire
6741	**reembolso**-*m*	refund	5116	**repetición**-*f*	repetition
5333	**reencarnación**-*f*	reincarnation	6783	**repetido**-*adj*	repeated
7482	**reencuentro**-*m*	reencounter	6848	**repisa**-*f*	shelf
5605	**referente a**-*adj*	regarding	5088	**repleto**-*adj*	full
5686	**refinar**-*vb*	refine	5937	**réplica**-*f*	replica
6061	**reflexión**-*f*	reflection	6472	**repollo**-*m*	cabbage
6016	**reforma**-*f*	reform	6925	**reposar**-*vb*	rest
5983	**reforzar**-*vb*	strengthen	6179	**represalia**-*f*	reprisal
6106	**refrán**-*m*	saying	5595	**represión**-*f*	repression
6742	**regar**-*vb*	water, spill	7392	**reprimir**-*vb*	suppress
6335	**regentar**-*vb*	manage	7297	**reproche**-*m*	reproach
5043	**regional**-*adj*	regional	5303	**reproducción**-*f*	reproduction
6427	**registrador**-*m*	registrar	7293	**reproducir**-*vb*	reproduce, copy
7238	**regocijo**-*m*	delight	6884	**reproductor**-*adj; m*	reproductive; DVD player
6286	**regresivo**-*adj*	regressive	6330	**reptil**-*m*	reptile
7252	**regulación**-*f*	regulation	6984	**repugnar**-*vb*	disgust
7374	**regularidad**-*f*	consistency	6100	**repulsivo**-*adj*	repulsive
6220	**rehacer**-*vb*	redo	6064	**requisito**-*m*	requirement
6999	**rehusar**-*vb*	refuse	5628	**resbalar(se)**-*vb*	slip
5047	**reinar**-*vb*	reign	5314	**resentimiento**-*m*	resentment
7361	**rejilla**-*f*	rack	6156	**resentirse**-*vbr*	feel resentful
7003	**relevancia**-*f*	relevance	7102	**res**-*f*	farm animal
7519	**relevar**-*vb*	relieve, substitute	6625	**resfrío**-*m*	cold
5582	**relevo**-*m*	replacement	7364	**resguardo**-*m*	receipt
5278	**reliquia**-*f*	relic	6674	**residencial**-*adj*	residential
5323	**rellenar**-*vb*	fill	5138	**residir**-*vb*	reside
6788	**relucir**-*vb*	shine	6313	**resonancia**-*f*	resonance
5581	**remar**-*vb*	row	7496	**resorte**-*m*	spring
6904	**remediar**-*vb*	remedy	6398	**respetuoso**-*adj*	respectful
7125	**remitente**-*m/f*	sender	5086	**resplandor**-*m*	brightness
6903	**remolino**-*m*	swirl	7128	**restablecer**-*vb*	reestablish

5990	restante-*adj*	remaining	6664	saga-*f*	saga
6316	restar-*vb*	deduct	5643	saldar-*vb*	pay off
6197	restauración-*f*	restoration	7429	salvamento-*m*	rescue
5381	restaurar-*vb*	restore	5603	sanar-*vb*	heal
5558	restricción-*f*	restriction	5397	sandalia-*f*	sandal
5560	restringir-*vb*	restrict	5784	sandía-*f*	watermelon
5838	resucitar-*vb*	resurrect	6011	sangrado-*adj*	bleed
6118	retomar-*vb*	resume	5925	sanguijuela-*f*	leech
6279	retórico-*adj*	rhetorical	6959	sanguinario-*adj*	bloodthirsty
7400	retornar-*vb*	return	5366	sanguíneo-*adj*	sanguine
6108	revelar(se)-*vb*	reveal	5152	sanidad-*f*	health service
7481	revertir-*vb*	revert	6384	sanitario-*m; adj*	bathroom; sanitary
5061	revivir-*vb*	revive			
6420	revuelo-*m*	stir	7195	saquear-*vb*	sack
6048	revuelto-*adj; m*	messy; scrambled eggs	7341	saqueo-*m*	pillage
			6436	sarampión-*m*	measles
6530	ribera-*f*	riverbank	6053	sarcasmo-*m*	sarcasm
5701	rígido-*adj*	rigid	7259	sarpullido-*m*	rash
6139	rigor-*m*	exactitude, rigour	5254	sartén-*f*	frying pan
5671	rito-*m*	rite	5482	satisfactorio-*adj*	satisfactory
7428	rivalidad-*f*	rivalry	6311	sauce-*m*	willow
5530	rizar-*vb*	curl	7041	secador-*m*	hairdryer
6276	robusto-*adj*	robust	5705	secar(se)-*vb*	dry
7498	roedor-*m*	rodent, mouse (coll)	7089	secretaría-*f*	secretary's office
			6899	secuaz-*m*	minion
6873	romanticismo-*m*	romanticism	7148	sedante-*adj; m*	sedative; sedative
6363	ronco-*adj*	hoarse			
6780	rosada-*adj*	pink	6485	seducción-*f*	seduction
5576	rotación-*f*	rotation	7098	segmento-*m*	segment
7452	rozar-*vb*	brush against	5501	seguimiento-*m*	tracking
5908	rubí-*m*	ruby	6897	seiscientos-*num*	six hundred
6451	rugir-*vb*	roar	5873	seleccionar-*vb*	select
6589	ruin-*adj*	despicable	5391	semáforo-*m*	traffic light
5244	ruiseñor-*m*	nightingale	5535	semanal-*adj*	weekly
7150	rumano-*adj; m*	Romanian; Romanian person	5743	sembrar-*vb*	sow
			6818	semejanza-*f*	likeness
7077	rumba-*f*	rumba	5637	senil-*adj*	senile
5987	rumorearse-*vbr*	be rumoured	6838	sensatez-*f*	good judgement
5852	rural-*adj*	rural	7338	sepulcro-*m*	tomb
			6473	sepultura-*f*	burial
	S		5190	sequía-*f*	drought
			7401	séquito-*m*	entourage
5746	saborear-*vb*	savor	5296	serbio-*adj; m*	Serbian; Serb
7441	sabotear-*vb*	sabotage	7027	serenata-*f*	serenade
5050	sacramento-*m*	sacrament	5573	serenidad-*f*	calm
5172	sacudir(se)-*vb; vbr*	shake; get rid off	5259	seriedad-*f*	seriousness
5658	sádico-*adj; m*	sadistic; sadist			

7169	**servidumbre**-*f*	servants
6460	**seta**-*f*	mushroom
5817	**siciliano**-*adj; m*	Sicilian; Sicilian person
7197	**sien**-*f*	temple
5735	**sífilis**-*f*	syphilis
5035	**significativo**-*adj*	significant
6203	**silbar**-*vb*	whistle
6275	**silbido**-*m*	whistle
7067	**silo**-*m*	silo
6714	**silueta**-*f*	silhouette
5690	**silvestre**-*adj*	wild
6672	**simbólico**-*adj*	symbolic
7079	**simbolizar**-*vb*	symbolize
7462	**simplicidad**-*f*	simplicity
5786	**simulación**-*f*	simulation
5087	**simulacro**-*m*	drill
6308	**simular**-*vb*	pretend
5338	**sinfonía**-*f*	symphony
5429	**singular**-*m; adj*	special; unique
7464	**sinónimo**-*adj; m*	synonym; synonymous
7217	**sintonía**-*f*	tuning
5430	**sirio**-*adj; m*	Syrian; Syrian
5897	**situar(se)**-*vb*	place
7153	**soberanía**-*f*	sovereignty
6654	**soberbio**-*adj*	proud
5831	**sobornar**-*vb*	bribe
7353	**sobrecarga**-*f*	overload
7358	**sobrepasar**-*vb*	exceed
5953	**sobresaliente**-*adj; m*	protruding; outstanding
5033	**socialismo**-*m*	socialism
5874	**socialista**-*adj*	socialist
7289	**sofocante**-*adj*	suffocating
5279	**solemne**-*adj*	solemn
5375	**solidaridad**-*f*	solidarity
7072	**solista**-*m/f*	soloist
6686	**sombrilla**-*f*	parasol
5335	**sombrío**-*adj*	somber
6199	**someter**-*vb*	submit
7119	**sonámbulo**-*adj; m*	sleepwalker; sleepwalker
5036	**sonda**-*f*	catheter
5611	**sonoro**-*adj*	loud
5122	**soplo**-*m*	breeze, breath
6705	**soprano**-*m/f*	soprano

5282	**sorber**-*vb*	slurp
7042	**sórdido**-*adj*	sordid
5589	**Sor**-*f*	Sister
6517	**sorteo**-*m*	raffle
5821	**soso**-*adj*	dull, boring
6753	**sostenido**-*adj*	sustained
6570	**stock**-*m*	stock
5139	**suavidad**-*f*	softness
5097	**subconsciente**-*m*	subconscious
6775	**subdirector**-*m*	assistant manager
5376	**subida**-*f*	rise
7189	**súbito**-*adj*	sudden
7162	**subsidio**-*m*	subsidy
7418	**succión**-*f*	suction
6116	**sucesión**-*f*	succession
6830	**sucesivo**-*adj*	successive
6132	**sucursal**-*f*	branch
5337	**sudeste**-*m*	southeast
5752	**sudoeste**-*m*	south-west
6823	**suela**-*f*	sole
6051	**sujetar**-*vb*	hold
6615	**sumar**-*vb*	add
6564	**sumergir(se)**-*vb*	immerse
6957	**sumisión**-*f*	submission
5566	**superioridad**-*f*	superiority
6511	**supervisar**-*vb*	supervise
5113	**supervisión**-*f*	supervision
5162	**suplente**-*m*	substitute
7137	**suprimir**-*vb*	suppress
5604	**supuesto**-*adj; m*	supposed; case
6610	**sureño**-*adj; m*	southern; southerner
6318	**sureste**-*m*	southeast
5667	**suroeste**-*adj*	southwest
5872	**susceptible**-*adj*	susceptible
5599	**suspenso**-*m*	failing grade, suspense (LA)
5779	**sustentar(se)**-*vb*	sustain, support
5405	**sustituir**-*vb*	replace
7394	**susurrar**-*vb*	whisper
5977	**susurro**-*m*	whisper

T

6953	**tabú**-*adj*	taboo
7141	**taburete**-*m*	stool

6764	**táctico**-*adj; m*	tactical; tactician
6171	**tajar**-*vb*	cut
7224	**tajo**-*m*	cut, work (coll)
5600	**taladrar**-*vb*	drill
6944	**talco**-*m*	talc
7147	**tallo**-*m*	stem
5739	**tapadera**-*f*	cover
5499	**tapar**-*vb*	cover
7080	**tapete**-*m*	rug
5876	**tapón**-*m*	plug, cover
6029	**tardanza**-*f*	delay
5350	**tarro**-*m*	jar
7420	**tea**-*f*	torch
5939	**teclado**-*m*	keyboard
6718	**tecla**-*f*	key
7439	**tedioso**-*adj*	tedious
6466	**tejar**-*vb; m*	tile; tile factory
6843	**tejer**-*vb*	weave
5040	**telefonear**-*vb*	call
6300	**telégrafo**-*m*	telegraph
5275	**temblor**-*m*	tremor
6085	**temerario**-*adj*	reckless
6009	**temeroso**-*adj*	afraid
5281	**temible**-*adj*	fearsome
6994	**temporizador**-*m*	timer
7056	**tenaz**-*adj*	tenacious
6916	**tendero**-*m*	shopkeeper
6055	**tenebroso**-*adj*	gloomy
7409	**teñir**-*vb*	dye
6285	**tenor**-*m*	tenor
7191	**tentáculo**-*m*	tentacle
5661	**tentador**-*m*	tempting
5982	**tentar**-*vb*	tempt
6911	**tentativa**-*f*	attempt
7326	**teología**-*f*	theology
6798	**teórico**-*adj; m*	theoretical; theorist
6680	**termómetro**-*m*	thermometer
6626	**terrateniente**-*m/f*	landowner
6182	**terrenal**-*adj*	earthly
6836	**terrorífico**-*adj*	terrifying
7299	**tesorero**-*m*	treasurer
5550	**testimonio**-*m*	testimony
7075	**testosterona**-*f*	testosterone
6230	**textura**-*f*	texture
6869	**tifón**-*m*	typhoon

6585	**tifus**-*m*	typhus
6521	**timidez**-*f*	shyness
5401	**tirado**-*adj*	stranded
6682	**tirante**-*adj*	tense
5557	**tirón**-*m*	pull
7390	**titanio**-*m*	titanium
6247	**titán**-*m*	titan
7233	**titulado**-*m*	graduate
5309	**tiza**-*f*	chalk
6559	**tocadiscos**-*m*	record player
5392	**tocador**-*m*	dressing table
7051	**tolerante**-*adj*	tolerant
7173	**tónico**-*m*	tonic
7182	**torbellino**-*m*	whirlwind
6784	**torero**-*m*	bullfighter
7304	**torpeza**-*f*	clumsiness
5587	**torrente**-*m*	torrent
6075	**torso**-*m*	torso
6665	**toser**-*vb*	cough
5324	**totalidad**-*f*	entirety
5829	**tóxico**-*adj*	toxic
6442	**trabar(se)**-*vb; vbr*	lock, start up; get tangled up
5555	**traductor**-*m*	translator
6217	**traficar**-*vb*	traffic
6291	**traicionero**-*adj*	treacherous
6405	**trámite**-*m*	process
6697	**tramo**-*m*	stretch
6294	**tranquilizante**-*adj; m*	reassuring; tranquilizer
5196	**transacción**-*f*	transaction
6921	**transcripción**-*f*	transcription
6811	**transcurso**-*m*	course
6971	**transfusión**-*f*	transfusion
5052	**transparente**-*adj*	transparent
6144	**transportador**-*m*	transporter
5294	**trasto**-*m*	piece of junk
5412	**trastornar**-*vb*	drive mad
5377	**trastorno**-*m*	disorder
5084	**travesía**-*f*	voyage
5853	**travesura**-*f*	mischief
5004	**trayecto**-*m*	journey
7295	**trazar**-*vb*	trace
6698	**trébol**-*m*	clover
6057	**trenza**-*f*	braid
5121	**trepar**-*vb*	climb

6966	**tribal**-*adj*	tribal
6209	**tribuna**-*f*	stand
5107	**trimestre**-*m*	trimester
6538	**trinar**-*vb*	chirp, be very angry
7058	**tripulante**-*m/f*	crew member
6136	**trivial**-*adj*	trivial
6719	**trompa**-*f*	trunk, horn
5994	**tropezar(se)**-*vb*	stumble
7425	**trote**-*m*	trot
5144	**tuberculosis**-*f*	tuberculosis
7328	**tuerca**-*f*	screw
7244	**tuerto**-*adj*	blind in one eye
7368	**tumulto**-*m*	tumult
5248	**túnica**-*f*	tunic
6540	**turba**-*f*	mob
6576	**turbar**-*vb*	disturb
7455	**turbio**-*adj*	muddy
6805	**turbulencia**-*f*	turbulence
6126	**turístico**-*adj*	tourist
7424	**tutela**-*f*	guardianship

U

6918	**ubicar(se)**-*vb*	locate, find
5384	**úlcera**-*f*	ulcer
6840	**ultimátum**-*m*	ultimatum
7246	**ultrajar**-*vb*	outrage
5919	**ultra**-*pfx; adj; m/f*	over; ultra; extremist
6513	**unánime**-*adj*	unanimous
5147	**uranio**-*m*	uranium
5762	**urbano**-*adj*	urban
7501	**urgir**-*vb*	press
5875	**urna**-*f*	vase
6438	**usuario**-*m*	user
7109	**utopía**-*f*	utopia

V

5374	**vaciar**-*vb*	empty
7069	**vaina**-*f*	scabbard, pod
5450	**vajilla**-*f*	tableware
6786	**valeroso**-*adj*	valiant
5292	**válido**-*adj*	valid
5262	**valija**-*f*	suitcase

5641	**vallar**-*vb; m*	fence; fenced enclosure
6356	**valorar**-*vb*	value
7220	**vandalismo**-*m*	vandalism
5225	**vanguardia**-*f*	avant-garde, vanguard
6263	**vano**-*adj*	futile
7477	**variable**-*f*	variable
7135	**variación**-*f*	variation
5675	**vasto**-*adj*	vast
6752	**vector**-*m*	vector
5756	**vega**-*f*	meadow
7057	**vegetación**-*f*	vegetation
5609	**vegetariano**-*adj*	vegetarian
5356	**veinticuatro**-*num*	twenty-four
5680	**veintidós**-*num*	twenty-two
7287	**veintiocho**-*num*	twenty-eight
7275	**veintisiete**-*num*	twenty-seven
6766	**veintitrés**-*num*	twenty-three
6842	**veintiuno**-*num*	twenty-one
6157	**vejiga**-*f*	bladder
7183	**velar**-*vb*	look after
6097	**velero**-*m*	sailing boat
5935	**vello**-*m*	fuzz
5198	**venado**-*m*	deer
6235	**vendaje**-*m*	bandage
7175	**vendar**-*vb*	bandage
5267	**venenoso**-*adj*	poisonous
5465	**ventura**-*f*	fortune
6397	**verbal**-*adj*	verbal
6737	**verbo**-*m*	verb
6924	**vereda**-*f*	path
7317	**verificación**-*f*	verification
5731	**verja**-*f*	fence
7031	**vertebral**-*adj*	vertebral
6512	**vertedero**-*m*	garbage dump
5059	**vertical**-*adj*	vertical
6022	**vértigo**-*m*	vertigo
5512	**vestimenta**-*f*	clothing
6877	**viable**-*adj*	viable
7174	**vibrar**-*vb*	vibrate
6342	**vicario**-*m*	vicar
5900	**viceversa**-*adv*	vice versa
5923	**vicioso**-*adj*	depraved, vicious
6419	**victorioso**-*adj*	victorious
5519	**vídeojuego**-*m*	vídeo game

6095	**vietnamita**-*adj; m/f*	Vietnamese; Vietnamese person
6469	**viga**-*f*	beam
6366	**vigía**-*m/f*	lookout
7396	**vigilia**-*f*	vigil
5142	**vigor**-*m*	vigor
5969	**vikingo**-*adj; m*	Viking; Viking
7272	**viña**-*f*	vineyard
5189	**vinagre**-*m*	vinegar
6623	**viñedo**-*m*	vineyard
5620	**violinista**-*m/f*	violinist
7222	**virar**-*vb*	turn
7093	**viril**-*adj*	virile
6864	**virilidad**-*f*	virility
5888	**virtual**-*adj*	virtual
6641	**virtuoso**-*adj; m*	virtuous; virtuoso
5717	**viruela**-*f*	smallpox
6121	**visibilidad**-*f*	visibility
5352	**visón**-*m*	mink
6825	**vitalidad**-*f*	vitality
7271	**vitrina**-*f*	display cabinet
5841	**víveres**-*mpl*	supplies
6251	**vizconde**-*m*	viscount

5904	**vocal**-*adj; f*	vocal; vowel
7473	**vocero**-*m*	spokesman
6627	**voltaje**-*m*	voltage
6067	**voltear(se)**-*vb*	turn around
6018	**voltio**-*m*	volt
5177	**votante**-*m*	voter

Y

7471	**yodo**-*m*	iodine
7074	**yogur**-*m*	yogurt

Z

6193	**zapatero**-*m*	shoemaker
7202	**zas**-*int*	pow, bang
7483	**zodiaco**-*m*	zodiac
5206	**zumbido**-*m*	buzz
5186	**zurdo**-*adj; m*	left-handed; left-handed person
7508	**zurrar**-*vb*	spank

Contact, Further Reading and Resources

For more tools, tips & tricks visit our site www.mostusedwords.com. We publish various language learning resources. If you have a great idea you want to pitch, please send an e-mail to info@mostusedwords.com.

Frequency Dictionaries

In this series:

Spanish Frequency Dictionary 1 – Essential Vocabulary – 2500 Most Common Spanish Words
Spanish Frequency Dictionary 2 - Intermediate Vocabulary – 2501-5000 Most Common Spanish Words
Spanish Frequency Dictionary 3 - Advanced Vocabulary – 5001-7500 Most Common Spanish Words
Spanish Frequency Dictionary 4 - Master Vocabulary – 7501-10000 Most Common Spanish Words

Our mission is to provide language learners worldwide with frequency dictionaries for every major and minor language. We are working hard to accomplish this goal. You can view our selection on https://store.mostusedwords.com/frequency-dictionaries

Bilingual books

We're creating a selection of parallel texts. We decided to rework timeless classics, such as Alice in Wonderland, Sherlock Holmes, Dracula, The Picture of Dorian Gray, and many more.

Our books are paragraph aligned: on the left side of the page you will find the English version of the story, and on the right side the Spanish version..

To help you in your language learning journey, all our bilingual books come with a dictionary included, created for that particular book.

Current bilingual books available are English, Spanish, Portuguese, Italian, German, and Spanish.

For more information, check https://store.mostusedwords.com/bilingual-books . Check back regularly for new books and languages.

Other language learning methods

You'll find reviews of other 3rd party language learning applications, software, audio courses, and apps. There are so many available, and some are (much) better than others.

Check out our reviews at www.mostusedwords.com/reviews.

Contact

If you have any questions, you can contact us through e-mail info@mostusedwords.com.

Printed in Great Britain
by Amazon

21268155R00133